THE
CARAVAN MANUAL

John Wickersham

Author: John Wickersham
Editor: Ian Heath
Cover design: Lee Parsons
Page build: James Robertson
Photographs: John Wickersham
Project manager: Louise McIntyre

First published 1993
Reprinted 1993, 1994
Revised 2nd Edition 1996, Reprinted 1997, 1999
Revised 3rd Edition 2000, Reprinted with minor amendments 2001
Reprinted 2002 (twice), 2003 (twice), 2005 (with minor amendments) and
2007 (with minor amendments)
Revised 4th Edition 2009

Published by:
Haynes Publishing, Sparkford, Yeovil, Somerset BA22 7JJ, UK

A catalogue record for this book is available from the British Library

ISBN 978 1 84425 678 5

Haynes Publishing, Sparkford, Yeovil, Somerset BA22 7JJ
Tel: 01963 442030 Fax: 01963 440001
Int. tel: +44 1963 442030 Fax: +44 1963 440001
E-mail: sales@haynes.co.uk
Website: www.haynes.co.uk

Haynes North America, Inc.
861 Lawrence Drive, Newbury Park,
California 91320, USA

Printed in Great Britain by J. H. Haynes & Co. Ltd

While every effort is taken to ensure the accuracy of the information
given in this book, no liability can be accepted by the author or
publishers for any loss, damage or injury caused by errors in, or
omissions from, the information given.

Gas Regulations

Gas Regulations and the way in which appliance manufacturers
interpret them regarding the installation of their products are
subject to continuing change. It is strongly recommended that
anyone contemplating the installation of a gas appliance should
consult the appliance manufacturer's customer service department
before undertaking any work themselves. This may reveal different
recommendations from those stated here, in which it is suggested that
a competent amateur could consider tackling the preliminary carpentry
and fitting work in accordance with the installation instructions.
However, it is suggested in the chapters concerned with gas systems
and appliances that work on the gas connection(s), flues and the final
testing of an installation should always be entrusted to a competent
and appropriately qualified gas engineer.

Contents

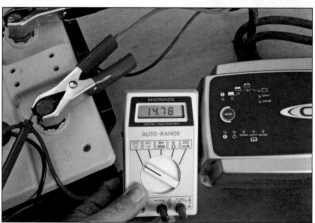

Foreword

The Camping and Caravanning Club recognises the importance of a well-maintained and regularly serviced caravan and we welcome the latest edition of *The Caravan Manual*. The publication has a wealth of information and attention to aspects of safety that will help our members get the most out of their caravan and assist with their safety on and off the road. As caravans become ever more sophisticated, so the manual has grown over the years to meet the need for knowledge from both newcomer and experienced caravanner. This fourth edition is no exception, with much new material to bring it up-to-date in a clear and readable format while also balancing the role of DIY with the need for professional servicing.

Simon McGrath,
Editor of Publications
The Camping and Caravanning Club

I know many people who are 'hands-on' practical caravanners and many who can write sensible English that's easy to understand. John Wickersham can do both, and that's a rare talent. This book is jam-packed full of useful information, illustrated with clear colour photography that will appeal to both beginners and experienced caravanners who simply want to know how things work. The Caravan Club always stresses the importance of proper, regular maintenance. With this excellent, updated edition of *The Caravan Manual* to hand you will soon see what needs to be done, what you can do yourself and what should be left to the experts.

Barry Williams
Head of Publications
The Caravan Club

Author's note

I recently came across a photograph taken in the 1950s of a teenager sitting on the steps of a caravan near Bournemouth. Little did the boy realise in those distant days that his fascination for caravans would one day lead him to write books about how they're built, repaired, and serviced as well.

At the time this holiday snap was taken, another teenage schoolboy built an Austin 7 'Special' in Somerset. Not content with the fruits of his labours, he then wrote down how the task was accomplished and in 1956 his book went on sale. Little did John Haynes realise that hundreds of Haynes Car Repair manuals would follow on later, and thousands of motorists would put them to use.

As one of the many users of these extraordinary repair guides, I was privileged to be invited to discuss a proposed caravan manual. That was in 1990 and the thought of committing 75,000 words to paper and producing 500 prints in my darkroom was obviously a truly tough task. However, the book went on sale after three years of work and achieved a pleasing response.

A lot has happened since that First Edition appeared – both in the caravan world and also the production of books. In fact this Fourth Edition bears little resemblance to the original text.

Thanks to the advent of digital cameras, I could ensure that this latest edition would be lavishly illustrated. Thanks to Haynes Editorial and Production staff, its layout looks stunningly good. Thanks to many caravan engineers and the courses they ran, the content is right up-to-date. And with the help generously given by the caravanning clubs, dealers, manufacturers and other enthusiastic owners, a body of information has been compiled that I hope you'll find helpful and easy to follow.

John Wickersham
January 2009

Unhappy with hotel accommodation, many people now enjoy the pleasures of caravanning instead. *(photograph courtesy of The Caravan Club)*

Introduction and overview

A touring caravan provides the means for travelling far and wide. The aim of this book is to help you keep your caravan in tip-top condition so your travels can be carried out in comfort and safety.

The number of people taking holidays in touring caravans continues to grow each year. The National Caravan Council has reported that over 500,000 caravans are in regular active use and The Caravan Club adds that 'Caravan holidays are the most popular "paid for" holiday choice in the UK, accounting for a 19% share of all holiday nights.'

Perhaps the growing appeal of holidays in touring caravans is a reaction to several recent events of worldwide concern. For example, some holiday-makers have become disenchanted with airport delays, security protocol, lost luggage and holiday hotel disappointments. These irritating realities have undoubtedly caused some people to look at alternative holiday plans. Coupled with this is the fact that more and more people have discovered that modern caravans are comfortable, well-equipped and built for use at any time of the year.

■ The caravanning clubs

Further confirmation of the popularity of caravanning is reflected by the monthly distribution of members' magazines from the two major caravan clubs. Figures calculated independently by the Audit Bureau of Circulations (ABC) revealed the following average net monthly circulation figures in 2007 for the Clubs' respective magazines:

> *The Camping & Caravanning Club Magazine* – 209,042
> *The Caravan Club Magazine* – 365,048

The total average distribution each month therefore adds up to a remarkable 574,090 copies.

Note: *Membership of these clubs includes owners/users of touring caravans, motor caravans, folding caravans, and tents.*

■ Caravanning in comfort

The reasons for taking up caravanning are both personal and varied. For some, a caravan mainly provides accommodation for an annual summer holiday. In contrast, other people use their caravans all year round – sometimes for touring and sometimes as a base when attending major events. The diversity of opportunities for travel is a key attraction, but one element is common to all participants – the desire to caravan in comfort and safety.

■ Servicing and repairs

Modern caravans are sophisticated and to ensure they provide comfortable accommodation with a safe set-up, they need to be serviced at regular intervals. Just as cars need servicing, so do caravans and their appliances. Needless to say, you also have to learn how to operate the appliances correctly and it's certainly useful to have a rudimentary understanding of the way they work. Features like this are covered in the chapters which follow.

Occasionally, something might fail to function. When this happens it's always useful to know what the repair procedures are likely to entail. This is important both for readers who want to carry out their own repairs as well as owners who prefer to take their caravan to a dealer. Having a broad understanding of what the repair involves helps you know if a job has been carried out correctly. Either way, guidance relating to many of the more common problems and the appropriate courses of action are provided in this manual.

■ Upgrading facilities

Some caravan owners also decide it would be desirable to *improve* the facilities in their caravan. A waste water system might be altered, for example, or its appliances might be due for replacement. Depending on one's knowledge, skills and workshop equipment, many projects can be tackled by competent owners. *The Caravan Manual* provides the appropriate guidance and, to support the advice, Appendix C lists manufacturers' addresses.

Since the First Edition of *The Caravan Manual* was published in 1993, hundreds of caravanners have successfully tackled their own repairs and servicing work. Needless to say, this has enabled them to save considerable amounts of money by using their own time and labour. However, a great deal has changed since the original publication.

■ New regulations and quality problems

Not only have many new products been introduced, European standards and new legislative measures have had an impact on this industry. Indeed, some of the products previously in use are no longer deemed to be safe, and a number of familiar items have been withdrawn from the market. A short section in the Appendix records some of the new standards that have recently been introduced.

Other developments have been brought about by changes in car design and construction. The greater use of electronic systems in modern vehicles, for example, has certainly had an effect on matters like wiring a car for towing.

On a less pleasing note, the relatively high incidence of damp in caravans continues to be a matter of concern. For instance, *The Caravan Club 1999 Quality and Reliability Survey* learnt from the 5,500 survey participants, that 2% of caravans had dampness *at the time of delivery*. In the Club's *Quality and Reliability Survey* conducted in 2005, 4,154 participated and there was again evidence of damp in 2% of new models. The 1999 survey also found that 11% of respondents experienced damp in their caravans during the first three years of use. In the *Quality and Reliability Survey* conducted in 2002 this condition was reported in 12% of caravans; in the survey of 2005 it was back down to 11%.

However, these figures hide the fact that the severity of reported faults has diminished. For example, the majority of problems appear in

The idea that caravans offer only basic comforts is now far from the truth.

double-glazed 'plastic' windows and water ingress occurs in the void between the inner and outer panels. Damage arising from damp penetrating around the frame and getting into the body panel structure is far less prevalent.

There is no doubt that manufacturers are committed to making improvements and the chapter on body construction which appears later was researched with particular diligence. Presumably a boat doesn't leak when it's brand new, and water shouldn't be able to find its way into a new caravan either.

■ The Fourth Edition

It's a long time since *The Caravan Manual* with its monochrome photographs was first published in 1993, and this latest edition bears little resemblance to the original. Most of the text has been completely rewritten and this new edition is published in full colour.

Notwithstanding these changes in presentation and content, this new manual continues to recognise that many readers intend to carry out their own repairs, servicing tasks and improvement work. With this in mind, it is not presented as a glossy textbook for display on the coffee table.

At the same time there are still warnings about operations which should only be tackled by trained and qualified service engineers. Advice relating to these issues should be heeded at all times. Note, too, that some tasks which used to be straightforward, like changing wheel bearings, now have to be carried out using factory machinery. This might seem a bad feature of recent models, but in reality modern sealed bearings seldom need changing at all.

As stated already, modern caravans are far more sophisticated than models built several decades ago and many of the innovations help to make our caravanning experiences even more enjoyable, comfortable and safe.

Towing advice

Safe towing is dependent on a well-matched pairing of car and caravan. The power of the towcar's engine, the weight-to-weight relationship and the load distribution are important matters. So too, is the driver's skill and experience.

The successful pairing of a towcar and caravan involves a number of elements. The aim here is to draw attention to the points you need to consider in order to obtain a well-matched outfit. It is an involved subject and sources of further help are also provided.

Sources of help

The Caravan Towing Guide

Some of the main considerations are given in a booklet entitled *The Caravan Towing Guide*, which is published by The National Caravan Council (NCC) in co-operation with *The Camping and Caravanning Club* and *The Caravan Club*. Information reproduced in caravan handbooks is usually based on *The Caravan Towing Guide* and copies are available directly from the NCC.

At the time of writing, a new edition of the Guide has just been produced (September 2008) by the NCC.

Caravan magazines

Further information can also be obtained from the caravanning magazines available from most newsagents.

On account of their monthly publication, caravan magazines are able to keep abreast of the latest models of cars and caravans. Towcar tests are reported regularly, so too are tests of new and used caravans. However, it is the magazines' data pages that are a particularly helpful point of reference.

In the towcar listings, information is usually given on vehicles' kerbweights; some tables also add information on towball noseweight limitations and others calculate the maximum weight of a fully laden caravan that each listed vehicle can tow.

In addition there are free supplements dealing with car/caravan matching and these usually accompany Spring issues of magazines. The supplements are written by caravanning specialists and the advice is especially helpful. Contrary to expectations, car manufacturers are not always forthcoming when questions are posed regarding their vehicles' towing potential.

Advice is also available from technical specialists employed by the caravan clubs and this is one of the many benefits available to members.

The Caravan Clubs

Even though their origins and objectives might be slightly different, the two major clubs are an exceptional source of help. Both The Camping and Caravanning Club and The Caravan Club have an enormous membership and their respective employees have extensive knowledge on towing matters. Moreover, they are able to draw on first hand experiences reported by their many members.

Both clubs also have guidance leaflets on towcars and caravans and both run very popular courses on towing skills. These courses are conducted away from the public highway and offer plenty of opportunity to acquire manoeuvrability skills in controlled situations.

Technical leaflets on other caravan matters are also free to members of both clubs and information appears in their monthly magazines. For example, *The Caravan Club* has around fifty detailed and substantive information leaflets with titles like: *Choice of Towcar, Choice of Trailer Caravan, Choice of Towing Bracket, Automatic Transmission for Towing, Rear View Mirrors* etc.

Caravan Owners' Clubs

If you purchase an older caravan, it is not unusual to find that the original handbook is missing. In some instances, a manufacturer may have ceased trading, or perhaps has been taken over by a larger company. This can mean you lack important information for your particular model, like the tyre pressures or details about weights. Both are critical contributors to safe towing.

This is where owners' clubs for particular marques are invaluable. Here is an opportunity to make contact with others who tow an identical model and to gain the help you need. The addresses of the Hon. Secretaries of Owners' Clubs are published periodically in the main consumer magazines.

Towcar of the Year Award

Since its inception in 1978, the annual Towcar of the Year Award run by *The Caravan Club* has put hundreds of new cars through rigorous tests in order to evaluate their suitability for towing. As the contest has evolved, so has its scope. As a general principle the contenders are usually placed in a series of different price categories, although in some years special class awards have also been given for all-terrain cars and multi-person vehicles (MPVs). Notwithstanding these divisions, all vehicles are ultimately compared across all classes in order to produce an outright winner.

The contest is conducted at a test track over two days. Weighing is carried out and ballast added to either car or caravan as deemed necessary. This achieves accurate noseweights on the test caravans and overall parity in the evaluation.

Features like ride quality, handling characteristics, hill starts, braking, traction, acceleration, suspension and general performance are assessed independently by a team of experienced judges. However, the evaluation isn't strictly limited to an assessment of a car's towing qualities on a demanding track. Recently a series of tests have evaluated elements like ground clearance, rear overhang from the back axle to the tow ball and the provision of stowing space for caravanning gear. The test team checks storage in each car and uses items that include an awning and water containers.

In recent years, entries have included around 40 or 50 vehicles, all of which must be new models from the preceding 12 months. As the information is cumulatively drawn together over successive years, valuable data is thus compiled. The box below

Noseweight is meticulously checked in the Towcar of the Year Award competition, and ballast is added in order to achieve (ideally) a coupling head weight that is 7% of the actual laden weight of the caravan. (See later section on Noseweight.)

shows overall winners since the contest was first carried out, and because the event takes place in September results are usually published in the late Autumn issues of caravan magazines.

Note: In 2007, *Practical Caravan* joined forces with *WhatCar?* and the *Camping and Caravanning Club* to create another competition entitled *Towcar Awards*.

Weight factors

Irrespective of the power of a car's engine, towing a caravan that is heavier than the vehicle is dangerous. The phrase about the 'tail wagging the dog' assumes a special meaning in the context of caravanning.

Weight matters are important and a potential for confusion is the recent change in terminologies. Before looking more closely at weight relationships, check the terms in the box on the next page.

Drawing on the terms relating to weights, it is recommended that the total weight of a caravan, with everything on board (actual laden weight or ALW) is no greater than 85% of the mass of the vehicle in running order (MRO). This is checked using the following formula:

**ALW of caravan ÷ MRO of car, x 100
= % weight of caravan to car**

This is a recommendation, but caravanners with extensive towing experience may tow a heavier caravan thus achieving a higher weight relationship, as long as the caravan does not exceed the MRO of the car.

After being put through many exacting tests at Millbrook track in Bedfordshire, the Skoda Superb 2.0 TDi was declared Towcar of the Year 2009.

A good towing car should provide stowage space for caravanning items, and this is being checked as part of The Towcar of the Year Award.

Towcar of the Year Winners

1978	Rover 3500
1979	Renault 20TS
1980	Peugeot 505
1981	Toyota Crown Super
1982	BMW 528i
1983	Volkswagen Santana
1984	Citroën BX 16TRS
1985	Volvo 360 GLE
1986	Ford Sierra XR 4x4
1987	Renault 21GTS
1988	Vauxhall Senator 3.0i CD
1989	Vauxhall Cavalier SRi 2.0i
1990	Vauxhall Cavalier 4x4 2.0i
1991	Rover 416 Gti 16v
1992	Volvo 940 SE Turbo
1993	Vauxhall Calibra Turbo 4 x 4
1994	Citroën Xantia 1.9 TD VSX
1995	Renault Laguna RT 2.0
1996	Vauxhall Vectra 2.0l 16v GLS
1997	Peugeot 406 GLX DT 2.1
1998	Citroën Xantia V6 Exclusive
1999	Audi A6 Avant 2.5 TDi
2000	Seat Toledo V5
2001	Volkswagen Golf V6 4Motion
2002	Peugeot 406 GTX 2.2 HDi Estate
2003	Skoda Superb 2.5 V6 TDI Elegance
2004	Subaru Forester 2.0 XT
2005	Mazda 6 2.0D Estate TS2 (136ps)
2006	Kia Sorento 2.5 CRDi XE
2007	Volvo V50 D5 Sport
2008	Ford Mondeo Titanium X Estate
2009	Skoda Superb 2.0 TDi

Putting both a laden caravan and its towcar on a weighbridge will indicate if the outfit is within the vehicle's Maximum Train Weight.

Note: *Car manufacturers sometimes specify the weight of a trailer that one of their models could tow on the basis of the power of its engine. Occasionally this disregards the weight advice.*

given. Even if the engine has the pulling power, you should not be misled into thinking that it is acceptable for a trailed caravan's weight to exceed the car's MRO. See TOWING LIMIT in the Weight (Mass) Terminology panel.

The weight issue is very important and in several parts of the country the police are now making road-side spot checks of trailed outfits and it is often found that many caravans are grossly over-laden. It is particularly important to monitor the actual weight of your caravan by taking it – with its full travelling load on board – to a weighbridge. Addresses may be found in the *Yellow Pages* and information is also available from a *Local Authority Trading Standards* or *Weights and Measures Department*.

Weight (Mass) Terminology

THE TOWING VEHICLE

MASS OF VEHICLE IN RUNNING ORDER (MRO): This is the manufacturer's defined weight of a vehicle and it normally includes these elements:
• fuel tank 90% full;
• adequate supply of liquids associated with its propulsion;
• weight of driver but no passengers;
• no load other than the standard provision of tools/equipment;
Add to this about 25kg for the towbar and tow ball.
Note: *Manufacturers' definitions vary and some don't include the weight of a driver. If the 'driverless Kerbweight' of the car is stated instead, calculate MRO by adding about 100kg to this figure, which roughly accounts for weight of a driver, towbar, tow ball and trailer wiring.*

GROSS TRAIN WEIGHT: Defined by the vehicle manufacturer as the maximum permissible combined weight of both the laden tow car and the laden caravan.

MAXIMUM PERMISSIBLE TOWING MASS (MPTM): Sometimes specified by a car manufacturer and usually referring to the maximum weight a car can tow based on its restart ability on a 1:8 (12.5%) uphill gradient.

MAXIMUM AUTHORISED MASS (MAM): Sometimes referred to as Maximum Permissible Weight or Gross Vehicle Weight. It is the permitted limit of a car with driver, passengers, luggage and imposed nose weight.

THE CARAVAN

(Terms introduced in conjunction with the European standards for caravans EN 1645 Pt. 2. *New terms apply from September 1998, i.e. 1999 models*)

MAXIMUM TECHNICALLY PERMISSIBLE LADEN MASS (MTPLM), formerly Maximum Authorised Mass or Maximum Technical Permissible Weight: Stated by the manufacturer, taking account of elements like tyre ratings, suspension weight limits, material rigidity etc.

BAILEY CARAVANS LTD		
RANGE	PAGEANT S S	
MODEL	MONARCH	
M.T.P.L.M.	1238	kg
MASS IN RUNNING ORDER	1062	kg
TYRE PRESSURE PSI/BAR	37/2.6	

Bailey of Bristol, South Liberty Lane, Bedminster, Bristol, BS3 2SS

MASS IN RUNNING ORDER (MRO), formerly ex works weight: Weight of the caravan with factory-supplied equipment as defined by the manufacturer.

USER PAYLOAD, formerly Caravan Allowable Payload: The weight limit is established by subtracting the MRO from the MTPLM. The User Payload comprises the following three elements:

i) Personal effects payload: items you take including clothing, food, drink, cutlery, crockery, cooking utensils, bedding, hobby equipment. The formula for the expected minimum provision is:

(10 x number of berths) + (10 x length of body in metres excluding draw bar) + 30
= minimum allowance for personal effect payload (kg)

ii) *Essential habitation equipment*: any items, including fluids, deemed by the manufacturer as essential for the safe and proper function of equipment for habitation.

iii) *Optional equipment*: the weight of optional items like cycle rack, spare wheel, and an extra bunk must now be itemised by the caravan manufacturer. The weight of items subsequently installed by the owner e.g. solar panels, will also fall into this category.

ACTUAL LADEN WEIGHT (ALW): This refers to the actual weight of a caravan when you use it and includes all personal effects, essential habitation equipment and optional equipment. The ALW of a caravan that's ready to be used for a typical holiday trip should be checked on a weighbridge to ensure it falls within the MTPLM. This figure is needed so that you can calculate the caravan's ideal noseweight and to establish the recommended weight ratio. Where possible a caravan's weight should be no greater than 85% of the car's mass in running order (MRO). Experienced caravanners might exceed this ratio but a caravan's ALW should never be greater than the car's MRO.

Periodically it is important to weigh a fully laden caravan on a weighbridge to confirm it doesn't exceed its MTPLM.

Load distribution

In addition to the overall weight loading of your caravan, items carried should also be stowed and secured appropriately. The illustrations below show the guideline you should follow, keeping note of the noseweight achieved as well.

Heavy items should be as near as possible to the axle – which often means carrying well-secured items on the floor.

Note: *It is wrong to rectify excessive noseweight by loading something heavy in the extreme rear of the 'van. Compensation might be achieved by doing this, but on the road the so-called 'dumb-bell effect' means that any tendency for snaking is then much harder to check. Fore and aft balance must be achieved by adjusting the loads carried near the axle.*

Noseweight

Noseweight limits are determined by the car manufacturer, taking elements like the suspension and the integrity of tow bracket mounting points into account as well. To achieve good stability, a substantial noseweight is needed, even when the caravan assumes the recommended level or slightly nose down stance. A strongly nose-down stance should be avoided since this affects steering. The traction on a front wheel driven car is affected too, as well as the angle of headlamp beams. To overcome this, it is sometimes necessary to fit spring assisters to the towcar.

To achieve the optimum stability of the outfit, noseweight is generally recommended to be 7% of the actual laden weight of the caravan. When the weight of a laden caravan is multiplied by 7%, you typically achieve a noseweight around 50–90kg. However, some cars limit the

When coupled up and with the correct noseweight, a car and caravan should achieve a level or slightly nose-down stance.

- ■ If the caravan is strongly nose down, the car's suspension needs stiffening.
- ■ If the caravan is nose up, loading is incorrect or perhaps the tow ball falls outside the range of permitted heights. (See panel on Drop Plates in Chapter 3.)

noseweight to 50kg and since this musn't be exceeded, the 'ideal' noseweight for heavier caravans might not be achieved. Other cars can take extremely high noseweights e.g. Citroen XM (110kg), Range Rover/Discovery post-1995 (150kg) – but these examples are unusual.

It should also be pointed out that caravans have occasionally been manufactured where the ex-works noseweights are excessive – even before gas cylinders have been added. Oddly enough, some models have achieved minimal noseweight and their owners have found it especially difficult to achieve the necessary forward weight. Readers' letters published in magazines highlight some of the more unusual problems experienced.

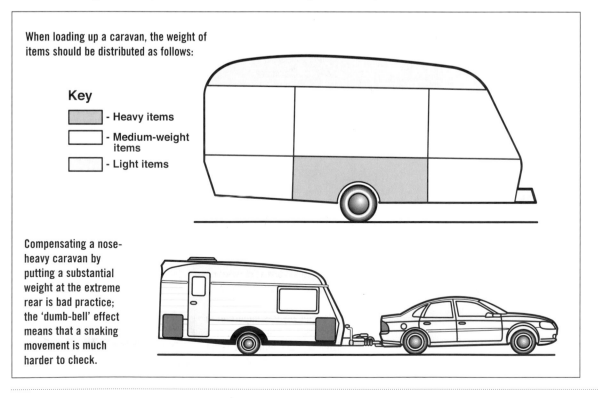

When loading up a caravan, the weight of items should be distributed as follows:

Key

- - Heavy items
- - Medium-weight items
- - Light items

Compensating a nose-heavy caravan by putting a substantial weight at the extreme rear is bad practice; the 'dumb-bell' effect means that a snaking movement is much harder to check.

Types of car

Notwithstanding the points already mentioned, there are still some further technical details about potential towcars to take into account.

Low torque preference

It is self-evident that a powerful engine is important, but the point at which an engine achieves its greatest power varies from model to model. The term 'torque' refers to the turning force of an engine and some cars achieve peak torque i.e. pulling power, when the engine is running at low revs whereas others are most powerful when the engine is achieving very high revs. For instance a sports car, a 'hot hatchback', and a GTi Saloon normally achieve greatest power and best acceleration when the engine is running at high revs.

This isn't much help to a caravanner since the law imposes stricter speed limits on a vehicle towing a trailer compared with one that is driven solo. Moreover, when cruising near the towing speed limit, you want to be in top gear, which of course will determine the speed of the engine.

In a 'sport performance' car, engaging top gear at relatively slow speeds will mean the engine's revs are low – which is not the point at which the vehicle's sparkling performance is achieved. As the analogy rightly indicates, race horses might be able to reach high speeds but they are not usually good at pulling heavy carts.

So the best type of towing vehicle is seldom a model designed to achieve high speed performance. In technical terms, you need a car whose engine achieves good 'low-end torque' – that is one which achieves its best pulling power when the engine is running slowly. The graphs from car manufacturers which match torque against speed will reveal whether an engine is likely to display this characteristic.

Model type

Today there are fewer cars which follow the more traditional style in which a large boot extends at the rear. In this arrangement, it means a tow ball is situated a long way behind the rear axle. The resulting down force from a coupled caravan is not helpful for the rear springs, particularly if the boot is also fully loaded. Herein is a benefit of a hatch-back design where the towball is much closer to the rear axle.

A similar benefit might be claimed for multi-purpose vehicles and more people are using MPVs as towcars; others favour 'all-terrain vehicles' for their off-road capabilities.

In most cases, off-road vehicles are built on a sturdy chassis which is a robust sub frame rather than a series of pressed steel box sections. Some refer to this as a 'true chassis'. However, its sheer rigidity is sometimes claimed to impose additional stress on a caravan – sufficient for some caravan manufacturers to invalidate the Warranty where this type of vehicle is used for towing.

The concern is based on the idea that a more conventional vehicle permits greater flexion, thereby easing the ride characteristics for the trailed vehicle. It is for this reason that some owners of all terrain vehicles fit a towball which incorporates a cushioning system. When pulling a caravan over a heavily rutted campsite field, this certainly could reduce the shocks that might be imposed on the structure of the caravan. One supplier of these couplings is Dixon-Bate Ltd whose address appears in the Appendix.

Driven wheels

Since noseweight has a tendency to push down the rear of a car and to lift the front, many caravanners prefer a rear-wheel-driven car. In fact experienced caravanners are often critical that so many winners of the Towcar of the Year Award are front-wheel-driven vehicles, but there is a reason for this.

Rear-wheel drive is becoming more and more unusual. For instance, in the 1998 Awards, there

---

Checking noseweight

A caravan's noseweight can be checked in one of the three ways pictured here:

Most accessory shops sell noseweight gauges like this.

Some AL-KO jockey wheels incorporate a weight indicator.

Noseweight can be checked using a reliable set of bathroom scales and a sturdy stick.

When using a gauge or wooden stick, make sure the caravan is on level ground with its jockey wheel lowered and the corner steadies retracted. Raise the coupling head using the jockey wheel in order to insert the gauge or stick. Then lower the nose using the jockey wheel so that the total downthrust of the coupling head is borne by the gauge or stick. Take the reading.

were 41 competitors and only one vehicle entered was rear-wheel-driven. It was equally significant that 12 of the entries comprised 4WD vehicles.

Quite apart from the merits of 4WD transmission for off-road vehicles, many 4WD saloons achieve notable cornering and overall traction performance on the roads as well. There is no doubt that this configuration – though not essential – is helpful when towing, and both Ford and Vauxhall 4WD models have been overall winners in the Towcar of the Year competition in the past.

Automatic versus manual transmissions

Traditionally the caravanner has preferred a tow car with a manual gear change. This is partly because vehicles with automatic transmission used to experience serious problems when the transmission oil overheated. Overheating can occur when towing in hot, hilly areas and in traffic jams. Nowadays a standard oil cooler overcomes this and if the problem persists, specialists like Kenlowe supply auxiliary gearbox coolers.

Notwithstanding this, the prejudice continues. There is no doubt that manual transmissions have much in their favour. On the other hand, *The Caravan Club* leaflet entitled *Automatic Transmission for Towing* is a long and detailed document that presents the value of automatic systems in a cogent and convincing manner.

Not only is the 'creep' facility of an automatic so good in a traffic jam – with the attendant relief on the leg normally used for the clutch, there are other advantages too. As the leaflet points out:

'Hitch a caravan behind a car and the case for an automatic gearbox to protect an engine, transmission and body shell from the type of shocks caused by clutch engagement become almost unanswerable. Solo and (particularly) towing, progress is very much smoother, including when reversing'.

Without doubt, the old resistance against using an automatic for towing is scarcely tenable in respect of modern vehicles.

Fuel

In this country, the use of liquefied petroleum gas in vehicles has never achieved the popularity it has in Holland. The debate here is concerned with the petrol versus diesel arguments. On one hand, diesel engines normally have good low-end torque which is fine for towing; on the other hand, petrol engines are often more economical and generally provide better acceleration if you want to overtake when climbing a hill.

There are many arguments but one thing that cannot be ignored is the punitive imposition of tax on fuels. If your caravanning is done principally in Britain, the cost of diesel fuel is not particularly attractive, but if you tour extensively in France, the picture changes dramatically.

From a technical viewpoint, there certainly isn't a heavy balance in favour of one fuel over the other. Rather more concerning is the loss of leaded petrol to owners with older tow cars. It is currently too early to judge the long term effectiveness of lead-replacement additives. These are formulated to reduce the potential damage to exhaust valve seats which is the key problem caused when using lead-free petrol. As regards their efficiency, only time will tell.

Note: *Modern engines are built with hardened steel valve seats so the use of unleaded petrol presents no problem.*

Suspension

Some vehicles are noted for soft suspension whereas others deflect less easily. Generalisations are difficult here and the best advice is to check what manufacturers recommend about suspension strengthening strategies. There are plenty of add-ons available from independent specialists but not all devices meet the approval of car manufacturers. Once again, the *Clubs* usually have information on particular models and their suspension requirements.

Types of caravan

Single versus twin axle

Finally the towing issue is partly determined by the caravan, too. Some achieve better balance than others and test reports in caravan magazines are helpful here. In truth, nearly all modern caravans tow well.

However, when it comes to straight line tracking, there is no doubt that a well balanced twin axle caravan is more likely to hold a straight course than a single axle 'van. The friction imposed by the four wheels helps to resist sideways deflections from passing vehicles. This is one of the advantages.

Of course the case is not clear-cut. A twin axle configuration is inevitably heavier and costly, too. Moreover the benefit endowed by tyre friction on the road is conversely a problem when trying to manoeuvre the caravan on site or at home. The 'scrubbing' of the tyres makes manual handling difficult and most owners of twin axle caravans recognise the importance of being accomplished at reversing their 'vans using the towcar.

To overcome this there are tricks like parking the wheels on thick plastic sheets and wetting these to permit a better degree of side slip when manoeuvring the caravan manually. In addition, Lunar fitted the Knott optional axle elevation system for several years on its Delta models. This hydraulic device lifted one set of wheels clear of the ground, thereby enabling the caravan to have the same manoeuvrability as a single-axle model. However, the product has not been fitted on recent Lunar caravans.

For several years Lunar offered an optional hydraulic axle elevation system on its Delta models. By raising both wheels on one axle clear of the ground this considerably improved manoeuvrability.

The Knott elevation system employs hydraulic lifting gear.

Towcar preparation

A number of tasks have to be carried out before a vehicle can be used for towing. Some can be done by DIY owners; other jobs are best left to qualified specialists.

Before a car can be used to tow a caravan, a bracket of suitable design is needed. A 12V socket or sockets will also have to be fitted, together with ancillary electrical components. These additions enable a caravan's road lights and other 12V accessories to function using a supply from the towing vehicle. Furthermore, some vehicles will tow more efficiently if the rear suspension is upgraded and various types of spring assister are available.

Fitting these items requires technical knowledge, practical skill and sometimes special tools as well. In the past many owners have fitted a towbar themselves and have also wired-up the electrical sockets. On older vehicles this was usually straightforward but in the last few years things have changed. For instance, the electrical systems in recent cars usually include sophisticated electronic components which, in turn, have made the task of preparing a vehicle for towing a demanding and exacting undertaking. In fact few owners would be wise to attempt electrical work unless they have attended a training course for professional towbar installers.

Installing a towbar is sometimes straightforward but it rather depends on the car. The fact that many models have rear moulded plastic skirts instead of traditional chromed bumpers often makes things difficult. Removing large body panels without causing damage is something that can even challenge experienced towbar fitters. In this trade, it's fully accepted that towing bracket installations on some types of car are far more demanding than usual.

Terminology

The structure fitted to a vehicle that is capable of towing a caravan is known by two names: 1) towbar, or 2) tow or towing bracket. Both terms are used in this book and no difference is implied. On page 19 there is also reference to brake levers fitted with a 'gas piston'. In automotive circles these are sometimes described as 'gas struts'.

This towbar from Witter was quite easy to fit and the procedure was clearly described.

Towing brackets

A number of specialists are engaged in the manufacture of towing brackets and it is worth spending time comparing the different products.

Manufacturers

Most car manufacturers offer towing brackets for vehicles in their ranges. This is scarcely surprising, since nearly all cars can tow a trailer of some kind or another. Notable exceptions, however, are the Ford Ka and the MGF; the manufacturers did not declare suitability for towing when the vehicles underwent EC Type Approval testing.

In addition to the vehicle manufacturer, there are also a number of independent towing bracket specialists. The quality of these products, like the price, varies considerably. Long established manufacturers such as Brink and Witter are examples of specialists whose brackets are well respected within the industry.

Then there are bespoke specialists like Watling Engineers near St Albans. This long-established Company will design and build a bracket for almost any kind of vehicle for which a Type Approved product is not a mandatory requirement. This includes hundreds of passenger cars registered in the UK before 1st August 1998. Models as diverse as the 1927 Bentley 3-litre Tourer, the 1952 Humber Snipe, the Pontiac Transam or even the Honda Gold Wing motorcycle are examples quoted in the prodigious list. Watling Engineers is a useful contact for owners of restored historic caravans who want to tow behind a 'classic car' of similar vintage.

Tow balls

When choosing a towbar, take account of the tow ball it supports. Three types are used when towing caravans:

1. Bolt-on flange tow balls
2. Swan neck tow balls
3. Detachable tow balls

The bolt-on tow ball is particularly popular in the United Kingdom; many French tow cars also have bolt-on units.

Most towing brackets made in mainland Europe have a swan neck tow ball and there are many different patterns.

Though more expensive, a detachable tow ball maintains the clean lines of a vehicle used for occasional towing.

Tow ball types compared

• The traditional British-style bracket is usually designed to accept a separate bolt-on 50mm tow ball which is attached to a face plate using high tensile bolts. The 50mm version was introduced in the early 1960s as a replacement for the 2in ball. This design, also popular in France, is sometimes referred to as a 'flanged ball' and in most instances its attachment is by two 16mm bolts fitted at 90mm (3.5in) centres. Occasionally, however, you might find four-bolt variations. Particular attention has to be paid to ensure that the attachment bolts are tightened correctly as described in the accompanying box on bolt-on tow balls.

• The swan neck version is normally made as an integral part of the bracket itself, and these tow balls are popular in many countries in mainland Europe. However, the design does not lend itself to the acceptance of certain accessories although clamps made to fit the neck section have been designed by some of the manufacturers of blade-type stabilisers such as Bulldog. Experience has shown that a few clamping devices don't clasp the neck as firmly as might be desirable and this is partly because there are several different profiles of the 'swan-neck' pattern. Variation in tube diameter is also apparent.

• Detachable tow balls have become increasingly common too, and some are neat in appearance and notably secure when fitted. Others are rather

Bolt-on tow balls

■ The stem section of bolt-on flange mounted balls is now manufactured in two versions, and a variation on the standard pattern became necessary when stabilising coupling heads were introduced. For example, if your caravan is fitted with an AL-KO Kober AKS coupling head stabiliser you will also need a tow ball whose stem projects rearwards and higher than a normal tow ball. That's because an AL-KO stabiliser head is considerably bulkier than a standard coupling unit and if attached to a conventional tow ball there simply isn't enough clearance. In consequence, as it articulates around the ball it is more likely to foul sections near the flange and the tow ball's attachment bolts.

■ The standard M16 (16mm) high tensile bolts at 90mm centres used to attach a flange-type tow ball must be tightened to the correct torque setting. A torque setting of 195Nm (143lb/ft) is typical, but check the actual figure for *your* bracket with the manufacturer. Furthermore, if self-locking nuts are fitted instead of standard ones the torque setting is 215Nm (158lb/ft).

■ Metal locking nuts like the Stover pattern can be used up to three times. However, Nylock self-locking nuts should only be used once. Alternatively, if spring washers are fitted to a standard nut, these should be replaced every time the fixing is loosened off.

■ In the last few years tow balls have been sold with a variety of surface finishes. Chromed versions are costly but their smart looks are surprisingly durable. A recent variation has been the introduction of a gold finish, which is only a cosmetic enhancement. There have also been black-coated versions, which have often caused problems when used with coupling head stabilisers.

To avoid damage to the friction pads in these products, AL-KO Kober's instructions state that the black coating on the ball must be removed with emery cloth before use with a coupling head stabiliser.

■ The quality of bolt-on tow balls has varied in the past and now there's an EC standard. When purchasing a new bolt-on tow ball, check for a compliance sticker as shown alongside.

This detachable BMW tow ball is stowed on a rack installed in the boot.

The attachment mechanisms of some removable balls are less compact than others.

Offering-up this AL-KO AKS 2000 coupling head stabiliser to a conventional tow ball fitted with a bump stop plate shows there's insufficient clearance to provide proper articulation. Using a standard flanged towball with an AL-KO coupling head stabiliser is extremely dangerous because one of the components is likely to get destroyed.

A bolt-on tow ball is advantageous if you want to fit an accessory like a bumper guard.

clumsy and there are a few products that are not particularly easy to fit or detach in a hurry. Naturally a detachable tow ball enables owners to maintain a vehicle's clean lines at the rear when it's not being used for towing. Unfortunately, however, some detachable products don't include a satisfactory mounting facility for the electrical sockets, and some lack the all-important eyelet needed for attaching a breakaway cable.

Adding accessories

An advantage of the bolt-on tow ball is that you are sometimes permitted to attach additional components like a bumper guard, stabiliser coupling, cycle rack or a mounting plate for 12N and 12S sockets. However, there is a strict limit to the number of accessory items that can be carried

On some vehicles there are captive nuts already *in situ* to accept a towing bracket.

between the ball and the mounting face plate on the bracket. Bear in mind that:
• it is the responsibility of the caravanner to check with the tow bracket manufacturer whether additional accessory items can be added;
• some major manufacturers have suggested that as long as the additional item doesn't move the towball more than 15mm (⅝in) away from the mounting face plate, the arrangement is acceptable;
• to permit the subsequent addition of accessory items between a tow ball and bracket flange plate, Witter now tests its towbars with a 25mm (1in) spacer in place on the test rig;
• when an accessory is added, it is usually recommended that at least three clear threads are visible beyond the end of the nut – that's a minimum protrusion of about 6mm (¼in). If necessary, a longer bolt of the required tensile strength should be fitted.

Legislation

When selecting suitable attachment points for a towbar, a bracket designer is confronted with the fact that modern vehicles:

i) are much lighter than older models, and
ii) are built with accident crumple zones.

This means there are only a few points of suitable integrity for the attachment of a tow bar. In recognition of this, a car owner should never attempt to make up his or her own bracket.

Before legislation relating to towbar installations was introduced, tow bracket specialists designed their products by drawing on knowledge that had been built up over a long period of time.

Under the latest legislation, all brackets passing type-approval tests are required to display an approval plate.

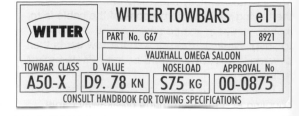

WITTER	WITTER TOWBARS	e11
	PART No. G67	8921
	VAUXHALL OMEGA SALOON	

TOWBAR CLASS	D VALUE	NOSELOAD	APPROVAL No
A50-X	D9. 78 KN	S75 KG	00-0875

CONSULT HANDBOOK FOR TOWING SPECIFICATIONS

Drop plates and flange-mounted accessories

Even though tow brackets are manufactured to produce a standard towing height, if you have a bolt-on tow ball then a drop plate or other accessory item might be easy to fit. However, you are only permitted to add components like these on a 94/20/EC approved bracket if testing was originally conducted with a plate or spacers installed.

Directive 94/20/EC specifies that the centre of a tow ball should be between 350mm and 420mm (13.8–16.6in) to the ground when the vehicle is laden to maximum weight.

Problems arise, however, with some older caravans which have an unusually low coupling. Equally, if a car is only partially laden, it might be helpful if the tow ball was slightly lower. In either case, a drop plate which lowers the ball height is permitted on vehicles registered *before 1st August 1998* in order to achieve an outfit where the caravan front is very slightly 'nose-down'. However, a drop plate must *never* be used to *raise* the height of a tow ball.

Sometimes their products were designed to fit the attachment points recommended by vehicle manufacturers, but quite often other mounting points were used as well.

Note: *These practices are still followed when designing and installing bespoke 'one-off' brackets for commercial vehicles, but this is expected to change in 2112.*

However, car manufacturers became increasingly aware that certain models in their ranges could become popular towcars, so they began fitting threaded captive nuts during vehicle assembly to coincide with the installation points on their 'own-brand' towbars. This practice is now increasingly prevalent, and although some cars don't have pre-fitted fixings in place a large number have dimple points in their steel panels to indicate the drilling points for bracket attachment.

As cars became much lighter the importance of using car manufacturers' designated towbar fitting points was also instrumental in creating a European Directive, which gained legal status in the UK. The panel alongside describes this in detail and new legislation immediately affected the design and attachment of towing brackets. So from 1st August 1998 adherence to strict standards became obligatory for almost all cars. The small number of vehicles not covered by the legislation includes low volume production vehicles (including most kit cars), and specially imported models (like the Mitsubishi Pajero) which do not bear an 'e' mark on the VIN plate.

To comply with the new law, a towbar prototype has to pass Type Approval tests if the design is intended for installation on vehicles registered on or after 1st August 1998. This applies to 'S' registered cars and later; moreover, to verify the status of a Type Approved tow bracket, a Euronorm-type plate or label has to be affixed to the unit. An example of a typical plate is shown on page 16. The implications for bracket design are:

i) Type Approved tow brackets must be attached to all the recommended fixing points identified by the vehicle manufacturer.

ii) Type Approved tow brackets must not obscure a vehicle number plate when not being used.

iii) To achieve Type Approval, towing brackets have to pass a Euronorm standard.

Breakaway cables

Braked caravans and trailers weighing over 750kg and less than 3,500kg have to be fitted with a sacrificial breakaway cable. In the event of a caravan accidentally becoming unhitched from the towing vehicle, the purpose of the cable is to instantly engage the caravan's brakes and then to snap. Whereas the link with the tow car is then severed, the caravan would be left with its brakes fully engaged.

To achieve this sequence of events, the correct coupling of a purpose-made breakaway cable

Legal points

■ European Standards for towing brackets have replaced the former British Standards in respect of passenger cars registered in the UK after 1st August, 1998, but note that the former British Standard BS AU 114b is still applicable for vehicles registered *before* this date.

■ The European Directive, 94/20/EC – now with legal status in the United Kingdom through an amendment to the *Road Vehicle (Construction & Use) Regulations 1986* – has brought significant changes to the design of towing brackets to be fitted to newer vehicles. The directive applies to all light passenger vehicles which have a *European Whole Vehicle Type Approval (EWVTA) Certificate of Conformity* and which have been registered in the United Kingdom on and after 1st August, 1998.

■ At the time of publication, commercial vehicles such as light commercial vans – including motorcaravans built on these base units – fall outside the legislation.

■ The Directive requires that only Type Approved towing brackets can be fitted to post 1st August 1998 vehicles registered in the UK. Fitting a non-Type Approved bracket can lead to prosecution, an invalidation of a vehicle warranty, and a likely invalidation of the vehicle's insurance cover.

■ Since one of the objectives of the new Directive is to encourage free trade, a vehicle manufacturer can no longer insist that you fit *only* the bracket listed under their accessory items. Provided the alternative product is of 'equivalent quality', you should not – in theory – be in conflict with the vehicle's warranty. It is the interpretation of 'equivalent quality' which is the problem area and some vehicle manufacturers are checking the wording of their warranties with particular vigilance so that there's no chance of ambiguity.

■ EU Regulation 55 has now superseded EC Directive 94/20/EC and took effect from 1st April 2007. This will gradually become embodied into all European Member State legal systems for the Type Approval of towbars. In effect this replicates all the technical requirements of 94/20/EC and merely amends one small element on towbar Type Approved labels. Whereas a product was previously marked with a rectangle containing 'e' plus the country code, it is now marked as an 'E' plus country code and is contained in a circle.

For many years owners have been advised not to attach a clip directly to an eyelet on the towcar. Movement during towing sometimes causes a bouncing clip to settle in an upright position on the eyelet and a modest tug can then force its spring tag to distort and pull open, whereupon it then gets detached.

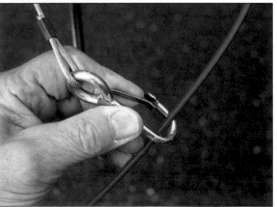

To overcome the possibility of a distorted clip, it is recommended that the clip is passed right through the eyelet. The plastic-coated wire should then be taken back towards the caravan and the clip is then attached to the cable itself, thereby forming a noose.

Although this system works satisfactorily, many towbars are not made with an eyelet. Other provisions can be made retrospectively, but all too often the eye itself is too small. That's why a clip is often fastened directly to an eyelet, and this sometimes causes slack cable to hang too close to the road.

In 2004, both AL-KO and BPW chassis manufacturers noted the problem and introduced a new cable (left) fitted with a clip that features a hinging spring gate. Its design is similar to the hinging gate on rock climbers' karabiners, and unlike the one on the right these clips *can* be coupled directly to an eyelet.

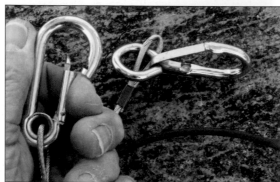

A breakaway cable must apply a caravan's brake efficiently if a coupling hitch were to become detached accidentally. To achieve an effective pull on the cable, its connection point on a towcar should be as near to the centre line as possible. The towing eyelet used here is much too far to the side of the car.

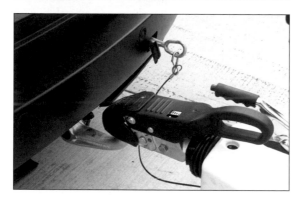

If a towbar has been supplied without an eyelet for attaching a breakaway cable, some owners fit an accessory described as a 'pigtail' (not to be confused with 'pigtails' used in electrical work). It should be no further from the centre line of a tow ball than 100mm (4in); this one is fine.

In the absence of coupling points, a breakaway cable is often looped once round the stem of a tow ball. Code of Practice BS AU 257 (1998) deemed this acceptable but it is not the preferred method of attachment. Were a coupling to jump from a tow ball, the cable could flip off before activating braking.

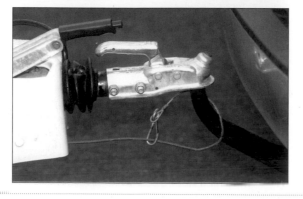

Replacing breakaway cables

The length of a breakaway cable fitted on an AL-KO Kober chassis is slightly different from the cable used on a BPW chassis. It's essential to fit the correct type and AL-KO has traditionally used a bright red plastic sleeve on its cables whereas BPW sleeves are blue. Cables are also sold by independent suppliers, although these are seldom any cheaper; in addition some specialists have raised questions regarding their length and whether the sacrificial breaking point of these products replicates the severance characteristics of AL-KO or BPW replacements.

It is certainly wise to fit a new cable supplied with one of the hinge-gate clips shown earlier, and many fitters obtain these direct from the appropriate chassis manufacturer. When a replacement is fitted it is also important to ensure that the route taken by the cable runs as straight as possible between the attachment points on (a) the towcar and (b) the caravan handbrake.

These four photographs show details about replacement:

If a cable appears distorted and if the plastic sheath shows signs of damage it is time to get a new one fitted.

Check the coupling point on the towing vehicle and confirm that it is no further from the centre of the tow ball than 100mm (4in).

Thread the replacement through the cable guide under the A-frame; unfortunately some guides lack the smooth edges of this example.

This coupling ring isn't hard to attach to a handbrake lever, but crimping the hook types on sale calls for heavy-duty pliers or a portable vice.

Above: Some doubts are expressed whether it is acceptable to loop a breakaway cable around the stem of a detachable tow ball. If your car has a detachable product, the National Caravan Council states: 'You must seek guidance on procedure from the towbar manufacturer or supplier.'

Below: Not only should a breakaway cable follow a straight route to its attachment point on a caravan brake lever, it must also have some slack – but not enough to let it drag on the road. It should be the correct length and you should never wind it twice around the stem of a tow ball as shown here.

Technical Tip

Several caravans have recently been badly damaged by burnt-out brakes; the drums have sometimes become so hot that they have been irreparably damaged. Research conducted by AL-KO Kober with police assistance found that the incidents were particularly prevalent with these car/caravan combinations:

a) where a caravan is fitted with a gas piston-assisted hand brake lever as described on page 54.

b) where a breakaway cable has insufficient slack when coupled to the tow car.

c) where a powerful 4x4 off-road vehicle is being used.

Even a modest tug on this type of hand lever causes it to engage a caravan's brakes fully; that is very helpful when you're parked but NOT when you're towing. The research also found that 4x4 types of towing vehicles are sometimes so powerful that drivers have not always realised that the caravan's brakes have started to bind. Equally significant has been the fact that on several vehicles of this type, the attachment point for the breakaway cable is positioned a long way forward of the towball. This causes the connected cable to be too tight and when a corner is turned it tightens even more and then activates the brake lever. If there's an assisting gas piston fitted, the lever immediately flies up to fully engage the caravan's brakes.

The National Caravan Council has since published a free Advice Sheet which lists the right and wrong ways to connect a breakaway cable. The sheet is distributed through dealers and is also displayed on the NCC website: www.thecaravan.net

is crucial. The photographs above highlight examples of good and bad practice together with some of the problems which arise when a towbar lacks a coupling eyelet of the required diameter.

There is no doubt that one of the errors made by many caravanners is the incorrect attachment of the breakaway cable. Fortunately the incidence of caravans breaking free from towcars is low… but it does happen.

Also be aware that if a breakaway cable is too taut it can lead to burnt-out brakes on a caravan as described in the accompanying technical tip panel.

Testing

Today, prototype brackets are rigorously tested before a new design is manufactured. However, the integrity of a bracket is of little merit if the key points of attachment on a vehicle are showing signs of rust. Sound fitting points are crucial.

During testing, a prototype bracket is fitted on a rig and submitted to a two million cycle fatigue 'Type Approved' test. This ensures the bracket design is sound, but it pays no regard to the

attachment itself. Car manufacturers, however, are now expecting a test to be conducted with a bracket fitted to a bare body shell to confirm that the whole installation is sound. This type of test adds considerably to the cost and if you buy a vehicle manufacturer's 'own model', this will undoubtedly be reflected in the price.

Safety matters have gained more attention in recent years and car manufacturers are also more aware now of the needs of the towing public. So they include their own towing brackets as accessory items and urge owners to choose them. However, brackets from many independent manufacturers are made to the same tested standard, and may be considerably less expensive.

National Trailer and Towing Association (NTTA)

The caravan industry is supported by a number of trade associations whose membership is made up of manufacturers, retailers, service specialists and so on. The National Trailer and Towing Association is a good example and, like many such organisations, it runs training courses for its members. However, it also advises the public on towing matters via its website at www.ntta.co.uk. For

The NTTA runs training courses to keep member towbar fitters up to date on installations and wiring techniques.

instance, when selecting a towbar fitter it is difficult for a caravanner to ascertain if an installer is conversant with the complexities of modern car wiring and is aware that caravan 12V connections have undergone changes in recent years; and although auto electricians at franchise dealers would be knowledgeable about new wiring systems in vehicles, they are not always aware of the changes (described later) that have occurred in pin allocations on caravan plugs.

To help caravanners and other trailer users choose a well-informed installer, the NTTA has therefore established a 'Quality Secured Accreditation Scheme' for towbar fitters. Approved 'QS' installers receive annual assessment visits, quality of work checks, staff experience verification and other checks. Without doubt, this accreditation scheme helps you choose a workshop or mobile fitter that's able to offer a first-class service.

DIY installations

As stated earlier, some towing brackets are suitable for DIY installation, although the electrical work on modern cars is usually better left to trained automotive electrical specialists. One of the chief problems relating to fitting a towbar is being able to dismantle rear body panels, some of which need modifying to accommodate a projecting tow ball. On several recent vehicles panel removal and alteration is not always easy.

That said, tow bracket installation instructions are usually clearly laid out, and Witter Towbars has taken this one step further by creating online animated fitting instructions. The initiative, called 'i-fit', is an interactive web presentation which leads an installer through the task step by step. In addition Witter's recent annual catalogues have provided over a hundred pages explaining legal issues, practical information and Type Approval developments. Other bracket manufacturers offer useful literature, too, and obtaining copies should always be a starting point for anyone wanting to prepare a vehicle for towing.

Check the components and fixings against the list on the instruction sheet.

Needless to say, every vehicle is different and the sequence of photos which follows can only provide a superficial insight into bracket installation work. The 2001 Vauxhall Corsa shown here was needed for towing a lightweight folding caravan and it was decided to install a bracket from an independent manufacturer.

General tools normally needed
- Selection of spanners and sockets
- Electric drill with sharp twist drill bits
- Conical hole-enlarging drill or rotary files
- Safe means for elevating the vehicle
- Calibrated torque wrench

Note: *To avoid scratches and general panel damage, special tools may be needed to remove rear body skirts and integrated moulded 'bumpers' on some vehicles.*

Safety
- Never work under a car that is merely supported by a jack. Either drive the rear on to some firm planks or robust ramps or use a hoist in a garage.
- Use eye protection, hand protection and any other items recommended in the installation instructions and power tool guidance literature.

Preparatory work
- Some brackets are now finished with long-lasting protective finishes. Witter brackets, for example, are shotblasted before passing through a seven-stage zinc phosphate pre-treatment. The later application of automotive specification resin paint provides notable protection – in the past many brackets were only given an application of undercoat primer or a parsimonious lick of topcoat. In fact many DIY installers would add further coats of a product such as Hammerite. So check the finish of your bracket and if you want to add further protection, check with the towbar manufacture regarding the compatibility of the paint you intend to apply.
- Open the kit of parts, lay out all the fixings, identify them and check that nothing is missing.
- When fitting a towbar to an older vehicle, releasing rusted bolts is often a time-consuming exercise. You might decide to apply lubricants or release agents some time before starting the job.

Note:
- *Good quality torque wrenches that are calibration-checked periodically are expensive so it's not unusual for a DIY installer to get a service specialist or towbar fitter to make the final checks before putting a towbar into commission.*
- *Some towbar centres often require a second fitter to conduct a tow ball torque check and both members of staff then have to sign the worksheet.*
- *The NTTA recommends that when tightening towbar bolts you should start with the smallest first and leave the large bolts until last. Doing this the wrong way round means that tightening a small bolt is unlikely to be able to move or 'settle' a bracket's framework if the large fixings were fully tightened first.*

Work in progress

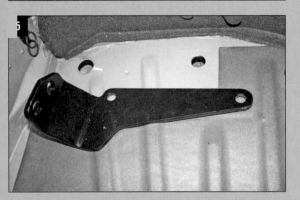

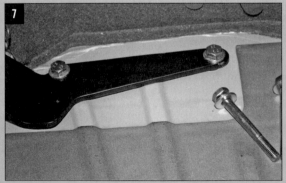

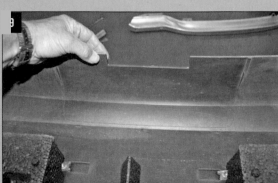

1. The difficulty of removing a rear bumper and underskirt panel varies from model to model. Care is needed when flexing the plastic.

2. On this vehicle a structural crossmember is unbolted, removed and replaced by the main section of the new towing bracket.

3. This Vauxhall didn't have captive bolts but drilling points were marked in the panels; a small section of rust treatment had to be scraped away before drilling.

4. Although it's best to drill a small pilot hole first, a good quality cone drill like this is used by fitters for enlarging holes in thin metal panels.

5. Strengthening brackets like this often have to be installed on the floor of the boot space or in the bottom of the spare wheel pan.

6. To prevent compressing two adjacent steel panels when tightening bolts it's normal to insert spacer tubes, which are supplied in the kit.

7. With a spacer in place, the bracket is loosely fitted. Bolts are normally finger-tightened before a methodical tighten-up and torque check later.

8. It's not unusual to fit bracket support sections like this, which are inserted inside a main box section component.

9. This was a fairly easy cut-out in the rear skirt to make space for the tow ball. Cuts are normally made with a sharp knife or small powered cutting wheel.

10. All bolts have to be torqued-up correctly as described in the installation instructions. These bolts on the tow ball are very important.

Having removed protective shielding and exposed part of the wiring loom, an installer checks which cables supply each of the rear lights.

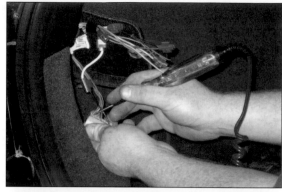

In this installation an audible buzzer is fitted to verify that direction indicators are working, although a subsidiary warning light is often preferable.

Snap-lock connectors ('Scotchlocks') must match the cable size, and to avoid corrosion should only be used inside a vehicle where it's dry.

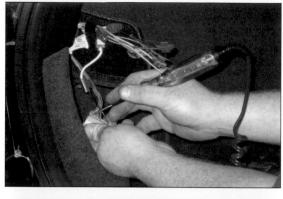

At the end of an installation, a fitter uses a check panel to confirm that the new plug/socket connections are working correctly.

Electrical modifications

It is a legal requirement that a caravan's road lights operate in conjunction with the lights on the tow car. Furthermore, when towing, there's also a need to keep a caravan battery charged and to ensure that the refrigerator remains in operation. To achieve these objectives, a towing vehicle has to be appropriately wired to provide the power.

Since the First Edition of *The Caravan Manual* was published in 1993 the electrical systems in cars have changed radically. For instance, it was fairly straightforward to make minor wiring alterations in most cars manufactured around that period in order to supply the electrical sockets for towing. The 12N black plug and socket were concerned with caravan road lights; the grey 12S plug and socket to provide power (a) to charge a caravan's leisure battery, and (b) to run its fridge.

In the past caravanners with a rudimentary understanding of auto electrics often wired these connections themselves. To operate a caravan's road lights, for example, extension cables were connected to the cables supplying a vehicle's rear lights and then taken through the car boot for coupling into a 12N socket. However, this is no longer possible on modern cars fitted with electronic control systems.

Nevertheless, if the car you propose to tow with is an older model without the kind of electronic aids described in later sections, the photographs above show the traditional way of connecting-up the cables needed for the pins on a 12N road light socket.

Traditional way to connect a 12N socket

The 2001 Vauxhall Corsa shown earlier had neither a bulb failure warning device nor sophisticated electronic control systems. For this reason it was acceptable to take some multicore cable, couple-up its separate seven wires to the 12N socket and connect the separate cables to the appropriate individual feed wires supplying power to the car's rear lights.

Installations like this were commonplace some years ago but this kind of wiring modification can no longer be carried out on vehicles fitted with electronic control systems.

Electronic control systems

One of the first features that brought an end to simple wiring modifications was the introduction of electronic bulb failure warning systems in cars. To be informed when a road light isn't working is a useful safety feature, but a car's sensing system ceases to work properly if you use the cable feeding a rear light on the tow car to provide power to run a caravan light bulb as well. Such bulb failure devices were initially only fitted on expensive cars but they are now fitted on vehicles in all price ranges.

Other electronic control systems have also been introduced and many of the latest cars are fitted with:

• Control units for maximising engine performance and economy.
• ABS systems to control braking on slippery surfaces and traction control systems (TCS).

• CANbus multiplex wiring systems in whole (or in part) instead of traditional wiring harnesses.
• Electronic Stability Programmes (ESP) in which a gyroscopic sensor detects unusual lateral movements, and sensors on the wheels monitor irregular rotation speeds; steering irregularities are also monitored. Automatic remedial control strategies including brake application, throttle adjustment and steering control are then instantly brought into action to restore normal stability.
• Trailer Stability Programmes (TSP) initiate further automatic control strategies if irregular movements are detected in a trailer. As soon as yaw sensors identify unfavourable swaying, a braking/speed adjustment and steering response system is again brought into action, albeit with recognition that there's a trailer involved.
• Hill Start Assist (HSA) prevents a vehicle rolling backwards whenever it comes to a standstill if negotiating a hill. The driver has no need to operate foot brake or handbrake because HSA comes into action automatically, and once it's clear to proceed, all a driver needs to do is to depress the throttle as usual.

Modern electronic controls systems offer great benefits but they mean that work on a vehicle's electric system is often the preserve of specially qualified engineers. In response to this some readers might be disappointed to learn that wiring-up external electrical sockets on many cars is certainly not a DIY task; errors can be costly and control malfunction might lead to serious accidents.

Of course, you can still monitor the operation of an installation and verify the correct function of multi-pin connectors. Equally if a socket on the rear of a car gets damaged it's not a difficult job to fit a replacement; it usually demands patience rather than electrical knowledge.

Also be aware that some vehicles are fitted

Wiring a socket demands patience and manual dexterity rather than electrical knowledge.

with a 13-pin socket at the time of manufacture, but these don't always recognise the needs of caravanners. For example, many imported German vehicles fitted with a 13-pin socket as original equipment may only have 8 pins connected-up. That's fine for a boat trailer, but it leaves a caravanner needing to have additional wiring carried out to provide 12V supplies for running a caravan fridge and charging a leisure battery when the vehicle's towing. Information on these two elements is given in *Chapter 7, Low Voltage Supply* and *Chapter 11, Refrigerators*.

As a further point, it is appropriate to provide an explanation why jobs hitherto tackled successfully by DIY enthusiasts are now realistically beyond the scope of most practical owners. Hence the aim of the following section is to give a brief insight into the complex systems being installed in modern-day cars.

CANbus multiplexing

CAN stands for 'Controlled Area Network'. In traditional vehicle wiring, a large number of cables are used to supply current to 12V accessories,

---

Routine checks

Although seldom used for installation work, this type of check device is fine for confirming operation of the pins in your car's towing sockets.

Periodically carry out a visual check of pins, especially during winter when grit and damp can cause a short circuit in poorly protected sockets.

Using the 12N socket drawing on page 32, a check with a tester was done to find if power for the caravan's left sidelights was reaching pin 7.

Some damp-inhibiting sprays cause damage to plastic plugs and sockets, but a squirt of Tri-Flow twice a year leaves the brass contacts clean.

Note: *The check device shown above has a tungsten filament illumination wire in the handle and these draw sufficient current to upset the Central Processing Units (CPUs) in some vehicles. However, these products are usually fine for checking pins in a towing socket. For more advanced installation checks, some fitters now use testers fitted with light emitting diodes (LEDs); when these are illuminated the draw of current is much less than the consumption of bulbs fitted with tungsten filaments.*

The ECS Electronic trailer module is a central processor unit (CPU) which is often used in electrical installations.

Employing computer technology and sophisticated components like this in cars means that auto electrical systems are remarkably complex.

and wiring 'looms', sometimes called 'harnesses', are the defining feature of such older wiring. However, by employing ideas used in computer technology the automotive industry has now introduced wholly different 12V supply and control systems. These draw on the principle that if one cable can carry out the work of many cables, there's a much smaller wiring harness and a corresponding saving of copper, weight, installation time and cost. The reduction of cables is achieved using a system referred to as 'multiplexing', and Toyota first experimented with this idea as long ago as 1955.

Today's circuitry is certainly reliable, and self-diagnostic benefits are useful too. Instead of bundles of cables being used to send power to individual 12V accessories a large single cable provides the power, and in some installations one of these runs round the whole vehicle. Once a power supply has been distributed, appliances then need to be switched into operation. This is where a multiplex system plays its part because a large number of data signals can be transmitted using what is referred to as a single 'bus' cable. Working in conjunction with this 'bus' cable are electrical switches (called 'relays') which are situated throughout a vehicle; these are triggered when they receive their activating data signal from the 'bus' cable.

In CANbus multiplexing systems, data signals are sent at high speed which can mean around 30,000 times a second. These data signals operate computer processing units (CPUs) which are instrumental in distributing the power needed to run electrical equipment such as lamps, motors, relays and so on. Decoders are key components in this process and their role is to recognise their particular call-up data code. On receipt of the relevant data, a decoder then activates a relay which duly supplies the power

required to set a particular electrical accessory into operation.

This is only a brief, simplified overview of the radical changes that have occurred in recent vehicle wiring systems. The benefits of CANbus installations are wide-ranging, and thanks to control facilities like computer-based engine management systems we enjoy much improved fuel efficiency and enhanced engine power. Improved braking activation and stability control facilities are invaluable safety features too.

The benefits of these innovations are indisputable but when it comes to wiring-up sockets to supply the road lights on a caravan there are many implications. Firstly, there are many older vehicles still in use which are not fitted with electronic control systems. Secondly, there are many variations in the circuitry of vehicles which are equipped with CANbus multiplex wiring systems. For example, some recent cars – e.g. the Honda Accord – even employ a mixture of both CANbus multiplex and conventional wiring within the same vehicle. In fact it is the dissimilarities of wiring strategies in modern cars that makes it hard to select the best way to create an appropriate supply to serve a caravan.

CANbus systems and towbar wiring

One outcome of recent developments is that more and more electrical installations are likely to be carried out at main dealer workshops, some of which have hourly labour charge rates that are more than double those of well-established towbar fitters. However, there are many highly qualified independent installers and a caravanner just needs to make sure that he or she uses a towbar specialist who has attended training courses such as those run by the National Trailer and Towing Association (NTTA).

A further implication of sophisticated car electronics is the fact that some 'universal wiring kits' sold by towbar manufacturers may not be suitable in certain cars. In consequence 'vehicle-specific kits' are preferred by many fitters, and to comply with vehicle warranty requirements some specialists are only installing the electrical packages supplied by main dealers. These are often costly, but their pre-fitted coupling plugs and sockets are designed to connect directly into units already located in the car and this undoubtedly makes installation work more straightforward.

Warranty issues aside, independent vehicle-specific kits of high quality are available from suppliers like Right Connections. Westfalia in Germany is another independent manufacturer, and this company is contracted to supply vehicle-specific wiring kits to manufacturers in the VAG group, which includes Audi and Volkswagen.

When it comes to basic installation principles, ascertaining whether a vehicle has a multiplexing system is often difficult. In addition, an auto electrician needs to find a permanent 12V supply and it is often best to take this directly from a vehicle battery. It should never be taken from a multiplex 12V power feed cable because this can lead to a distortion of data signals which, in turn, may upset a vehicle's management system.

To avoid this kind of problem it is hardly surprising that towbar specialists often choose to install vehicle-specific wiring kits complete with pre-fitted electrical connectors. On the other hand, it is sometimes possible to completely bypass a car's existing wiring system when wiring-up sockets for towing. This alternative strategy has been successfully used by many towbar installers since the late 1980s.

Bypass wiring systems

The basic principle behind a bypass wiring system works as follows. If you were to take a 12V live (positive) supply direct from a vehicle's battery to a multi-pin 12N socket together with a neutral (negative) connection, you would completely bypass the car's wiring and diagnostic installation. Of course, this would mean that all the road lights served by the towing plug and socket are permanently live and all lamps on the caravan would operate simultaneously. Individual switching is then needed for the supply to work as required, and this is achieved by adding relays which are electrically-controlled switches.

It was pointed out earlier that if you were to connect a caravan lighting cable to the feed wire providing 12V power to one of the rear light units in your car, this would upset a bulb failure detection facility. However, if, when a car light is in operation, you only take a *tiny* amount of current – i.e. just enough to activate a relay and nothing else – a bulb failure warning device might not detect this. So in a bypass system the type of relays fitted are able to perform their switching function by 'stealing' only a very small amount of current from a car's supply cables serving the lights. In fact they may only take around 10mA (0.01A) to activate and a vehicle's bulb failure device seldom detects such a very small loss.

These are the key features, then, of a standard bypass system:

• Power to run the caravan's road lights is drawn directly from the car battery using a newly installed independent supply cable and an in-line fuse.
• Relays which control the 12V flow to the different pins in a 12N towing socket are triggered by a small current drawn from the feed cables that serve the towcar's rear lamps.
• Master control units that carry out these switching operations are available from several manufacturers and distributors.

The PCT 'Towing Interface' is shown alongside as an example of a master control unit used in bypass systems. Clear markings on the case and supporting instructions indicate how the unit is fitted.

Broadly speaking, this is a well conceived way of operating the road lights on a caravan without

Relays

Relays are used in both cars and caravans. At its simplest, a relay is merely a switch, except that it isn't operated manually. The switching action is normally activated by an electric current. This has a number of advantages over a conventional switch.

First a relay can create a switching action automatically when fed with a triggering current. This means that the user doesn't have to remember to operate a manual switch, so a relay can stop current going to a caravan refrigerator from a car battery as soon as the engine is switched off. The driver doesn't need to remember to disconnect the supply.

It is also important to recognise that when a relay is used, a large current feeding an appliance can be switched on or off by using a very small current to activate the switching system.

Most relays are made with a mechanical make and break system. A current fed to a coil creates an electro-magnet which in turn pulls a spring-loaded make/break lever – which then works just like a manual switch. This type of relay has been fitted for many years in cars, and in some caravans too. However, solid-state relays with electronic switching are being used more and more.

Self-switching relays, now very popular with towbar fitters installing 12S systems, incorporate electronic sensing circuits to activate the current to the relay coils. The sensing circuits monitor the voltage coming to the relay through the supply line from the battery and only switch a relay ON when the alternator is providing its full charge. Equally, the relay switches OFF when the extra voltage provided by the alternator charge is terminated, i.e. when the engine is no longer running.

making alterations to a car's wiring system. Unfortunately, however, the installation of bypass systems is still not straightforward on some types of car. For example, cables which feed the rear lights on recent BMW, Mercedes and Lexus cars carry a pulsing power supply and this is likely to cause a standard relay to 'chatter' on and off. To cope with the problem, additional circuitry is needed to smooth out electrical pulses.

Prior to embarking on an installation it is normal to disconnect a vehicle battery before fitting electrical accessories, but this can have several implications on modern vehicles, especially when 'battery saver' devices are used. For instance, in diesel vehicles you should first turn on the ignition which activates the heater plugs and then wait for them to cut out before coupling-up a battery saver. On a number of vehicles you should also take the key out of the ignition before disconnecting a battery. Remember, too, that one-touch electric windows may also need reprogramming after a battery has been disconnected and reinstated. Even the installation of a bypass system requires knowledge about the vehicle being adapted.

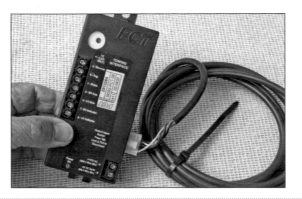

The ZR 1328A 'Towing Interface' from PCT is easy to wire into vehicles in which a bypass system won't interfere with their electronic circuitry.

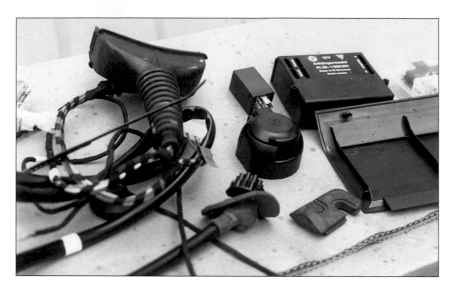

components together using pre-fitted connector blocks is often fairly straightforward. Provided a manufacturer's instructions are clearly presented, and as long as dealers are subsequently willing to download the necessary software onto a new set-up, it might be less daunting than it all sounds at first.

Note: *To find out more about multiplex CANbus systems, see Chapter 5 of* The Trailer Manual *by Brian Bate, published by Haynes.*

General wiring advice

Notwithstanding recent developments in vehicle wiring, some caravanners will want to tow using an older car that doesn't have electronic systems. For that reason several general principles are given here about cable, connections and fuses.

Safety
• When tackling electrical installations, it is wise to disconnect a vehicle's battery. On some cars, however, this upsets radio and security system memory functions. Battery savers are available for dealing with these elements but check if their use is acceptable on your car.
• If connecting-up a trailer warning light on the dashboard, take appropriate steps to ensure that an emergency airbag isn't triggered accidentally. It is believed that there has been a fatality as a result of suffocation from false activation.
• Check all safety warnings in the vehicle owners' manual.

Cables
• Cable with a core of the appropriate diameter and rating is essential when wiring 12V accessories. If a cable is too thin and it's running over a considerable distance, a voltage drop is produced which can be severe enough to upset the operation of appliances such as a caravan refrigerator. This subject is discussed again in Chapter 7.
• On bypass systems in a car, the NTTA recommends that a 12V supply cable should not be of less than 3.0mm² nominal cross-sectional

In addition, it is now being reported that some recent cars can even detect the loss of the 0.01A needed to activate bypass system relays. At present problems like this are unusual and bypass systems have been successfully fitted by many towbar installers since the late 1980s. Products used for these installations are supplied by specialists like Kewal, PCT, Ryder, Towing Electrics and Towsure, and the cost of components is notably good.

Nevertheless, more and more towbar fitters are now installing vehicle-specific wiring kits as opposed to bypass systems. One possible shortcoming in a standard bypass arrangement, for example, is the fact that it might not initiate on-board features like a trailer stability programme (TSP). In contrast, when a vehicle manufacturer's own wiring kit is installed, the coupling of a trailer plug is identified by the car's software whereupon the stability programme is immediately brought into action.

Paradoxically, if the use of vehicle-specific wiring kits continues to gather momentum this might lead to a renewed increase in owner-installation work. Circuits inside electronic boxes are certainly complex but plugging these

Be careful when working under the dashboard; emergency air bags have sometimes been triggered accidentally.

area (26.5A current rating/44 copper strands of 0.3mm in the core). Cables of this rating are recommended for operating a caravan fridge and to charge a leisure battery via the 12S socket connections. But note: large caravan fridge-freezers now being fitted in some models may draw nearly 20A, and to ensure they run efficiently even thicker cable may be needed to minimise voltage drop. Some installers achieve this by running double lengths of 3.0mm² (44 strand cable) in large fridge-freezer supply systems to effectively create a 6.0mm² cable.

• If a cable is too thin it can also get hot; if the insulation then starts to melt the consequences can be serious.

Fuses

• A fuse provides over-current protection to both components and circuits; these should always be mounted where they are easily accessible for checking and replacement.

• Types of fuse vary in quality, accuracy and reliability. For example, glass tube fuses are not very accurate and the springs fitted in their holders can get weak, thereby causing uncertain connections. Ceramic fuses were often used in older cars too, but they are not very accurate either and can sometimes overheat; they can also corrode quite easily.

• Blade fuses that are mounted in purpose-made holders are now the motor industry standard. These are much more accurate and are sold in many different ratings.

• When deciding what fuse is appropriate for protecting an appliance, a traditional rule of thumb is to find the maximum current draw (Amps) for the appliance and then to uprate this by 10%. The resulting calculation is unlikely to match a fuse rating exactly so the figure is adjusted upwards to establish what fuse is required. (Example: If an appliance takes up to 6.0A, the addition of 10% raises this to 6.6A. There's no fuse rated at 6.6A but the next size up is 7.5A so that would be fitted.)

Cable connections

A good electrical connection is always important

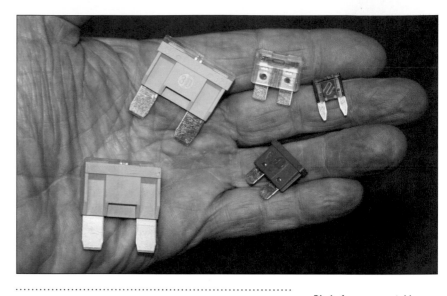

and a universal term for describing a sound result is to say that it is 'gas tight'. This is achieved, for example, if the compression of cable strands within a connector is so positive that there's no contact with the air and no attendant risk of subsequent corrosion.

However, when carried out by a skilled person a soldered joint is regarded by most auto electricians as the best way to join cables. A quicker method is to use crimp connectors, and when used externally these types of coupling are often covered with heat-shrink insulation sleeving.

Internal connections in dry locations in a vehicle can also be carried out using snap-lock connectors as shown in the panel on page 28. These are made in different sizes to suit the main cable and the joining 'tap cable'; it is most important to select the correct ones. The colour-coding depicts the suitability relative to the cable size expressed in mm² as follows:

Permitted sizes of main and tap cables in connectors of different colours
Red   0.5–1.5mm²
Blue   1.5–2.8mm²
Yellow   2.8–6.0mm²

Blade fuses are notably accurate, come in a wide range of ratings and have become the motor industry standard.

Soldered connections are especially good when carried out by a skilled electrician.

When soldered or crimped connections are used externally they should be completed using heat-shrink insulation.

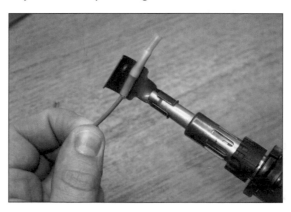

Connectors

Snap-lock connectors or 'Scotchlocks' derive a feed from a cable by making a small penetration through its insulation sheath. Although a hinged plastic flap covers the metal tag which penetrates the copper core, there will always be a small cut left in the insulation if the coupling is later removed. This is one reason why some electricians dislike these components.

Crimp connections are more positive but necessitate cutting the original cable in order to fit a double female connector socket and 'bullet connectors' on all the coupling cables.

Snap-lock connectors are colour-coded to suit different sizes of cables.

A metal tag in a snap-lock connector incises through the insulation of the cable providing the 12V supply.

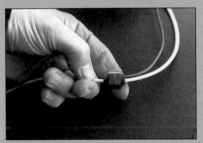

Once the snap-lock tag is squeezed through both wires, a protective flap covers the exposed metal.

Crimp connectors are preferred by many auto electricians but a sound joint is only achieved if a good quality ratchet-type crimping tool is used.

Multicore cable

In order to operate both the road lights and a caravan's auxiliary items – e.g. the fridge – when towing, two types of seven-core multicore cable are sold to suit the respective 12N and 12S connections. With the advent of 13-pin connections, a 12-core cable is also being marketed, recognising that only 12 of the pins are normally allocated.

12N black-sheathed cable
• Purpose-made seven-core cable sheathed with black insulation should be used.
• Alternatively, eight-core 12N cable is needed if you decide to fit a mechanical switching socket to control fog lamps as described later.
• The white earth cable has a cross-sectional area of 2.0mm² to yield a continuous current rating of 17.5A. Its core is made up of 28 filaments.
• The other coloured cables have a cross-sectional area of 1.0mm² to yield a continuous current rating of 8.75A. These are made up of 14 filaments, each of which is 0.33mm in diameter.

12S grey-sheathed cable
• Even though several pins have no allocation in a 12S socket, you should use seven-core

cable sheathed with grey insulation. Approved 12S cable is slightly larger in girth than the 12N cable to suit the demands of the appliances. For example, whereas a caravan sidelight bulb might be rated at 5W, an average size caravan refrigerator is around 95W.
• The white earth cable has a cross-sectional area of 2.5mm² to yield a continuous current rating of 21.5A. It is made up of 36 filaments.
• The coloured cables have a cross-sectional area of 1.5mm² to yield a continuous current rating of 13.0A. These cables are each made up of 21 filaments.
• In the earlier section entitled 'Cables' it is recommended that 12S supply cable for refrigerator operation should be no less than 3.0mm² nominal cross-sectional area (26.5A current rating/44 copper strands of 0.3mm in the core). It is therefore clear that the red 1.5mm² feed in a multicore 12S cable which is designated for the fridge constitutes a weak link in the overall supply that runs from the vehicle battery to the appliance. In recognition of this and to avoid a significant voltage drop, the length of multicore cable should always be as short as possible. However, some auto electricians take advantage of the fact that some of the seven cables are not used at all and couple up one of the spares with the red cable, thereby doubling-up the total current rating of the feed to the fridge.

12-core cable for 13-pin plug/socket connections
• At the time of writing, UK 2009 model caravans are being fitted with 13-pin plugs as standard, instead of a 12N and a 12S plug. These are connected with 12-core cable which has to comply with strict rating requirements. In effect, seven of the cables inside the sheath should have a cross-sectional area of 1.5mm²; the remaining five should have a cross-sectional area of 2.5mm².
• As the table further on shows in respect of pin allocation on 13-pin connectors, the 2.5mm² cable is needed for connection to pins 3, 9, 10, 11 and 13.

Earth connections on the tow car

It is critically important to make sure that any earth connections on a car are clean, sound and electrically efficient. These represent the all-important negative coupling of an electrical appliance and the metal body of cars is normally used to act like a very large cable. Incidentally, very few cars now use the metal body to provide a live coupling.

Poor connections between a cable and an attachment point on a metal panel of a car are surprisingly common. The points of contact should be free of paint and rust and non-experienced DIY electricians often fail to achieve good electrical earth connections. Equally if there are connections on several electrical fittings that need to be attached to the body, each cable in turn should be routed individually to the sound earthing point. Don't join the cables together and then lead only one of the bunch to the earthing point.

Fog lamp disabling devices

When a towcar is coupled to a caravan in foggy weather, it is less distracting for the driver if the vehicle's fog lamps are disabled. Failure to do this causes the powerful fog lamp or lamps on the car to reflect brightly from the front of the caravan. The installation of a disabling facility addresses this problem and places less load on the towcar's alternator.

On modern vehicles with CANbus multiplex systems the disabling facility is normally built-into the programmed trailer operating mode whenever a caravan's electrical sockets are coupled-up.

However, on older cars not fitted with multiplex systems there are two ways of achieving the objective, both of which involve cutting existing cables in the vehicle's wiring loom. If the Hella switchable socket is fitted, this has a mechanical switch built in to a special 12N socket, as shown in the schematic drawing alongside. More recently electrically-operated cut-out relays have been used, and the wiring for a Ryder TFC1 device is also shown here.

The supplementary supply serving a caravan

So far, most of this section on wiring has focussed on road light operation on the towcar and its caravan. However, a towing vehicle is also wired-up so that some of the output from its alternator can be diverted to charge the caravan leisure battery. In addition, a refrigerator that might be running on gas or mains electricity when a caravan is parked on a site must only be operated on a 12V supply when it's being towed. Both of these features call for special wiring in the towcar that is entirely separate from the system dealing with the road lights. Until 13-pin sockets started to be fitted on 2009 caravans these domestic issues were undertaken solely by the 12S coupling.

The idea of having a supplementary (12S) socket was first introduced in the late 1970s but the allocation of its seven pins went through a significant change affecting caravans manufactured from 1st September 1998 onwards. This is discussed later and shown in the socket diagrams too. For the moment, the main concern here is how the 12S supply is connected up with a tow car.

Source of 12V supplies for refrigerator and leisure battery charging

The 12S seven-pin socket on a car (or its more recent 13-pin successor) has to provide a 12V supply, and it's important that the voltage loss at the pins is as small as possible. Voltage drop is reduced when thicker cable is used and to avoid an unacceptable loss the NTTA recommends that each supply feed uses 3.0mm² minimum (44 strand) automotive cable.

It is further recommended that the supply is drawn directly from the vehicle's battery with a 20A in-line fuse fitted in the cables as near to its live (positive) pillar as possible. Don't be tempted

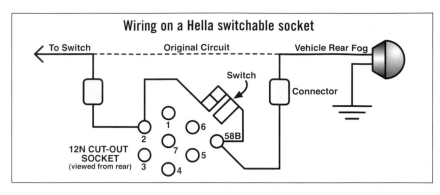

Wiring on a Hella switchable socket

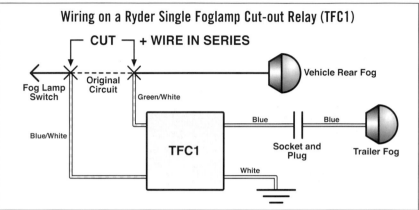

Wiring on a Ryder Single Foglamp Cut-out Relay (TFC1)

to take a supply from a 12V cable supplying a boot light in the towcar because the vehicle manufacturer will have only selected cable with a rating for running this item. It certainly won't be suitable for supplying high consumption products like a refrigerator and a battery charger.

It's the same if you find a connecting block or a cigar-type socket in the back of a car for running 12V accessories. Once again it is highly unlikely that a vehicle's cable supplying these blocks is suitable for running the caravan items mentioned above. That's why cables of 3.0mm² are specified and taken directly from the vehicle's battery.

Controlling the supply to a 12S socket

An automatic switching facility is also needed in the supply that serves a 12S socket. For example, you should only operate a refrigerator on a 12V supply when the engine is running; if it were permanently connected, a fridge would soon discharge a towcar's battery completely.

Equally the caravan's leisure battery also needs to be isolated from the vehicle when you're operating the starter motor. Stealing power from a leisure battery when starting an engine will greatly reduce its life – it isn't built to deliver high currents for short spells like a vehicle battery.

Isolating/activating the 12S supply

For many years the supply to a 12S socket was controlled by electro-magnetic relays, and the twin relay fitting kits from Hella, PCT, Maypole and Trend are often used. These relays are normally fitted in the engine compartment and, if wired correctly, they should switch the 12V supply into action as soon as the engine is running. To

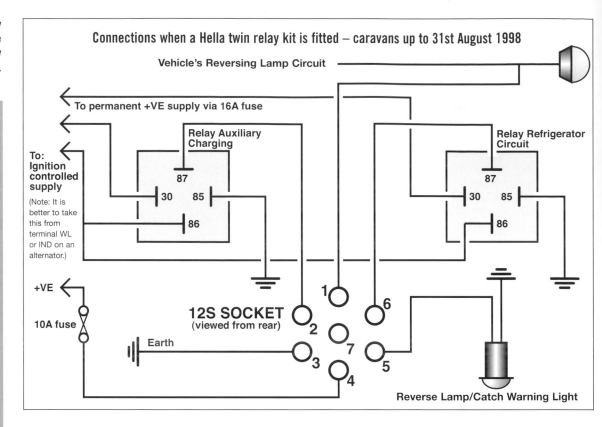

Connections when a Hella twin relay kit is fitted – caravans up to 31st August 1998

Vehicle's Reversing Lamp Circuit

To permanent +VE supply via 16A fuse

Relay Auxiliary Charging

87
30 85
86

To: Ignition controlled supply
(Note: It is better to take this from terminal WL or IND on an alternator.)

Relay Refrigerator Circuit

87
30 85
86

+VE

10A fuse

Earth

12S SOCKET
(viewed from rear)

1
2
3
4
6
7
5

Reverse Lamp/Catch Warning Light

When a Hella twin relay kit is purchased, the connections are clearly shown on the wiring leaflet.

Heavy duty flasher unit

Adding a caravan's direction indicators into a vehicle's electrical system used to cause overloading problems so it was necessary to fit a replacement 'heavy-duty flasher unit'. These units also included a terminal tag which was used to connect the additional (and legally required) warning light or buzzer which confirms when a towed caravan's direction indicators are operating correctly. Heavy duty replacement units were typically supplied by Hella. However, the need for this modification ceased as soon as indicator operation became activated by a computer processing unit (CPU). Since this cannot be changed, additional CPUs or by-pass relays have to be fitted to drive a caravan's lights.

The TEC3M from Towing Electrics is an auto switching combination relay often used in 12S supply systems.

activate the relays a supply has to come from the vehicle's alternator and ideally this is taken from the ignition light circuit. To achieve this, terminal 86 on a Hella relay should be connected to terminal WL or IND on the alternator. Moreover, typical Bosch, Lucas and Delco alternators normally have an ignition light terminal.

It is not good practice to ignore the alternator's connection and to take the relays' trigger supply from an ignition-controlled accessory instead. This would mean that the starter motor is then able to 'steal' power from the caravan's leisure battery *before* the engine is running. However, this is not the case if the supply is connected to an ignition-controlled supply which the car manufacturer has designed to be temporarily disabled when the starter is turning over.

Regrettably, some installers have ignored these points and owners of pre 1st September 1998 caravans who check their 12S socket pins with a test lamp often find that pin 2 is live when the ignition key is turned to the point where the light on the dashboard is illuminated. That reveals the installation

was incorrectly carried out; pin 2 should only become live when the engine is actually running.

However, endeavouring to connect a relay trigger wire to an alternator is certainly not easy on some French, Japanese and Italian vehicles. It is also difficult on vehicles like BMW and Volkswagen, where the alternator connections are encased in a shielding material.

These difficulties prompted the introduction of an altogether different method of switching on the supply to a 12S socket which uses a device called a 'self-switching relay'. The component comprises a monitoring device *and* a relay combined. Its operation takes account of the fact that when an engine isn't running, a voltage reading at the live (positive) pillar of a fully-charged vehicle battery should be around 12.7V. However, when the engine is running and its alternator is functioning correctly there should be a reading of 13.2–13.7V. These differences are noted by a monitor sensor which, in turn, triggers its accompanying relay accordingly. Products like the Ryder TF1170 range of 'Smart' self-switching combination relays have been popular for several years and the photograph alongside shows the TEC3M 30A Auto Switch Combi Relay supplied by Towing Electrics.

So far in this chapter, guidance has related to the business of making connections in towcars. This should now be considered in the light of changes to the sockets themselves.

12N Socket changes

It is certainly a long time since cars were fitted with just a five-pin plug and socket coupling. As soon as caravans needed a 12V supply to run an interior light or two, this was changed to a seven-pin connection and the components are referred to as 12N sockets and 12N plugs, where 'N' stands for 'Normal'.

Of course, a basic trailer still uses just a single 12N connection, but on caravans this practice ceased from October 1979 onwards. However, there are still owners enjoying caravans built before this date, so it's appropriate to give the pin allocation on a single 12N connection. Bear in mind that gas lighting was still in vogue in the early 1970s, and since there were only two or three 12V lights indoors the towcar battery was used to provide their power. The idea of having a separate 'leisure battery' fitted in a caravan had not been adopted at this stage.

Pre-October 1979 caravans
Apart from pin 2 supplying a caravan's lighting indoors, all the other pins on the 12N connection were concerned with road lights as follows:

Pin 1 *(sometimes marked L)* –
    Yellow cable; left indicator
Pin 2 *(sometimes marked 54G)* –
    Blue cable; caravan interior lighting
Pin 3 *(sometimes marked 31)* –
    White cable; earth, i.e. negative return
Pin 4 *(sometimes marked R)* –
    Green cable; right indicator
Pin 5 *(sometimes marked 58R)* –
    Brown cable; right-hand tail light
Pin 6 *(sometimes marked 54)* –
    Red cable; stop lights
Pin 7 *(sometimes marked 54L)* –
    Black cable; left-hand tail light and number plate illumination

Several issues prompted the need for change, one of the main ones being the introduction of fog lamps on cars as an obligatory provision from October 1979. This requirement also applied to caravans built after that date – although there is no legal obligation to fit fog lamps retrospectively on older models. In addition to the fog lamp issue, caravans were also being fitted with more 12V accessories indoors. Furthermore, the supply feeding a refrigerator needs to have a higher rated (i.e. 'thicker') cable than the ones fitted in 12N, black-sheathed, multicore cable.

Post-October 1979 caravans (up to 31st August 1998)
To meet the new demands, pin 2 on the 12N connections was given over to running a fog lamp and a completely new seven-pin plug/socket system was then added. This was called the 12S system, where the 'S' denotes 'supplementary' connections. Here are some of its features:
• A plastic 12S plug is distinctively coloured either white or grey; the 12S plastic sockets have a white cover flap, though occasionally you may come across a cover flap in grey plastic.
• To prevent making wrong connections, the male/female brass tube contacts in the centre of

the cluster of a 12S plug/socket are reversed. This means you cannot insert a 12S plug into a 12N socket and vice versa.
• The 12S multicore cable is thicker than its 12N counterpart. This is because cable of higher rating is needed to supply a caravan refrigerator and the charging facility for the caravan battery. There is also a need for the shared white earth return cable to be thicker.
• The 12S multicore cable is covered in a grey sheath so that it doesn't get confused with the thinner, black-sheathed multicore cable connected to a 12N plug or socket.

From the introduction of this new connection in 1979 and right up to 1st September 1998, nearly all British caravan manufacturers allocated the pins in accordance with a standard approved by the National Caravan Council. In most cases, only four connections were used, namely pins 2, 3, 4 and 6.

However, when new European Regulations were anticipated (and implemented in the United Kingdom on 1st September 1998, as described later), some manufacturers decided to introduce alterations much earlier. For instance, the 12S plugs on Bailey Caravans were wired differently in 1996 and the 12S plugs on caravans from ABI, Crown and Elddis some time later, as wiring diagrams in their owners' manuals revealed.

Notwithstanding these individual changes, the 12N and 12S connections in the majority of caravans between 1979 and 1998 were wired as follows:

12N pin allocation (up to 31st August 1998)
Pin 1 *(sometimes marked L)* –
    Yellow cable; left indicator
Pin 2 *(sometimes marked 54G)* –
    Blue cable; caravan fog lamp(s)
Pin 3 *(sometimes marked 31)* –
    White cable; earth, i.e. negative return
Pin 4 *(sometimes marked R)* –
    Green cable; right indicator
Pin 5 *(sometimes marked 58R)* –
    Brown cable; right-hand tail light
Pin 6 *(sometimes marked 54)* –
    Red cable; stop lights
Pin 7 *(sometimes marked 54L)* –
    Black cable; left-hand tail light and number plate Illumination

12S pin allocation (up to 31st August 1998)
Pin 1 Yellow cable; reversing lights or for a catch on an inertia brake
Pin 2 Blue cable; leisure battery charging
Pin 3 White cable; earth, i.e. negative return
Pin 4 Green cable; permanent power supply from the car battery
Pin 5 Brown cable; sensing device but often left spare
Pin 6 Red cable; refrigerator supply
Pin 7 Black cable; no allocation.

This is shown diagrammatically overleaf when looking directly at the pins in the 12N and 12S sockets.

Some towing brackets only carry a plate to accept a single socket so a modification is needed.

On some vehicles, a removable body panel reveals a location for the towing sockets.

Pin allocations for 12N and
12S sockets
(up to 31st August 1998)

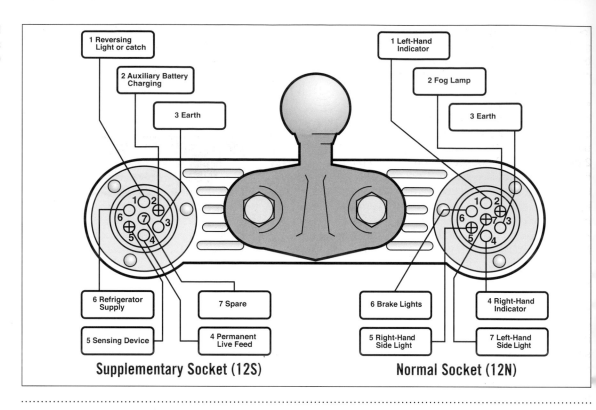

Supplementary Socket (12S)   **Normal Socket (12N)**

1 Reversing Light or catch
2 Auxiliary Battery Charging
3 Earth
6 Refrigerator Supply
5 Sensing Device
7 Spare
4 Permanent Live Feed

1 Left-Hand Indicator
2 Fog Lamp
3 Earth
6 Brake Lights
5 Right-Hand Side Light
4 Right-Hand Indicator
7 Left-Hand Side Light

Why were 12S pin allocations changed?

When European Standard EN1648-1 was introduced in the United Kingdom on 1st September 1998 the changes only affected the pin allocations on the 12S socket and 12S plug.

The intention was to cut the number of live, current-carrying cables and these were reduced from four to three. Some specialists claim the alteration was prompted by the belief that current-carrying cable can create a magnetic field, which might adversely affect the operation of certain electronic control devices being fitted in cars.

The term used to describe this concern is 'electro-magnetic compatibility', or EMC. It is also one of the reasons why passengers in modern aircraft have to comply with requests not to use personal electronic products at key points in a flight. In the context of cars, some specialists are sceptical and question whether disabling one of four current-carrying cables is really going to make any significant reduction in the likelihood of upsetting electronic control systems. That's a fair point, but the change was made just the same.

Summary of 1998 revised 12S pin allocations (caravans post-1st September 1998)

Pin 1 Yellow cable; reversing lights or a catch for an inertia brake
Pin 2 Blue cable; spare
Pin 3 White cable; earth, i.e. negative return
Pin 4 Green cable; 12V live feed and leisure battery charging
Pin 5 Brown cable; sensing device but often left spare
Pin 6 Red cable; refrigerator supply
Pin 7 Black cable; earth, i.e. negative return for the fridge

You will note that some of the pin allocations are the same as before, although some of these are seldom used. For example, pin 1 (yellow cable) is for reversing lights and many caravans are not fitted with these. It's also designated for a 'reversing catch', and these were fitted before auto-reverse brakes were introduced in the late 1970s. Similarly, pin 5 (brown cable) is allocated

1 Reversing Light or catch
2 Spare
3 Earth
6 Refrigerator Supply
5 Sensing Device
7 Refrigerator Earth
4 Auxiliary Battery Charging and Live Feed

Supplementary Socket (12S)
Post-1st September 1998 connections

Pin allocations for 12S
socket from 1st September
1998 onwards.

for 'sensing devices', and again this connection is rarely used. Pin 3 (white cable) is also unchanged but *is* important, being an earth connection (i.e. the negative return). New allocations were as follows:

• **Pin 2** (blue cable). Until the alterations, pin 2 had been allocated for the provision of a charging current for the leisure battery. This task was then passed on to pin 4 instead, which meant that pin 2 on both the 12S socket and on the 12S plug fitted on post-1st September 1998 caravans no longer had a designated use.
Note: *If the towcar is still wired to offer a pin 2 charging function – but you are towing a newer 'van – there is no need to disconnect it. The charging function would be useful if you subsequently sold your towcar to a caravanner who owned an older caravan.*

• **Pin 4** (green cable). This supply was now given a dual function. When a towcar's engine isn't running it provides a permanent live feed to serve some caravan 12V appliances, but not the refrigerator. However, when the engine is running a relay in the caravan now diverts the 12V supply to charge its leisure battery. To serve this double function, it is beneficial if the cable coming from the vehicle's battery is 3.0mm^2 minimum (44 strand) automotive cable.
Note: *Diagrams of wiring circuits inside caravans are shown in Chapter 7. Since the switching of the pin 6 supply is done inside the 'van, battery charging takes place even if the towcar is wired to the previous standard, with a relay-operated charging feed going to pin 2.*

• **Pin 7** (black cable). This addition provides an extra earth facility so that the full complement of 12V appliances doesn't rely on a single cable coupled to pin 3 for the neutral (i.e. negative) connections. Using the centre pin in the cluster, i.e. pin 7, the additional earth cable is specifically intended for the refrigerator.
Note: *The implication of allocating pin 7 as an earth for the fridge means that if you purchase a caravan from the 1999 model year or later, you must make sure that pin 7 is connected to a sound earthing point in the towcar. If it isn't connected-up, your caravan fridge will not work on its 12V setting.*

Mixing and matching old and new 12S systems

The fact that pin allocation on 12S connections was changed in 1998 inevitably means that problems arise if you pair an older car with a newer caravan or vice versa. If you appoint a knowledgeable towbar specialist to fit a 12S socket on your car, they should ask about the age of your caravan and wire up the socket to suit. But some never bother to ask this question and that can lead to problems. For instance, if a new caravan is being towed by a pre-1st September 1998 car that has been wired-up in the manner appropriate for its age, pin 7 on the vehicle's

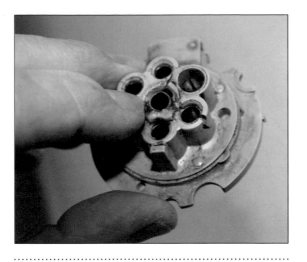

Persistent arcing between the centre pin and socket on this 12S connection has caused the plastic to melt.

socket will be left spare. In consequence the caravan fridge won't work on its 12V setting.

It is most regrettable that caravan owners should need to point this out to an auto-electrician, some of whom are quite unaware that pin allocations changed around 1998.

Pin burn-out problems

Alterations to well-proven systems sometimes introduce unexpected problems; 'pin burn-out' was a case in point. As has been explained above, after 1998 the centre pin of a 12S socket was specifically allocated for connecting the earth wire for a fridge. However, it is unfortunate that this is the most likely pin to get damaged during the pitch and toss of towing. It also hasn't helped that large refrigerators have become popular because these appliances draw more current. Nor is it helpful that the black wire in a multicore cable has a cross-sectional area of 1.5mm^2 and only yields a nominal continuous current rating of 13.0A.

Added to these aspects is the fact that the connecting male pin in a 12S plug and its counterpart female tube in a 12S socket may not fit very tightly. A loose connection between the two can then cause sparks to jump across the gaps, and this phenomenon – called 'arcing' – causes the pins to get hot. Many caravanners report that their 12S plug gets warm on a trip and the photo above shows the severe damage that often occurs.

To reduce the likelihood of pin burn-out, you can enlarge pin 7 on the 12S plug with a knife so that it fits in the socket tube more tightly. Some towbar fitters also make the following wiring improvements in the 12S plug and socket:

1. Presuming you do not have a sensing device for pin 5, connect the brown wire in the multicore cable from the back of the 12S socket to a good earth point on the vehicle.
2. Couple up pin 5 to pin 7 in the 12S plug using 2.0mm^2 28 strand 17.5A cable. This doubles-up the vehicle's earthing provision (i.e. negative connection) that serves the fridge by using two cables instead of one.

3. If pin 2 is unused (although it might still be connected to the split charge relay) this can be joined to pin 6 in the back of the 12S socket using 2.0mm² 28 strand 17.5A cable. This doubles up the live (i.e. positive) connection to the refrigerator by using two cables instead of one.

This strategy helps to reduce the voltage loss in cables, which means there is less resistance and this, in turn, means there's less likelihood of a build-up of heat. However, a different approach for improving the 12S electrical connection would be to fit a 13-pin coupling instead.

Thirteen-pin couplings

There has been considerable unease about another change to caravan electrical couplings. However, the problem of burnt-out 12S plugs couldn't be ignored and the benefit of adopting a universal European standard makes obvious sense. Furthermore, anyone who has used a 13-pin plug with its twisting and tightening action cannot fail to be impressed by the positive way in which these plugs and sockets link together.

Historically, 13-pin sockets have been fitted on several imported vehicles for more than ten years, but the UK caravan industry declined to fit 13-pin plugs as standard until September 2008. In effect the change applied to 2009 caravans, and when these models were first shown to the public in the summer and autumn of 2008 a mixed reception was anticipated.

Recognising that many caravanners already had towing vehicles fitted with 12N and 12S sockets, Bailey responded with an innovative answer. Although the Company offered its 2009 models with a 13-pin plug mounted on a length of 12-core sheathed cable as standard, this had block connectors at the inboard end which coupled-up to the electrical system. This meant it could be quickly detached and replaced with Bailey's alternative twin cable product, which is fitted with 12N and 12S plugs instead. The opportunity to purchase an alternative coupling

It's easy to unplug the multicore cable from the electrical unit situated inside a Bailey 2009 caravan. Thus you can fit either single cable with a 13-pin plug or twin black and grey cables with 12N/12S plugs

These ISO 11446 thirteen pin plugs couple-up much more positively than the 12N and 12S products.

eliminates the need to use adaptor cables, which add a clumsy bunching of wires on a caravan's A-frame.

Not surprisingly, the use of adaptors was considered from an early stage in European discussions and different ways of linking seven- and 13-pin systems were compared. For instance, a 13-pin socket manufactured by WeST can accept either its partner 13-pin plug or a 12N plug.

However, it was ultimately decided to adopt the single function 13-pin product which complies with ISO 11446 and is sometimes referred to as the 'Jaeger system'. This term will soon be lost because many other manufacturers are now producing ISO 11446 products, including FEP.

WeST sockets accept either a 'partner' 13-pin plug or a 12N plug.

An ISO 11446 approved 13-pin socket made by FEP, a German manufacturer.

This inexpensive adaptor couples with a 13-pin plug, which then fits a 12N socket on a car. Of course, it only operates a caravan's road lights.

Adaptors

It will be a long time before existing 12N/12S couplings are completely replaced by 13-pin sockets, and during the interim, adaptor cables will be in regular use. Here are some of the products being sold by caravan dealers, auto-electrical stores and towbar specialists.

Making connections

Wiring a 13-pin plug or socket calls for dexterity, patience and careful preparation of its multicore cable. Sharp eyesight helps, too, because markings in the moulding of the plastic couplings that show pin numbers are not always as prominent as you'd like. Some manufacturers are supplying 12-core cable but Autac of Macclesfield has developed purpose-made 13 core cable to the gauge specifications shown on page 36. The colour coding follows the recommendation laid down in the annex

This adaptor cable allows twin 7-pin plugs on a caravan to be coupled to a car fitted with a 13-pin socket, but it adds untidy cabling at the front of a 'van.

This adaptor is the reverse of the previous one and permits caravans fitted with a 13-pin plug to couple up to a car fitted with twin 7-pin sockets.

of ISO 11446. Furthermore, if you choose the right end of a length of cable you'll find that each coloured wire falls in line with the connecting sockets of the plug or socket that you are coupling-up.

Pin numbers are usefully and clearly depicted on the hinged lid of this FEP socket.

Marks showing the pin numbers in the plastic moulding on the rear of this FEP socket are not so easy to see.

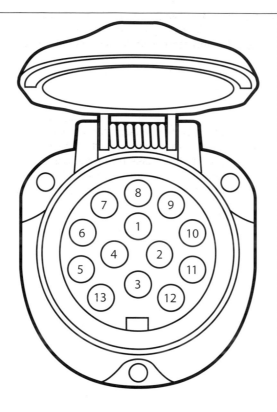

Numbering of the contacts in a 13-pin ISO11446 socket when viewed from the rear of a towing vehicle.

PIN ALLOCATIONS AND CABLE SIZES (ISO 11446 & 4141-3)

Pin no	Colour	Function	Cable cross-sectional area
1	Yellow	Left indicator	1.5mm²
2	Blue	Rear fog lamp(s)	1.5mm²
3	White	Earth for pins 1–8	2.5mm²
4	Green	Right indicator	1.5mm²
5	Brown	Right-hand sidelight	1.5mm²
6	Red	Brake lights	1.5mm²
7	Black	Left-hand sidelight and number plate	1.5mm²
8	Pink	Reversing light(s)	1.5mm²
9	Orange	Permanent power/charging	2.5mm²
10	Grey	Refrigerator (Ignition controlled)	2.5mm²
11	White/Black	Earth for pin 10	2.5mm²
12	White/Blue	No allocation	—
13	White/Red	Earth for pin 9	2.5mm²

The 13-pin sockets on cars

Notwithstanding the positive coupling features of these products, it is disappointing that many cars equipped with standard 13-pin sockets only have eight of the tubes wired up. Some even have five tubes missing completely.

The tubes which have been connected run all the road lights, including reversing lamp(s). That's fine for anyone towing a trailer but it doesn't help the caravanner who needs four more connections coupled-up to run a refrigerator and charge a leisure battery. In consequence these connections have to be carried out before all the functions on a caravan are working.

Spring assisters

Another matter to consider is the towcar suspension. Depending on a caravan's laden weight, the National Caravan Council (NCC) advises that noseweight falls somewhere between 50–90kgs (110-198lbs). Drawing on experience, *The Caravan Club* recommends a noseweight around 7% of the actual laden weight of the caravan – which typically falls within the NCC guideline.

Either way, this imposes a significant load on a vehicle's rear suspension and if the boot or hatchback is full as well, the springs may be under a far greater loading than normal.

Removing heavy items from the boot and carrying them in the caravan may help, but this could result in overloading and/or instability. The loading potential of a caravan is often fairly modest.

In practice, many vehicles manage without alterations to the springs.

Some cars, like models from Citroën, have load-sensitive suspension systems with ride height compensation. But there are also vehicles which suffer badly and too much tail end sag could be dangerous.

One problem with the rear sagging is that headlight beams are correspondingly deflected up into the air – at great inconvenience to oncoming drivers. Front-wheel-drive vehicles can also lose traction and wheel spin on acceleration will often be experienced. Equally there can be problems with braking and tyre adhesion when cornering. Without doubt, this is the time to consider firming-up or replacing the springs.

Owners' Manuals: The first step is to check the towing advice section in the vehicle manual. A second step might be to discuss this with a franchise dealer.

Shock absorbers: When looking for an answer, some owners wrongly attribute the problem to the vehicle's shock absorbers. However, a shock absorber is simply a damping device to prevent the vehicle bouncing along on its springs; most shock absorbers contribute little, if anything, to the firmness of the suspension system. It is the springing system which needs reinforcement.

Suspension diversity: One problem with producing 'universal' suspension aids is the fact that vehicles have a variety of systems including coil spring, leaf spring, torsion bar, hydro-elastic and hydraulic systems. This is why a discussion with a franchise dealer is recommended.

Spring assisters: A number of products are designed to strengthen a vehicle's springs. However, some mechanics claim that the attachment of rubber supports on coil springs introduces stress points which can hasten a fracture. This is why you should check their acceptability with a main dealer. On the other hand, there's no doubt that many caravanners find products from specialists like Grayston or Aeon successful in achieving the objective.

Spring replacement: On an older vehicle, whose springs may have deteriorated, fitting new replacements might be the immediate answer. Upgrading the springs is another option but whilst this might be fine when towing, ride quality is likely to be too hard when driving solo. Sometimes progressive rate coil springs are available which overcome this element. These have a lighter gauge section that deflects when the load is modest, after which more robust parts subsequently take effect when the load is more substantial.

Additional coil springs: Another strategy is to add additional springs. Products from the Dutch manufacturer MAD are well known – as are the products from Monroe. In the case of Monroe's units, these include variable rate coil springs which offer progressive resistance as the load increases; these are mounted on the outside of a telescopic shock absorber thereby producing a 'two-in-one' configuration. The Monroe Load Leveller, as it is called, is made in versions to fit a large number of vehicles.

Air spring addition: Alternatively Monroe Ride Levellers are shock absorber units which incorporate an inflation facility to increase ground clearance. The units can thus be adjusted to suit solo driving or towing. A pressure gauge indicates the level selected and the units are joined by plastic tubing to an inflation point. This is positioned so that a standard air line or foot pump can be connected to provide inflation. A de-luxe version of the Ride Leveller system includes a compact on-board 12V compressor with a dashboard control switch.

Bump stop springing: A completely different way to overcome the problem is to replace standard bump stops with larger units that offer a concertina action. When the tow car is loaded, these make contact with the steel stop plate but assume the role of additional springs on account of their construction.

All-in-all there are a number of solutions, and the caravan clubs hold a large fund of information drawn from their members regarding their tow cars and preparatory tasks that need carrying out as a pre-requisite to towing. Normally, however, detailed advice is only available to club members.

Adding supplementary coil springs from MAD is one way to reinforce a tow car's rear suspension.

A Monroe Ride-Leveller shock absorber is inflated to suit the particular weight of the towed caravan.

Coil spring assisters from Grayston have been used successfully by many caravanners.

Caravan chassis and running gear

For many owners, these are the least interesting parts of a caravan. On the other hand, safe and certain towing is dependent on a well-designed chassis matched with a good suspension and efficient brakes.

Chassis design has changed significantly in the last twenty five years. In the 1970s, caravan chassis were undoubtedly robust; but by modern standards they were also comparatively heavy. Structural members were welded together and the steel sections were usually painted rather than galvanised.

Around 1980, chassis design and construction changed in a very short space of time. This was partly intended to reduce the weight of caravans – prompted in turn by the fact that car manufacturers were producing lighter vehicles with better performance and improved fuel efficiency.

So with the help of computer-aided design systems, caravan chassis specialists created lighter structures without compromising strength. The era of the lightweight caravan chassis had arrived.

Pre-1980 chassis and running gear

A number of older caravans still provide sterling service, and it would be wrong not to include brief reference to their chassis and running gear. This can be helpful to a 'first timer' contemplating the purchase of an elderly model.

The B&B (Bird & Billington) chassis used prior to 1983 was a popular design.

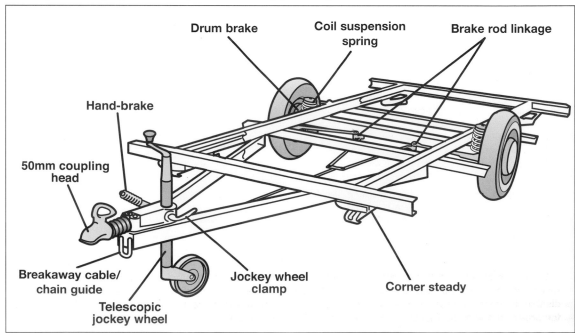

Drum brake

Coil suspension spring

Brake rod linkage

Hand-brake

50mm coupling head

Breakaway cable/ chain guide

Telescopic jockey wheel

Jockey wheel clamp

Corner steady

Background

In the 1960s and 1970s, nearly all caravan manufacturers ordered chassis from specialists such as Ambergate, B&B (Bird & Billington) and Peak. One manufacturer whose strategy was different was CI Caravans (Sprite Group) of Newmarket. This Company built their own chassis, although the brakes and suspension – referred to as *running gear* – were supplied by B&B, Harrison or Axles Ltd.

Practices changed around 1982 when most caravan manufacturers started to use a new 'lightweight chassis' designed and built by AL-KO Kober. Once again, CI Caravans, famous for the Sprite models, chose not to follow the majority and continued building a heavier traditional chassis. The policy was unchanged until 1990, after which many of the Company's 1991 models were subsequently built on a lightweight chassis with undergear supplied principally by F.T.F. and sometimes by Knott (UK) Ltd.

Running gear

As regards running gear on 'old-type' chassis, the suspension used coil springs and telescopic shock absorbers. Brake assemblies were often made by Lockheed Girling and there were a number of models using the same drums and brake shoes that were fitted to Morris Minor and Austin A40 cars. This often proves helpful when looking for spares.

One problem often experienced is a failure of the shock absorbers due to fluid loss. Anyone buying an older caravan should check for signs of seepage; replacement 'shockers' can be fitted, but the work is not easy.

Over-run braking

The over-run brake mechanism and coupling head assembly is different from more modern units as well. Coupling heads are normally of cast construction – whereas most recent models are made from pressed steel. However, the most significant difference is a brake disabling lever that has to be manually engaged before a reversing

Before reversing, a lever was used to disable the brakes on older types of over-run system such as this B&B Beta IV unit.

manoeuvre can be carried out. Without doubt, the need for a passenger to alight in order to operate a lever prior to every reversing manoeuvre is extremely inconvenient. Moreover, it is now illegal to fit such a system on a modern caravan.

Chassis maintenance

The section on page 43, entitled *Working safely under a caravan*, should be read before contemplating chassis maintenance.

Usually the steel members need to be painted periodically to prevent rusting. In particular, forward-facing cross members need regular inspection since these receive the brunt of stone chip damage from the towing vehicle.

As with most jobs, preparation is important and surface rust should be removed using a wire brush. A rotary brush driven by an electric drill is better than a hand brush, *but it is essential to wear safety goggles*. Filaments of wire often become detached and fly in any direction.

Once surface rust has been removed, there are several pre-painting treatments available. Some leave a coating of phosphate as a base for subsequent applications of undercoat and cellulose

Over-run braking – how it works

When horse-drawn carts were driven down steep hills, the load would roll forwards, giving the poor old horse an undignified push in the rear. Were it not for the invention of the over-run braking system, a caravan would do exactly the same thing to a tow car. This would *also* happen every time you applied your car's brakes. So how does it work?

By mounting the caravan's coupling head on a sliding steel bar, an automatic brake operating mechanism can be activated. Here's the sequence of events:

1. Tow car brakes are applied; the caravan rolls forward unchecked.
2. The coupling head's mounting tube or rod remains fixed and as the caravan comes forward, the rear-most part of the rod presses against a short lever.
3. Lever movement actuates the brake rod which then pulls the cables that finally apply the brakes.
4. On a well-adjusted system, the caravan's brakes will respond almost immediately, thereby working in conjunction with the car.

The only problem with this device is that you get exactly the same effect of pressure against the rear of a towing vehicle when starting to reverse an outfit. On older caravans you therefore have to operate a lever to disable the over-run system prior to reversing. On newer caravans, a mechanism in the brake drum disables the brakes automatically as soon as a reversing manoeuvre is detected.

Electrolytic action

If dampness penetrates between two dissimilar metals, one is usually damaged by an electrolytic action. In effect a primitive battery is formed whereby one metal acts as an anode and the other a cathode. The water acts as an electrolyte.

To avoid damage caused by the contact of two dissimilar metals, a neoprene spacer has to be fitted. A classic problem occurs if you bolt a steel accessory item – like the 'L' shaped support plate for a leaf spring type of stabiliser – directly on to an aluminium draw bar. If there is no separating neoprene there's a serious risk of localised damage to the aluminium chassis.

topcoat. Another popular treatment is a special protective metal paint called Hammerite. Available in both smooth and 'hammered' finishes, this can be painted directly on to bare – or even rusty – metal in one thick coating. Check the instructions carefully; remember to buy Hammerite thinners/brush cleaner, and note that the product dries quickly.

Spare parts

Spares for pre-1980 chassis and running gear are becoming increasingly scarce. Some items were held by AL-KO Kober but stock is now supplied by Johnnie Longden Ltd whose address is in the Appendix. In some instances parts need to be sourced through a caravan breakers.

Aluminium chassis

Different yet again is the aluminium chassis. For instance some of the caravans from Lunar, Swift and Cotswold were built on an aluminium structure matched with either AL-KO or Knott axles, overruns and brake linkages. These came from several chassis specialists; from around 1983, Lunar's Clubman and Delta models were built on a product made by TW Chassis Ltd of Lostock Hall, Preston, and a number of Cotswold and Swift models have been built on a Syspal chassis manufactured in Broseley, Shropshire.

However, it was Lunar that became most closely associated with the aluminium chassis and weight-saving was one potential benefit. Unfortunately, timber floor supports were normally used to contribute to under-floor bracing and this tended to counter the weight-saving intention.

Undoubtedly the use of aluminium sections has advantages, but two problems should be noted:
1. When towing in winter, road salt can damage an aluminium structure more than galvanised steel. In salty conditions, the surface soon becomes pitted and coated with oxide – so hosing off the chassis members is a recommended chore.
2. Problems occur in respect of damage to an aluminium section if it comes into contact with steel. The mismatch of material leads to an electrolytic action; so any junction needs a spacer such as a heavy duty neoprene gasket which is explained in the box on the left.

Today, aluminium chassis are no longer used. In 1998 Lunar switched to lightweight galvanised steel chassis for virtually every model and products from AL-KO Kober and Knott are now exclusively used instead.

Lightweight steel chassis

The change to lightweight, computer-designed chassis occurred in the early part of the 1980s when AL-KO Kober, a German Company, took over the B&B operation based in Leamington Spa. However, the changes were more far-reaching than just the chassis structure itself.

In the UK caravan industry, AL-KO Kober immediately adopted a prominent role as far as chassis manufacture was concerned. In addition, BPW, a German specialist with worldwide prominence in commercial trailer axle and running gear production, also manufactures lightweight caravan chassis and undergear. The BPW product is used by many caravan manufacturers in mainland Europe and was later fitted on all Explorer Group caravans in the UK. It has also been used on Fleetwood caravans for a number of years, although recent Fleetwood models have been built using the AL-KO product exclusively.

Background

The new approach to design and construction involved a radical change in the suspension as well as the chassis. It also coincided with new thinking on the construction of caravan floors; bonded ply composite panels were being developed.

On a lightweight chassis, the main members are in direct alignment between the coupling head and the outermost ends of the axle tube. This shows an AL-KO two-piece chassis, bolted together forward of the axle.

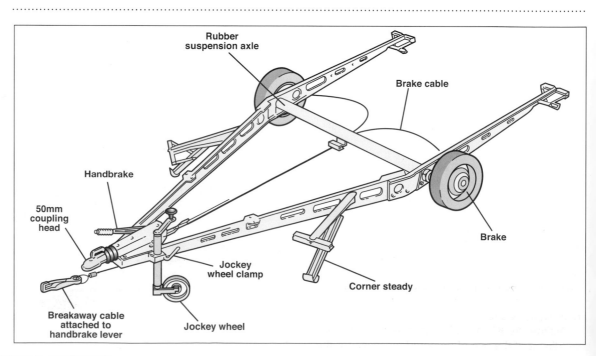

Prior to this, a caravan builder would start with a completed chassis fitted with running gear, to which was added wooden joists and a thin plywood floor. Today, most manufacturers start with a prefabricated floor panel comprising a bonded sandwich of plywood and block foam insulant. This is inverted and the chassis members and axle are then assembled and bolted in place. There is no welding involved.

Strength

Even though far less material is used in a lightweight chassis, strength is achieved through the interplay of three principal components:

- the chassis members,
- the axle tube,
- the composite floor panel.

The layout of the chassis members is important. In contrast with the earlier heavy structures, there are no cross members. Moreover, the main longitudinal chassis members run in a straight line from the coupling head at the front to the outermost ends of the axle tube. This means the pulling action of the towcar is in alignment with points slightly inboard of the caravan wheels. This geometry is an important feature.

Other strength-giving elements which also save weight include fold backs on the edges of the longitudinal chassis members.

Axle position

The all-important matter of nose-weight is partly determined by a caravan's axle position; so this is computer-calculated, taking into account the intended layout of the finished caravan. For instance if a caravan manufacturer is designing a model with an 'end kitchen', this will be taken into account when calculating the precise location of the axle. Kitchen appliances are among the heaviest items in a caravan and play an important part in respect of stability, too.

Chassis assembly

When the AL-KO Kober chassis first appeared in Britain, it was constructed with bolt-together sections that had to be assembled at the caravan factory. However, some manufacturers, e.g. ABI, specified continuous main members made without any joins. Subsequently, the use of one-piece chassis members was sometimes adopted.

Finally in early 1999, AL-KO Kober introduced the sectional 'Vario Chassis' that can be assembled using several alternative coupling positions, thereby providing a more universal application. Hence by working to AL-KO Kober's build plan, the components supplied can be assembled to suit a number of models in a manufacturer's range.

Neither AL-KO nor BPW chassis require any welding and the use of prepared recesses for the

Chassis members and running gear are assembled on an inverted floor panel.

assembly bolts ensures that the finished structure achieves a high degree of dimensional precision.

Design evaluation

In spite of the weight-saving features of modern AL-KO and BPW chassis, some traditionalists still prefer the older form of construction. There are advantages and disadvantages in respect of the lighter units:

Advantages
- Whereas some AL-KO Kober chassis were painted in the early 1980s, most are galvanised.
- Both the AL-KO and the BPW galvanised chassis are virtually maintenance-free.
- The weight/strength relationship is most favourable.

Disadvantages
- You could position a jack under almost any main member on an old-style chassis. On a lightweight chassis, jacking can *only* be carried out by:

  a) using a factory-designed side jack fitted into lifting brackets on the chassis;

On a modern lightweight chassis there are no cross members, but the axle tube is one of the contributors to rigidity. This is the AL-KO Delta axle discussed on page 47.

Introduced in 1999, the AL-KO Kober Vario chassis can be used for caravans of different dimensions.

Technical Tip

On lightweight chassis built in the 1980s, the manufacturer recognised that some owners would wish to fit a single-leaf type of stabiliser like the Scott or Bulldog models. It was then deemed acceptable to attach its mounting bracket on the chassis member provided the two fixing holes were drilled in horizontal alignment. When this is done, the holes have to be formed in the mid point of the member measured vertically. However, two holes drilled one above the other have never been permitted since this could lead to chassis failure.

Whilst drilling an early chassis in exceptional circumstances might be approved by AL-KO, the manufacturer does not recommend it, so stabilisers now use clamp-on brackets instead.

With later chassis, requirements are even more stringent.

No drilling of *any* kind is permitted on a 1990s AL-KO Kober chassis and disregarding this will invalidate the chassis warranty. Moreover, in Germany and Holland, drilling a chassis is deemed illegal unless the altered design is submitted for special Type Approval.

b) positioning a portable jack under the outer end of the axle tube;

c) jacking directly under the steel plates that secure the axle tube to the main side members.

• It is not permitted to drill a lightweight chassis built in the 1990s, see the Technical Tip box on the left.

Galvanising protection

When first galvanised, steel chassis members sometimes suffer from a surface discoloration referred to as 'wet storage stain'. Galvanised components need time to cure completely, during which time the coating changes from a shiny finish to a dull grey. If used prematurely on a salted road during winter, a new chassis should be washed-off after use in order to prevent 'wet storage stain' forming on the surface. In practice this doesn't cause the chassis to deteriorate, but it *does* give an unsightly appearance to chassis members.

The stain can also occur after a prolonged lay-up period – especially if air circulation around the chassis members has been restricted. Caravan skirts and front 'spoilers', for example, can hinder air movement. If this occurs, unsightly deposits can be removed with a stiff nylon brush.

In time, however, the zinc coating on a new chassis reacts with the atmosphere, and becomes a dark grey colour. This shows that the zinc treatment has developed its full protective potential and further incidence of wet storage stain is unlikely.

The protective benefit of galvanising is notable. Indeed it should never be painted because this tends to allow moisture to become trapped between the galvanised surface and the subsequent layer of paint.

Maintenance and repair

A galvanised chassis is virtually maintenance-free. At most, an owner merely needs to brush away road dirt. However, if a chassis gets dented or distorted, repairs should be carried out by a specialist. In the case of a modern sectional chassis, the specialist is sometimes able to unbolt and replace a damaged component and check alignment. Without question, this is *not* a do-it-yourself repair.

On the other hand, if surface abrasion exposes part of the steel underneath, you can treat this with

a cold galvanising compound. Typical products comprise granules of zinc suspended in a liquid binder. These are usually brush-applied after which the binder evaporates, leaving the zinc behind. Products are sold in auto accessory shops and even Builders' Merchants – cold galvanising compounds are often used for treating wrought iron fences.

Corner steadies

The much abused 'corner steady' has a tough life. This is *not* a jack and if you try to lift a caravan using corner steadies you will not only distort the mechanism; you are likely to damage the chassis and might also split the floor panel as well.

Some corner steadies often take an age to lower and the quick-operating types are comparatively costly. As a rule, these are only fitted to more expensive models.

Many caravanners also take small wood blocks to place under each steady, although load distribution is also achieved using corner steady plates sold by accessory suppliers like Towsure. Some plates can be permanently attached to each leg.

Maintenance

Even when used correctly, the spindle threads can soon get rusty. The mechanisms must therefore be lightly greased on a regular basis and the steadies raised and lowered as often as possible – especially during a long period of outdoor storage. Be careful

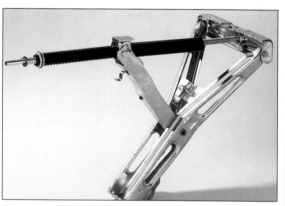

Fast acting corner steadies from AL-KO Kober can be fitted as replacement items.

A permitted jacking point is directly below the steel plates that secure the axle tube to the main side members.

Some corner steady plates can be attached permanently to many types of corner steady legs.

Lead-in tubes are often being fitted to help when locating a corner steady brace in the dark.

not to *over-grease* the spindle because this attracts grit. A multi-purpose grease made to DIN 51825 standard is recommended by AL-KO Kober; only a thin smear on the spindle threads is advised.

Accessories

Various corner steady locking systems are available but few would deter a competent thief. There are also add-on tubes to steer an operating brace directly on to the head of the spindle when it's dark. Some caravanners even take re-chargeable drills fitted with a special socket to speed-up operation.

Working safely under a caravan

Whether repainting an older chassis, adjusting brakes or working on any other job that necessitates access under a caravan, it is *absolutely essential* that the elevation support systems are completely fail-safe.

One approach is to drive a caravan on to a pair of scaffold planks. Having raised both sides equally, two or three further planks can subsequently be added, thus raising the height progressively. The corner steadies should then be lowered and the wheels chocked. Provided the ground is firm, this controlled elevation to a modest level has much to commend it.

An alternative is to use a jack, chocks and sturdy axle stands. Start by elevating one side of the caravan with a jack – make certain that the hand-brake is on, corner steadies are *raised,* the wheel on the far side is firmly chocked and a steady balance is provided by the jockey wheel. A stand can then be inserted under the axle, inboard from the road wheel. The procedure is then repeated on the other side. Once the caravan is elevated, corner steadies can then be lowered, using wood blocks where necessary and both wheels chocked. Note the following:

• Under no circumstances use the corner steadies to elevate a caravan.
• Some plastic wheel chocks can slip badly on certain surfaces – such as smooth tarmac. Use robust chocks, bearing in mind that heavy timber chocks shaped to the wheel curvature might be worth making.

• Axle stands vary in quality. Some DIY stands have a very small base and offer inadequate stability to support a caravan.
• Soft and/or sloping ground can render an arrangement unsafe.
• Never rely on a jack alone when working under a caravan.

Jacks

For work at home or for emergency roadside repairs, the AL-KO Kober scissor jack was purpose-made with a support to match the profile of a modern axle tube. This is no longer available and the AL-KO side-lift jack has taken its place.

The first AL-KO Kober side-lift jack was introduced in the early 1990s and can be fitted to the Company's chassis made from 1980 onwards. This involves drilling, so from 1992 AL-KO chassis side-members were manufactured with two preformed holes to receive the jack's inverted 'L'-shaped attachment bracket. However, the system required caravan manufacturers to fit a small piece of strengthening timber in the core of floor panels at the time of manufacture. If they failed to include this provision, a Mk I side jack mustn't be installed retrospectively.

In response to this, AL-KO then launched the Mk II version, which was stronger and didn't need floor strengthening. Today there are two versions of the Mk II bracket to suit lighter and heavier caravans. The smaller one can cope with a maximum weight of 1,600kg, while the sturdier bracket is for caravans weighing up to 2,000kg.

Corner steadies

Never try to lift a caravan using corner steadies – this will distort the mechanism and possibly result in a split floor panel.

The AL-KO Kober compact scissor jack was made to fit the shape of the chassis tube.

Left: This AL-KO side-jack has the smaller bracket for caravans weighing up to 1,600kg.

Above: This sturdier bracket is for caravans weighing between 1,600–2,000kg.

Once its jacking brackets have been fitted to a chassis, the dual-function Trailer-A-Mate is easy to use.

Stronger brackets than this might be needed to elevate heavy twin-axle caravans.

Side-lift jacks

When using this type of jack, you are strongly recommended to keep your caravan attached to your towcar. This is especially important during a roadside wheel change. You should also engage the caravan's handbrake lever and chock the opposite wheel.

AL-KO Kober instructions add: 'The caravan *must* be connected to the tow ball of your towing vehicle before commencing jacking.' Furthermore, you must not transfer a Mk I side-lift jack to a caravan that doesn't have the required floor strengthening. To do so could cause considerable damage.

Hydraulic bottle jacks sold in auto stores would be useful if they included a top support bracket to cradle either the hexagonal axle tube from AL-KO or the square-section axle tube from BPW. However, an all-important support 'cradle' is seldom available, and if your caravan gets a puncture there is often insufficient ground clearance under its axle to introduce a bottle jack.

Other jacks are advertised from time to time, such as the Trailer-A-Mate hydraulic product from Australia that also doubles-up as a jockey wheel. A scissor-type hydraulic lifting device called the Kojack appeared in 2007 but at the time of writing the brackets intended for attachment to a chassis using AL-KO's punched holes are only made in one size.

Coupling heads and over-run assemblies

The earlier section on over-run braking explained that modern coupling heads are usually made from pressed steel, whereas older units were made from a heavy casting. There are exceptions, of course, and some cast units are still manufactured.

Also continuing to grow in popularity are coupling head stabilisers which have built-in

friction pads. Provided a tow ball is completely grease-free, these pads grip the ball tightly thereby reducing a coupling's ease of articulation. However, as long as a suitable tow ball with a long stem is fitted there is no reduction in a caravan's actual range of lateral movement. (See panel in Chapter 3 entitled: *Bolt-on tow balls*.)

More expensive caravans built on an AL-KO chassis are often fitted with a red-trimmed AKS stabilising coupling head as standard. Models built on a BPW chassis have a dark blue WS3000 stabiliser manufactured by Winterhoff. By having its friction pads mounted fore and aft in its coupling head, the Winterhoff product attenuates movements in both the lateral plane (i.e. horizontal swaying) and the vertical plane (i.e. pitching). The pre-2001 models from AL-KO only had pads bearing on the right and left sides of a tow ball, so there was no damping effect on vertical 'pitching' movements.

The later stabiliser coupling from AL-KO Kober, referred to as the AKS 3004, has two further pads mounted front and back together with a wear indicator. The device is also fitted with a coupling indicator button. Both elements are shown in the accompanying photographs; also note that in Chapter 12, one of the repair projects focuses on friction pad replacement on an AKS 3004.

Modern coupling heads

A feature of modern coupling heads (rather imprecisely referred to as 'hitches') is the fact that

Cast coupling heads were commonplace on older caravans – though a few couplings today are of cast construction.

Many caravans are fitted with a pressed steel coupling head which features a red/green button to confirm when the unit is correctly coupled.

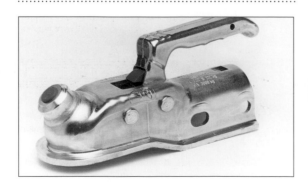

Like many AL-KO accessories, this coupling head stabiliser bears distinctive red trim.

The Winterhoff stabiliser fitted on many BPW chassis is finished in dark blue.

Unlike early AL-KO stabiliser couplings, the Winterhoff product has friction pads positioned fore and aft of a tow ball.

This indicator on an AL-KO AKS 3004 stabiliser coupling reveals if a tow ball is worn or if the front and rear pads of the device need replacing.

A safety indicator on the top of an AL-KO AKS 3004 stabiliser coupling shows green when it has engaged correctly with the tow ball: red indicates that coupling has not been achieved.

locked. This security device prevents the locking cam inside the enclosure from being moved.

Modern over-run assemblies

The function of an over-run system was explained in the box on page 39. The design of this all-important brake activating system has improved in the last two decades and legislation has played a part, too. For instance in EEC countries, caravans manufactured from October 1982 onwards are not permitted to have an over-run system which employs a spring mechanism for smoothing the operation. The ruling requires that a hydraulic damper is used.

Maintenance

The lubrication of all moving parts on an over-run assembly is important and the accompanying diagram shows typical greasing points. Whereas the uppermost pair of grease nipples are easy

they usually offer 'one-hand' operation. Whether it's a release button system or a unit whose handle has a release position, the design enables you to attach or release the coupling head single-handed.
Note: *You might damage a coupling mechanism if you take all the nose-weight by lifting on a handle in its unreleased position.*

Two particularly notable safety features found on more recent products such as the AL-KO AKS 3004 are:
• a tow ball and mechanism wear indicator,
• a positive coupling indicator button with red (danger) and green (coupled) markings to verify the coupling head has engaged on the ball.

Some products also incorporate a brass insert that is fitted into the body of the coupling and then

This grease nipple (shown in the accompanying drawing) can be easily missed; it is often hidden by excessive grease and dirt.

On the coupling head forming part of AL-KO's Euro over-run brake assembly, there's a grease nipple on the underside close to this spring.

An over-run assembly must be serviced regularly and three grease nipples are fitted on most units.

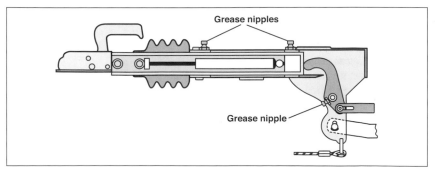

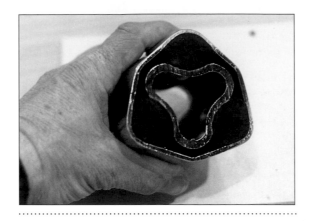

Three lengths of rubber are inserted into an AL-KO Kober caravan axle tube at the time of manufacture and this forms the rubber-in-compression suspension.

A fitting point for an additional shock absorber has been included on an AL-KO Kober chassis since the early 1990s.

to identify, a third grease nipple usually fitted underneath can be difficult to locate. In fact it often gets missed altogether – partly because road dirt and remnants of grease obscure its location. Similarly, on caravans where AL-KO's Euro over-run brake is fitted (described on page 55) there is a further elusive grease nipple on the underside which is located near its spring. The recommendation of AL-KO Kober is to use a multi-purpose grease which meets DIN 51825 standards.

As a further measure, it is appropriate to protect the over-run unit and coupling head with a waterproof cover whenever a caravan is laid-up for an extended period. However, try to attach the cover in such a way that air can circulate around the whole assembly.

The AL-KO Kober Octagon telescopic shock absorbers are easy to fit and many owners install them without difficulty.

Axles and suspension

Several types of suspension system have been fitted to caravans. These have included leaf springs, torsion bar suspension and coil springs. Earlier reference has been made to pre-1980 chassis where coil spring systems and hydraulic dampers were used.

Nowadays the suspension system employs

lengths of rubber which are forced into compression as a caravan rides the bumps. The diagram below shows that within both ends of a six-sided tubular axle, three lengths of compressible rubber are seated within an inner tube which has tri-lobal flutings.

The BPW suspension system is different and uses four lengths of rubber which are mounted within a four-sided axle tube. However, the operating principle remains the same as the AL-KO Kober product.

Provided the rubber suspension isn't over-stressed, it will afford excellent service. Moreover, since it is self-damping, shock absorbers are not normally needed. However, they have sometimes been fitted to heavy caravans and are also necessary on the AL-KO Kober Delta and the BPW SWING Vtec axles which have a conspicuous arrow-like appearance as shown in the photograph on pages 41 and 54.

To accommodate four lengths of rubber, a BPW axle tube is square in cross section; its maximum carrying capacity is shown on the axle label.

The rubber in a caravan suspension deforms in varying degrees as the suspension arm rises and falls.

Rebound or Free position

(25% below horizontal)

Normal laden position

(5% below horizontal)

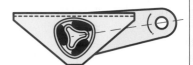

Maximum bump

(15% above horizontal)

In view of these self-damping characteristics, it is a paradox that shock absorbers are commonly fitted to many post-1993 caravans built on AL-KO Kober's Euro-Axle system. Installation points are also provided on models that haven't had them fitted and AL-KO supplies 'Octagon Shock Absorbers' which can be easily attached. The reason for this trend is that shock absorbers are standard in Germany and many British caravanners have wanted to follow suit. Nevertheless, AL-KO Kober's UK technical staff make the position clear; the performance characteristics of the rubber suspension mean that 'shockers' are not normally necessary.

Maintenance

A notable benefit of a compressed rubber suspension is that no routine maintenance is required. However, you can extend the life of a suspension system by taking precautions whenever the caravan is being unused for a long period.

Since rubber always returns to its original shape after a load has been removed, the manufacturer recommends that whenever a caravan is stored for long spells, it should be supported on axle stands. In consequence, its weight is no longer borne by the suspension. Some caravanners pursue a similar strategy for extending the life of the tyres by fitting products such as 'Winter Wheels'. However, these supports only take the weight from the tyres; they do not take the load from the suspension.

'Delta' (AL-KO) and 'SWING Vtec' (BPW) axles

A special feature of a modern caravan's axle tube is that its tubular structure contributes strength to the chassis members. However, axle tubes are not always straight. For example, the AL-KO Kober Delta and the BPW SWING Vtec axles have a prominent arrow-head shape as shown on pages 41 and 54. This is used on several of the more expensive caravans sold both here and abroad. Research has shown that the Delta-shaped axle achieves better stability than is obtainable on conventional designs, particularly when a car and caravan are negotiating a sharp bend. In this situation, the caravan wheel on the outside of the corner increases its toe-in and negative camber angle. This creates an improved alignment between the vehicle and the caravan

AL-KO Kober 'Euro-Axle'

The 'Euro-Axle' was first used for caravans in the 1994 model year and remains current. In truth, the term is imprecise because it also embraces alterations to wheel bearings, the suspension arm and stub axles.

With regard to the axle tube itself, this is now galvanised rather than painted and a metal data label affixed to the tubing bears the letter 'E' in a circle within the entry box headed CAPACITY. The same rubber suspension system is retained.

Other features include:
• A stub axle which is bolted to the suspension arm rather than welded. This means the final position of the wheel on the road – called 'toe-in' – can be adjusted at the factory to fine tolerances using sophisticated machinery. The setting-up work is strictly a factory operation and the attachment bolt is security marked.
• The backing plate of the brake is zinc treated rather than painted. It is also bolted to the suspension arm, thereby offering greater choice for the brake cable's point of entry.
• Sealed-for-life bearings are factory-fitted in the brake drum. A bearing is expected to last for around 100,000km (approx. 62,500 miles) and is pre-greased and double-sealed. In the unlikely event of bearing failure, the drum has to be sent to the factory; a service centre would not have the equipment to fit a replacement bearing.
• To accept the sealed bearings, the stub axle is now larger in diameter.

Wheel bearings

Another development of significance to owners concerns wheel bearings. For many years, the wheels on caravans – like those on cars – revolved freely on tapered roller bearings. In fact this type of bearing was commonplace until the early 1990s.

The inner and outer bearing units are seated in the brake drum which in turn is held to the stub axle by a castellated nut. This descriptive term refers to the fact that its notched shape is reminiscent of a castle tower. Indeed it is these notches that provide a point of retention for the split pin that ensures the nut will not shake loose. The accompanying photograph (top) shows the bearing assembly.

....

Tapered roller bearings used to be fitted to caravans; but these were superseded when sealed bearings were introduced in the early 1990s.

The sealed bearings now fitted into the brake drum of modern caravans can only be replaced by returning the drum to the chassis manufacturer.

Modern sealed bearing units are superbly engineered and are expected to last for around 100,000km (62,500 miles).

Bearing damage

Bearings are most likely to get damaged if a caravan is being towed with the handbrake partially engaged accidentally, or by an incorrectly fitted breakaway cable. Damage can also occur if the brake system is set too tightly during servicing. These situations cause the drum to run hot and the grease in the bearings then starts to melt. When this happens the bearing soon gets damaged.

Provided the retaining nut is tightened to permit free rotation of a wheel without play and as long as new split pins are fitted every time a bearing is reinstated, the system is hard to fault. Periodically the bearings should be greased using multi-purpose grease meeting DIN 51825 specifications, noting that it is important not to over-pack the grease cap. These procedures follow established automotive practice.

Notwithstanding the success of the system, sealed-for-life bearings were introduced around 1992. Caravans built on BPW chassis with Knott running gear ran on sealed bearings first; subsequently the use of sealed bearings formed part of the AL-KO Kober's Euro-Axle components used on many 1994 models.

With a lifetime guarantee, these superbly engineered bearings are unlikely to give problems. Unfortunately, however, if a replacement is needed it is a factory-only job and the drum has to be sent back to the manufacturer.

One-shot flanged nuts like this have been used by AL-KO Kober since 1994.

Although BPW brake drums used to be retained by one-shot nuts, reusable castellated lock nuts have been fitted since 1998.

Drum retention nuts

Rather than having a castellated retention nut and a split pin, a modern caravan's brake drum is held in place with a type of nut that grips the stub axle threads very tightly. BPW initiated this change around 1992 and used a one-shot flanged nut that is manufactured with a mildly oval shape. This enables it to achieve a tight grip on the stub axle threads, but this type of nut must not be used a second time.

AL-KO Kober also adopted this retention system in place of castellated hub nuts when the Euro-Axle was introduced on 1994 caravan models. The Company advises that prior to fitting a new nut, a mineral grease (AL-KO Part No 800.052) should be used sparingly on the stub axle threads. Once fitted and tightened to the correct torque level, a red marking paint (AL-KO Part No 800.015) is then used on the nut, thereby confirming at a future inspection that it has been correctly tightened and has neither been pre-used nor loosened. Torque setting for an AL-KO flanged nut is 290 (plus or minus 10) Nm.

In 1998 BPW made a further change and introduced a castellated tined (i.e. spiked) lock nut instead of a one-shot flanged nut. This type of nut *is* reusable *as long as air tools are not used* for its fitting or removal. Moreover, a calibrated torque wrench is essential to ensure that it is tightened to a critical 280Nm.

Although these fixing nuts are considered far better than castellated nuts secured with a split pin, the changes meant that few DIY owners are now able to remove a drum to inspect the brake assembly, to clean away dust, or to fit replacement shoes. Not only is considerable force needed to remove the new types of fixing, but retightening a replacement nut to the stated torque setting is critically important and requires a special tool.

Caravanners who own a torque wrench for tightening their caravan's wheel nuts often presume the same tool can also be used for torque checking the drum retention nuts. However, that is not the case, because the respective torque settings are quite different. To secure a hub nut you need a good quality torque wrench whose accuracy is checked and calibrated annually and which achieves the torque settings quoted above. A model like Norbar's product costs around £300.

This often comes as a bitter blow to competent and experienced self-help enthusiasts who have hitherto kept their brake assemblies in good order using a rudimentary tool kit.

Brakes

Part of this section concerns maintenance of braking systems but there are also a number of general points that deserve attention.

General features

Virtually all caravans employ a drum brake system. Other brakes have been tried, however, and the

German chassis makers, Peitz, introduced a disc brake in the 1980s. Cotswold was the first British caravan manufacturer to fit these units and the 1986 Celeste could be ordered with Peitz disc brakes as an optional extra. More recently, disc systems have been shown on BPW chassis at major exhibitions. However, hydraulically-operated disc brakes are comparatively costly and are more inclined to seize-up when fitted on a vehicle that remains unused for extended spells. For this reason, nearly all European caravans have cable-operated drum brakes.

Points about the operation of drum brakes include the following:
• During towing, a caravan's brakes operate automatically via the over-run system – described earlier in this chapter on page 39.
• An auto-reverse braking system causes engaged brake shoes to release automatically when a caravan moves backwards.
• As explained in pic on the right, the button-type handbrake lever fitted on many post-1980 caravans is not correctly engaged until it reaches the vertical position. This takes considerable effort to achieve and on more expensive models a gas piston is often fitted to assist when the lever's being pulled. Engagement is also easier if the Euro self-adjusting handbrake has been fitted.
• When storing a caravan for a long period, it is best to park on level ground, chock the wheels and leave the brake in the off position.
• Modern brakes use asbestos-free linings and AL-KO Kober has fitted these since April 1989. Labels to indicate the absence of asbestos are sometimes affixed to the backing plate of a brake assembly.

Many caravans are fitted with levers which have a push button on the end of the hand-grip; to achieve full braking security on a slope these *must* be raised to a vertical position to engage fully.

The AL-KO Kober Euro over-run automatic self-adjusting handbrake was introduced in the UK in 1999; note its distinctive curving shaft and absence of a ratchet release button near the handle.

Asbestos-free linings have been fitted on AL-KO Kober brakes since April 1989.

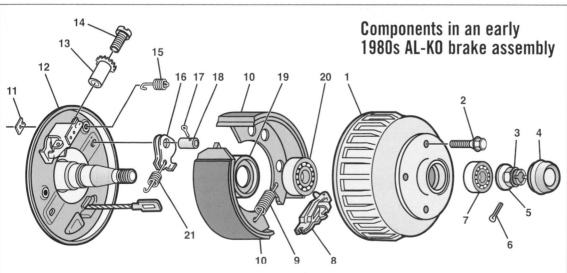

Components in an early 1980s AL-KO brake assembly

The brake assemblies built with tapered roller bearings are often serviced by DIY owners because no special tools are needed.

1 Brake drum	7 Outer tapered roller bearing	13 Starwheel adjusting nut
2 Wheel bolt	8 Expanding clutch	14 Adjusting screw
3 Castellated nut	9 Brake shoe tension springs	15 Shoe mounting pressure springs
4 Grease cap	10 Brake shoes	16 Spring loaded reversing lever
5 Lock washer	11 Cover plates	17 Floating pivot pin
6 Split pin	12 Backplate	18 Split pin

The key components in a modern braking system

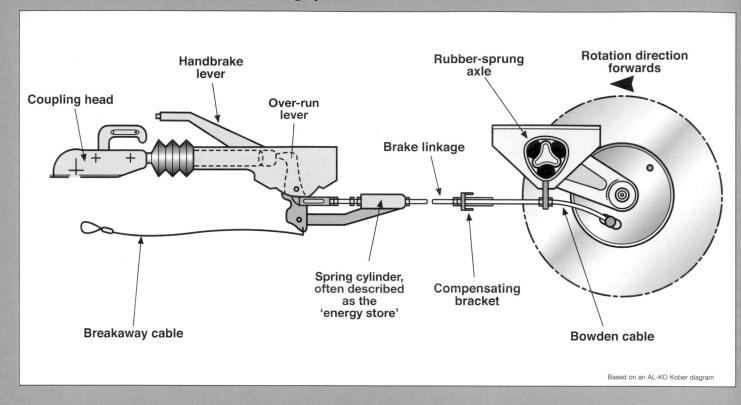

Handbrake lever

Over-run lever

Coupling head

Rubber-sprung axle

Rotation direction forwards

Brake linkage

Spring cylinder, often described as the 'energy store'

Compensating bracket

Breakaway cable

Bowden cable

Based on an AL-KO Kober diagram

A close look at drum brake components and functions

The backing plate on the AL-KO type 2051 system which is fitted to medium range axles up to 1,300kg and some large tandem axles.

View of the brake assembly on a type 2051 unit, bearing in mind that this has been set up especially for illustration purposes.

AL-KO uses a four-digit number to identify a braking system and the following explains how to identify a unit if this is illegible.

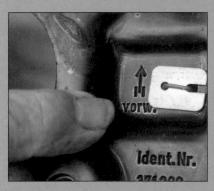

This arrow punched on the back of the plate indicates which way a wheel rotates when a caravan is moving in a forward direction.

The springs which hold a pair of springs together must be correctly fitted; it often pays to take a photo before dismantling them.

In the upper part of the brake, this expanding mechanism also provides the point of attachment for the end of the cable.

There are different ways of fitting cables to expanding brake activators; on this example a cable eyelet couples onto this hook.

The brake shoes on some BPW brakes are held in place with a clip; AL-KO shoes are usually held in place with a coil spring.

On an AL-KO backing plate a metal tag provides attachment for a brake shoe retention spring, but replace these if they are rusty.

On the backing plate there should be small plastic plugs; the ones nearest the edge are peep-holes for checking shoe wear.

From the other side the inspection port aligns with the end of a shoe; but even with a torch, checking wear isn't particularly easy.

When this bung is removed, inserting a screwdriver enables brakes to be adjusted. An arrow shows how to tighten brakes.

The screwdriver blade has to engage with the teeth on this 'starwheel'. As it is turned you'll hear a click from its locking spring.

The automatic release of the brakes when reversing a caravan with AL-KO or BPW brakes is activated by this cam.

Known as a 'spring-loaded reversing lever' this component will rotate when the shoe starts to bear on the drum when backing.

Provided the components are clean, the lever pivots around this pillar and its eccentric shape enables the shoe to move inwards.

One end of the trailing brake shoe is seated within the reversing lever and rests on a wheel that must also rotate freely.

When the caravan moves forward again, this spring pulls the lever back to its normal position so that the shoe can bear on the drum.

Identification of AL-KO Brake Systems

All AL-KO brake systems are identified by four-digit numbers which should be quoted when ordering parts. These are located on the outside of the backplate. Prior to 1994 (black-painted backplates), the number is situated towards the centre. In 1994, the introduction of the Euro System (gold coloured backplates), the number is situated on the outside edge. These systems are:

> 1635, 1636 and 1637 Systems – lightweight axles up to 900kg and most tandem axles sets.

> 2035, 2050 and 2051 Systems – medium range axles up to 1,300kg and some large tandem axles (e.g. ABI Superstar).

> 2360 and 2361 Systems – heavy range axles up to 1,850kg but tandem sets on trailers only, not on caravans.

If the four-digit number cannot be read due to age or corrosion, the procedure for establishing which system has been fitted is to measure the brake drum and shoes. For example, measure the diameter of the brake drum in centimetres (i.e. 16cm) and the width of the brakes in millimetres (i.e. 37mm). This indicates a 1637 System. This rule applies for all AL-KO Brake systems. Note: *On 1635, 1636 and 1637 systems, the brake shoes are handed left and right. All other AL-KO systems use matching pairs.*

Auto reverse systems

The invention of an over-run brake which releases automatically when an outfit is reversed has been a great asset for caravan and trailer owners. Several products achieving this objective have been developed and a few older caravans were fitted with the AP Lockheed system. This features trailing brake shoes which are mounted loosely within a carrying cradle. Whenever the wheel rotates backwards, these shoes slide along the cradle, and move away from the friction surface of the drum. However, the Lockheed system is not currently used on new models.

Nowadays nearly all caravans are fitted with either AL-KO Kober, Knott or BPW auto-reverse brakes; whilst the objective is the same, the operating mechanism is different.

Shoe withdrawal

Reverse operation in these units is dependent on a specially shaped spring-loaded cam or 'reversing lever' which touches one end of the trailing brake shoe. This is shown in the photograph sequence on page 51 and also in the exploded diagram on page 49. As soon as the expanding shoes touch the drum, the fact that the wheel is rotating in a *reverse* direction causes the cam-shaped spring-loaded reversing lever to pivot. On account of its eccentric shape, as soon as the reversing lever pivots, the trailing shoe releases pressure from the friction surface of the drum. The wheels then turn easily.

Shoe reinstatement

As soon as a caravan is subsequently towed in a *forward* direction, a spring on the cam now pulls it back to its normal position. Once the cam is back in its usual place, the trailing brake shoes will now bear against the drum in the usual way whenever the brakes are applied.

Checking brake assemblies
a) Pre-sealed bearing models

Before sealed bearing units were fitted in the early 1990s, you could remove a brake drum quite easily to clean the assembly and to check or change the brake shoes. Some owners do this themselves and if you have a pre-1994 AL-KO Kober Euro-Axle or a pre-1993 Knott system, the job is not difficult.

Start by jacking up the caravan, setting it on axle stands and removing a wheel, taking full note

Difficulty in reversing

1. If the brakes are set too tightly, difficulty will be found when reversing the caravan because this can prevent the reverse mechanism from operating properly.
2. The minimum permitted thickness of an AL-KO brake shoe is 2mm. Linings which wear below this critical thickness can also interfere with the correct operation of the reversing mechanism.

Auto-reverse braking and handbrake engagement

When a caravan is moved backwards, its brakes are automatically released. This is fine when you're reversing your caravan – the auto-reverse system on post-1980 caravans is a great asset – but there is a problem if an unhitched caravan is parked on a backward facing slope.

In this situation, the handbrake must be correctly applied. If there's the *slightest* backward movement, the auto-reverse mechanism comes into play and the brakes are automatically released. On a hill, a caravan could unexpectedly roll away.

To counter this, caravans that have a hand lever with a ratchet release button are equipped with a back-up system. This comprises a coil spring housed in a metal tube which forms part of the brake rod assembly. This is often described as the 'energy store' and in the drawing on page 50 it is labelled 'spring cylinder'. To benefit from this back-up facility it is essential that you *fully* engage the brakes – *hence the need to haul the handbrake lever into a vertical position.* This gives you a 'second chance' and here's how it works.

If the caravan moves backwards and the brakes release, the spring in the energy store is then suddenly released, thus re-applying the handbrake. This provision can prevent a parked caravan from rolling backwards down a hill, but of course it's essential to reset the handbrake lever to the vertical once again. Better still – chock the wheels. The Euro brake also creates a spring activated re-engagement 'back-up'. However, its linkage employs completely different geometry and the spring it compresses is located under the piston assembly. In order to show this photographically, the Euro over-run assembly in the picture was turned over to reveal its key components.

of the safety points given in the earlier section, *Working safely under a caravan* on page 43. Then:

1. Remove the grease cap.
2. Withdraw the split pin from the large castellated nut on the end of the stub axle.
3. Undo the nut with a socket spanner, removing it together with the large washer.

Note: *On the 2050 and 2051 AL-KO brake systems, no washer is fitted under the castellated nut. On the 1635, 1636 and 1637 systems the dished washer must be fitted with the concave side outermost.*

4. Tap away the brake drum and lift it from the stub axle.

Note: *Use a leather hammer where possible to prevent drum damage. In exceptional cases, a puller might need to be hired to remove a drum.*

5. The outer bearing is easily removed from its seating. It will often be dislodged with the first sign of drum movement.
6. Check condition of shoes and remove any excess dust. A product like Tetroson brake and clutch cleaner can be used.

Note: *On earlier brake shoes with brackets (prior to April 1989), the friction material contained asbestos. Under no circumstances should the dust be blown away. Remove it carefully with a rag, making sure that it is not inhaled and wear a protective mask.*

Reassembly reverses the operation:

1. Tighten the nut with a torque wrench to between 30–35Nm (22–26 lb/ft);
2. Back off the nut 180° (half a turn);
3. Re-tighten nut 90° (quarter of a turn);
4. Fit a new split pin folding over each leg in opposite directions;
5. Ensure the grease cap is not more than half full of multi-purpose grease meeting DIN 51825 specifications;
6. Grease should also be applied in the hub between the bearings.

If you don't own a torque wrench, a way of confirming that the centre nut is sufficiently tight is to carry out the following check:

1. Ensure the caravan is stable on its axle stands.
2. Replace the wheel.

Checking brake assemblies on a system fitted with taper roller bearings

1. Remove the grease cap.

2. Withdraw the split pin from the large nut on the end of the stub axle. Undo the nut with a socket spanner, removing it together with the large washer.

3. Tap away the brake drum and lift it from the stub axle. It is better, however, to use a leather hammer.

4. In some instances a brake drum has to be removed with a puller.

5. The outer bearing is easily removed from its seating.

6. Check condition of shoes and remove any excess dust. A product like Tetroson brake and clutch cleaner can be used.

The ability of a brake to hold a caravan on a slope can vary from model to model. However, this element is covered in an EU Directive that states that trailers (which includes caravans) constructed on or after 1st January 1968 must have a parking brake capable of holding the trailer when stationary on a gradient not exceeding 1-in-6.25 (16%).

3. Tighten the nuts (or bolts) as much as you are able on the stands.
4. Grasp the tyre firmly on either side and apply hand pressure to ensure there is no looseness in the bearings.
5. Play that might not have been apparent when you checked the brake drum is more likely to be evident when grasping a wheel.

Note: *Do not shake the wheel so vigorously that the caravan is under risk of falling from the axle stands. Remember that the wheel fixings have not been properly tightened for road use.*

b) Sealed bearing models

In essence, the job of removing a brake drum on a caravan fitted with sealed bearings is not difficult provided you have the following items:

a) A calibrated torque wrench that can set the fixing nut to a setting of 290Nm (plus or minus 10Nm) This is equivalent to 214lb/ft (plus or minus 7.5lb/ft). The setting is 280Nm on a Knott axle (204lb/ft).
   Note: *The torque wrench often purchased from AL-KO Kober to check the tightness of wheel nuts (or bolts) will not operate in this range. A Norbar wrench suitable for the job and available from AL-KO Kober costs around £300.*
b) A 32mm socket is needed to fit the nut.
c) Replacement 'one-shot' nuts are needed.

Here lies the problem as far as the DIY service engineer is concerned. You cannot do the job with normal hand tools and the essential torque wrench would have to be purchased or hired.

Provided you have the tools for the job, jack up the caravan, setting it on axle stands and removing a wheel, taking full note of the safety points given in the earlier section on page 43, *Working safely under a caravan.*

Then, follow this procedure:

1. Remove the dust cap (note that this isn't any longer called a 'grease cap'.)
2. The dust cap on a sealed bearing system should be dry inside. If grease is visible it should only be the tiniest smear caused by unavoidable seepage.

3. A 32mm socket with a long lever is needed to undo the flanged hub nut; it will be *very* tight.
   Note: *There's no split pin or castellated nut on the Euro-Axle system.*
4. Tap the drum away from the stub axle.

Note: *On very large single axle caravans a heavy duty 2361 brake system is used. Because of the weight of the drum, a special removal and refitting tool is needed (AL-KO Part No. 605.267) to prevent the bearing from being damaged.*

Re-assembly points

1. When the new nut is fitted, a small amount of mineral grease should be applied to the stub axle threads (AL-KO Part No 800.052).
2. It is essential that the nut is tightened to the *torque* specified. A calibrated torque wrench is needed as described above, and the nut should be tightened to a setting of 290Nm (plus or minus 10Nm) on an AL-KO Kober system: 280Nm on a Knott system.
3. Any surplus mineral grease must now be removed.
4. The nut should be marked with a special red paint available from AL-KO Kober to signify it has been replaced and correctly torqued up (Part No 800.015).
5. The dust cap should be tapped back into place – completely dry, of course.

Gas piston handbrake

Acknowledging that a handbrake demands a reasonable amount of strength to engage correctly, AL-KO Kober manufactures a gas piston version which has often been standard on many Continental caravans. To fit a gas piston assembly as a replacement, the entire over-run has to be replaced and the brake rod changed.

The great benefit is the fact that a gas piston forces the handbrake firmly into a fully engaged position as soon as the brake release button is depressed. It takes a certain amount of pressure to return the lever to its normal unbraked position later, but the technique of doing this is mastered after a little practice. Without doubt, the product is a great help to anyone uncertain about securing a

Some caravans, like the Knaus Sport and Fun model, are fitted with gas piston handbrake levers.

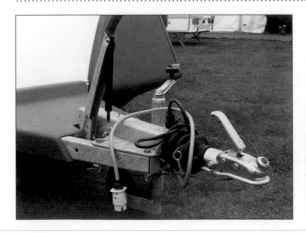

On a modern chassis, the central brake rod couples to a pair of cables at the axle tube. Note the Delta axle here.

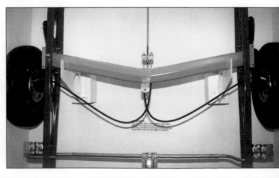

caravan parked on sloping ground. However, the Euro over-run automatic brake is even better.

Euro over-run brake

In 1999, AL-KO Kober showed the Euro over-run automatic self-adjusting handbrake at several exhibitions in the UK. This product has been described and illustrated earlier in this chapter, but its special feature is a mechanism which identifies forward or backward wheel rotation when a caravan is parked. It responds immediately to movement, reacts automatically and its spring applies increased pressure to hold a parked caravan in place.

In the UK, models in the Vanmaster range were the first to have this product fitted; today many of the more expensive caravans in manufacturers' ranges have a Euro self-adjusting handbrake. Without doubt it represents a big step forward in over-run mechanisms.

Brake rods and cables

Whereas earlier caravans had brakes operated exclusively by rods, current practice is to use a rod followed by cables for coupling into the brake drums. These are called Bowden cables.

The cables couple to the rod in the vicinity of the axle tube and connection is achieved using a floating plate referred to as a 'balance bar'. It is the balance bar which plays a part in confirming that the amount of braking going to each wheel is balanced. If the brakes are correctly set at the drums, the balance bar should lie in parallel alignment with the axle tube.

In addition the outer sheath of the Bowden cable is fixed to a plate welded to the axle tube.

Rod support

It is important that the central brake rod is fully supported and AL-KO Kober recommends that either metal brackets or flexible support straps are fitted at intervals no greater than 1.3m (51in) over its entire length. The recommendation of BPW is different and the Company advises that a bracket should be fitted 1.0m from the axle and another on the front part of the floor panel at the forward end.

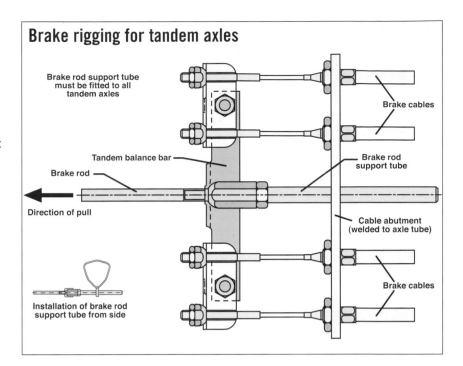

Brake rigging for tandem axles

Brake rod support tube must be fitted to all tandem axles

Brake cables

Tandem balance bar

Brake rod support tube

Brake rod

Direction of pull

Cable abutment (welded to axle tube)

Brake cables

Installation of brake rod support tube from side

The point is that if support is lacking, when you are driving along a bumpy road, an excessive rise and fall of the brake rod can pull on the cable and intermittently activate the brakes – causing unwanted wear.

Regrettably, a number of caravan manufacturers have failed to provide the amount of support specified. Fortunately support straps are often available from service centres and a practical owner can carry out the necessary remedial work, but owners of twin axle caravans should also note the next point.

Balance bar support

On a single axle caravan, the balance bar is comparatively light. However, on a twin axle caravan, the assembly is much heavier and on a bumpy road surface this can bounce up and down causing unwanted intermittent braking. To prevent this occurring, there should be an additional brake rod support tube that extends rearwards from the balance bar. This should fit within an enlarged hole in the centre of the cable fixing plate welded on

A brake rod support tube that passes through the cable abutment plate on the chassis tube is an essential component on twin axle caravans. N.B. These are alternatively called 'tandem axle' caravans.

When the brakes are correctly set at the drums, the balance bar should lie parallel to the axle tube.

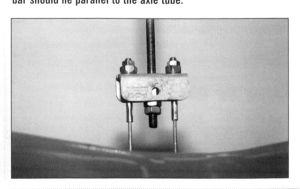

This brake rod support tube has been fitted on a single axle caravan to prevent intermittent braking caused by a bouncing balance bar and rod.

Disconnecting a Bowden cable at the brake drum

1. A support throat helps to attach the brake cable at the rear of the bracing plate.

2. When replacing a cable, the top section of the support throat is lifted away.

3. The cable is now clearly visible at the backing plate.

4. The attachment nipple on the end of the cable has now been disconnected from the brake assembly.

Before adjusting the brakes, the coupling head must be pulled fully forward.

to the axle tube. The component is shown in the diagram on the previous page.

Unfortunately this all-important support tube has not been fitted on some earlier twin axle caravans. It is a component that is easily added, however, and AL-KO Kober can supply the part.

Cable renewal

Normally a Bowden cable lasts for many years although damage can occur if it gets caught on a high obstruction. Provided safe access can be arranged under a caravan, and as long as you have the knowledge and the necessary tools to remove the drums (discussed earlier), brake cables are fairly easy to replace. The photograph on page 55 shows the balance bar

attachment; the sequence above shows the connection at the drum.

Brake adjustment

In one key respect, brake adjustment is the same for both rod only and rod/cable systems, i.e. that work *must* commence at the drums. Some owners erroneously think that they can take up play by adjusting the rod just behind the handbrake. This is not the case. Work at the forward end of the entire system is the *last* part to be adjusted.

Procedures and setting distances may vary between different products and the description here relates to post-1980 AL-KO Kober systems Check running gear guidance for other models, particularly with regard to clearances.

a) Preparatory tasks

Safe access will be needed underneath the caravan; check the guidance given earlier.
• Park the caravan on firm, level ground.
• Make sure it cannot move. Chocks are needed because the brakes will not be operable during the adjustment.
• With a sustained pull, draw the coupling head forward to its full extent.
• Release the handbrake *completely*. If a badly-fitted fairing hinders its range of movement, you may need to elongate the opening.
• Jack up one side of the 'van and support the axle tube on a robust axle stand.

- Lower all the corner steadies to provide further support.
- When the security of the caravan has been confirmed, have an inspection lamp or torch to hand. Markings can be hard to see. The job is also more comfortable if you've got an old piece of carpet to lie on.

b) Drum adjustment

- Remove the plastic bungs from the access holes in the backing plate (see page 51).
- Look through the outer hole to confirm that the linings are not badly worn. You will need a torch and only a rough assessment is possible.
- Select a screwdriver whose blade is small enough to pass through the inner hole to engage with the star wheel.
- Rotate the adjuster until brake resistance is felt when the wheel is turned in a forward direction, i.e. as if the caravan were being towed *forwards*. See the Technical Tip box on page 58.
- An arrow stamped on many backing plates indicates which way to turn the adjuster to increase braking. Otherwise the direction is established by trial and error.
- Once firm resistance is felt, back off the adjuster. Slacken off the mechanism just enough to allow the wheel to turn freely in a forward direction.
- The process is now repeated on the other brake drum – or the remaining three drums if working on a twin axle model.

Note: *BPW brakes incorporate a gear drive which couples the 'star-wheel' to an 8mm square-ended adjuster nut on the backing plate. This is sometimes called a 'set nut' and a similar system was used on the older Lockheed brakes. In consequence a spanner rather than a screwdriver is needed to adjust the brakes. In addition, a special tool (or a 4mm drill bit) has to be inserted through a hole in the backing plate – this ensures that the reversing release cams are in a fully forward position. Then the shoes are adjusted using a spanner, as shown alongside.*

c) Brake cable and balance bar check

- Now turn attention to the plate welded to the axle tube which secures the sheath of each brake cable. If brake adjustment has been done correctly, the cable inner, when pulled, should extend between 5 and 8mm. To check this properly, disconnect the locking nuts that secure the brake cable inner to the balance bar. Now pull on the cable and check the amount of movement.
- Reconnect the cables and adjust the locking nuts so that the balance bar lies parallel to the axle tube. On twin axle caravans there's a tandem balance bar and full alignment must be achieved.

d) Installation check

- It is important that the brake rod is parallel to the caravan floor when viewed from the side.
- It *must* be well-supported over its entire length

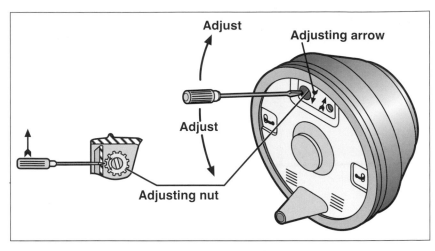

Adjusting an AL-KO Kober brake using a screwdriver.

In broad terms BPW and Knott brake assemblies are very similar to AL-KO's product. However, the star wheel adjusting mechanism is different.

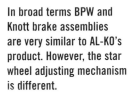

Firstly a 4mm steel spike has to be inserted into the backing plate (sometimes a drill bit is used); then an 8mm spanner is used on the adjuster nut which is linked to the star wheel.

Before checking brake adjustment, this balance bar on a twin axle caravan needs to be dismantled. Note that a rod support tube has not been fitted on this 1990 caravan.

A technician pulls on the brake cables to confirm that the shoes are being activated. When correctly adjusted a brake's cables should start to operate the shoes when pulled between 5–8mm.

When checking braking, a caravan wheel must *not* be turned in the reverse direction, i.e. as if the 'van were being backed. If you make this mistake, the auto-release mechanism automatically releases the pressure applied to the shoes – just as it does when you're reversing a caravan – and the wheel will then rotate freely. So checking brake resistance must always be done by rotating a wheel in the direction it would turn when the 'van is moving forward.

When correctly adjusted, the over-run lever should just make contact with the over-run shaft.

There should be a clearance gap of 1mm between the lever and the 'energy store' tube.

in accordance with the chassis manufacturer's recommendation.
• With twin axle AL-KO Kober models – which have a double balance bar – there *must* be a support tube bolted to the rearward face of the bar. This should pass through the abutment plate welded to the axle, to stop the unit sagging as shown in the diagram on page 55.

e) Forward end adjustment
• The brake rod may need fine adjustment to ensure that at the front, the over-run lever *just* touches the rear of the towing shaft.
• On an AL-KO standard system, focus your attention on the spring cylinder and tighten the self-locking nuts to achieve a 1mm clearance between the nuts and the cylinder. (This is not applicable if a gas strut handbrake lever has been fitted.)

f) Final checking
• Check the brakes engage at the appropriate point on the handbrake ratchet as described in the box on page 56. If they engage prematurely, the auto-reverse mechanism is unlikely to operate correctly and the brakes might lock when backing the 'van.
In a workshop it isn't easy to confirm whether a

caravan's over-run mechanism is going to activate its brakes with full efficiency. A manual push of the coupling head is unlikely to provide accurate information, and to resolve this some caravan service specialists make up a controlled compression tool instead. For instance, the one illustrated below was constructed using an old jockey wheel and a dummy tow ball. When fitted to a caravan, the jockey wheel handle of the device is able to depress the shaft in a controlled manner so that brake activation can then be checked as required.

Replacing brake shoes
Before brake shoes are removed, it is always wise to take note of the assembly before starting the job. For example, on the older Lockheed brake it is advisable to make a sketch of the fitting position of the brake-shoe springs. The array of holes and slots in the shoes can lead to confusion when you later re-assemble the units.
On brake systems fitted to more recent caravans, the shoes are held to the backing plate with small coil springs and a location tab that seats on the outside of the backing plate. These are often rusty, so have some replacements ready.
Before fitting the new shoes, remember to back

When correctly adjusted, AL-KO Kober standard brake systems should start to engage on the second or third click on the hand lever ratchet.

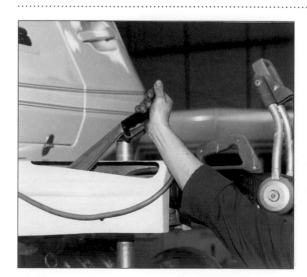

Some service engineers make up a test rig using a spare jockey wheel. This will depress a caravan's coupling head in a controlled manner, thereby allowing the activation of the brakes to be checked.

off the adjuster fully before endeavouring to refit the drum. Check the Tip box on page 53 regarding brake grease. When the drum is finally replaced, operate the hand lever several times to allow the shoes to settle.

Once the assembly is reinstated, adjust the brakes following the procedures described earlier.

Brake burn-out

A few seasons ago, several incidents occurred in which caravans' brakes were unknowingly engaged as a result of incorrectly fitted breakaway cables. In consequence, brake assemblies overheated, grease in bearings melted and in some instances they were totally destroyed.

When AL-KO Kober heard about these incidents, the Company responded by conducting roadside research with Police assistance. Once data had been collected a working party of industry experts was convened representing the Camping and Caravanning Club, the Caravan Club, the National Caravan Council, the National Trailer and Towing Association and the Society of Motor Manufacturers and Traders. Here are some of its findings:

• Breakaway cables are often attached incorrectly, and in some instance they even engage a caravan's handbrake when it's being towed.
• Analysis of the incidents revealed that premature application of a towed caravan's brakes by a breakaway cable is more likely to occur on models whose handbrake is fitted with a gas spring.
Note: *The benefit of gas spring (or 'gas strut) assistance is the fact that an owner merely has to exert a brief pull on their caravan's hand lever, after which the gas spring takes over and* fully *applies the brakes. It's a good system, but an over-tight breakaway cable can similarly trigger full brake engagement when a caravan is being towed.*
• The data also revealed that there's a greater incidence of premature braking when off-road vehicles are used for towing. This is partly because their bracket attachment point for a breakaway cable is often mounted a long way from the ball itself, so the connected cable is often too taut. Inevitably the cable will easily tighten when negotiating tight corners, thereby engaging the brakes.
Note: *It was mentioned in Chapter 3 that a cable's attachment point on the towing vehicle should be no more than 100mm (4in) from the centre of a tow ball. Unfortunately on some designs of towbar this provision is lacking.*
• It was also found that many off-road vehicles are so powerful that a few owners didn't even realise that their caravans' brakes had been fully engaged by the hand lever. Fortunately, many owners saw and smelled smoke coming from the brake drums and stopped in time to avert major damage. Others didn't.

To advise owners of these matters, a free leaflet was subsequently compiled and circulated to caravan dealers. It is also published on the websites of the National Caravan Council and the caravanning clubs.

If a driver doesn't realise that his caravan's brakes have been locked in the fully-engaged position, it's not long before there's billowing smoke and the assembly burns out.

Automatic anti-snaking caravan braking

In 2007 AL-KO introduced a new safety device which monitors lateral instability in a trailer and applies its brakes automatically, thereby helping to bring it back into line. The product is known as the 'AL-KO ATC' and it can be fitted either when a caravan is manufactured or retrospectively on most AL-KO chassis. Shortly afterwards BPW introduced a similar electronic stability device known as the IDC for its own caravan chassis.

Taking the ATC as an example, lateral acceleration sensors in the device detect both large and small side oscillations, whereupon the caravan's brakes are operated electrically. Though this helps to suppress instability, such devices should not be regarded as eliminating the need to load-up a caravan correctly.

As the accompanying photographs show, the device is bolted to the Bowden cable support flange on a caravan's axle and projects towards the rear.

This display on an exhibition stand uses an inverted AL-KO chassis to show how an ATC device is fitted.

This underside view shows the device during a retrospective installation at AL-KO's UK workshop.

Once a towcar is connected, the results of a pre-operation test are shown by this LED; continuing information about status is also displayed.

The shoulder profile on a wheel fixing must exactly match the seat in the wheel.

A forward-facing plunger connects with the brake rod and power is drawn from the towcar via its plug/socket couplings. When braking is deemed necessary the device draws 15A, and since this places a significant demand on the supply system it briefly takes priority over other 12V habitation supplies like the battery charger.

Verification of the status of an ATC product is shown by an LED light mounted on a caravan's A-frame fairing.

Further information about ATC and IDC operation is available from their respective manufacturers and it is important to point out that once these products are fitted they are claimed to be maintenance-free.

Wheels

Wheels should be fitted whose permitted load is appropriate for a caravan's maximum technically permissible laden mass (MTPLM) – previously called maximum allowable weight. Since a caravan's weight is shared by two wheels (four in the case of a twin axle model), the MTPLM should be divided by two before making a check with the maximum load rating stamped on the wheel. The division would be by four in the case of a twin axle model.

Wheel fixings

As regards the means of attachment, the fixings that hold a wheel in place are either nuts or bolts. The latter are now standard, presumably on the basis of production cost. But irrespective of the *type* of fixing employed, it is very important that its shoulder profile matches the seat formed in the wheel. This is important. The recess for the fixing, referred to as the 'seat' or 'seating,' is not standard and there are a number of variations. It is critical that the surfaces mate exactly.

Moreover, when a fixing starts to tighten on a steel wheel it is intended to deform the seating very slightly. Since the metal has a natural springiness the seating reacts and helps to grip the shoulder of the bolt or nut. Provided the fixing isn't over-tightened – which would lead to damage – this grip helps to hold the wheel securely.

The same reactive effect cannot be achieved

by an alloy wheel which is more rigid than steel. This is why the wheel fixings have to be tighter. Incidentally if you decide to have alloy wheels fitted, enquire if different fixings will be needed to match the seats. There have been instances where this has been overlooked.

Wheel trims

Since the shoulders on the fixings need to mate in close register with the wheel seats, it is bad practice to introduce *anything* between these two surfaces. In clear disregard of this requirement, some caravan manufacturers recently introduced bridging brackets that are fastened under two wheel bolts. The brackets include a threaded central hole for securing plastic wheel embellishers. The system is not satisfactory. Nor, for that matter are many wheel embellishers. Most end their life on roadside verges and their unexpected break for freedom is a danger to pedestrians, cyclists and other vehicles. A well-designed wheel will be attractive enough not to need a clip-on plastic cover, but embellishers are commonplace and it is wise to secure them by adding plastic cable ties available from DIY and auto stores.

Wheel and tyre matching

Bear in mind that there's a relationship between a wheel pattern and the type of tyre fitted. For example, a tubeless tyre must be matched with a wheel having a 'safety rim'; this is specifically designed to achieve the air-tight junction required. So you must insist when buying a spare wheel that it is identical in every respect to the type originally fitted on your caravan.

On many caravans over fifteen years old, the wheels do not have safety rims and cannot be used with a tubeless tyre. However, it is often permissible to fit a tubeless tyre together with an inner tube. The suitability of the matching arrangement should be checked with a tyre dealer.

Safety bands

Most wheels are made with a deep well and this can become a problem if you have a serious puncture. The edges of the tyre can slide into the well, which means they lose contact with the rim

Threads on fixings

Nowadays, caravan wheels are usually held in place by a threaded bolt and it is advisable to brush the threads periodically to remove dust. The same is recommended for the threads on studs. However, the application of a film of grease is not recommended because a torque setting to denote the tightness needed for a fixing is usually quoted on the presumption that its threads are dry.

Furthermore, grease on the threads might contribute to premature loosening and subsequent wheel loss.

Graduated settings on a torque wrench are checked as the adjusting knob on the end of the lever is rotated.

of the wheel. The result is that the metal wheel rim itself then rolls on the road surface, whereupon the caravan can slide about through lack of friction.

To overcome the problem, many people have a well-fitting collar fitted and the Tyron Safety Band is one of the best-known examples. In the event of a sudden puncture, this prevents a tyre dropping into the well and pulling away from the rim. In consequence, tyre rubber remains in contact with the road instead of the metal of the wheel rim. A degree of road holding is thus maintained while the outfit is slowed down. Naturally the tyre will sustain serious damage, but maintaining control is clearly important.

Wheel and caravan security

As a method of reducing caravan theft, AL-KO Kober has devoted considerable time to developing a security system which locks a caravan's wheels and prevents them from rotating. After extensive research, finished products were fitted on several 2006 models whose running gear had a lock receiver pre-welded to the stub axle. In addition alloy wheels of a particular pattern were needed to house the partner locking plate.

The security afforded by the system later achieved a 'Diamond Standard' following independent attack tests conducted by the Sold Secure test house. Further developments included the introduction of purpose-made covers to suit steel wheels, and covers to match several more patterns of alloy wheel. Retro-fit kits were also introduced for some types of AL-KO chassis that hadn't previously been fitted with a lock receiver. However, the modification work is comparatively complex and needs to be carried out by experienced specialists.

Working to a similar theme, the German Company Winterhoff later designed and manufactured the 'Wheel-Lock Diamond' to suit most post-2004 BPW chassis used for Explorer Group caravans.

Wheel braces

At one time, the brace provided with caravans was hopelessly inadequate for removing a wheel by the roadside. After 1988 the situation improved

when The National Caravan Council amended its Caravan Certification Scheme to include a requirement that all participating manufacturers should provide a satisfactory wheel brace.

In practice the word 'satisfactory' is vague and

As a pre-requisite for accepting an AL-KO or BPW wheel lock, a receptor device is an essential component.

The Safety Band system from Tyron prevents a punctured tyre from falling into the well of the wheel and pulling away from the rims.

Wheel rim sizes

For many years, single axle caravans ran on 13in wheel rims. This often led to difficulties when purchasing replacement tyres, especially in parts of mainland Europe. In response to this many UK manufacturers decided to fit 14in wheels instead and the transition took effect in the early 2000s. For instance, Swift and Elddis started to fit 14in wheels on 2001 models; Bailey fitted them on 2002 models. Keep this point in mind if purchasing a pre-owned caravan built around that time.

The locking plate shown here was purpose-made to suit this particular pattern of alloy wheel.

Removing a wheel

Note: *This sequence shows procedures with an older caravan where only a portable scissors jack is available. The operation is certainly easier using the types of side jack described earlier in the chapter, but many caravans are not fitted with chassis brackets that accept these alternative lifting devices.*

Also note that this sequence was carried out on a sound surface which permitted the use of axle stands. Dealing with a roadside puncture, as described below, is much more challenging and potentially more dangerous.

1. Lower the jockey wheel, apply the caravan brake firmly, then chock the wheel on the opposite side; slightly loosen the wheel fixings.

2. Ensure all the corner steadies are raised.

3. Locate the jack; a scissor type is compact enough to slide underneath.

4. The caravan is raised and an axle stand inserted. Then the caravan is lowered so the axle rests in the cradle of the stand. Finally, lower the corner steadies to provide stability.

5. The fixings are now fully loosened and withdrawn; the wheel is removed.

Roadside wheel changing

This is very different from wheel changing in the safety of a service centre. Also note that the law in an increasing number of European countries makes it obligatory to carry a high-visibility safety jacket (or waistcoat) at all times, e.g. in France. This *must* also be worn during roadside work. Anyone ill-equipped and faced with a roadside breakdown is advised to summon the Emergency Services.

The photographs above show procedure on the presumption that an axle stand is available to achieve better stability than you can achieve with a jack alone. By the roadside, you might need to use the levelling blocks normally carried in your caravan instead. Equally there could be roadside debris to help with chocking. Every possible precaution *must* be taken to keep the 'van stable and to ensure that you are safe from passing vehicles. Hence it is very important that you only jack up a caravan by the roadside when it remains hitched to the towcar. Shock waves from passing vehicles can rock a caravan off its jack. The whole wheel-change operation should be completed as hastily as possible. Under no circumstances crawl under the 'van.

Having completed the tasks shown in the sequence illustrations, wheel replacement involves the following:

- Make sure the brake drum presents a clean, flat surface.
- Centre the wheel by doing up the fixings by hand.
- Tighten further using a brace, but watch jack stability as you do it.
- Raise corner steadies; remove axle stands.
- Lower the caravan to the road surface; remove jack.
- Tighten the fixings further in the order north, south, east, west – or by the clock face – 12, 6, 3, 9 o'clock positions.
- Finally set the tightness with a torque wrench.
- In the case of wheels with five fixings, progressively tighten each opposite nut in succession.

In a remote roadside breakdown when a torque wrench is unavailable, use the brace, bearing in mind that you should exert effort, but that the operation should not be seen as a tough test. If using a telescopic wrench, it is certainly possible for some athletic men or women to over-tighten the fixings and to cause wheel damage.

Having made an assessment of tightness, proceed immediately to a garage to have the torque checked. Experts then advise that this setting is re-checked after either 30 miles or 30 minutes' driving.

In many European countries it is obligatory to wear a high-visibility safety jacket when carrying out roadside repairs.

you often find that a tyre fitter has over-tightened the fixings. Accordingly it is wise to purchase a telescopic wheel wrench which is sold with sockets to suit four different sizes of fixings. The sockets thus suit both the car as well as the caravan and an 'extending bar' wrench affords excellent leverage. However, a calibrated torque wrench is always needed when replacing a wheel to ensure the fixings have been tightened correctly.

Tightness of fixings

Also safety-relevant is the issue of wheel fixing tightness. There have been a number of instances where wheels have become detached from caravans and a similar problem is also well-known by drivers of goods vehicles. As a rule this seems to happen more often to a near-side wheel, i.e. one which revolves in the same direction as the loosening direction of a wheel nut.

Research has not produced conclusive evidence why this happens but the need to have the fixings tightened to the appropriate torque setting is indisputable.

- If the fixing is not tight enough, it can shake loose and the wheel can come off.
- If the fixing is too tight, the seating on the wheel can get damaged and this can again lead to the loss of a wheel.
- The correct tightness is most important and this can only be checked by using a torque wrench whose calibration is verified regularly.

Check the settings recommended for *your caravan* in its handbook. Typical settings are detailed in the box alongside.

Spare wheel

This is an essential item which is not provided with some caravans at the time of purchase. The importance of obtaining a matching spare has already been emphasised and the suggestion that a suitable alternative can be found at a car breakers is ill-founded.

Methods of carrying a spare vary. Some manufacturers e.g. Lunar, have made stowage provision in the front locker, although nose weight needs checking carefully if this location is adopted. Avondale developed an under-floor wheel pan which is accessed from inside the 'van. Vanmaster has included a sliding drawer system accessed from outside. One well-known manufacturer took the ill-advised decision to mount the spare on the rear wall of the caravan which can lead to instability problems. The majority of caravans, however, are fitted with an under-floor carrier.

Wheel carriers have been developed by AL-KO Kober and several independent manufacturers.

In general a carrier uses a telescopic arrangement so that it can be slid out from underneath the caravan. This is fine – *as long as* the tubes are kept well greased. If overlooked, the tubes soon seize up completely.

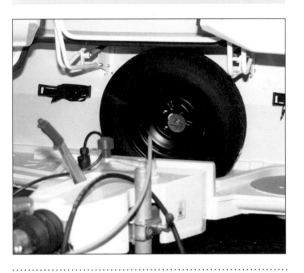

Locating a spare wheel in a forward locker is very convenient, but it must not cause excessive nose weight.

Carriers can be fitted to many caravans built on a modern lightweight chassis and the photographs overleaf show a DIY installation.

Wheel brace

A telescopic wheel wrench is sold with sockets to suit four different sizes of fixings, and is suitable for use on a car or caravan.

AL-KO Kober spare wheel carrier

The small nuts on a spare wheel carrier will be tight to do up and will feel as if they are cross-threaded. This is not the case. The threads are intentionally deformed to achieve a tighter grip. This prevents them from shaking loose while travelling.

Fitting an AL-KO Kober spare wheel carrier

1. The caravan must be safely elevated. This is critical.

2. Components are assembled using normal spanners.

3. Before installation, make sure the telescopic tubes are well greased.

4. Dummy run – the chassis attachment components are checked.

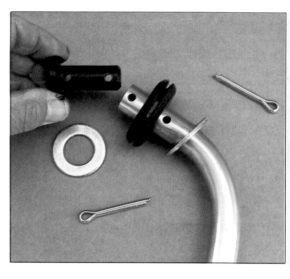

5. A rubber grommet is inserted into the pre-punched hole in the chassis.

6. The fixed end of the carrier is offered-up and fastened into place.

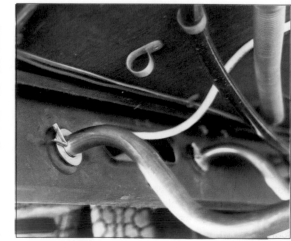

7. The spare is held to the double rails using a large spigot.

8. The carrier is rested on the ground and checked.

9. A locking bolt for the main securing nut is fitted to the chassis.

10. The carrier is now raised and the plastic securing wheel is fitted in place.

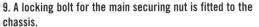

Tyres

Caravan tyres are safety-critical items and are manufactured to exacting European standards. The user will also be prosecuted if the tyres are faulty as explained in the box on page 66.

Tyre life

Bearing in mind that in the case of most caravans, the entire weight has to be borne on *two* wheels, the assertion is often made that life is much easier for tyres fitted to cars. Also caravans tend to remain stationary for longer periods and this places demands on the tyres. So caravan tyres nearly always need replacing due to the walls deteriorating; the tread, in contrast, can look scarcely worn.

Consequently, the serviceability of caravan tyres should not be judged solely on tread depth. Specialists state that you should never use tyres on a caravan which are more than seven years old. They point out that tyres more than five years old are due for replacement; their deterioration by then will be significant, irrespective of tread depth.

As a guide to owners, there's usually a date marked on a tyre although this hasn't been shown on the BRMA diagram reproduced on page 67. In truth, this is not an obligatory requirement.

An example of such a marking is shown in the photograph on page 66, where the figure '2607' indicates that this tyre was manufactured in the 26th week of 2007. Since these date markings are sometimes difficult to identify it makes sense

for an owner to keep a diary of the dates when new tyres were installed.

Tyre care

Deterioration occurs when a caravan is stationary for prolonged periods, and it undoubtedly helps to relieve the tyres by supporting the 'van on axle stands. If these provide full support, removal of the caravan's wheels for storage in a place away from sunlight is particularly helpful. Provided the strategy doesn't infringe the conditions of an insurance policy, this precautionary measure will afford a degree of security as well.

Alternatively, it helps if the caravan is periodically moved a short distance – either forwards or backwards. This ensures that different parts of the tyre wall are distended during the period of storage.

Keep a constant check on tyres too, looking at both the side walls as well as the tread. An inspection lamp will be helpful when checking the inner face. Cuts, bulges and penetrating flints can lead to a sudden loss of air, and a driver is legally obliged to ensure the tyres are sound. However, remember that age-related failure is often sudden and there might not be warning signs of a pending problem.

Pressure check

Handbooks should indicate the pressures needed for the tyres installed and these must be checked frequently. A reliable dial-type gauge is recommended.

Remember that tyre pressures should be checked when the tyre is cold. The pressure will rise when the vehicle is used and this is taken into account when a 'cold pressure' reading is specified by a manufacturer. Do *not* make adjustments for hot conditions or sustained fast towing situations.

Commercial tyres

Caravans are either fitted with car or commercial tyres. However, recently, manufacturers have been more inclined to fit the latter type; their higher permitted pressures offer the potential to carry larger loads.

A problem associated with this is a tendency to

recommend the same inflation pressure for all the caravans in a particular range and this has been the subject of investigation by The Caravan Club. When a caravan with a substantial MTPLM (maximum technically permissible laden mass, formerly referred to as the maximum authorised weight), is towed with its tyres inflated to a high pressure, the combination might be fine. But if the same tyre at the same pressure is specified for a model with a *much lower* MTPLM, there's a risk of the caravan suffering from an excessively bumpy ride. This can lead to furniture and fitting damage inside.

As a result of problems reported by members, The Caravan Club sought the support of the National Caravan Council after which caravan manufacturers were urged to be more model-specific when quoting tyre pressures.

Load and speed limits

Tyres are built to cope with different load limits and different maximum speeds. On modern tyres, a load index figure appears in the coding moulded on the wall and reference to a load index table reveals the maximum load-carrying performance applicable when the vehicle is driven at the tyre's maximum speed rating. The diagram opposite shows what the moulded rubber markings on the side wall signify.

Having identified the load limit figure, read the kg limit from the Load Index table opposite and then double it for a single axle caravan (multiply by four for a twin axle 'van). Then compare this with the manufacturer's quoted maximum technically permissible laden mass (previously referred to as Maximum Authorised Weight) to ensure the carrying capacity of the tyre exceeds that of the caravan's MTPLM (formerly MAW). Bear in mind that tyres are only one element contributing to a caravan's quoted MTPLM. Chassis and suspension design are other elements.

In certain circumstances, for maximum towing speeds not exceeding 62mph (100km/h), e.g. in the UK where the statutory speed limit is 60mph, bonus loads may be applied to tyres. However, in the interest of maximising safety margins, it is recommended that bonus loads are not taken into consideration for tyre selection purposes.

As regards speed ratings, alphabetical designations have been used for a number of years to indicate the maximum speed at which a tyre can carry the load calculated from the Load Index table. Speed ratings in the range applicable to caravans are listed below and both R and S rated tyres are popular choices:

J	=	62mph (100km/h)
K	=	68mph (110km/h)
L	=	75mph (120km/h)
M	=	81mph (130km/h)
N	=	88mph (140km/h)
P	=	94mph (150km/h)
Q	=	100mph (160km/h)

R = 105mph (170km/h)
S = 113mph (180km/h)
T = 118mph (190km/h)

Since the maximum towing speed limit in Britain is 60mph on motorways, it might seem logical to purchase a 'J' rated tyre. However, if you take your caravan to France, it is illegal to have a rating lower than the maximum permitted speed (81mph on many of the motorways) even if you have no intention of towing at anywhere near that speed. So if you intend towing abroad, a tyre with a speed rating of 'M' or higher is needed.

Buying replacement tyres

When buying new tyres, make sure they are:
- the correct size
- the correct type
- of the appropriate speed rating
- of the appropriate load rating.

   Even though commercial tyres offer higher load-carrying possibilities, switching from car-type tyres has a number of implications. The potential for increased tyre pressures might present problems.

   Equally, switching to a larger sized tyre in the hope of increasing the loading limit is unwise since there might be insufficient room under the wheel arch. For example, there must be at least 30mm (1³⁄₁₆in) of free space at all extremes of wheel movement – and this could be unachievable if a larger tyre is fitted. In other words before making a change to the type of tyre fitted, seek the advice of the caravan clubs, a tyre specialist or the British Rubber Manufacturers' Association.

Load Index Table

Load Index	Kg	Load Index	Kg	Load Index	Kg	Load Index	Kg
60	250	71	345	82	475	93	650
61	257	72	355	83	487	94	670
62	265	73	365	84	500	95	690
63	272	74	375	85	515	96	710
64	280	75	387	86	530	97	730
65	290	76	400	87	545	98	750
66	300	77	412	88	560	99	775
67	307	78	425	89	580	100	800
68	315	79	437	90	600	101	825
69	325	80	450	91	615	102	850
70	335	81	462	92	630	103	875

Technical Tip

The recommended pressures for caravan tyres vary quite considerably. For instance, models running on car tyres might have a typical pressure quoted in the handbook of around 33psi (e.g. the 1998 Avondale Leda Chiltern) whereas models running on commercial tyres might require a pressure of 52psi (e.g. the 1998 Avondale Leda Pentland). So reference to the handbook is important and if this has 'gone missing' when a caravan is purchased second-hand, the Caravan Clubs can often advise members about correct tyre pressures.

BRMA CAR TYRE SIDEWALL DRAWING

Car tyre markings
(Reproduced with permission of the British Rubber Manufacturers' Association).

For updated information on tyre markings see www.tyresafe.org.uk

SIZE DESIGNATION
NOMINAL SECTION WIDTH (mm)
ASPECT RATIO
RIM DIAMETER (INCHES)

SERVICE DESCRIPTION
LOAD INDEX
SPEED SYMBOL

165/70R13 79T

RADIAL

MADE IN GREAT BRITAIN

REINFORCED

* LOAD AND PRESSURE REQUIREMENT

COMMERCIAL NAME OR IDENTITY

"TRADE NAME" "KP 200"

MAX. LOAD 437 kg (963 lbs) MAX. PRESSURE 300 kPa (44 psi)

DENOTES TYPE OF CONSTRUCTION

ASPECT RATIO IS THE TYRE SECTION HEIGHT EXPRESSED AS A PERCENTAGE OF THE SECTION WIDTH

REINFORCED WHERE APPLICABLE

TWI

TREADWEAR 160 TRACTION A TEMPERATURE B

COUNTRY OF MANUFACTURE

* UNIFORM TYRE QUALITY GRADING REQUIRED BY USA CUSTOMER INFORMATION REGULATIONS

MANUFACTURERS NAME OR BRAND NAME

PLIES SIDEWALL 2 RAYON
PLIES TREAD 2 RAYON 2 STEEL

DATA CODE

DOT ABC DEF 343 ◄

(E11) 021234

* NORTH AMERICAN DEPARTMENT OF TRANSPORTATION COMPLIANCE SYMBOL

LOCATION OF TREAD WEAR INDICATORS (MARKINGS VARY WITH MANUFACTURER)

* TYRE CONSTRUCTION DETAILS

TUBELESS

M&S

TWI

* NORTH AMERICAN TYRE IDENTIFICATION NUMBER

TUBELESS OR TUBE TYPE (NB. IF NEITHER IS SHOWN A TUBE MUST BE FITTED)

ECE TYPE APPROVAL MARK AND NUMBER. THE ALTERNATIVE EEC APPROVAL MARK IS e11

TYRES SPECIFICALLY DESIGNED FOR MUD AND SNOW (WINTER)

Exterior body maintenance

Cleaning techniques, window replacement, dealing with delamination and locating leaks are subjects discussed in this chapter. Before jobs like this can be tackled, however, it is important to understand how a caravan is constructed.

When lighter chassis were developed around 1980, their radical new designs went hand-in-hand with changes in body construction. In fact the interplay between a chassis and its accompanying composite floor panel makes a critical contribution to the total structure.

Previously, the heavy type of chassis used for a caravan was a self-sufficient foundation; the ply and timber joists that sat on top were merely a rudimentary form of staging. Now there is interdependency so that both floor and chassis work together to provide rigidity. Strength is thus achieved in a different way, and yet the total weight of the two elements is considerably less than it has previously been.

Constructional features

The floor section, side walls, front walls, rear walls and roof are usually built differently – a fact which has implications for both maintenance and repair work.

Floor panels

On the older type of chassis, longitudinal timber joists support a panel of treated plywood – typically 13mm (½in) ply. The advantage of this is there's little to give trouble. However, the structure is quite heavy and lacks thermal insulation – which means you get cold feet when caravanning in winter. Some DIY owners improve this shortcoming by glueing block polystyrene between the joists. A product like Jablite, used in the building industry for floor insulation and available from builders' merchants, is a popular product for this upgrading work.

In contrast, the floor panel fitted to a lighter chassis is completely different in construction. It has no supporting joists underneath, and

strength is achieved by using a prefabricated composite panel instead. This comprises a three-layer 'sandwich' in which two layers of thin, treated plywood (typically 5mm ³⁄₁₆in) are bonded to an insulating material in the middle. The core often consists of styrofoam insulation with timber battens around the perimeter and strengthening wooden cross-members as well. When the styrofoam and the reinforcing timbers are bonded to the plywood with special adhesive, the resulting composite board has remarkable strength.

The advantages are that the floor is light, strong, and well insulated. A disadvantage, however, is that strength is seriously impaired if the bond between the ply and the core material starts to fail. Dealing with 'delamination', as this condition is known, receives attention later in the chapter.

Side walls

The traditional way to build a post-war caravan was to start by constructing a skeleton framework using timber struts. This was clad on the outside with aluminium sheet, and finished on the inside with faced hardboard or thin pre-decorated plywood. An insulation material was usually fitted in the void between the inner and outer skins. However, if a fibre-glass 'quilt' or 'Rockwool' insulant is used, it tends to slump in the void, leaving cold spots. More rigid products like block polystyrene are preferred.

Until recently some manufacturers still adopted this form of construction, particularly low volume specialists who built high quality models, e.g. Carlight Caravans. However, the majority of manufacturers now use prefabricated bonded panels for the side walls and these are formed in an industrial press just like the bonded floor sections.

The difference from floor panels, however, relates to the materials used for the 'sandwich'. The interior surface is 3mm decorative ply, the core is often polystyrene, and the outer surface

Some high quality caravans like the models from Carlight were always constructed using a skeleton framework of wooden struts.

(Photograph courtesy of Carlight Caravans)

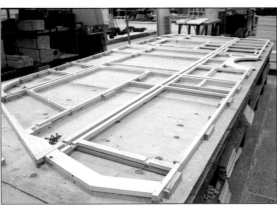

To achieve accuracy in construction, the traditionally built wall framework of a Buccaneer caravan was assembled in a jig.
(Photograph courtesy of Andrew Jenkinson)

Most caravan side walls are now made using prefabricated composite bonded panels.

is usually sheet aluminium. Wooden battens will be used within the sandwich as well, especially around apertures like windows or locker openings, to provide a strengthening surround. The wood provides a solid framework which is necessary when fitting hinges, catches and so on.

Some manufacturers bond small galvanised sheets at key points in the sandwich to provide fixing points for furniture; others insert additional timbers. These are important because rivets and self-tapping screws would not achieve a secure hold in the thin decorative ply that faces the interior part of the side walls. Similarly, timber strengthening battens are built into the core to reinforce the overall rigidity of the panel.

Front and rear walls

Although the front and rear walls are sometimes built with the same type of bonded board used for the side walls, most are constructed using a ply and softwood framework. This provides a base on which to mount moulded panels, which in turn gives a particular model a distinctive appearance. The shapely front and rear sections provide a visual improvement over the featureless side walls.

Two types of material are used for these front and rear panels as discussed later.

Roofs

In most caravans, the roof is constructed with a framework of wooden strutting and shaped plywood formers. The structure is sometimes assembled in a jig before being offered up. Thin decorative 3mm

Sealants are used to bond and waterproof junction points where different body sections are joined together.

A boat-style roof structure is being made here using timber struts that are assembled in a jig.
(Photograph courtesy of Andrew Jenkinson)

Roofs are usually filled with a fibre-glass wool insulant and then capped with either aluminium sheet or a GRP moulding.

This helps to shed water more effectively on account of the pitch.

The traditional 'lantern-style' roof in which a raised section is bordered by small roof-light windows is only seen on older caravans. In recent times this was a registered design of Carlight caravans and lantern roofs were fitted by the Company until manufacturing ceased at its Sleaford factory around 2004.

A further constructional feature was the introduction by Bailey Caravans of bonded panels that were installed in the roofs of 2006 models. A pre-formed insulated board undoubtedly creates a more robust structure than is achievable with conventional timber strut framework clad in ceiling ply and an aluminium outer skin. Although this type of roof is not intended for carrying heavy weights, its strength was convincingly shown when three members of Bailey's staff and three officials of The Caravan Club stood on one as a publicity stunt.

Creating this type of structure is not without its challenges. For example, the lack of a void in the main part of a caravan's roof means that all electrical cables needed for ceiling lights have to be pre-installed in the right positions when the bonded sandwich panels are manufactured.

Doors and windows

Few owners realise that the door on their caravan is unlikely to have been made by the caravan manufacturer. Most doors are provided by specialists who supply the caravan industry with units to suit their particular models.

Windows, similarly, are items that are 'bought-in'. At one time a window comprised an aluminium frame and a piece of glass. In 1978, however, it became illegal to fit 'non-safety' glass. Moulded acrylic windows which fulfilled this requirement seemed an obvious answer – and eliminated the need for an aluminium frame fitted with rubber weather strips. 'Plastic' windows were instantly adopted and have been used ever since.

At first, moulded acrylic windows were single section panels and these were fitted to many

ply may be used to line the ceiling although faced hardboard is sometimes preferred because its flexibility will negotiate curved sections more readily.

On the outside, sheet aluminium is the most common cladding material although some manufacturers have fitted one-piece glass reinforced plastic (GRP) roof panels instead, e.g. Avondale.

Some caravan roofs are built with flat sections whereas others adopt the inverted 'boat' style where a ridge runs longitudinally along the centre.

The bonded panel roof now being fitted on some Bailey caravans isn't intended to be walked on but it is far stronger than a conventional roof made using timber struts and cladding.

models built in the early 1980s. However, double-glazed versions were a more logical choice in view of the greater level of insulation being achieved by using bonded wall panels. So in spite of their considerable cost, double-glazed units became the standard fitment.

Although the acrylic plastic windows fitted on most touring caravans don't have a frame, some models in the Explorer range are equipped with Seitz S4 framed windows. These units comprise an outer frame with its double-glazed panel and a corresponding cassette frame that is fitted inside. This houses two recoiling rollers for a blind and mesh fly screen respectively. The outer and inner frames are screwed tightly together, thereby achieving a weather-resistant fit around the aperture. Seitz S4 units, more frequently seen on motorcaravans, are costlier than frameless windows but are notably good. In reality few caravan owners would choose to fit them retrospectively in a refurbishment project. However, readers requiring more information should note that the installation of Seitz S4 windows is described with step-by-step photographs on pages 94–7 of *Build Your Own Motorcaravan* by John Wickersham, Published by Haynes.

Materials

Not only is it helpful if you know how your caravan is constructed, it is also useful to differentiate between the materials used. This is important if damage occurs and a repair is needed.

Sheet aluminium

When sandwich construction first arrived, it was found that timber battens within the core of a wall panel could be seen on the side elevations if you looked closely at a caravan. To hide this, manufacturers used aluminium sheet that had a surface texture. Rippled, pimpled and stucco surface finishes are common examples and if an outside wall gets dented, you cannot replicate the appearance if a body repair filler is used.

Some years later, fabrication techniques improved and some manufacturers e.g. Avondale and Compass, reverted to plain aluminium again. Many others have since followed and textured surfaces seem to be going out of fashion.

Glass reinforced plastic (GRP) sheet

When the technique of manufacturing thin glass reinforced plastic (GRP) sheet was mastered, this provided an alternative to aluminium cladding. The material is thin and so flexible that it is supplied on a roll. When the Abbey Domino was launched in 1995 with its GRP impact-resistant sidewalls, a new chapter in construction was opened.

Other models like the Abbey Chess and Solitaire soon followed, but the use of aluminium

The Seitz S4 windows used on some caravans in the Explorer range have an outer frame which houses the acrylic double-glazed panel; this is tightly connected to an inner frame that houses a blind and fly screen.

sheet still predominates in caravan construction. It is worth noting that the GRP alternative has been more widely used by manufacturers of coachbuilt motorcaravans such as Auto-Sleepers, Bessacarr and Swift.

One disadvantage with sheet GRP is that it lacks the high gloss finish of painted aluminium. On the other hand, dented aluminium usually involves major repair work because large areas usually have to be overlaid with a completely new sheet. In contrast, damaged GRP can often be repaired using conventional car bodywork fillers. For this reason many people believed that GRP sheet would become increasingly popular: but it didn't. Some repair shop staff seemed

Aluminium sheet with a pimpled surface is often used on imported caravans like this TEC model, but dealing with an accidental dent is not a DIY repair job.

The side walls of the Abbey Domino are clad in GRP impact-resistant sheet.

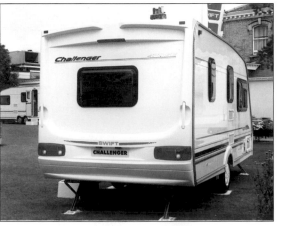

The one-piece rear panel on this model is made from GRP, which has the advantage of being easily repairable.

Identifying ABS and GRP

These distinctive types of plastic used for body panels are easy to identify. The rear surface of ABS and acrylic-capped ABS panels is very smooth. In contrast, the rear of a GRP panel has a roughened surface. On closer inspection you can often see the strands of glass used as the reinforcing binder in the lamination. The inside surfaces of items like locker doors, side skirts and front fairings are therefore the 'give-away' feature.

However, there are exceptions which can mislead an owner. On the gas locker doors of Vanroyce caravans (which are no longer in production), two GRP moulded panels were bonded back-to-back. Hiding the roughened reverse face of a panel was a cosmetic nicety and the door was also more sturdy as a result.

The inner surface of this wheel arch cover is smooth, confirming that it is made from ABS plastic.

The roughened surface on the inside face of this locker door indicates that the component is moulded using GRP.

to find difficulty carrying out 'invisible' repairs using polyester resins so caravan manufacturers reverted to the use of aluminium cladding.

Moulded glass reinforced plastic

Glass reinforced plastic, or 'fibre glass' as it is affectionately known, is a long established material used in the construction of cars, boats, light aircraft – and caravans. Note that in this application, we are referring to *moulded* GRP sections as opposed to the thin, flat, flexible GRP sheet mentioned above.

When a contoured panel is built by an experienced laminator using a well-finished mould, the final product will not only look smart; it will also give exceptional service. Most better-quality caravans have moulded panels on both the front and rear. Some caravans often have GRP side skirts and chassis cover-fairings too.

The main feature is ease of repair. Many specialists can undertake GRP repair work and DIY owners often achieve smart results as well. This is discussed later in the chapter.

The rear of this caravan is built using a bonded panel for the upper part and a GRP moulding for the lower section.

Acrylic-capped ABS

Acrylonitrile-butadiene-styrene is a tongue twister by anyone's standards; so this type of plastic is more commonly referred to as 'ABS'. Versions of ABS often have a matt finish and are used for items like wheel arch embellishers. A similar material is used for vehicle bumpers, wing mirrors and a host of other automotive accessories.

By capping the material with a coating of acrylic, the surface finish is much shinier and this is more suitable for caravan front and rear panels. Equally, the material is also used for bathroom cabinets, washbasins and even moulded shower cubicles.

On caravans built two or more decades ago it is sometimes found that rainwater has worked its way under the acrylic skin on ABS panels, thereby forming blisters of water. Subsequently there may be localised areas where the shiny coating chips away. This defacement is one of the shortcomings and it appears that there is no permanent cure.

Repairing cracks in acrylic-capped ABS is another matter of concern. For a number of years, it has been believed that when an acrylic-capped ABS front panel of a caravan receives damage, the entire section will have to be replaced. This can come as a great shock to an owner who has merely split a small part of the front underskirt on a high kerb. Car owners have similar shocks when they find how much it costs to replace a damaged ABS bumper; and so do motorcyclists whose race-replica bikes sustain a small crack in a fairing.

In response to this, chemists have been working on plastic repair kits and these have recently become available. It is too early to say how successful a repair will be on the thin acrylic-capped panels used on caravans. One service centre, West Riding Leisure of Huddersfield, developed expertise in ABS repair work some time ago, but most caravan service centres still prefer to replace an entire panel. It is certainly true that to date, few service engineers have attended training courses in ABS repair procedures. This is a great pity.

Sealants and mastics

The ability of a caravan to resist weather damage is largely dependent on the sealants used in its construction. An ever-present problem is the fact that different materials expand and contract at different rates in different temperatures. Thermal stresses are a potential threat.

Then there are mechanical stresses – a caravan is subjected to relentless movements when towed along bumpy roads. So the sealants selected to bridge the junctions between adjoining materials have to permit flexion without loss of adhesion or self-destruction. It's a tall order.

Products are classified in accordance with their intended function, chemical formulation, and method of application. Whereas some are non-setting sealants, others are known as adhesive sealants; these take around 24 hours to cure and achieve their full strength.

Products like Sikaflex 221 and Sikaflex 512 Caravan are used extensively in the automotive, boat and caravan industries because of their remarkable ability to maintain an unfailing bond in spite of differential movements – even when the adjoining materials are dissimilar. For example,

This type of Remi sliding roof window fitted on some Avondale and Bailey caravans affords access to apply an extra film of Sikaflex 512 Caravan around its perimeter.

today's car windscreens are seldom held in place using a rubber surround. Instead they are bonded to the metal bodyshell using a black adhesive sealant. Note that Sikaflex emphasises that at least 4mm of adhesive sealant should be applied. In other words if you cramp-up or screw down a fitting so tightly that sealant oozes out and leaves less than 4mm in place, its strength will be greatly reduced.

Unfortunately adhesive sealants usually take more than an hour to start setting and several more hours to achieve full strength. That's why caravan trim sections are fitted by manufacturers using screws and a normal bedding sealant. However, that doesn't prevent DIY owners carrying out screw-free installations at a later date.

Naturally, few owners wouldn't want to refit fixtures that are satisfactorily keeping out the

Type	Example	Purpose	Form	Available from
Silicone sealant	Dow Corning 785 Sanitary Acetoxy mildew-resistant silicone sealant.	Sealing sanitary ware like shower trays, wash basins and non-porous surfaces.	Cartridge (310ml) to fit standard DIY dispenser gun.	Builders' merchants.
Bedding Sealant	Carafax Caraseal IDL 99 non-drying bedding sealant.	To provide a flexible bedding layer on which to mount external fittings like ventilators, awning rails, and trim strips.	Cartridge to fit standard DIY dispenser gun.	Caravan accessory shops.
Ribbon-type bedding sealant	W4 mastic sealing strip.	For the sealing and re-bedding of caravan and motorhome fittings.	Sold in 5m (approx.) rolls with a non-stick backing paper.	Caravan and motorhome accessory shops.
Adhesive sealant	Sikaflex-512 Caravan, Technique adhesive sealant systems.	For creating permanent bonds between dissimilar materials which attain a high level of adhesion and a barrier to the passage of moisture.	Cartridge to fit standard DIY dispenser guns.	Automotive specialists and selected caravan accessory suppliers – addresses from Sika Ltd.

Sold in several colours, silicone sealant is mainly used for sealing around sanitary ware like shower trays or wash basins.

A non-drying bedding sealant is used to weatherproof components which might need to be removed from the body at some future point.

A non-setting sealant sold in ribbon form is sometimes easier to position than a similar product applied from a cartridge gun.

Sikaflex-512 Caravan sealant is used here to seal a lamp fitting, but its adhesive properties also commend it for bonding body panels.

Awning rails get tugged in winds. Once this beading of sealant was applied, a gloved finger and spittle created a smooth bevel edge before it started setting.

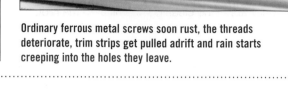

Ordinary ferrous metal screws soon rust, the threads deteriorate, trim strips get pulled adrift and rain starts creeping into the holes they leave.

rain. That said, Sikaflex 512 Caravan can also be used to add a supporting edge around existing ventilators, roof windows and awning rails to increase their weatherproofing performance.

The harsh fact is that damp does find it's way into caravans, and sometimes at a surprisingly early point in their life. Reasons for this problem can be attributed to:

- Bad design in the body construction;
- Unsatisfactory surface preparation;
- Bad workmanship when sealant is applied;
- A wrong choice of sealant;
- A product drying-out, becoming brittle and losing elasticity;
- Use of screws which puncture the metal cladding;
- Failure to specify stainless steel screws;
- Seepage through capillary action between adjoining panels.

As mentioned later, this is why regular damp testing with a good quality meter is always important. Rectifying any points of weakness should then be carried out without delay.

Routine cleaning

Inevitably a caravan gets dirty and if parked under a tree for a prolonged period it will be coated with algae and a fair share of bird droppings. Under some species of tree e.g. limes, the surface will also become coated with a sticky film.

When being towed, mud, grease and tar stains will spoil its appearance, too. Routine cleaning is a necessary chore.

Washing

Many owners resort to a bucket-and-sponge approach which is fine – but tedious. Standing on a set of steps to reach the roof can also be precarious so many owners purchase a soft brush fitted on an extendable tubular pole. These products are often on sale at caravan exhibitions and there are versions which have a facility for coupling-up a hose to the handle.

Some caravanners also decide to purchase a high pressure hose complete with a cleaning chemical dispenser, but in the hands of an inexperienced user this strategy can lead to all sorts of problems. The power of water can be extremely damaging and it's not unusual for ageing plastic decals to get broken by the jet; in extreme circumstances windows get cracked as well. Remember, too, that the layer of paint on aluminium panels is surprisingly thin.

Also at risk are the sealants which provide a bedding for trim strips and other wall-mounted components. When ageing sealant loses its flexibility, the power of a water jet can blast pieces away. This is when the leaks are likely to start.

Provided you recognise these points, high

To reach difficult areas of their caravan, many owners purchase a purpose-made soft brush on an extendable pole to make washing easier.

When parked for long spells under trees, a caravan soon accumulates stains, bird lime and algae deposits.

pressure hoses can be a great asset. Specialists who use these machines regularly advise you to:

- spray the cleaning chemical from the bottom and work upwards;
- use increased power for stubborn stains – but only where it is safe to do so;
- exercise caution around vents, windows, locker lids and the door;
- finally apply the cleaning chemical to the roof;
- rinse the entire surface with fresh water.

Cleaning items

When adopting other cleaning techniques and applying polish, the following items are strongly recommended:

A hard compound rigid sponge is good for cleaning interior faced ply surfaces. These are often used by interior decorators.

A hard bristled brush is useful for cleaning wheels and around the coupling.

A long handled cranked brush sold for painting the back of radiators is ideal for agitating liquid cleaning chemicals when applied around fittings.

Open-weave cloth made from 100% cotton stock. For polishing, avoid material that contains lint; items of clothing like old T-shirts are not recommended for this reason.

When tackling a major clean, start with the really dirty jobs and then move to the finishing operations. For instance, in a full schedule, the recommended order is:

1. Clean the wheels and tyres.
2. Clean the door and locker shuts.
3. Remove individual tar spots.
4. Remove stubborn stains and black streaks.
5. Apply shampoo to the body and windows.
6. Polish sections of the body.
7. Polish the windows.
8. Apply cleaner to black plastic items.
9. Apply tyre dressing.

Specialists who market cleaners suitable for the different materials used in caravan construction include Auto Glym, Fenwicks and Mer. As the box alongside explains, caravans have a number of common problems, particularly the incidence of black streaks.

When following the order of cleaning recommended, note that there are plenty of proprietary products for wheel cleaning e.g. Mer Alloy Wheel and General Wheel Cleaner. Equally there are tar removal and tyre refurbishment treatments, but whereas this part of a cleaning operation is done first, application of a tyre dressing should be left until last.

Around the body generally, Auto Glym Caravan and Motorhome Cleaner is very effective for removing algae from trim strips and bird lime marks. Once applied, the cleaning action should be

It is important not to get too close to trim strips or handles when using a pressure hose at a high setting.

A specially-formulated product from Auto Glym known as Caravan and Motorhome Cleaner is easy to apply and shifts many types of dirty marks.

When Auto Glym Engine Cleaner is applied to algae-coated and black-streaked trim strips, it should be agitated with a brush before rinsing off.

Stain removal

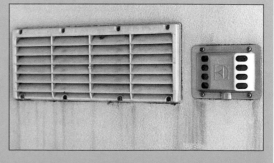

Black carbon stains that form below caravan guttering, ventilators and other wall-mounted fittings can be successfully removed with Auto Glym Caravan Cleaner. The container has a piston dispenser so that stained areas can be sprayed with the chemical. It should then be agitated with a brush or sponge and finally rinsed off with clean water. For even worse streaks use Auto Glym Engine Cleaner. In addition to its function cleaning engines, the product is especially good for removing grease from tyres and cleaning plastic covers, discoloured vents, exhaust marks from the tow car, caravan ovens, barbecue equipment and even stains on the outside of saucepans.

A proprietary vehicle polish is applied to this GRP locker door to achieve a long-lasting shine.

A number of rubber treatments are available for cleaning and re-establishing the flexibility of rubber seals.

accelerated by using the cranked brush mentioned earlier to agitate the chemical. When the deposits are shifted, rinse off with clean water.

The application of a shampoo conditioner is recommended next, but when it is time to rinse away the suds, avoid using a high pressure hose. This has the effect of 'bouncing off' the conditioning film that most shampoos leave after application. However, gentle flooding on aluminium panels enables some conditioners to electrostatically bond to the surface, thus affording protection.

Windows should be tackled next and there are many cleaners that are suitable on the glass units fitted to older caravans. Acrylic windows are different. These 'plastic' windows are easily scratched and the first task is to ensure that preceding shampoo and rinse work has removed all the dirt and dust. Then you can apply a product specially formulated for plastic windows such as Auto Glym Fast Glass. This is sprayed on to the window and then promptly spread across the surface with a piece of paper kitchen roll. In equal haste it should be removed with another piece of clean kitchen roll. The cleaning fluid mustn't be allowed to dry – so avoid doing this job in direct sunshine.

As regards polishing work, it is best to leave patterned aluminium, such as a stucco surface finish, with the sheen left by the shampoo. The point is that some paints applied to aluminium can be lifted by polishes. This is not the case on

moulded GRP or acrylic-capped ABS and a coat of polish will achieve protection that may last for six months or more.

Always take note of product instructions and when applying a polish, be careful to keep it from black plastic components like door handles and rubber seals around the windows. The black sheen on plastic door handles can be revived with a product like Auto Glym Bumper Care or Mer Bumper & External Vinyl Cleaning Gel and this is applied after the polishing is complete. There are also rubber-care products intended for maintaining the cleanliness and flexibility of window seals.

To finish the task, a final application of a tyre treatment like Auto Glym Tyre Conditioner completes the valet. Rubber paints that were once used are less popular nowadays. Tyre conditioner is sprayed on to the rubber and its white streaks initially look unpleasant, but these mustn't be touched and the conditioner is merely left to dry for ten to fifteen minutes. Later, the revived surface makes a tyre look like new again.

Body panel sealants

Cleaning a caravan and removing stubborn marks is a time-consuming job. This has led to the development of body-sealing products which create a surface barrier on painted surfaces and plastic mouldings. Although these products cannot prevent dead flies, bird lime and green algae accumulating on a caravan, their removal requires just a very quick wash with the help of an approved shampoo. In some instances a shower of rain can create a self-cleaning effect when a caravan is parked.

The application of a sealant to a pre-cleaned surface is not a new idea. Franchise dealers selling cars like Ferrari, Mercedes, Porsche, Volvo and others normally offer these treatments as an 'optional extra'. The manufacturer of A-Glaze sealant, for example, has also treated motorised yachts, express coaches and passenger aircraft in order to reduce cleaning operations to the minimum.

It was only natural to extend sales by offering

An A-Glaze kit for caravans and motorhomes includes a surface preparation treatment, the sealing product and a shampoo for use later.

Paintseal Direct offers a professional application service which includes upholstery treatment inside; it's not available, however, for DIY use.

the A-Glaze product as part of a DIY treatment kit for caravan owners as well. In a similar way, Paintseal Direct offers a professional application service in which specialists apply CPC protective treatments that contain Du Pont fluoro polymers and Teflon. However, the Paintseal product is not sold for DIY applications.

Neither product is cheap and the preliminary preparation is an exacting task which may take a day to complete. However, these sealants are sold with a warranty and Paintseal's professional application service on a new caravan carries a five-year guarantee. Without doubt, sealing products make routine cleaning much easier although they are best applied when a caravan is new. Moreover, they are not usually applied to body panels with a textured surface.

- It is important to keep the cloth damp. A plant spraying atomiser, available from Garden Centres, is very helpful here.
- Before final buffing, wipe away any residue of the compound – again using a damp cloth or damp sponge.
- The final buffing should be done with a clean, dry cloth.

Note that Farécla Caravan Pride Colour Restorer can sometimes be used on painted aluminium surfaces, but this should be checked on a small corner of a panel because the depth of paint is often extremely shallow.

Reviving dulled GRP and acrylics

Over a period of years, it is not unusual for moulded GRP and acrylic panels to lose their sheen. A point is reached when polish doesn't revive the appearance and many cutting compounds are far too abrasive.

A product that will revive a dulled finish very successfully is Farécla Caravan Pride Colour Restorer. This was introduced to the caravan market in early 1999 but the product is a long-established favourite in the marine industry, albeit under the name of 'Boat Pride Colour Restorer'.

The product is a standard grade finishing paste and whereas a professional would apply Colour Restorer using a slow-speed buffing machine whose pad had been liberally dampened with water, the treatment can also be applied by hand. The procedure is:

- Use a damp rag and apply the Colour Restorer in straight backward and forward motions. Change direction quite regularly to ensure you achieve even coverage.

Window repair and replacement

One of the biggest disincentives to purchasing a pre-1978 caravan is the fact that if a window gets broken, it is unlikely to be repairable. Aluminium framed glass windows are no longer manufactured for caravans and the only source of a replacement is a specialist breakers.

Replacing broken windows is expensive and delivery delays are not unusual. The damage here occurred in the shared caravan/lorry park at a motorway service station.

Removing scratches in acrylic windows

Driving too close to hedgerows often leaves scratch marks on acrylic windows – but these can usually be removed. Anyone who has seen demonstrations at exhibitions by staff from Farécla will know that Caravan Pride Scratch Remover restores a high gloss surface to a scratched plastic window. This fine rubbing compound can be applied either with a slow-rotating buffing machine or by hand. Procedures are shown in the photographs below and important tips are given in the box on the facing page.

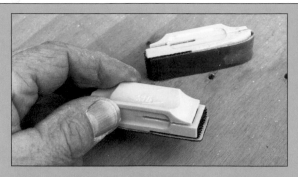

1. Deep scratches are normally removed by starting with 1200 grade wet-and-dry paper mounted on a small block. The water acts as a lubricant.

2. Use an open-weave cloth made from 100% cotton stock and ensure it is wet. A garden spray bottle is useful for delivering a fine mist to the rag.

3. Apply Scratch Remover over the entire surface and be meticulous about regularly re-applying a fresh mist of water to the surface from a spray bottle.

4. A machine is quicker but only use a purpose-made polisher. This revolves much more slowly than a drill with a mop attachment.

Removing and replacing an acrylic window

Replacing windows is quite an easy operation on most caravans. It is especially straightforward when the mounting is on a flat surface but more involved if the window is seated in a deep, moulded recess. In the latter case, the aluminium moulding that holds the unit has to be eased away from its seating. Some types of fully-flush window units are more difficult to deal with and you should seek advice on removal procedures from the manufacturer. The photographs show a typical replacement operation.

1. An end cap often needs to be removed and the window centralising block fitted just below it must be detached. Be careful not to drop any tiny screws.

2. Window stays and fittings will need to be detached by undoing their self-tapping screws. All items will be transferred to the new replacement unit.

3. If the aluminium support strip needs pulling away from the wall to provide withdrawal space, remove the plastic insert and then undo the trim's retaining screws.

4. After easing the aluminium support strip away from the recess on this moulded front, a cracked window was then slid out of its channelling.

Obtaining a more recent plastic window ought to be easier, but this can also be difficult if a caravan manufacturer has ceased trading. Once again, this may mean contact with a breakers, and The Caravan Centre, Blaenavon, South Wales, stocks a wide range of second-hand windows.

Alternatively, EECO is a caravan window specialist whose service involves sending a carrier to collect the remnants of a broken window, and then making a replacement in the same colour and to the same pattern. Even at busy times, the new unit can be delivered in two or three weeks.

Apart from breakage, other problems include the formation of condensation between double glazed units and external surface scratching. Finding a permanent cure for the condensation problem is less easy, but before buying a costly replacement it is worth removing the window, withdrawing the tiny sealing plug and leaving the unit in a warm airing cupboard. When the condensate has dried, the plug is reinstated using a plastic-specific model-making adhesive.

In contrast, dealing with scratches is more certain of effecting a permanent cure.

Problems with damp

Caravans have suffered from leaks for years; this is not a new problem. Some of the problems were discussed in the earlier section on sealants and it is scarcely surprising that weak spots appear when a 'van is towed along bumpy country lanes; as the saying goes, 'prevention is better than cure'.

Checking for damp

Owners are strongly advised to have an annual damp test carried out on their caravan. Whilst this is normally included in a full service schedule, some caravan workshops will also conduct a damp test as an individual service item.

Unfortunately a few dealers carrying out damp testing do not observe some of the procedures recommended by The National Caravan Council. To carry out the operation correctly, the following points must be adhered to.

• The test equipment

A damp meter is required that is submitted for calibration checks on a regular basis and whose specification meets the following criteria:

A measurement range of 6% to above fibre saturation within wood, regarded as a nominal 100%.

An operating temperature range of –10°C to +45°C.

Resolution of +0.1%

Suitable types of professional meters used at many service centres include models from the Protimeter range which record the amount

of damp in a checking area as a percentage. It is also necessary for service specialists using these instruments to understand their full diagnostic scope and to interpret the readings correctly. In reality, most caravan owners would be advised to entrust this work to staff at an approved workshop. In fact a caravan which is still under warranty must be checked at a workshop that meets its manufacturer's approval.

It is acknowledged that inexpensive damp meters are also sold at DIY stores, some of which the author has subjected to simple performance tests. It was concluded that models with red/yellow/green display LEDs are unable to yield comparable diagnostic information to that obtained from a model expressing damp as a percentage. One model tested was offered up to a sodden wooden fence post in the garden after a downpour and revealed a satisfactory reading.

Meters are battery-powered and most models have twin probes which are sharp enough to press into interior plywood, albeit leaving tiny marks on the surface. These are avoided if radio frequency meters are used instead.

Most damp meters have twin probes with sharp points which are used on the plywood inside a caravan.

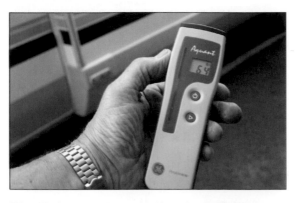

This radio frequency damp meter leaves no marks when readings are taken.

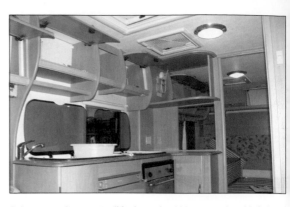

Prior to starting a test, all lockers should be opened and left for a while so that the caravan's internal temperature stabilises.

A service specialist trainee is taught to push probes under rubber window surrounds to leave as few surface marks as possible.

This radio frequency meter is methodically used all around window openings so that a dozen or so readings can be taken around each aperture.

• Preparation relating to the caravan

All internal doors and locker lids should be opened and the caravan left long enough to achieve a uniform temperature throughout the interior. Taking steps to see that a caravan's temperature is stabilised also helps to ensure that the interior is free of condensation. Equally if a conventional meter is used its probes must be free of moisture too.

• Points for taking readings

Service specialists should carry out tests in accordance with the NCC's line diagrams; moreover, at each area of attention indicated on the drawings a meter should be offered-up all around the component. Fifty or more readings are taken on the inside of a caravan by a thorough service specialist, and a dealer should provide customers with the series of line drawings of the internal walls/ceiling with areas of concern clearly marked.

• Interpreting the findings

Since timber has a natural moisture level it would be wrong to expect zero readings on a damp meter. Advice to service specialists from The National Caravan Council offers the following guidelines to percentage readings:

0–15%   Acceptable moisture content

16–20%   Further investigation is needed. Owners should have a repeat set of readings carried out three months or so after the test.

Over 20%   Indication of areas where remedial work is required at the earliest opportunity.

Over 30%   Damage to the structure of a caravan may be taking place. Urgent remedial work is needed.

Note: *Visible evidence in the form of moisture stains or mildew sometimes supports the percentage reading. However, false readings can be given if there is still condensation in a caravan which has recently been in use. And as mentioned earlier in the chapter, some bonded walls have small galvanised metal plates embedded in the core to provide attachment points when installing furniture units. These can also generate a false reading.*

The wisdom of arranging regular damp tests using a meter is indisputable, but it is also prudent to make periodic visual checks as well. For instance you can:
• remove the screws from ventilators and check the sealant is achieving a good bond;
• look carefully at surface-mounted grab handles which have more pull and push threat to their bedding sealant than anything else;

If you unscrew a vent, it will adhere firmly against the caravan if the bedding sealant is still flexible.

Check carefully around light fittings; water can penetrate the body when neoprene washers lose their resilience.

Rust marks in the lens of this light show that rain is making a forced entry.

The timber was badly rotted around this window and a new framework had to be fitted.

• look around road lamp fittings. This is a common point of water ingress, especially if a neoprene washer behind the lens starts to deteriorate;
• use your nose inside! A musty smell is always the 'give-away' that mould is developing in the damp behind the wall panels;
• check the route taken by water discharging from the front and rear slope of the roof on a dewy morning. A critical point is the horizontal trim strip above the windows which covers the join between moulded front (or rear) panels and the lower edge of the roof cladding material. If you see water disappearing behind this strip and not re-appearing underneath, it is a certain sign that water is draining via an attachment screw into the void behind. If you remove the trim strip, rusty screws usually confirm the points of entry;
• check around the side windows. Rainwater can also creep behind the horizontal strip from which a plastic window is suspended and it then spreads all around the aperture.

Results of water ingress

If rain does get into the caravan, the outcome is serious as the accompanying photographs

illustrate. In many cases appalling degradation occurs because of a failure in the bedding sealant behind decorative trim strips and the awning rail. Note too, that a caravan built using bonded wall panels is just as susceptible to damage as an older caravan which has a void between the inner and outer cladding.

However, it is the front and rear walls of a caravan that often fail first because this is where most of the water discharging from a roof is channelled. The accompanying photographs show work at Crossley Coachcraft and the recurring problem of front-end damage from damp.

Results of rainwater damage

Outside: Failed sealant on the trip strips and awning rail has led to severe damage.

Inside: Water has rotted wood in the walls and the polystyrene is also very damp.

(Photographs courtesy of Sika Ltd)

Before rebuilding part of the timber sub-frame, a caravan front must be completely taken apart.

The rotted part of the frame will be cut away and replica sections made.

Precautionary measures

Whilst early-warning readings on a damp meter show that damp is present, many owners take steps to ensure this problem doesn't happen in the first place. The photographs (left) show a trim strip being re-bedded on fresh ribbon sealant which is a comparatively easy DIY task.

In addition it is often suggested that awning rails should be re-bedded every five years or so. The sequence below shows a re-bedding operation where Sikaflex 221 is being substituted for a conventional mastic. Although a few screws are initially needed to hold a rail in place while the Sikaflex adhesive cures, the product achieves an exceptional bond without a need for screws.

It is wise to check under trim strips every few years and to apply a fresh bed of mastic sealant if necessary.

When ribbon mastic is applied, a protective backing paper has to be removed before the fitting is reinstalled.

Structural damage

Two things bring about a need for major repair work: stress fractures arising from a design fault and the more common problem of accident damage. Major structural damage would normally be undertaken by a specialist in body repairs but some DIY enthusiasts have the background experience and resources to tackle this type of work.

Re-bedding an awning rail

1. Once the screws are removed, the rail is removed as a unit.

2. The mastic shown here is still in reasonably good condition, but there are places with poor coverage.

3. Remains of the old mastic are removed with a cleaner; white spirit is often effective.

4. The aluminium seam is meticulously cleaned as well.

Photographs courtesy of Sika

5. Once all remnants of old sealant are removed, Sikaflex 221 or Sikaflex 512 Caravan is applied around the wall perimeter. Masking tape can be used to show the rail's position.

6. Sikaflex 221 or Sikaflex 512 Caravan is similarly injected on to the back of the rail; this will be temporarily held with tape or a few self-tapping screws while the sealant is curing.

Design faults

This problem is uncommon, but in the early years of sandwich wall construction, a number of caravans were built with a rear kitchen and a rear door. Some models subsequently developed aluminium stress tears above the door aperture. The condition was aggravated by the weight of kitchen appliances and the fact that they were located at the very back of the living area. On a rough road, the pitch and toss of towing soon finds weak spots.

If there's merely a polystyrene core above the door opening, this creates a point of great weakness and shearing is inevitable. The cure is to insert and bond a timber lintel into the core. Then the upper part of the wall is overlaid with a new aluminium skin to hide the area of repair.

Suffice it to say, a timber lintel is now fitted in most caravans at the time of construction.

Accident damage to GRP

It can be distressing to visit a body repair specialist like Crossleys (often referred to as Crossley Coachcraft), whose workshop is in Leyland. However, experienced coachbuilders can bring back wrecked caravans from the very brink of a breaker's yard.

Surface damage to GRP is not so worrying and many DIY car owners will be familiar with products sold for repairing rotted car sills, damaged wings and so on. Examples of products include:

Isopon P40 (Trade version U-Pol B)

This is a polyester resin paste containing a mulch of chopped glass fibre strands to give strength to a weak or damaged panel. It can be used to repair splits in GRP as a first-stage operation – thereby giving a material strength before the finishing filler is applied later. To repair a small split in a GRP fairing cover, for example, you would:

i) remove the cover and gouge deep scratches in the roughened rear face with an old chisel or wood rasp

When mixing P40, a 'blob' the size of a golf ball is mixed with three 'blobs' the size of garden peas.

ii) support the splits by applying Sellotape or brown parcel tape on the shiny side
iii) apply a mix of Isopon P40 to the rough side of the moulding with a decorators' knife.

A product like Isopon P40 is prepared on a scrap of plywood by adding a catalyst paste to the polyester/glass compound. Given temperatures around 16C° (60°F), the mix ratio is a 'blob' of P40 the size of a golf ball with three 'blobs' of catalyst paste the size of garden peas. The two items should be mixed thoroughly on the board and a decorators' knife is useful. The catalysed mix should be used promptly and applied with the knife to the unseen side of the fairing.

Acetone cleaner can be purchased at modest cost to clean the mixing knife; alternatively, and at risk of reprimand, you can use expensive acetone nail varnish remover obtainable from any well-equipped handbag.

Isopon P38 (Trade version U-Pol Extra)

This is a filler paste used to recreate a smooth surface on a damaged area of GRP. It lacks the strength of P40 but is applied to the outer side of a panel to recreate an attractive finish.

Safety

■ Polyester products are flammable and can damage human tissues.
■ Barrier creams are sold by GRP specialists to provide protection.
■ Catalysts (often called hardeners) can cause serious damage to human tissue, especially when coming into contact with the eyes.
■ All safety advice in product instructions must be followed.

A GRP front can be repaired successfully by anyone familiar with lamination techniques using products supplied by a specialist like Trylon.

Surface damage to this GRP skirt can be fully repaired using either a filler paste, followed by matching paint, or using a pre-coloured gel coat.

Repairing a damaged GRP surface using coloured gel coat

Loose remnants of the damaged cracked gel coat are removed from this caravan front using a steel disc or an old chisel.

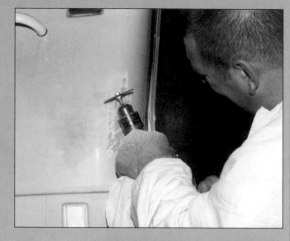

Having cut back the damaged surface to the glass fibre reinforcing mat, a polyester filler paste is mixed with catalyst (i.e. 'hardener') and applied.

Once the filler has completely cured, the surface is rubbed over with either a sanding disc or a hand-held block covered with abrasive paper.

In this repair the service workshop was able to purchase some colour-matching gel coat from the caravan manufacturer. This eliminates the need to paint the damaged area.

NOTE: *Chips of brittle gel coat can fly into your face so it is recommended that eye protection is worn. This operator should also have used hand protection.*

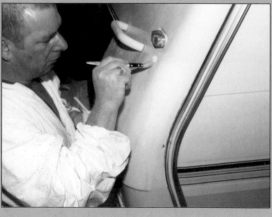

Using the damaged fairing as an example, once the P40 is set, the tape on the shiny side of the panel is removed. Any stray material is smoothed off with coarse glass paper and the shine is removed from around the repaired section. The filler is mixed in a similar manner to P40 and then knifed over the prepared area to recreate any contours.

When it has cured (a term meaning hardened) the filler is rubbed down with abrasive papers using progressively reducing grades of coarseness. Once the surface is smooth, the filler is finally painted.

Polyester resins and chopped strand mat

More ambitious repairs are often tackled by DIY enthusiasts who have experience of glass fibre laminating work. Anyone who has built or repaired a GRP canoe, for example, will be fully conversant with the way a glass fibre panel on a caravan can be reconstructed.

A specialist like Trylon in Northamptonshire, has supplied the DIY builder/repairer with the necessary materials for over thirty years. The Company supplies polyester laminating resins, gel coat resin, filler powders, colour pigments, reinforcing chopped strand mat, catalyst, acetone cleaner, brushes, laminating rollers and instructions about safety, storage and use.

Guidance given by Trylon about the use of these materials is invaluable, and a number of practically-minded caravanners have found that seemingly irreparable GRP caravan fronts or backs can be successfully rebuilt.

As regards less serious surface abrasion, the outer surface known as 'gel coat' may get damaged in a minor collision. Pre-coloured gel coat resin suitable for surface repairs is sometimes available from a caravan manufacturer's after-sales department. This is mixed with a catalyst, applied to the damaged area and then immediately covered with Sellotape.

The adhesive tape retains the gel in place which is especially necessary on a vertical surface but it also keeps air from the resin while it cures and if you don't do this the gel coat can remain tacky on the surface. Around 24 hours later the tape is removed and the surface smoothed with wet-and-dry papers of diminishing coarseness until a shine is achieved.

An alternative to gel coat is to use surface filler like Isopon P38. This subsequently has to be painted, and many car repair suppliers have paint-mixing facilites so that an exact colour match can be achieved. The specially mixed paint will even be put in an aerosol can if required.

Accident damage to acrylic-capped ABS

Rather surprisingly, the procedures for repairing ABS panels are not particularly dissimilar from the methods of repairing GRP. On the other hand, the chemicals are certainly different.

The photographs show a repair carried out just prior to the launch of Gramos Microfil Extreme ABS plastic repair system in 1999.

Note: *Gramos repair kits are now available to the general public and can be purchased from Kingdom Industrial Supplies. At the close of 1999, new repair kits were also launched by Bradleys whose specialism in the repair of ABS materials has been well established in the car industry. Bradleys also manufactures special paints for application to this type of plastic surface (see Appendix addresses for these contacts).*

Replicating unobtainable ABS and GRP mouldings

When a caravan moulding is damaged beyond repair owners will have to obtain a new component. However, manufacturers only stock replacement parts for a limited period and in some cases manufacturers cease trading. This not only causes problems if an external panel is irreparable; it also causes concern when owners need to replace an internal product like a shower tray or wash basin which turns out to be unobtainable.

In response to this, several specialists have established re-moulding services, V&G based at Whittlesey near Peterborough being one of the best-known. The Company is sufficiently well-respected for a manufacturer like Swift to pass on to it the GRP moulds of caravan fronts and other components which Swift is no longer stocking as spares.

Although V&G doesn't re-create components in ABS plastic, its speciality is to produce a new GRP mould using the remnants of damaged ABS or GRP components. Having made a mould it is then possible to replicate an unobtainable component, albeit in GRP. The fact that the original product might have been made in ABS plastic is seldom a problem. In truth, a GRP

A mould for producing a caravan front in GRP takes up a lot of space but the yard at V&G near Peterborough has dozens of types in store.

Repairing a split in an acrylic-capped ABS panel

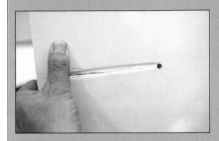

1. Holes are drilled at the ends of the split to prevent further stress damage; the damaged area is also deepened in order to accommodate the repair compound and roughened with P80 grit paper to achieve a key.

2. Surface cleaner is applied to the damaged area, wiped over with a lint-free cloth, and left to dry. Primer Adhesion Promoter is sprayed on next and allowed to dry for 30 minutes.

3. Self-adhesive fibre reinforcing tape is cut to size and stuck to the rear of the damaged panel.

4. A two-part bonding filler is dispensed from a standard sealant gun through the spiral nozzle supplied so that the components are blended. This is applied to the split, to finish just below the surface.

5. When the bonding filler has fully cured, the area is rubbed down so that no filler appears above the surface.

6. Primer adhesion promoter is applied to the surface once again in readiness for the addition of a final top filler.

7. The filler paste is dispensed on to a board and a measured amount of red catalyst is mixed in thoroughly with a plastic applicator.

8. The filler is applied over the damaged area using the applicator and feathered off at the sides. This will be smoothed off when dry with abrasive paper; a matched etching paint suitable for this material will be applied and a colour-matched top coat added finally.

The finished face of this mould for a locker lid is given a good coating of polish before a replica moulding is made.

To prevent a mould from distorting, a framework of strengthening timber is constructed to stabilise the panel.

With its badge, nameplate and locks in place this replica product looks very much like the one it replaces.

When an owner's original washbasin cracked badly, V&G created this copy mould to make a replacement.

This brand new GRP front for an obsolete caravan is colour matched, polished and ready for installation.

copy is often much stronger than the component it replaces.

The illustrations above show some of the work that V&G has undertaken for caravan owners.

The A-frame covers on caravans are often quite fragile; this mould produces much stronger replacements.

Delamination

The strength in a piece of plywood is achieved because its layers are all bonded firmly together with adhesive. If the glue fails, the weakness of the individual laminates is demonstrated in no uncertain manner.

It's exactly the same with the bonded panels used in caravan construction. Individually the 3mm ply or sheet aluminium forming a wall is flexible and fragile; and the block polystyrene used in the core is as brittle as a biscuit.

When bonded the strength is remarkable but if the layers start to come apart, there's a serious problem, and delamination will occur.

In practice it is delamination of floor panels that is the more common failing. If you hear creaking in the floor and notice a spongy feeling in certain areas, take immediate action. Typically delamination is most common in areas of heavy use – just inside the door, and around the area of the kitchen sink. Some owners find that small areas on the inner section of plywood rise up like a blister.

The condition might develop later in the life of a caravan, but there are cases reported of delamination starting in a floor panel on a caravan's very first trip. This is covered, of course, within the warranty but it proves that newer models are not always free from failure.

Fortunately repairs are not only possible; they are even completed successfully by confident and determined owners.

Procedure

Rebonding a delaminating panel is achieved by injecting a purpose-made bonding adhesive into the area where separation has taken place. Kits containing Apollo's rebonding chemicals known as AX 8136 Parts A and B are available from some caravan dealers and specialist suppliers like Leisure Plus.

Another range of products including the special TX formulation kit is available from Trade Grade Products. Whereas the rebonding chemicals are normally injected into the floor from *inside* a caravan, the TX product can be injected from the underside of floor panels. The advantage of this strategy is the fact that carpet and vinyl coverings don't have to be removed.

In practice, delamination repairs are not difficult to carry out, but if a mistake is made, rectifying the fault might not be possible. For this reason some caravan accessory shops are not prepared to sell repair kits to members of the public. Equally Apollo is exclusively a manufacturer and doesn't have a retailing arm for selling its products directly to caravan owners.

The kind of errors that can be made include:

• Forgetting to mix both chemicals together to activate the curing process.
• Drilling holes through both layers of floor ply so that the chemicals drain out on to the ground below.
• Allowing the chemicals to start hardening

before any blister bubbles in the interior ply have been forced back down using a heavy weight.
• Permitting surplus bonding agent to ooze out of the drilled holes and to dry on the floor. Once the chemical has set, it's very hard to remove hardened spillages later.
• Overlooking a manufacturer's all-important safety advice regarding necessary precautions that must be taken when using the bonding chemicals.

To summarise, the instructions supplied with a repair kit should be carefully checked. Also look

Blistering on the aluminium skin all along the side of this caravan is an example of advanced delamination.

Procedure for dealing with delamination in the outer aluminium skin on a wall

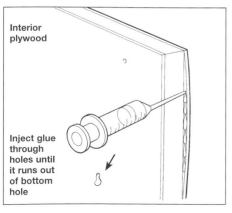

Interior plywood

Inject glue through holes until it runs out of bottom hole

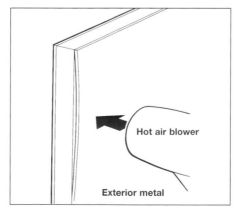

Hot air blower

Exterior metal

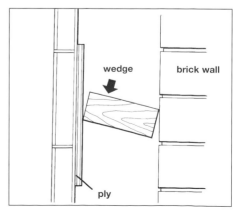

wedge

brick wall

ply

Repairing a delaminated floor

1. With the floor covering removed, sponginess in the floor panel adjacent to the kitchen units confirmed that delamination had taken place.

2. The straight edge of a spirit level sometimes reveals that there's a slight rise in the delaminating plywood.

3. A repair kit comprises a two-pack bonding agent from Apollo Chemicals, plastic syringes, and beech dowel pegs.

4. You mustn't drill through the ply on the underside of the floor panel, so tape is used as a depth indicator on the twist drill.

5. On this repair, 42 holes were drilled in a measured block that completely covered the delaminating portion of the floor.

6. By temporarily inserting a dowel and pushing it down you establish how much the pegs need to be trimmed before injecting the chemical.

7. Mix in small batches at a time; the two chemicals are measured, mixed in the stated proportions, and then drawn into a syringe.

8. Inject the bonding agent. Hardly any is taken in by the sound areas, but where there's a zone of delamination, a large quantity disperses into the void.

9. When the agent leaks out of a hole, tap in a dowel peg. Wipe away any excess on the floor at once – it's hard to remove when it's dry.

10. Lay a sheet of brown paper over the area, followed by a sheet of thick boarding, then place something heavy such as bricks on top.

at the step-by-step photographs above, which show a repair operation being carried out on a 1993 Avondale caravan. Having established what the job entails, only embark on DIY repairs if you feel confident to tackle the work that's involved.

Localised patch repairs on bonded wall panels

If your caravan wall sustains a dent no bigger than the palm of your hand, re-skinning the entire side seems a disproportionate response. It is certainly

Delivery times on a replacement panel of pre-painted aluminium sheet often run to six weeks or more.

When a hole is torn in the side or a major strengthening repair has been carried out, the entire area will be overlaid with a new aluminium panel.

true that body fillers used for car repairs can sometimes recreate a reasonable finish, although a colour-matched paint is needed for completing the job. However, difficulties arise if the dent is in a textured surface, and it's often pointed out that patches of filler soon break away from an aluminium panel.

In practice these predicted fractures are not always apparent. When the author decided to fill a damaged area in textured aluminium, an attempt to recreate the pattern in the filling compound was not a success. But apart from this mild disfigurement, the patch itself remained sound for a further 12 years, at which point the 'van was sold. Cracks never developed, there were no signs of rainwater ingress and the paint matched well.

Another strategy involves a professional process known as the HBC system in which a flexible copy skin is created from a nearby textured zone. After a dent has been filled, the replica patch is then bonded on top of the damaged area and its feather edges are dressed skilfully to match the surrounding aluminium skin. It's a clever process but the tools and training needed to carry it out are costly and are not intended for DIY users.

At present few dealers appear to offer the HBC patch-repair service and the usual repair procedure is to re-skin the entire wall. If this is recommended for your caravan, bear in mind that dealers often have to wait around six weeks for the delivery of a matching, pre-painted panel of sheet aluminium.

Applying a new aluminium skin

This is really a job for a specialist body repairer. Once bent, aluminium sheet cannot be beaten flat again because the material stretches. So if a caravan wall is dented on the outside, a recessed area has to be filled and Apollo A5045 two-part adhesive is often used. This doesn't react with the polystyrene core in a bonded wall – which may happen if a polyester resin-based filler is used.

Having restored a flat surface, the entire area has to be overlaid with another sheet of aluminium. The fact that caravan walls are often divided up with trim strips means that a small section can often be applied rather than the entire side.

The specialist will remove the awning rail and all the trims, apply masking paper where necessary, and then spray both surfaces with several fine applications of a product like Apollo A11. When the new pre-painted aluminium sheet is offered-up, a notable bond will immediately be achieved. What's more, the fact that there's a wall section covered with a double skin of aluminium is seldom discernible.

Pressure then needs to be applied and various wedges can be arranged by parking the caravan adjacent to a wall. However, Crossley Coachcraft has developed a large inflatable mattress which is mounted to a vertical wall inside the Leyland factory. When a freshly skinned 'van is parked close to the wall, the mattress is inflated with a compressor. It is a clever arrangement because it ensures that a sustained pressure is exerted uniformly over the entire side of the caravan.

Once all the trim pieces are reinstated, it is then only a day or so before the owner can be enjoying his or her caravan once again.

A completely new middle section of aluminium has been bonded on top of a damaged panel. Later the 'van will be parked closer to the wall and the black mattress will be inflated to apply consistent pressure to the entire area while the adhesive is setting.

(Photograph courtesy of Crossley Coachcraft)

Interior maintenance and improvements

Interior design is an important factor when choosing a caravan. In the first part of this chapter the focus is on furnishings; in the second part, attention turns to the furniture.

In the past, the interiors of many British caravans have been traditionally styled and have included items like fitted carpet, plush velvet curtains and patterned upholstery. There has also been a proliferation of florid fabrics which have not been to everyone's taste.

However, in the last few years Continental influence has prompted the development of models which are not only less ornate but are also more practical for use on muddy sites by outdoor enthusiasts. For example, many UK caravans now have a vinyl floor covering together with shaped and edge-trimmed loose-lay carpet that can be removed whenever required. Bearing in mind that caravanning near the beach or in the countryside inevitably brings sand, mud, grass cuttings and other elements into your living space, this makes very good sense.

Interior furnishing materials

Whether to opt for a plush, precious interior in which slippers are needed or one that lends itself to an active lifestyle depends on the purchaser. Either way, keeping it clean and comfortable is appropriate and a knowledge of furnishings and fabrics is helpful.

Foam

Most caravans are supplied with foam interiors in the seats and seat backs. Upholstery specialists often refer to these collectively as 'cushions' and openly admit that the foam supplied with some new caravans is not of particularly good quality. The seats may seem reasonably comfortable at first, but after a few seasons, the foam inside loses its resilience and the cushions start to 'bottom out'.

This is apparent if you sit down abruptly. Poor resistance offered by the foam causes you to bump against the plywood base underneath. One remedy is to replace the original foam with a high density product. Though costly, this provides good support and will retain its elasticity for many years.

Another solution is to have an extra top-up layer bonded to the original foam. Several specialists offer this service and since the existing foam has lost its resilience, the thin extra layer can often be added without making alterations to the covers. Taking this idea further, a number of 'sandwich' constructions are possible to suit particular situations and this alternative approach is included in the box alongside on foam classifications.

Some upholsterers also recommend an addition of 'fibre wrap'. This soft polyester padding is a thin material which softens sharp, angular edges on cushions. It undoubtedly improves appearances although it only makes a minimal contribution to comfort.

Foam classifications

Foam: Typically this is a synthetic product manufactured to different specifications. High-density foam is guaranteed to retain its shape and comfort for a long period. Foams are available in soft, medium or firm grades and these designations relate to the amount of support provided. As a guide:

Soft is suitable for backrests but is not advised for use as a seat or bed base.

Medium is sometimes specified for backrests or, possibly, as a mattress for a child. It is unlikely to provide sufficient comfort or support for an adult.

Firm is usually too hard for back or arm rests, but is the best choice for a seat that will also be used as a mattress. It is both comfortable and durable. It is possible to combine any of the above grades to meet individual preferences. A good specialist can produce a sandwich mix – for example a bonded three-layer cushion which has a hard centre section and layers of softer foam on either side.

Dunlopillo uses latex which is the sap from rubber trees. It is naturally fire-retardant and non-allergenic. Though costly, Dunlopillo is a superior foam offering excellent support, long life, durability and good ventilation properties. It is commonly used in domestic furniture but is seldom seen in caravans.

Hard and soft foams can be bonded together to meet specific requirements.

Bunk beds often use 'split folding' cushions which are joined across the middle. Their foam depth is usually 50–75mm (2–3in).

On the subject of comfort, the fact that seats also have to double-up as beds introduces another difficulty. Some seats are contoured with a raised portion on the forward edge known as a 'knee roll'. They may be heavily buttoned, too. Neither feature is helpful when the seat changes its function to that of a mattress.

As regards the depth of foam, this varies considerably and anything from 50mm (2in) to 150mm (6in) is used. Foam for a sleeping base intended for adults is usually 100mm (4in) deep, but there is a growing tendency to specify 150mm (6in) foam on more expensive caravans for the master bed. On bunk beds made up using 'split folding' units, the foam is generally 50–75mm (2–3in).

Irrespective of dimensions or densities, all foam used for furniture has to achieve a 'combustion modified' designation for reasons of safety. See the box alongside for details of legislation.

As a further addition, many upholsterers recommend that foam is covered by a layer of thin stockinette material. This addition makes the task of fitting a cover much easier because it greatly reduces the friction of the foam against the inner face of the fabric.

Spring interior cushions

In response to owners' comments, several caravan manufacturers now offer spring interior cushions as an alternative to a foam filling. Spring interior units may also be fitted at a later date by an upholstery specialist. However, the cost is quite high and owners often restrict the alteration to those seat cushions which will be used for the double bed. Moreover, there is another reason for this strategy.

There is no doubt that spring interior cushions are fine for a bed, but when used for seating, there is sometimes a tendency for the forward edge to lack rigidity. Poor support behind the knee joint can be unsatisfactory and this point should be checked before replacing foam fillings.

Mattress support bases

The main contributor to comfort is the foam or spring interior core that is used in seats and beds. However, the overall success of a bed is also dependent on the structure which supports the mattress. This is linked with the problem of under-mattress damp which can be especially prevalent at certain times of the year.

Without doubt, the least satisfactory base for a bed is a sheet of flat plywood; this is often used in conjunction with a table top that helps support the mattress as well. It's not just the fact that neither item is able to contribute any form of springing. They also don't allow air to pass between the underside of the mattress and the top

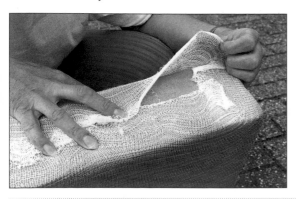

By covering foam with a thin stockinette, the cover will slip on much more easily.

Upholstery specialists can fit spring interiors as an alternative to synthetic foam.

A slide-out bed base. The hardwood slats offer resilience as well as providing ventilation to the underside of the mattress.

of its supporting base. This lack of air movement leads to large damp patches forming on the underside of the mattress. During cold weather the accumulation of moisture can get pretty bad and a mattress has to be lifted every morning so that it can start to dry out during the day. The use of fibrous underlays which help to reduce condensation is discussed later in the chapter.

An alternative to a ply base is the use of a series of softwood battens that are spaced using webbing straps. These allow air to reach the underside of a mattress but fail to provide much springing. They also have an annoying tendency to slip off the supporting rails at the sides, with rather dramatic results.

Much better are slatted bases comprising an aluminium frame which supports flexible laminated hardwood spars. These are made with an upward curvature and have a resilience which helps the mattress as well. Since they tend to flatten when supporting a heavy human, their ends are retained in a plastic fitting which allows them to slide as their splay increases.

A completely different approach is to support a mattress on an array of plastic plinths. An example is the Froli system from Germany, which is surprisingly easy to fit. Although there are several versions of Froli units, a clever feature on some of the supports is the fact that you can increase or reduce their flexibility in order to create the degree of firmness you like. The blue ones shown here look rather like flowers, and it is a replaceable insert in the centre of their 'petals' that permits this 'fine-tuning'. Different inserts alter the softness or stiffness of each unit, which means you can create a bed offering greater or lesser support for your back, hips and legs. Furthermore if Froli units are used to support a double mattress your partner can alter his or her side of the bed to create the amount of support they prefer.

Although this system is often used in motorhomes, it's less frequently employed for beds in caravans. Having said that, there's no reason why a discerning caravan owner shouldn't fit a Froli system as part of an improvement project.

Flexible mattress supports from Froli

Built with one of the several types of plastic support systems in the Froli range, this bed has both resilience and ventilation.

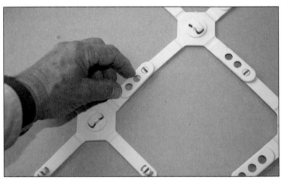

It is normal to start with a 9mm ($3/8$in) lightweight plywood board on which the clip-together framework is mounted, spaced as required.

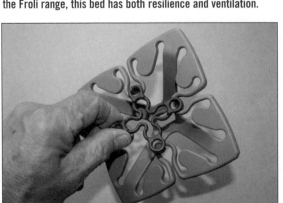

This red support brace that clips into the middle of each 'petal' can be changed for one offering greater or lesser flexibility to suit your preference.

Each of the prepared 'petals' is offered-up to the plastic straps, located and then turned through 90° to fix it in place.

Interior fabrics

Various fabrics are used for cushion covers although velour has been especially popular in recent years. However, tweed materials and cotton-type products have had varying moments of popularity, too.

In addition to the main fabric there's also variation in the type of edging strip used around upholstered cushions. Terms like ruche and piping are explained below in the box entitled, 'Trade terminology'.

Where covers are stitched in place, cleaning becomes more complicated and you are obliged to deal with them *in situ*. In the event, several cleaning chemicals are effective although there's an obvious advantage if covers are fitted with a zip so that dry-cleaning can be carried out.

As regards curtains, velvet with a stitched-in lining material seems to have continuing popularity even though many caravanners don't draw their curtains when blinds are fitted. A lining material enhances their appearance, but can lead to washing difficulties because one of the fabrics might shrink slightly more than its partner. Dry-cleaning would be preferred, but most caravan curtains are made with sewn-in plastic attachments and these are not accepted at most dry-cleaners. So if curtains have to be washed, a popular answer is to stitch them into a pillow case and then run them through a washing machine on a very cool wash programme.

Note: *Many fabrics are treated with stain-resisting and fire-retarding treatments. Depending on the product, these are likely to retain their properties for one or two dry-cleaning operations. If you want to get your upholstery treated with a stain resisting product, the Paintseal Direct service described in the previous chapter also includes the application of a CPC fabric treatment which features a DuPont Teflon formula.*

Stretch covers

At one time, stretch covers were made from rather poor materials, but nowadays there are attractive,

Paintseal Direct's external panel sealing service also applies a stain-resisting treatment to indoor fabrics.

thicker, high quality examples at competitive prices. Modern fabrics and improvements in the manufacturing processes mean that stretch covers have a more permanent and more striking appearance.

Some stretch covers offer two wearing sides – an advantage for distributing areas of wear and tear; many are also machine washable. So some caravanners use them as a way of protecting the original coverings – especially if they have children at the 'sticky finger' stage or if they own a dog.

If you order stretch covers, zip fastenings are often available, but remember to specify zips at the time of ordering because tie tapes are quite common. The minor problem of covers slipping

Many stretch covers are machine washable.

Trade terminology

Bottoming out: When foam loses resilience a caravanner will often feel the wooden base underneath when sitting down abruptly.

Raised front cushions: Also known as knee rolls or graduated cushions, these products have a foam section bonded along a forward edge to offer a raised profile. It can add to the comfort of a seat but is less pleasant when the cushion forms part of a bed.

Piping: Cord stitched around cushion edging gives protection from excessive wear. Straight piping is plain and purposeful; a twisted cord is more ornate.

Ruche: Serving the same purpose as piping, ruche is a decorative tape. The fluffy edging trim often seen in caravans is referred to as 'cut ruche'.

Top stitching: A decorative feature accomplished by stitching through both the outer fabric and a thin backing layer to delineate shapes in a patterned material such as flowers or leaves.

Buttoning: When covered in matching fabric, buttons are decorative features but they also help to prevent covers from slipping out of position.

Split folders: The term refers to cushions that open up like a book in order to form a wider unit – typically to make a bed width.

Fire retardant foam: Since 1990, all foam used in UK furniture has been required to meet a British Standard in order to meet a minimum fire rating.

Fire retardant fabric: A treatment mandatory on all fabrics since 1991.

The term 'ruche' refers to the different types of edging trims.

Zips are better on caravan stretch covers than tie tapes.

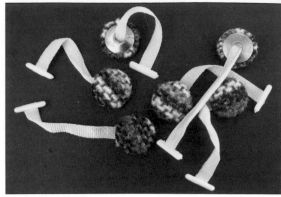

Professional upholsterers can supply buttons which are fitted using a large needle; these prevent a cover from sliding around the foam.

out of place is easily overcome if upholstery buttons are fitted – and many specialists supply DIY buttoning kits. The buttons have a long tail with a 'T' tag which has to be driven right through the cushion using an upholstery needle. Whilst this addition serves a practical function, it adds a decorative detail as well.

Note: *When measuring-up prior to placing an order, confirm with the manufacturers that they will be making the allowance for stretch when the covers are made.*

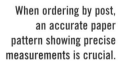 

Specialists like The Caravan Seat Cover Centre near Bristol carry large stocks of materials and send out samples to enquirers.

When ordering by post, an accurate paper pattern showing precise measurements is crucial.

Ordering new covers

Manufacturers of made-to-measure covers can usually supply tweeds, cotton print fabrics or velour. If you send for samples, it is immediately apparent that a remarkable selection of fabrics is available. Indeed it's not unusual to recognise some patterns as the ones being used in current caravans.

Bear in mind that the choice of fabric is only one consideration. Further decisions need to be made about points of detail. Top stitching, buttoning, piping or cut ruche add individual features that combine decorative effects with practical performance.

If you decide to have your caravan re-upholstered, some specialists are able to work from information and measurements supplied by the customer; others prefer to have the cushions available in order to guard against inaccuracy in the finished product. If using a mail order supplier, you should supply carefully cut pattern pieces and precise measurements for each cushion.

Methods of ordering and despatch vary; some companies use carriers whilst others operate a 'callers only' service. Several companies can also supply replacement foam, spring interiors and 'extras' such as curtains and scatter cushions.

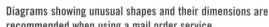

Diagrams showing unusual shapes and their dimensions are recommended when using a mail order service.

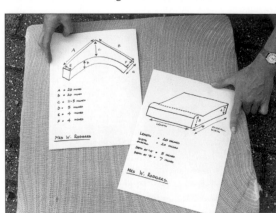

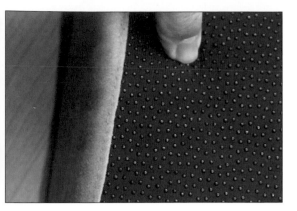

To prevent cushions from slipping on a flat base, some German products are finished underneath with a rubberised lining material.

To allow an owner to get their seat covers dry-cleaned, some upholstery specialists fit concealed zips on the back edge.

Making and fitting covers is an involved operation and completion may take a full day. As part of their service, some upholsterers allow you to park and stay overnight in a factory car park while the work is being undertaken.

Unless specified at the time of ordering, the majority of covers are supplied with a plain lining material for the underside of the cushion. This should be non-slip, durable and will help to reduce costs – though you can't rotate the cushions to even out the wear. Dark fabrics are preferred because any rust stain from bed box hinges is less discernible. Don't forget to indicate clearly on all patterns which are the top, sides, or fronts of the cushions. Clear line diagrams can help here.

Many covers now have concealed zips along the back edge, although tapes and envelope ends can be provided upon request. Some companies will stitch the covers in place; but this makes removal for cleaning more difficult.

Mattress underlays

It was mentioned earlier that cushions resting directly on a flat plywood base cannot benefit from ventilation underneath. In consequence, the underside of a mattress often develops damp patches. A remedy for this is to mount the mattress on a fibrous underlay which permits the passage of air. Several products are manufactured for this purpose, including a natural coir underlay supplied by the Natural Mat Company. Other examples include Vent air-mat from Hawke House Marine and DRY Mat™ from Ship Shape Bedding.

DIY approaches

Many upholstery specialists supply materials to customers who want to tackle their own refurbishment work. In fact stretch covers are successfully made-up by many experienced owners.

However, making your own *permanent* covers is a different task altogether. Owning an industrial sewing machine is essential and tasks like fitting ruche edgings can be extremely laborious. A few indomitable DIY upholsterers achieve good results, but not many match the standard of the professional who has the advantage of industrial machinery.

If you are renovating an older caravan, another strategy is to buy manufacturers' surplus cushions, and companies which specialise in surplus stock

A number of specialists will sell surplus cushions bought directly from the caravan manufacturers.

The fibrous Ventair 15 mattress underlay is designed for both caravan and boat owners; it can be cut to size with scissors.

often have trade stands at major caravan rallies. Firms like Magnum Mobiles & Caravan Surplus and O'Leary Motor Homes Sales & Hire are examples.

Carpets

It was mentioned earlier that in British caravans, fitted carpets have been the usual type of floor covering. When a caravan is manufactured, carpet is laid on the plywood floor surface and the furniture is then built on top.

Although this has been the more common approach, an increasing number of manufacturers are recognising that many owners enjoy active leisure pursuits like cycling, fishing, walking and water sports; some have dogs and young children

Removing stains

Everyone spills something or brings in dirt from outside at one time or another. The golden rule is to deal with the damage immediately and there are several points to keep in mind:

■ Apply a stain remover as soon as possible – if a specific treatment is available rather than a general purpose cleaner, so much the better.

■ If in doubt about the way a fabric might react with a cleaning chemical, use the product on a small corner first to check compatibility.

■ Always remove individual stains before washing an entire item.

■ Keep an emergency cleaning kit in your caravan.

■ Always apply a treatment with a clean, white cloth – like an old piece of sheet. If you use a patterned cloth, dye can run into the fabric you're cleaning.

■ If there's a surface deposit, scrape this away using a blunt knife before applying the cleaning compound.

■ When removing a mark from a velour fabric, always work in the direction of the pile to avoid surface damage.

■ Be gentle in the approach using a dabbing action where possible. Fabric fibres can be damaged if a rough, rubbing action is employed.

■ Be sparing when using fluids and keep the area blotted periodically to lift marks and to avoid deep penetration into the material.

■ Try to remove as much of the cleaning treatment as possible. Some chemicals leave a mark of their own.

■ If a trace of water is needed on the area of damage, a mist spray bottle is ideal. These are sold at garden centres.

■ Safety advice: wear surgical gloves, open windows to release fumes, extinguish flames (some chemicals are flammable), keep cleaning chemicals in labelled containers, and never mix chemicals together – the result might be explosive.

as well. In response to this, manufacturers such as Avondale, Bailey, Explorer and Swift now supply models which have removable carpet pieces with an underlay of vinyl floor covering. These have stitched edges and are easy to remove for cleaning. It is a far more flexible arrangement. If the forecast for a weekend predicts rain and a farm site has been booked, it makes sense to leave the carpet pieces at home for that particular trip.

Tackling common stains

In many cases, stains can be removed using kitchen products and the list that follows describes typical problems. The recommendations presume the mark is dry.

Beer
Using a solution of one part white vinegar to five parts cold water gently sponge the area. Blot well before repeating with cold water. Allow to dry naturally; don't apply heat because this can permanently set a beer stain.

Blood
Brush the stain lightly to remove surface deposits. Sponge using salt water solution followed by a mild ammonia and water solution before finishing with clear water. Blot well at every stage and avoid heat when drying.

Chocolate
Gently scrape away any residue. Any remaining blemish should respond to washing powder that you've mixed into a paste with water – apply with the knife in your cleaning kit and leave for thirty minutes, then carefully scrape it all away.

Egg
Scrape off any dried residue; then apply a paste of biological powder and water and leave for thirty minutes. Brush off before thoroughly sponging with clean water and blotting well. This is another case where you should avoid heat because it can set the stain permanently.

Grease
This is a stain whose remedy can cause colour problems. As a rule it's best to use a recognised grease solvent first, such as Mangers De-Solve It or Homesure Carpet and Upholstery Remover before shampooing the area. Be prepared to re-treat the area at a later date – grease spots have a habit of reappearing.

Ink
Gently dab the area with either clear methylated spirits or a proprietary ink remover. Blot frequently throughout the treatment to avoid spreading the mark and take care in case fabric colours run. Finally use a suitable fabric shampoo.

Jams and marmalade
Soften stain by applying glycerine for up to thirty

minutes. Sponge away with clean water then follow up with a solution of one part white vinegar to five parts water. Blot well throughout.

Sauces and ketchup

Soften with glycerine; remove excess then sponge with a 50–50 mixture of white vinegar and water. Biological washing powder and water may help to remove any remaining dye marks but be prepared for problems; some sauce stains are exceptionally hard to remove.

Tar

Where possible, remove any surface deposits before applying glycerine to soften the remaining mark. Leave for about an hour before blotting and then apply a proprietary product such as Mangers De-Solve It. Be careful not to drive tar further into fabric fibres; use a gentle lifting action instead. Incidentally, a product traditionally used for removing tar is lighter fuel, but this is highly flammable.

Urine

This is a difficult mark to remove successfully and professional help may be needed for any lingering odours. To loosen the stain, soda water can be applied and then blotted thoroughly. Follow this by using a proprietary product. Work even harder on the potty training.

Vomit

Gently but thoroughly sponge the area with water into which a few drops of ammonia have been added. Apply a paste of washing powder and water, leaving this for thirty minutes. Brush off the paste, then rinse and blot the area with fresh water.

Wine

Remove as much colour as possible using a white vinegar and water solution. Alternatively if you can't get white vinegar, prepare a mix of lemon juice and salt. Then apply a washing powder and water paste and leave for around thirty minutes. Brush this away before continuing with clear water.

Note: *Professional advice is available on*

customer help lines operated by manufacturers of proprietary stain removers. Check details on brand labels.

Seasonal cleaning

Several products are suitable for cleaning caravan covers. Many are used to clean car seats as well, bearing in mind that velour is not unknown in vehicles.

Where possible, try to plan any shampoo work on a hot day so that the cushions will dry as soon as possible. Although some padded wall sections may be difficult to remove for cleaning, most cushions can be taken to an outdoor table for attention.

Many cleaners are easy to use. For instance, Car Interior Shampoo from Auto Glym is sprayed on to the cover, agitated cautiously with a soft nylon brush, then removed with a clean, white, absorbent cloth.

Use a blunt knife to remove jam before it hardens, then either use a proprietary product or follow the glycerine and white vinegar process described alongside.

Apply treatments with a clean, white cloth such as an old sheet. If you make the mistake shown here, colour from the cloth can be released onto the fabric.

Cleaning kit

A cleaning kit might include the following:

1. A general purpose cleaner from a chemists or hardware shop.
2. An aide-memoire listing household products which can be used for stain treatment. Examples include: ammonia, biological detergent, clear methylated spirits, glycerine, lemon juice, salt and washing-up fluid. White vinegar also removes some stains – and relieves wasp stings as well.
3. A nylon scouring pad.
4. A small nail brush.
5. White absorbent cloth.
6. An old house knife with a blunt-ended blade.

Car Interior Shampoo from Auto Glym is sprayed on to the face of a cushion.

After gentle agitation with a soft nylon brush, the shampoo – and dirt – is removed with a clean cloth.

The black veneered chipboard is considerably heavier than the hollow door below.

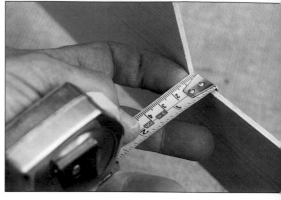

A 3mm decorative lightweight ply is used extensively in caravans.

Interior furniture

To be successful, furniture in a caravan should be:

- structurally sound
- light in weight
- attractive in appearance.

Sometimes the quest to save weight leads to a compromise in strength. Furthermore, when a caravan is being towed, interior fixtures are submitted to relentless stress. So occasionally there may be a need to carry out some running repairs.

Construction

The need to keep everything light means that there is little similarity with the kind of furniture used in our homes. For instance, veneered or laminate-covered chipboard is not used because it is much too heavy. Composite boards like MDF are not particularly light either.

To minimise weight, caravan manufacturers use extremely thin (3mm) decorative ply. This is finished with a white surface for use on walls or ceilings; alternatively it is faced with a paper that has been printed with an imitation wood grain. Unfortunately the product can normally only be purchased through a caravan accessory specialist or from a manufacturer spares section direct.

There is no doubt that the caravan cabinet maker employs great guile in disguising the product. All doors are usually built with a

End-of-line stock purchased from manufacturers by Magnum Caravan Surplus includes hundreds of frames for cupboard fronts which merely need a central panel.

hollow construction and their apparently 'heavy' appearance is a clever illusion.

The fixings used to hold constructions together will vary, but staples predominate. These can be applied quickly and are less damaging when a framework is being assembled or clad with a covering. Paradoxically, the sudden impact from a staple gun is likely to be less damaging than repeated blows where a hammer is used to drive home panel pins.

Making alterations

It is not unusual to find that a few alterations are needed in a caravan. Perhaps a shelf would be useful; or maybe the kitchen could be modified to make space for a microwave oven or a larger capacity fridge. Many practically-minded owners make successful alterations, but it is crucial not to add unnecessary weight to the caravan. The 'user payload' limit which defines how much equipment can be loaded into a caravan is often surprisingly restrictive. So bear in mind that an increase in weight through modifications will correspondingly lead to a reduction in the amount of holiday equipment you can carry in your caravan.

To fulfil the requirements of weight saving, a number of strategies can be followed. A first step is to approach surplus stock specialists who travel to outdoor shows; two specialists have already been mentioned in the section on replacement upholstery on page 96. Lightweight doors, work-top lids and other items are often on sale and frequently you can recognise which models they were used in originally.

Altering hollow doors

In addition to buying from surplus stock dealers, you can sometimes purchase hollow doors from a caravan manufacturer – especially unwanted spares from an obsolete model. They might not be the right dimension but as the accompanying photographs show, you can reduce them in size quite easily. However, the process is speeded up and the finish is likely to be more satisfactory if you own a precision saw bench.

Reducing the size of a hollow door

1. Using a saw bench fitted with a TCT blade, a clean cut is made through this hollow door.

2. An insert has been prepared to an exact thickness and will be glued into place using woodworking adhesive.

3. The insert should be held firmly in place with a G cramp and left overnight for the adhesive to dry.

4. When the side has been planed down and squared off, a thin lipping strip is used to cover the edge.

Edging strips

Doors, shelves and work tops are usually finished around the edges with either a thin strip or a more substantial moulding. Strip veneers that are applied using a domestic iron are not usually long-lasting; nor, for that matter, do they offer much protection against knocks.

A protective lipping is much better and this is one place where hardwood might be permitted even though it is likely to be slightly heavier than a softwood edge-moulding.

If you own a precision saw bench fitted with a tungsten carbide tipped (TCT) blade, preparing lipping is easy. Whilst an edging strip might be 6mm (¼in) or more, it can be prepared even thinner.

Anything of 6mm or thinner can be attached with an impact adhesive like Evo-Stik. But it still helps to support this with a mechanical fixing. Steel panel pins are one possibility and so are brass pins sold at marine chandlers. However, veneer pins are even less visible and provide a neat finish.

Whichever fixing is preferred, they all have a tendency to split a veneer or thin lipping. The time-honoured tip is to nip off the point with pincers – driving home a blunt point does reduce the chance of splitting the material. A better answer, however, is to drill a pilot hole and if you don't possess very fine twist drills, use a veneer pin as a drill in its own right. Nip off the head so

it sits securely in the chuck of a hand drill and keep up the revolutions. The point of the pin won't penetrate as well as a twist drill and it's likely to get hot – but it will form a perfect pilot hole.

Adding a shelf

Another improvement job is to fit an additional shelf. Whether this is a small structure to hold little more than an alarm clock or something larger for a CD collection, the construction should again create strength without unnecessary weight. Chipboard is out of the question.

Strength can be achieved in a number of ways and even something as seemingly flexible and

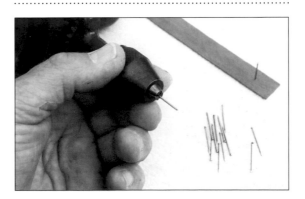

To prevent splitting veneer or edge lipping, pilot holes can be drilled using one of the veneer pins.

A hardwood lipping is prepared on the saw bench and grooved to house the light 3mm ply.

When glued to the front of the ply, rigidity is achieved without unnecessary weight.

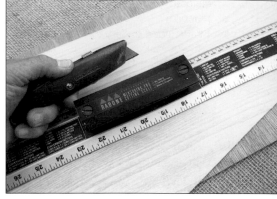

To achieve a clean edge, it is better to cut 3mm ply with a sharp woodworking knife than with a saw.

fragile as 3mm plywood can be strengthened using battens and supports. The photographs above show a length of lipping that has been grooved in a circular saw in order to prevent the ply from flexing. If a further batten is fitted to support the rear of the ply and attached to a side wall, the resulting structure will be pleasingly sturdy, even though its weight will be almost negligible.

Revisions to cabinets

Nearly all lockers, cupboards and cabinets are constructed with a skeleton structure of light timber and then clad with decorative ply. If obeche is available, this is an extremely light wood and yet it is strong. Otherwise, ordinary deal or a similar softwood can be used, but choose lengths with as few knots as possible.

To ensure a carcass framework is rigid, adjoining sections of timber should be glued and screwed, even if they are not jointed but are merely butted together. A woodworking adhesive like Evo-Stik Resin W (interior grade) is one of many suitable products and is easy to work with. When fastening structures to the floor or walls, you might decide to use a cartridge-injected adhesive like Sikaflex-512 Caravan, Gripfill or Evo-Grip. These products are now widely used in the building trade.

As regards fixings, twin-threaded countersunk 'Supascrews' are more rust-resistant than steel screws; equally, Reisser hardened steel screws

are a delight to use. However, in locations where there's likely to be moisture such as a washroom, brass screws are more appropriate. A selection of G cramps is strongly recommended, too, so that support can be given to structures overnight while an adhesive is setting.

When a framework is completed, the addition of ply will not only enclose the structure; it will also serve as a bracing material which helps to hold the construction together. The best way to cut 3mm ply to size is to use a cutting scale and a sharp woodworking knife. Several passes over the ply will be needed.

Catches, fittings and accessories

Some hardware items sold at DIY stores are suitable for use in caravans; others are not. Magnetic catches, for example, are less successful in a caravan since the furniture is subjected to so much stress movement.

Catches can often be purchased from a caravan accessory shop and the after-sales departments of caravan manufacturers can sometimes help as well.

When it comes to plastic vent covers, restraining catches and mainstream caravan items, CAK carries an extensive range of products. Many fittings used by manufacturers can be purchased using the company's mail order service.

Another mail order specialist is Woodfit, whose service to DIY cabinet makers is legendary.

To save weight, all cabinets, lockers and bed bases are made with a skeleton framework.

Several makes of cartridge-applied adhesive are available for anchoring structures to walls or floors.

The Warwickshire specialist CAK sells a remarkable array of ventilators, handles and catches, which are displayed at caravan shows held at the NEC, Birmingham.

Woodfit's catalogue lists huge ranges of hinges, catches, door handles and so on. It also includes drawer runners, moulded cutlery trays, waste bins and the kind of wire baskets on runners that are fitted as blanket boxes and vegetable storage units in many 'up-market' caravans. If you are embarking on a major renovation project, the catalogues from CAK and Woodfit are worthy works of reference.

Bathroom units

If you decide to rebuild a bathroom or add a shower, some caravan dealers can supply plastic washbasins, cabinets, shower trays and so on. Or you can use the CAK mail order service and there are plenty of products in stock. You will also find many products on sale in a well-stocked breaker's yard like The Caravan Centre at Blaenavon.

Equally, the specialists who deal in surplus stock bought from caravan manufacturers might be able to help. For example, Magnum Mobiles & Caravan Surplus carries a wide range of items, as mentioned on page 98. These items may need adapting to fit your particular caravan, but it is presumed that anyone tackling a project of this magnitude has already recognised that radical alterations are going to be needed.

Kitchen improvement

Anyone buying an older caravan may feel the kitchen deserves modernisation. If the budget is limited, caravan breakers often carry stocks of ovens, hobs, sinks and draining boards.

It doesn't take a lot of work to install a new sink and draining board, provided the basic framework forming the kitchen units is sound. Fitting replacement cooking appliances is not difficult – at least as far as the woodwork is involved. But making connections into the gas supply system should only be tackled by a competent gas engineer – as emphasised in Chapter Ten, *Gas supply systems and appliances*.

Interior blinds

Most modern caravans are fitted with cassette blinds and fly screens as standard. If these are not included in an older model, they can often be fitted retrospectively.

One of the problems with a spring retractable blind, however, is the tendency for the spring to lose its tension. This happens if it remains under tension for prolonged periods – for instance when the blinds are lowered during winter storage. It is better for the spring if blinds are left in a raised position; but then the upholstery fades.

On many types of cassette blind the spring can be re-tensioned or slackened. The procedure varies according to the product, and the accompanying photographs show the mechanism on a stand-alone Seitz Rastrollo cassette; these blinds are fitted in many recent caravans.

Once access has been gained to the spring,

Washbasin replacement project

The Caravan Centre at Blaenavon in South Wales carries large stocks of washbasins; some come from nearly new accident-damaged caravans.

The basin used here came from Magnum Surplus at Grimsby. To support a new pillar tap the ABS plastic was strengthened underneath with 9mm ($\frac{3}{8}$in) ply.

The surplus washbasin was purchased with a plinth to hide the waste water pipe; patience was needed to complete its assembly in the confines of a shower room.

To smarten up the walls in this room, standard plastic-faced wallpaper was purchased; this achieves a good bond if you use several coats of a PVA adhesive/sealer.

shown alongside, it can be tightened or loosened by turning the steel spindle in the middle.

Although a special tool is available to rotate the central spindle, most owners use pliers or make something up to turn its flattened end. However, before this is possible an end cap has to be removed from the cassette itself, and here lies a problem. Some caravan manufacturers build furniture right up to the end of the cassette which then completely obscures the cap. When this occurs, the entire blind assembly needs to be removed in order to make adjustments.

Having removed the cap, the spindle will pop out and unwind; you then turn it as required to reset the spring's tension and finally ease it back inside the cassette in order to engage its locked position.

As stated already, different products have slightly different procedures, but trial and error soon achieves what is needed. What a pity that some caravan manufacturers overlook the need to keep the all-important adjustment access points within reasonable reach of human hands.

The spring which is held within the cassette is withdrawn here to show the assembly. Note that to tighten the mechanism it doesn't have to be removed completely like this.

Note that there are two caps and two separate rollers – one for the blind, the other for the flyscreen. The central spindle is wound up or released as needed then pushed back to lock inside the cassette.

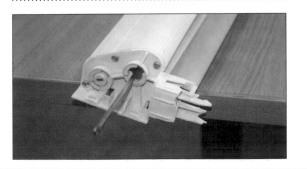

The 12 volt supply system

A caravan fitted with its own battery and 12 volt supply system offers many benefits. However, a low voltage system needs to combine efficiency with safety. It is also important to keep a battery in a good state of charge.

It seems surprising that gas lamps were still being fitted in caravans in the early 1970s. However, this form of lighting became obsolete when Lab Craft, an electrical engineering specialist, found a way to run fluorescent lighting units from a 12V supply.

By boosting the Direct Current (DC) supply to around 130V and changing it to Alternating Current (AC), Lab Craft found it was possible to ignite a fluorescent tube. This economic and efficient way of providing lighting in caravans was immediately acknowledged.

Fluorescent tubes running from a 12V source are still fitted in modern caravans today. However, the use of halogen lighting became popular in the late 1990s, even though these systems consume quite a lot of current and bulbs get remarkably hot. So when the price of light emitting diodes (LEDs) dramatically dropped these were adopted with enthusiasm around 2005. They not only stay remarkably cool, they also draw less current than halogen bulbs.

Lighting is certainly important, but, as this chapter reveals, there are many other products that also depend on a 12V DC supply.

Safety

Changing a faulty tube in a fluorescent light fitting is normally straightforward. But you must ensure the 12V supply is turned off at source; inside the casing of a fluorescent unit the supply is boosted to around 130V.

When the cover is removed, you will find that some tubes have tags fitted on their connection pins. More recent tubes are held in a slot with a push and twist arrangement. Either way, fitting a new tube is not difficult.

Single socket supply from the towcar battery

When caravans were first fitted with a 'strip light', this was the only component needing a 12V supply. Hence in 1970s caravans, Pin 2 on the black 12N socket (primarily intended for road lights) was allocated so that caravan lighting could be powered by the towcar's battery. Careful use meant that the battery would retain sufficient charge to start the engine after an illuminated evening in the caravan.

If you purchase a second-hand caravan built during this period, there is no reason why you shouldn't just use a 12N connection system – as long as your car is appropriately wired. Pin connections are given in Chapter 3, *Towcar preparation*. Unfortunately, however, the idea of having a fridge, a supply for a 12V TV, an electric water pump and a shaver point is an attractive proposition. But if these appliances are added, it is then necessary for a caravan to have:

- an independent battery,
- a fused distribution unit,
- separate supply circuits,
- battery charging facilities.

Once a 12V system is extended in this way, the wiring becomes far more elaborate. Moreover, an additional 12S or 13-pin socket will have to be fitted to the towcar to support the system.

The 12S (supplementary) socket

When legislation required caravans manufactured after 1st October, 1979 to have a rear fog-lamp, it was decided that Pin 2 on the black 12N socket, hitherto used for caravan interior lighting, would provide its electrical feed. This prompted the need for a second socket to supply interior services, leaving the 12N plug to deal exclusively with a caravan's road lights.

Named the 12S (supplementary) socket, this

new connection is described in Chapter 3. Pin allocation is explained together with revised 12S connections applicable to caravans manufactured after 1st September, 1998 in response to European Standard EN1648-1.

In summary, a 12S connection provides:

- a permanent live feed from the towcar's battery to power interior appliances if required;
- a feed to run the refrigerator on 12V which is live when the engine is running;
- a feed from the alternator to charge the caravan battery when the engine is running;
- an earth return (two earth returns in the case of post 1st September, 1998 'vans).

In addition, the 12S socket has one road lamp connection – Pin 1 – to operate reversing lamps, although these are not fitted on many caravans.

The 13-pin socket

As reported in Chapter 3, caravans manufactured in the UK from 1st September 2008 have been fitted with 13-pin plugs which combine the functions of the 12N and 12S connections.

Pin allocation in 13-pin plugs and sockets is given in the earlier chapter, and whilst the coupling arrangement represents a radical change in a car/caravan partnership, it makes no difference to the internal wiring described later.

Circuit designs

Starting at the towcar, when the grey multicore cable from a 12S plug has been taken along a caravan's draw bar, it usually terminates in a forward locker. In most caravans the individual feeds from the multicore cable are then separated and wired into a connecting strip. This marks the starting point of the internal wiring system.

In caravans built in the last thirty years, a 12V circuit draws its supply from one of two sources – *either* the vehicle battery via the car's towing socket, *or* the caravan's own auxiliary battery. A switch is also fitted into the system so that a caravanner is able to choose which battery will provide the power. A three-position rocker switch

When the supply is provided by either the car or the caravan's own auxiliary battery, a selection switch is needed in the circuit.

---

is usually chosen in which the central position isolates the supply completely.

In practice the preferred supply is from the caravan battery (often referred to as a 'leisure' battery on account of its unique construction). The vehicle battery should be regarded as a temporary provider since over-use may mean that vehicle starting is affected.

A supply fuse should be fitted, too, in order to guard against overload; this is described in the Safety box above.

Having obtained a 12V supply, this is then divided up into separate routes like the branches leading away from the trunk of a tree. Each branch is independently protected by a switch and a fuse, the rating of which is appropriate for the appliances being served. For instance a radio/tape player has a particularly low consumption, so it is normally protected by a 5A fuse. On the other hand, a water pump has a higher consumption, and a 10A fuse is usually fitted.

The purpose of having a switch to control

Recent caravans are fitted with a built-in battery box and the control panels are often mounted behind the container.

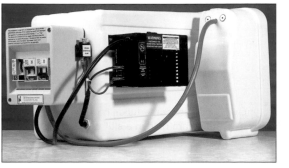

The mains consumer unit and charger are mounted on the rear of this Zig battery box.

(Photograph courtesy of Zig Electronics)

Electro-magnetic compatibility (EMC)

Anyone who has flown recently will know that airline operators strictly forbid passengers from using certain electronic appliances during the flight. It appears that a magnetic field might be created by some products which could upset the aircraft's crucial control systems.

As motor vehicles become increasingly controlled by electronic control units, similar fears are being expressed about cars. Important devices like engine management systems and ABS brakes are undoubtedly reliant on electronic circuitry. So the subject referred to as electro-magnetic compatibility is important.

These concerns about circuit interference are partly behind the latest European standards applicable to touring and motor caravans. Some caravan electrical experts claim that this is one of the reasons why caravans built after 1st September, 1998 carry one less current-carrying cable in the 12S socket. Pin 2, previously assigned to provide a charge to a caravan battery, is now left spare.

In addition, as soon as a post 1998 caravan is coupled up and the towcar engine is running, 12V appliances, with the exception of the fridge, are automatically disabled.

each branch is to offer separate control within the system. For instance if you needed to look at a troublesome water pump on a dark evening, you could switch off this part of a 12V supply without having to interrupt the feed to your interior lights. Some caravan control units do not have separate switches, but a supply can usually be isolated by withdrawing its fuse from the control panel instead.

The subdivision of the main supply into separate routes is achieved using a fused distribution unit. In the United Kingdom, units have been made by BCA Leisure, Plug-in-Systems, Sargent Electrical and Zig. (**Note:** *Plug-in-Systems is no longer retailing caravan products.*) Some distribution units are conspicuous in their location: others are more discreet and may be mounted behind a hinged cover. In some instances, a fused control unit forms part of a purpose-made battery locker – the Zig PowerMate and the BCA Power Centre are examples.

Another feature included in a circuit is a battery condition indicator, which shows its state of charge. Some of these are stand-alone items whereas others form part of the fused distribution unit. Either way they provide a warning when recharging becomes necessary.

Some condition indicators show a battery's state using a meter although many distribution units are fitted with two light-emitting diodes instead. A green light on the panel confirms the battery is in good condition; a red light warns that recharging is needed. **Note:** *The appearance of a red warning light is not very informative because it doesn't indicate if a recharge is needed urgently or fairly soon. A voltage meter is much more helpful and an interpretation of volt readings is given on page 111. Also helpful is a line of LEDs which display the loss of power as it progressively diminishes.*

The final feature to note about 12V supply systems relates specifically to caravans built after 1st September 1998. These now comply with standard EN 1648-1 and one of the requirements set down in this European Norm is that all internal electrical appliances, *with the exception of the refrigerator*, will cease operation when the caravan is being towed. The reason for this requirement is given in the panel on the left and the way the supply is automatically disabled is described later.

Typical low voltage systems

Even if the broad theory behind a 12V supply seems straightforward, an assembly of multicoloured cables presents a daunting prospect to most owners. In order to show the key features of a typical circuit, Plug-in-Systems used to take a large display board of coupled components to outdoor exhibitions. This showed how individual products were wired-up as they would be in a caravan.

To support this miniaturised wiring display, the Company also issued a drawing which illustrated the scheme as it would be represented in a diagrammatic form. It was a helpful presentation and the main features of the Plug-in-Systems display were used when the circuit below was drawn up. The diagram shows a typical circuit used in caravans manufactured prior to 1st September 1998. After this date the recommendations of EN 1648-1 were implemented, and the revisions are shown in the additional drawing given on the next page. **Note:** *Plug-in-Systems supplied components to several caravan manufacturers including Swift. However, the Company has now moved into different commercial fields.*

A clear wiring diagram is always useful and it is

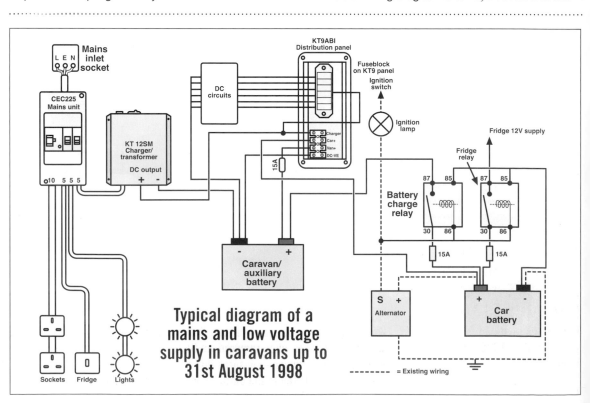

Typical diagram of a mains and low voltage supply in caravans up to 31st August 1998

regrettable that some caravan manufacturers fail to include this information in their owners' handbooks.

Revisions in 1999 models

In order to comply with a new European standard, EN 1648-1, caravans manufactured after 1st September, 1998 incorporate two important revisions. The decision to cease using a charging cable via Pin 2 in a 12S connection was discussed in Chapter 3 and necessitated changes in the caravan 12V wiring. So too, has the decision that the 12V circuits should be disconnected when a caravan is being towed – with the exception of a 12V supply to the refrigerator.

The reasons behind these changes are related to the problem of Electro-Magnetic Compatibility (EMC). This is described in the box opposite.

It is important to note that whereas changes were effective from 1st September,1998, some manufacturers implemented the anticipated revisions *even earlier*. For instance Bailey Caravans had different 12S plug wiring in 1996 models; Elddis and ABI models had changes appearing around 1998, as their Owners' Handbooks revealed.

The changed system operates as follows: when the towcar is coupled up and the engine is running, the caravan refrigerator should receive a 12V positive supply via Pin 6 of a 12S socket or Pin 10 of a 13-pin socket as normal. This feature has not altered.

However, this supply to the fridge provides the signal to a 12V circuit that the caravan is in tow. In electrical terms, the fridge feed triggers an automatic

switch known as a relay and it is this component which disconnects the live feeds going to all other appliances – light units, water pump, 12V sockets and so on. A typical wiring circuit containing this relay (labelled Relay TWO) is shown below.

Most of the latest caravans have a further relay, too, which controls the new double function of Pin 4 on a 12S connection. Note that the dual role of Pin 4 could be controlled by a battery selection switch but to prevent a caravanner having to remember to set this manually, manufacturers normally fit a relay to switch the function automatically (labelled as Relay ONE).

When a car and caravan are coupled up, under the latest regime, Pin 4 on a 12S connection or Pin 9 on a 13-pin connection operates as follows:

1. When the engine is *not* running, this pin connection represents the route by which a 12V supply can be drawn from the towcar's battery as an alternative source to the caravan leisure battery.

2. When the engine *is* running, this pin provides a charging supply for the caravan leisure battery and the supply line in the caravan is duly diverted by Relay ONE as shown in the drawing.

Note: *Whichever mode is in operation, bear in mind that this pin in a towcar's socket is permanently live. That's why it should have a water-resistant spring cover, which plays an important part whenever the caravan is uncoupled.*

Relay locations

A relay is a miniature switch which is activated by an electric current. Although an increasing number

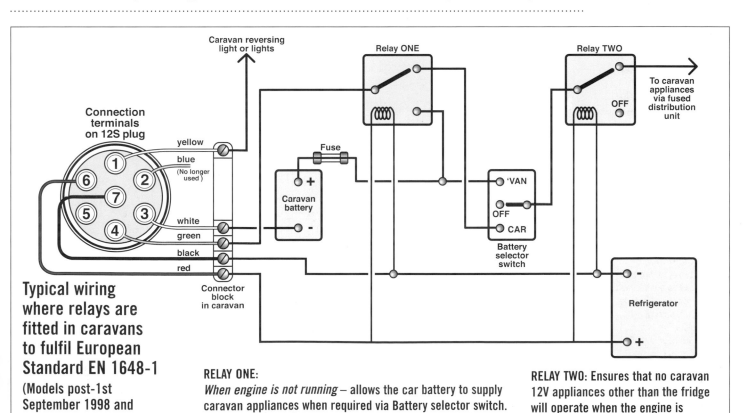

Typical wiring where relays are fitted in caravans to fulfil European Standard EN 1648-1
(Models post-1st September 1998 and some caravans built prior to this date)

RELAY ONE:
When engine is not running – allows the car battery to supply caravan appliances when required via Battery selector switch.
When engine is running – ensures that a charge from the car's alternator is fed to the caravan battery automatically.

RELAY TWO: Ensures that no caravan 12V appliances other than the fridge will operate when the engine is running IRRESPECTIVE of battery selector switch position.

TYPES OF RELAY
On receiving an energising 'trigger' current, different relays perform different functions. For instance Relay ONE on Page 105 diverts a flow of current either along one route or another. However, Relay TWO, when energised, switches OFF a supply of current. Different again are the relays in the drawing on Page 104. When energised these switch ON a supply of current.

of electronic switching devices are appearing, most types contain a small coil that becomes an electromagnet as soon as it receives a current. In its magnetic state it pulls a tiny contact lever which acts as a switch to make, break or divert the flow of current in a circuit.

Occasionally relays develop a fault and need to be replaced which isn't a difficult task. A more testing problem is finding out where the relays are located.

In the case of caravans fitted with the BCA Power Centre – e.g. Coachman and older Fleetwood models, the relays have been fitted inside the control unit itself. In some Compass caravans relays have been fitted in a special socket made to accept a relay, and these were usually installed in a forward bed box. Some Elddis caravans have been fitted with an electric module that contains the relays and this is fitted in a forward locker to afford good access.

Suffice it to say, there is no standardisation at present and owners suspecting a fault are advised to seek help from either a main dealer or the caravan manufacturer's Customer Service Department.

Components in the system

Using the preceding information on circuit design, an owner wanting to add more 12V accessories or planning to rewire and improve an older caravan will now understand modern systems. Most appliances have good wiring instructions and control items like a battery selection switch or a fused distribution unit are clearly labelled on the casing. Nevertheless, if you plan refurbishment work of this magnitude, take heed of the safety points identified in the box on page 107.

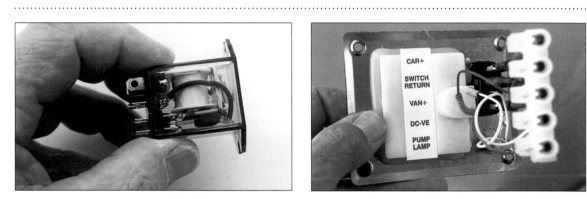

The small coil that operates an electro-magnetic switch is clearly seen in this relay.

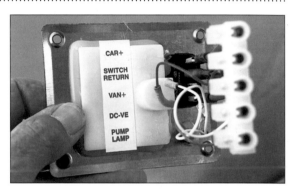

Connections on this Plug-in-Systems battery change-over switch are clearly labelled.

Sometimes caravan relays are fitted inside a control unit – as in the case of the BCA Leisure Power Centre.

It is easy to change a relay when the component is mounted on a connector that has been fitted in a locker.

On a fused distribution unit like the Plug-in-Systems PMS3, connections are distinctly marked on the rear.

Cable

One of the potential weaknesses in caravan wiring is the problem of voltage drop. This is often caused by the use of unsatisfactory cable. Notice that the term 'cable' is used here in preference to the word 'wire'.

If cable is too thin, too long or a combination of both, there will be an appreciable drop in voltage. For instance if a fridge performs poorly in 12V mode when you are towing, one of the tests is to check the input voltage at the connector block on top of the appliance. This is done using a multimeter when the towcar is coupled and the engine running. The reading should be at least 12V; if it is lower than this, the connecting cable needs to be replaced with a thicker cable of higher rating.

A similar test is to take a voltage check using a multimeter across the terminals of a caravan's leisure battery when it's being charged from the towcar's alternator, i.e. when the caravan is coupled and the engine is running. Car alternators typically produce around 14.5V and the reading across a battery's terminals should certainly be appreciably higher than 13V. In fact a poor charge rate is far more likely to be caused by an inadequate coupling cable or poor 12S/13-pin connections rather than a poorly performing alternator.

These examples affirm that it is crucial to use correct connecting cable.

To gain a fuller grasp of the system it is also helpful to understand a few electrical terms. The box below explains some key words.

Connecting accessories

When coupling up appliances, both the thickness of the supply cables and their length are significant. The previous section has pointed out that:

- a thick cable is needed to ensure there's a good flow of current. If the cable is too thin, there's a resistance to current flow and a safety risk, as explained in the accompanying box.
- cable length also needs consideration – the longer the run, the greater the drop in voltage. So if your leisure battery is situated a long distance from the base vehicle alternator, a significant voltage loss is inevitable when charging the battery while towing the caravan.

As regards the type of cable needed, a caravan 12V system is often wired using automotive cable. This has good flexibility because it is made from separate strands or 'filaments' and these have a standard thickness of 0.33mm². However, caravans wired with a custom-made wiring harness manufactured by BCA Leisure will have mains quality 12V flexible cable which has a thicker insulation sleeve. This is a more costly strategy but it means that in multiple cable runs, both 230V and 12V supplies are permitted to run alongside each other in a pre-made 'wiring loom' or 'harness'.

As regards cable rating, this is governed by the number of copper strands that make up the

Automotive cable suitable for 12V wiring is sold at any well-stocked caravan accessory shop.

Cable gauge is shown on the label here, but you can also work it out by counting up the strands.

conductor, and whereas a low consumption appliance like a fluorescent light only needs a thin cable, a high consumption appliance, like a refrigerator, needs thicker cable.

Cable rating is indicated on its packaging and information is sometimes expressed in respect of its cross-sectional area in mm². Alternatively

Electrical terms

When explaining electrical theory, many textbooks compare the flow of electricity to the flow of water. For instance, you can get a high pressure jet of water coming from a very narrow hose. Alternatively you can have a very large bore hose that releases water in huge quantities even though the pressure here may be much lower. If you combine the two and large quantities flow at great pressure, the rate at which water discharges from a pipe is impressive.

These three situations can be compared to the flow of electricity and the terms volts, amps and watts.

Volts (V) – This unit of measurement is concerned with pressure. In a practical situation, a cable offers a resistance that can lead to a loss of pressure. Moreover, the longer the cable, the greater the drop in voltage.

Amps (A) – Amperes or 'amps' measure the amount of electricity referred to as the 'current'. In practical terms, a caravan fridge needs a large amount of electricity to work properly (around 7–10A depending on the model). In consequence it needs a relatively thick connecting cable. In contrast, an interior strip light only needs a small amount of electricity (0.7 amps); so it works quite successfully with a much thinner connecting cable.

Watts – (W) This is the rate at which electrical energy is used and some appliances are more greedy than others. Watts are a combination of both the amount of current (amps) and the pressure of flow (volts). The formulae to remember are:

watts = volts x amps   amps = watts ÷ volts   volts = watts ÷ amps the label might quote an 'approximate continuous current rating' in amps. On a practical note, if a label is missing, you can confirm cable rating by carefully counting its copper strands. This presumes they are of standard size. Table A below shows the use of different rated cables in caravans.

As regards the length of cable used, the simple advice is, 'the shorter the better'. Table B below expresses the implications in practical terms by quoting the maximum current in amps that a cable can provide taking into account the *total length* of the live and neutral cable connecting an appliance to the power source.

Connections

Sometimes additions are needed in a caravan. For instance, you might want to fit a diaphragm pump, and a manufacturer like Whale specifies that this must be connected using 2.5mm² cable. It would therefore be entirely inappropriate to connect this up to a 12V cable serving a lamp over the kitchen work top. As the accompanying table shows, light units are usually supplied with 1.00mm² cable.

In any case, an appliance like a water pump would need to be wired up in conjunction with the pump switch and fused supply on a caravan's 12V distribution unit. So the supply and return cable should be fed through from here, endeavouring to find the shortest practicable route.

On the other hand, if you want to add some reading lamps in your caravan or halogen spot lights, it is usually acceptable to couple these up to the supply cables feeding a nearby lamp unit. This will involve the use of a connector.

Of the many types of connector, three types are commonly used:

1. Snap locks (Scotchlocks).
2. Crimp connectors.
3. Block connectors.

Some electricians dislike snap lock connectors but the National Trailer and Towing Association (NTTA) points out that these products are suitable for use inside vehicles in dry locations. However, the size of a connector must be correctly matched to the size of cable being used. As a guide, follow these recommendations:

	Main cable (mm²)	*Joining 'tap' cable (mm²)*
Red Scotchlocks	0.5–1.5	0.5–1.5
Blue Scotchlocks	1.5–2.8	1.5–2.8
Yellow	3.0–6.0	3.0–6.0

Some electricians working with 12V wiring systems prefer to use crimp connectors and once again these are sold in a series of sizes to suit cable of specific diameters. As a rule these are easier to hide than the bulkier snap lock fittings.

In other circumstances block connectors can be useful, and these have the advantage that couplings can be easily disconnected and joints re-formed when needed. Again, however, the size of the connector needs to be appropriate for the gauge of cable. It is not good practice to cut off some of the copper filaments of a cable in order to insert it into the coupling tube of a connecting block.

Normally the choice of connector is determined by the location of the joint. Then there's a need to secure the cables, and where possible a run of cable should be discreetly hidden and carefully secured. Where access is achievable, clips should be fitted as follows:

- On horizontal runs – at intervals no greater than 250mm (10in).
- On vertical runs – at intervals no greater than 400mm (16in).

Table A – Confirming cable rating

No of strands	Cross-sectional area in mm²	Current rating in amps	Application in caravans
14	1.00	8.75	Interior lights.
21	1.50	12.75	Cables serving extractor fans, but check the model.
28	2.00	17.50	Feed to fridge (minimum) see note.
36	2.50	21.75	Feed to battery from a charger. Feed to a diaphragm water pump e.g. Whale Evenflow.

Note: *For a number of years, Dometic installation manuals stated that if 2.0mm² cable is fitted, the cable run mustn't exceed 8m. Longer cable runs – between 8 to 10.5m – need 2.5mm² cable to avoid an unacceptable drop in voltage. More recently, however, Dometic has increased the recommended type of cable even further. For example, to operate the RM7601 and 7605 appliances on a 12V supply, 10mm² cable is now being specified by the appliance manufacturer. Whether caravan manufacturers are observing this is open to question.*

Table B – Maximum current (amps) permitted for cable of different cross-sectional areas on the basis of length

Cable size	Maximum cable lengths (supply and return)		
	4 metres	8 metres	12 metres
1.00 mm²	9.4A	4.7A	3.1A
1.5 mm²	14.1A	7.0A	4.7A
2.0 mm²	18.8A	9.3A	6.3A
2.5 mm²	23.5A	11.7A	7.8A

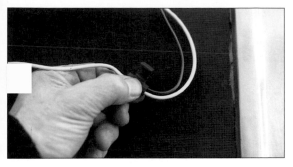

Snap locks allow a new cable to be coupled into an existing feed wire.

Many electricians prefer to use crimp connectors when adding accessories.

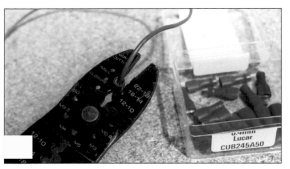

Crimp connectors are easy to fit, and are favoured by many electricians.

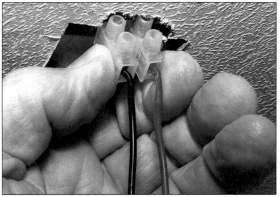

A standard screw connector block is used here for an additional ceiling lamp.

Fuses

In 12V vehicle wiring, three type of fuses will be found in recent and older circuits: glass tube fuses, ceramic fuses, and blade fuses. In the caravan industry glass tube fuses have been popular; these are cheap, but they are not accurate. In addition, the spring in tube fuse holders often gets slack.

The standard product now used in the automotive trade is the blade fuse. These tend to be a little more expensive but they are notably accurate. Blade fuses are also manufactured in many ratings and their markings are clear. Colour coding is as follows:

1A – Black	7.5A – Brown	20A – Yellow
2A – Grey	10A – Red	25A – White
5A – Orange	15A – Blue	30A – Green

Improving the lighting

When renovating a caravan, one of the most popular projects is to improve the internal lighting. Fluorescent lights continue to be popular on account of their low current consumption and tubes are easy to change. So are the tungsten filament 'car-type' bulbs used in some spotlights, but compared with their light output the consumption is greater.

Halogen lighting has proved popular in recent years but consumption is again high; moreover, the units get hot and changing a bulb calls for good dexterity. On account of their frugal consumption and minimal operating temperatures, light emitting diodes (LEDs) have become a more popular choice, especially now that different colour glows are available. Good quality LEDs also have a remarkable life.

Blade fuses are notably accurate and have become the motor industry standard.

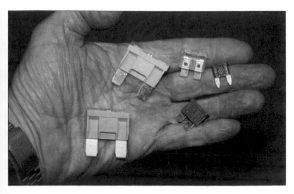

Some of the holders designed for blade fuses have a tight-fitting cap for extra safety.

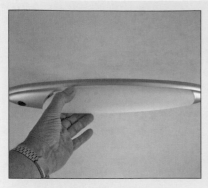

Recent fluorescent lamp fittings have a more attractive design than the bulkier fittings originally used.

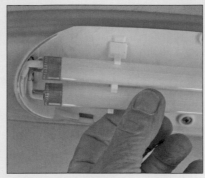

Unclipping the cover is easy and there's no difficulty changing a tube. But make sure the power to a unit is OFF.

This reading light can swivel in its holder and it is easy to change the 'car-type' tungsten bulb. Its consumption, however, is high.

Recessed halogen lamp fittings have become popular but consumption is high, the bulbs get hot and they break easily.

Good quality LEDs rarely need replacement and they consume very little current. This ceiling lamp has 78 warm-glow LEDs.

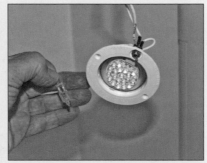

You reduce the life of a halogen bulb by touching its glass, but there's an LED conversion kit which fits some holders.

This is a 21 LED unit but there are smaller ones and products offering warm-glow illumination. Pins are spaced like halogen units.

Although pins snap off as easily as the ones on halogen bulbs, an LED unit can be touched and eased home with a screwdriver.

The panel of illustrations shows some examples of lamp units including LED replacement products. These small 'tablets' of LEDs, available from suppliers like CAK, are designed to fit into some of the more popular lamp housings originally used for halogen bulbs.

Leisure batteries

A caravan 'leisure' battery should not be regarded as a 'fit and forget' accessory. On the contrary, a battery needs periodic attention and special measures have to be taken if it is likely to remain unused for an extended period.

There are also important differences between a 12V leisure battery and a 12V vehicle battery. In summary:

A vehicle battery is designed to produce a surge of power to operate a starter motor. This is a demanding task, but once the engine is running, the battery gains an immediate recharge from the vehicle's alternator.

A leisure battery has to provide current over an extended period – and some time might elapse before recharging is possible. However, a recharge mustn't be delayed too long. Battery manufacturers also strongly advise owners not to discharge a battery completely – this can cause permanent damage.

The continued pattern of charge/discharge (referred to as deep cycling) is something that a *vehicle battery* cannot endure for long. The lead plates will soon get damaged and the all-important paste held within them can fall away. In a *leisure battery,* the plates are constructed with separators which retain the paste more effectively. This is reflected in the price although in the long term a leisure battery is a more economic proposition.

In Elecsol leisure batteries, carbon fibre is used in the plate construction as well. This is an unusual development and Elecsol batteries normally give notably long service. Without doubt, the inclusion of a five year warranty is proof of the manufacturer's confidence in the product.

As regards electrical performance, most specialists assert that a lead-acid 'wet' battery with cell top-up facilities achieves the best results. However, several Continental caravan manufacturers are starting to fit sealed gel batteries. Apparently this is to improve user safety; when a 'wet' battery tips over, its acid can cause damage and may lead to personal injury. For this reason gel batteries are normally installed on jet skis and quad bikes, but whether they are the preferred choice for caravans is debatable.

One advantage with a gel battery is the fact that it is completely sealed and has no need for a ventilation tube. However, it must *never* be charged at a higher voltage than 14.4V. Also be aware that gel batteries usually cost considerably more than comparable 'wet' batteries and are often heavier. In the UK, a traditional lead-acid 'wet' battery is clearly the more popular product for use in caravans.

When the level of the electrolyte falls, it should be topped up with de-ionised water.

It is recommended to smear battery terminals with a thin coating of grease.

Guidance on use

To get the best from a leisure battery, the following recommendations are put forward by manufacturers:

• The electrolyte must be checked periodically and if the level falls below the top of the plates, it should be topped up with de-ionised water. This is available from car accessory shops.
• A battery must not be left in a discharged state; ignoring this is likely to leave the battery irreparably damaged.
• If a caravan is parked for an extended period, its leisure battery must be kept in a charged condition. To achieve this it is usually removed and transferred to a bench for charging. Alternatively some owners use a trickle charger like the Carcoon product, which can be left permanently coupled to a battery.
• Completely sealed non-spill gel electrolyte batteries e.g. the Varta Drymobil, are less common and you should seek the manufacturer's advice about care and maintenance.
• When removing a battery, disconnect the negative terminal first: when installing a battery, connect the negative terminal last.
• The terminals should be smeared with grease, like Tri-Flow, or petroleum jelly (Vaseline).

Checking condition

Battery condition is usually checked with a meter although specific gravity testing is an alternative. A voltage reading is best taken directly from the battery terminals, but several points need to be borne in mind:

• It is recommended to use a digital voltmeter since these are easy to read and the level of accuracy is usually good. Whereas digital multimeters used to be expensive, they can now be purchased for under £10.
• Make sure *all* appliances are disconnected. Even a permanently connected clock can falsify a reading.
• If a battery has just been disconnected from a charger, or you've recently been towing your

caravan, the reading will not be a true indication of battery condition. It is necessary for the battery to settle before taking a voltmeter reading and this means waiting for at least four hours. The reason for the delay is that an elderly battery has a problem holding its charge; if you can wait even longer, e.g. 12 hours, the voltmeter will provide an even better indication of battery condition.
• Whilst a battery is described as providing a 12V power supply, the description is misleading. In fact a reading of 12V indicates the battery is discharged. The state of charge is as follows:

Voltmeter reading	Approx. charge state
12.7V or over	100%
12.5V	75%
12.4V	50%
12.2V	25%
12V or under	Discharged

Battery life between charges

The 'capacity' of a battery is expressed in Amp-hours (Ah) and this indicates how long it can provide an output before needing a recharge. As a rule, the external dimensions of a leisure battery are related to its Ah capacity and whilst a 90Ah battery product needs a recharge less frequently than a 60Ah version, there isn't always sufficient

A digital multimeter is well worth purchasing; some built-in voltage indicators in caravans are not always helpful.

Technical tips

Variations in battery performance between charges:

■ The stated capacity of a battery, expressed in Amp hours, presumes the temperature is 25°C (77°F). For every 1°C (approx.) drop in temperature, there's a 1% fall in battery capacity. So when a battery which is nominally rated as 60Ah is operating in a temperature of 15°C (60°F) it effectively becomes a 54Ah battery.
  Problems are even more acute for winter caravanners. Not only will a battery work harder to provide lighting and fan-assisted heating on long, dark evenings; the actual capacity of the battery is considerably less than its Ah rating might suggest.
■ Performance between charges deteriorates as a battery gets older.
■ If several appliances are used simultaneously, the faster rate of discharge reduces the effective battery performance still further.
The labels on German batteries often show this by giving different Ah capacities according to the rate of discharge.

During charging, a battery sometimes gives off hydrogen. This gas is lighter than air, explosive, and has a distinctive odour. Should the gas accidentally ignite – and a cigarette can cause this – the casing of a battery may be blown apart and corrosive acid forcibly ejected. Eye injury and flesh burns are likely.

There are two ways of venting hydrogen to the outside. If a battery is housed in a purpose-made locker, an outlet vent will have been included in the design and located *above* the top of the battery. This is because hydrogen rises. The alternative is to couple up a venting tube, and most leisure batteries have a connector nozzle and a length of flexible tubing.

Provided the tubing is tightly coupled, it can be led through a hole in a side wall or through the floor, thereby dispersing the hydrogen to the outside. If dispersal is done via a tube, the outlet can now be situated at a low level because the gas is contained within the tube and forced downwards.

It was mentioned in the earlier section on gel batteries that since these are sealed and not submitted to a charge rate higher than 14.4V they do not require a venting tube.

Calculating Ampere hours

Equipment	Rating in watts	Hours in use during 24-hour period	Watt hours
Two 8W lights	16	5	80
Two 10W spot lights	20	1	20
Water pump	50	0.2	10
Colour TV	50	5	250
		Total watt hours	360

Divide watt hours by volts to get ampere hours:
$$360 \div 12 = 30 \text{ Ah}$$

stowage space. In some purpose-made battery boxes fitted to caravans, there is only space for a 60 or 75Ah version.

In practice, this may not present a problem. If you tour with your caravan and are regularly on the move, the periodic charge received from the towcar is very beneficial. However, if you tend to site your caravan on a pitch for a week or more, a 90Ah battery has clear practical advantages, particularly if there is no mains hook-up.

To assess how long a battery will provide power between charges, a simple calculation makes a rough, but helpful estimation. The procedure is:

1. Establish the wattage of appliances. Typical examples: A single tube strip light – 8W; a spotlight – 10W; a water pump – 50W; a colour TV – 50W. **Note:** *The wattage of colour TV sets varies so check the label. Recent flat-screen sets with a built-in DVD player are rated with an input figure as low as 20W.*
2. Work out how many hours (or fractions of an hour) the appliances will be used in a 24 hour period.
3. Calculate watt hours for each appliance by multiplying wattage by hours in use.
4. Add together the total of watt hours.
5. Divide watt hours by volts to get ampere hours (Ah).

This calculation shows that if your caravan is fitted with a 60Ah battery and the ambient temperature is 25°C (77°F), the pattern of use given in the accompanying table means that the battery will be approximately 50% discharged after one day. If you continue to run it for a further 24 hours it will be completely flat, but that could be damaging.

Battery manufacturers point out that batteries last much longer if recharging commences as soon as they drop below 50% of their total capacity. In other words a 60Ah battery isn't going to provide an impressive service. A 90Ah battery would be more useful, of course, presuming that your battery box offers sufficient space to accommodate one of these larger products. Be aware, however, that it takes longer to recharge a 90Ah battery than one rated at 60Ah.

Also remember that these calculations are only approximate. As the technical tip panel points out, battery performance is influenced by several factors including temperature, age and rates of discharge. In truth, many caravanners report disappointment that their leisure battery needs recharging far more frequently than they had expected. Also bear in mind that 'budget-buy' batteries seldom achieve the performance of more expensive high quality products.

Other factors play a part, too, as discussed in the technical tip box on the previous page.

Leisure battery location

The closer a leisure battery is to the towcar's alternator, the better the charge rate when you are towing.

The reason for this, as discussed earlier, is that a long run of connecting cable leads to a fall-off in voltage and a poorer charge rate. Admittedly a thicker gauge of cable helps to reduce voltage loss on long cable runs. But the long run of cable from the engine compartment of the towcar and the leisure battery in the caravan reduces charging efficiency very significantly. In fact the term 'trickle charging' is used to describe this situation.

To achieve a better charge rate when towing, some caravanners used to transfer a leisure battery to either the boot or hatchback area at the rear of their cars. This then had to be coupled-up to the vehicle as follows:

1. The battery's positive terminal has to be connected using a battery clamp and a 2.5mm^2 or 4mm^2 lead coupled-up to the positive charging cable serving the car's towing socket. This is the charging cable which supplies Pin 2 in a pre 1st September 1998 12S socket or Pin 4 in a post 1st September 1998 12S socket.
2. The battery's negative terminal is coupled using a 2.5mm^2 or 4mm^2 cable that is connected to a sound earthing point in the towcar.

Although this strategy will shorten the runs of charging cable serving the leisure battery, there must be a good securing system so battery acid isn't spilt; it is also strongly advised to arrange venting for the hydrogen relief tube. If anyone is smoking in the car when hydrogen is emitted during charging there could be a serious risk.

Since the cable run between the alternator and battery is now greatly reduced the charge rate is higher. This is referred to as 'boost charging'.

To make this transference of the battery to the car comparatively simple, Lab Craft produced the TP2 battery box which has been used by caravanners for many years. Whenever the car is used for a solo drive, TP2 owners transfer the battery in its carrying box to the vehicle, connect using Lab Craft's plug, and achieve a boost charge.

This is a thoughtful system and it's unfortunate that this notable product is no longer being manufactured. New regulations led to its withdrawal in 1999, and today few caravanners move a leisure battery into a towcar even if it does achieve improved charging.

Other points regarding the location of a battery are:

• A battery should never share a locker with gas cylinders. Rather surprisingly some caravans made in the 1980s were built with a battery fixing point in the forward gas locker. (Gas cylinder valves can leak and a spark from a battery terminal could cause an explosion.)
• The preferred location is in a purpose-designed locker, fitted with security straps and vented to the outside.
• Traditional bolt-on connectors sold in auto shops are recommended, although spring battery clamps sold at caravan accessory shops are better still. Avoid using crocodile clips on battery terminals. A clip might become dislodged and a spark across a poor connection can be powerful.
• A battery location must have ventilation. The reason for this is given in the safety box on page 112.
• When adding an auxiliary battery in an older caravan, it may have to be fitted in a bed box or in the bottom of a wardrobe. All safety measures should be noted. Make sure the battery is firmly installed so it cannot tip over and ensure there is ventilation. The easiest answer here is to buy a battery with a gas venting tube and to feed this through a narrow hole drilled in the floor.

Charging

Methods of charging a leisure battery can be achieved using the following:

• a portable or fixed mains charger,
• the engine alternator,
• a petrol or diesel generator,
• a wind or solar system.

Mains chargers

As regards mains chargers, the following points are worthy of note:

• The amp output of a charger influences how quickly a battery is revived. Too high an amperage, however, is not good for a battery. As a rule of thumb, if you divide a battery's Ah rating by ten, this is the maximum recommended amp output rating of a charger.

The TP2 portable battery box with its built-in mains charger and car-coupling socket was popular for many years but manufacture ceased around 1999.

Spring-loaded battery clamps are fully recommended; never use crocodile clips.
....

• A leisure battery needs a different charging régime from that required by a vehicle battery. This is why an inexpensive portable car battery charger isn't recommended. On the other hand, some of the better types incorporate a selection switch; this provides the appropriate régime for either a car or a leisure battery.
• A battery can be 'over-charged' and when this happens, a situation inaccurately referred to as 'boiling' may occur. As a result, the water content of the electrolyte (diluted sulphuric acid) will start to evaporate. If this happens, the concentrated acid can damage the lead plates; so as soon as charging is completed, the battery must be topped up using de-ionised water.
• There are several separate cells in a battery, each of which has its own top-up point. Sometimes one of the cells will fail and this can upset an automatic charger's sensing system. Instead of switching off automatically when the other cells are recharged, it maintains its full output on account of the failed cell. This is another situation causing the battery to boil and to emit hydrogen.
• When on a mains hook-up, some people keep a built-in caravan charger running all the time. This is acceptable with older chargers that incorporated a transformer. However, some manufacturers of 'switched mode' electronic chargers might

Technical tip

The hydrogen gas produced when a battery is given a charge greater than 14.4V is potentially dangerous. But paradoxically, 'gassing' is good for a battery because it helps to cure a condition in which the plates inside get coated with sulphate. When this happens battery efficiency is greatly reduced and leisure batteries are often scrapped prematurely as a result. To extend their working life, manufacturers strongly recommend periodic charging for brief periods at higher voltages such as 14.8V, at which point gassing occurs.

However, you cannot do that when a battery is still connected up in a caravan and simultaneously running 12V accessories. Although low voltage appliances can cope with up to 13.8V, anything higher could be damaging. For this reason, built-in caravan chargers are designed not to exceed a 13.8V output, even though a leisure battery would benefit greatly from the occasional higher charge rate. Herein lies a problem which can only be resolved by periodically disconnecting the battery and transferring it to a bench for a reconditioning charge.

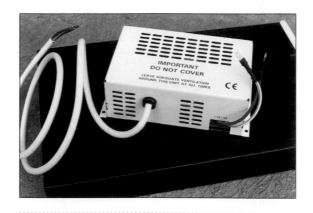

The BCA battery charger is a compact unit that can be left running when coupled to a mains hook-up.

recommend the charger is turned off when the battery level indicator shows a satisfactory condition. The charger from BCA Leisure forming part of the Power Centre unit is an exception and can be left on permanently without detriment.

• Normally a 12V supply should not be drawn directly from a mains-operated charger *without* having a connected battery in place. This is because a charger's output fluctuates and some 12V appliances *must* have a stable supply. Having a battery in circuit smoothes out irregularities and prevents damage to the accessories it has to run. There are exceptions, however, and BCA Leisure

asserts that its power supply units *can* be used without a battery in the circuit.

Stage charging

It has been explained earlier that a leisure battery coupled to a caravan cannot be charged at more than 13.8V because it may be running 12V accessories at the same time. Unfortunately this conflicts with battery manufacturers' advice; in order to recharge a battery fully and to reduce damage to its plates through sulphation, it is beneficial to provide periodic, though brief, reconditioning start-up charges of around 14.8V.

To address this problem, BCA Leisure has designed a power unit which produces two outputs when a caravan is coupled-up to a mains 230V supply. One output is for charging the battery: the other is for running 12V accessories. This product, called the Duo Charger, was first installed in 2008 Coachman caravans, and when the unit was exhibited at major exhibitions its output was shown using digital voltmeters.

An alternative, but somewhat clumsy, strategy is to disconnect a caravan battery during a lay-up period and, if necessary, transfer it to a work bench. Then it can be reconditioned using a portable charger which offers an automatic stage-charging cycle.

Manufacturers emphasise that to achieve a full charge level, a battery should receive a periodic reconditioning voltage around 14.8V.

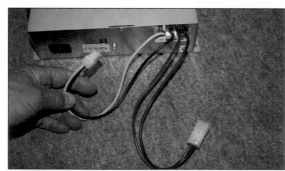

The Duo Charger from BCA Leisure has two feeds – one for battery charging and the other for running 12V components.

When the Duo Charger has been shown at exhibitions, the display has included two voltmeters to show the respective outputs.

When a caravan is out of use for an extended spell its battery can be removed, charged and stored in a good condition.

The range of Selmar Guardian Leisure chargers serves a variety of products. This stage charger is for 20–75Ah batteries.

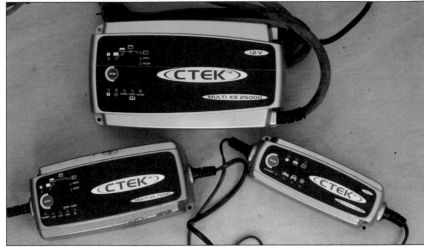

Different products for different needs; CTEK even offers eight-step chargers with a pulse maintenance mode.

Multi-stage chargers, sometimes called 'step chargers', are available from specialist suppliers, e.g. RoadPro, and caravanning retailers, e.g. Towsure. When purchasing a charger, make sure that its specification is suitable for the Ah rating of your caravan's leisure battery. On a good quality charger, this information is given in its specification leaflet and it's often indicated on a label fastened to its casing.

Depending on the sophistication of their circuits, the least expensive products provide three charge levels which are switched into action automatically during the cycle. A model that has been manufactured and improved over the years is the Selmar Guardian Leisure SGA4A 7A portable unit which is appropriate for 20–75Ah batteries. Other models suitable for larger batteries are also included in Selmar's range.

Another noteworthy range of advanced chargers, which first achieved recognition in the marine market, is manufactured by Sterling Power Products. Also impressive is the CTEK range, which can recharge

any type of lead-acid battery, including gel types. Even heavily discharged batteries can usually be recommissioned with a CTEK product.

Whereas some of the CTEK chargers are portable products, others can be installed permanently in a caravan to act as a fixed power supply. However, that function is only recommended for discerning caravanners who understand technical issues and are prepared to select the appropriate setting as and when needed. For instance, multi-stage models have a mode selector which you operate yourself. In other words if you were to accidentally start using your caravan's 12V appliances when the 14.7V setting had been selected, damage would undoubtedly occur.

That's the reason why the standard 'fit and forget' charger in a caravan has a 13.8V limit and includes no facility for manually altering its output. On the other hand, if you're prepared to adopt a hands-on approach, the preferred setting on a CTEK mode button can be selected, whereupon you then leave the charger to embark on its automatic stage-by-stage reconditioning work.

To give an example of a stage regime carried out by the inexpensive CTEK Multi XS 3600 three-stage fully automatic model, here is the pattern it follows. (This charger is suitable for batteries up to 125Ah capacity.)

i) Bulk: It starts with 3.6A constant current until 14.7V is reached.
ii) Absorption: Voltage is held at maximum level but current (Amps) is allowed to drop.
iii) Pulse: On reaching 0.4A, a pulse maintenance phase is adopted.

Thereafter, if the battery's voltage drops below 11.8V the charge cycle is restarted automatically. **Note:** *When using chargers that provide a higher-than-usual voltage, check the battery's electrolyte level frequently and top-up the cells as and when necessary with de-ionised water.*

Well-specified stage chargers are able to use their electronic circuitry to evaluate the needs of a battery and to prescribe the appropriate charging

This CTEK model offers a standby mode, 14.4V (for gel batteries) or 14.7V (for 'wet' batteries), a 13.6V supply mode and a 16V boost rate. Note that the 16V boost rate might damage some leisure batteries.

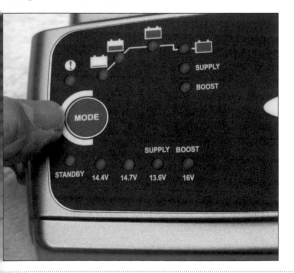

Technical tips

CHARGING VOLTAGES
Opinions differ regarding the optimum initial voltage best suited to different types of batteries when they are heavily discharged. To ensure a battery is not damaged by an excessive voltage, always observe its manufacturer's recommendations. A high boost rate, for instance, might damage some types of leisure battery.

The Carcoon trickle charger is designed to be left connected to a battery all through a lay-up period.

Several 230V portable generators are also equipped with a 12V DV outlet that can be coupled to a battery that needs charging.

régime. They also have a trickle charge facility so that a battery can remain connected during a winter lay-up; its circuit monitors battery condition and only starts providing a charge when the voltage drops below a certain level.

You can also purchase trickle chargers as a separate item and these are often used by Classic Car owners when a vehicle is laid-up in the winter. A well-known version used by car enthusiasts is manufactured by Carcoon.

The engine alternator

The charge from a vehicle alternator is usually quite high and this can provide the needs of both the car and caravan batteries when you're towing. For example, if a leisure battery is left in a caravan it will receive a gentle (i.e. 'trickle') charge via the car's 12S or 13-pin socket while the caravan is being towed. However, voltage loss due to the length of connecting cables limits

its effectiveness, and it was mentioned earlier in the chapter that a higher 'boost' charge is often attainable if a battery is transferred to the rear of the towcar. In practice it's a tiresome chore and few owners carry this out.

Petrol generators

It's well over a decade since caravans were first equipped with 'switched-mode' electronic battery chargers in place of the older, heavier types which had a transformer inside the casing. The newer products offer many advantages but are easily damaged if coupled up to an unstable 230V mains supply.

Unfortunately, many types of petrol generator tend to create an unstable supply, and a sudden surge of power – referred to as a 'spike' – can ruin a switched-mode battery charger. Surges often occur, for example, during a generator start-up and when a choke is disconnected. There is also the possibility of a surge when an electric kettle reaches its boiling point and automatically switches off. At this point the generator has one less high consumption appliance to run and you will hear the note of its engine change.

The charger may thus get damaged when an older type of generator is in use and when its mains supply outlet is coupled up to the caravan's 230V inlet. To avoid this problem, many generators have a 12V outlet too, and if you couple this up directly to the terminals of your leisure battery you bypass the caravan's mains charger and it cannot get damaged.

A further precaution is to get a petrol generator started and running for several minutes until its engine reaches normal temperature and is running smoothly. That's the point at which it is best to couple up its mains output to your caravan's input socket.

Bearing this problem in mind, Honda has pioneered a new type of circuit which is fitted in the Company's latest portable leisure

The Honda EU 10i employs inverter technology, which creates a very stable mains supply. These sought-after products should be secured against theft.

generators, like the Honda EU 10i and the EU 20i. This employs what is described as 'Inverter Technology', and Honda claims that the surge-free 230V output from these models is even more stable than you'd normally get from the National Grid. These are undoubtedly high quality generators, but an influx of cheap products being assembled in the Far East has attracted many owners, who later report problems with their caravan charger. You might pay more for a model like the Honda EU 10i but it is a superior product in all sorts of ways.

Solar and wind generators

The idea of getting 'something for nothing' is very attractive. On the other hand, these types of generator will only provide a trickle charge for a battery.

If you park a caravan on an exposed site or at a storage location in a region known to have sustained windy weather, a wind generator would be able to provide a battery with a useful trickle charge. Marlec systems are well known. However, these appliances are more useful for marine applications than they are for caravanning.

On the other hand, solar panels are dependent on light rather than weather and you can certainly keep a battery topped up in favourable conditions if you purchase:

- a good quality panel with a high wattage rating,
- a voltage control unit, and
- the appropriate installation components.

Note: *In Chapter 12 the installation of a flexible lightweight frameless 70W panel is described in detail.*

Strictly speaking, the term 'solar' is inaccurate because photo-voltaic cells also produce some electricity in cloudy weather. They do not depend on sunshine, nor for that matter do they need heat. In fact the bright light in cold arctic locations is more effective than the hazy light often found in the heat of a Mediterranean location.

During a winter lay-up, a large roof-mounted solar panel may be able to keep a battery in fair condition, although shorter daylight hours do not help. In the longer days of summer, the output is very much better. In fact some users report that when a large panel like a Siemens SR90 5.30 A/90W panel is coupled up to a 90Ah battery, it is possible to be completely self-contained.

Several products are available, complete with installation kits, but the initial cost of a high output panel is substantial. Indeed the notion of 'something for nothing' is certainly not the case in this instance.

Solar panels are available from several leisure specialists that can supply caravanners with compact units for portable use or large high-output models for roof mounting. A control unit prevents a solar panel from over-charging and can also report both battery condition and solar output.

The mains supply system

Modern caravans are equipped with appliances that operate from a 230 volts AC supply. This chapter explains in detail how a mains system is installed and used.

In 1977, The Caravan Club arranged to have twelve mains power sockets installed on one of its sites. The idea was unusual in those days and few caravanners would have anticipated that in a short space of time, most large sites would be similarly equipped. Even some of the five-van certificated sites available for use by members of the two national caravanning clubs are now being fitted with 230V pillars.

Hook-up facilities are commonplace throughout Europe, although you are less likely to encounter the coupling pillars found in marinas where payment for the electricity consumed is made using a swipe card facility.

Since these early trials, a lot has changed. For instance:

• it is no longer appropriate to speak of 240V; today the nominal voltage is 230V AC with a permitted variation of +10% and –6%.
• virtually all modern caravans are fitted with a mains system as standard.
• in caravans made from 1995 onwards, manufacturers have been obliged to include an approved hook-up cable.
• standardisation of items like hook-up sockets is happening throughout many European countries, although an adaptor should still be taken abroad.

On this site in France, the mains hook-up pillars have both traditional French sockets and sockets for blue plugs which comply with EN 60309-2.

Some sites have hook-ups where the electricity used is shown on a digital read-out; payment is made using a credit card 'swipe' facility.

Notwithstanding the present popularity of 230V provision, some older caravans are not wired for mains; so the work entailed in fitting an approved supply system is described later in this chapter.

Also covered are the procedures for connecting safely to a supply, and the way to calculate what electrical appliances can be used without overloading a site's supply capability.

Assessing the appliances you can use

On arrival at a site reception office, enquire how many amps are available from the hook-up points. Occasionally you may even come across a two-tier provision and two pricing bands. To convert the information to watts, multiply the current rating (usually expressed as ampères or amps) by the voltage (230V). In other words, a site offering 5A would be suitable for operating appliances whose total wattage doesn't exceed 1150W.

Practical implications

The term 'amps' refers to the *amount* of current available whereas most electrical appliances are marked in watts – which refers to their rate of consumption. For instance, a household light bulb

Safety

In one of its technical leaflets, *The Camping and Caravanning Club* states that 'Electricity is a very good friend but an even worse enemy'.
This is an important reminder. Fortunately the standards of equipment in Britain and the practices adopted are generally very good, but in some parts of Europe you may come across less impressive arrangements. If a hook-up point looks doubtful, it may be wise not to couple-up to a supply.

Be careful too, if you see slender lengths of twin flex cable coupled into mains hook-up points. Some may be merely joined with insulation tape and when you take into account the sudden downpours that characterise Continental thunderstorms, the situation becomes more worrying still. Always exercise vigilance; you will find some sites that have rudimentary installations whereas others exemplify the very best in electrical standards.

might be rated at 60W whereas a Truma Ultrastore 10-litre water heater running on 230V is much higher at 850W. A conventional domestic kettle used at home may be rated as high as 2500W – typically expressed as 2.5kW where 'k' refers to a thousand. As a general rule, the wattage of appliances is shown on a label – or marked on the glass dome of a light bulb.

The remarkable difference in the rate of consumption between a light bulb and a conventional electric kettle is very clear. Bearing in mind that some sites only provide a maximum of 5A, it is immediately apparent why you have to leave normal domestic appliances like kettles, pop-up toasters, and deep fat fryers at home. If you want an electric kettle on holiday, the answer is to buy one of the special caravan types rated around 750W. Low wattage kettles or heating jugs work well – they merely take longer to boil.

However, what will happen if you exceed the stated limit of a hook-up? Happily, there's unlikely to be a danger element if the installation is safe. Should you overload the supply, the site's safety cut-out comes into operation, leaving you with no electricity at all. On many sites you'll then need to summon a member of the staff who will reinstate the supply. Naturally they are unlikely to respond if they're 'off-duty'. However, many British sites have the resetting switches accessible and sometimes caravanners are permitted to reactivate the trip switch themselves.

To avoid overloading your hook-up pillar's limit, you just have to carry out a simple calculation. The procedure is to:

• establish the amp supply at the site reception office,
• multiply this by 230 (the voltage) to establish how many watts are available.
• check the wattage of all mains appliances in your caravan,
• monitor what you have running at any one time, adding up the total wattage of each appliance and confirming that you are keeping well within the site's limit. *But note the later section on problems that can occur at times of peak demand.*

A rough idea of typical power ratings is given in the box above.

If the task of adding together the wattage of appliances seems onerous, you can avoid this chore by fitting a current monitoring and cut-off device called a Fuse Control. The installation of a Fuse Control is included in Chapter 12. Not only does its display show the current consumption (amps) when appliances are running, but you can also set it to trip *before* the tripping point of your site's hook-up pillar. For instance, if a 10A supply is available you can set the Fuse Control to trip when your consumption reaches 9.5A. This precautionary measure ensures the site supply remains intact, and when you've disconnected one of the mains-powered accessories that contributed to the overload the device can be duly reset, whereupon the supply can be reinstated.

Assessing what appliances you can use

Remember that some sites provide as little as 5A (1,150W) and in rural areas in France a few sites provide even less. On the other hand, many of the sites owned by The Camping & Caravanning Club and The Caravan Club offer up to 16A (3,680W) from each hook-up point.

As regards 230V electrical appliances and accessories, these are typically rated at:

Flat screen colour TV	22–25W
Light bulb	60W
Refrigerator (depending on model)	120–135W
Battery charger (depending on battery charge level)	200–800W
Truma Ultrastore 10-litre water heater	850W
Microwave oven	1,300W
Domestic kettle	2,500W

Note: *The power consumption of a built-in battery charger is less easy to calculate. When a battery is heavily discharged the draw of current is considerably higher than when a battery only needs a trickle topping-up charge.*

When adding up the wattages of the appliances in use *at any one time,* make sure you don't overlook less conspicuous items like a built-in battery charger, and any of the appliances that offer a 230V operating mode such as a refrigerator, space heater and water heater.

On some hook-up pillars the switches that reactivate the supply of current can be accessed by the caravanner.

To ensure that you don't exceed the current (amps) available from a hook-up, the combined wattage of all your appliances must be added.

To avoid calculating the consumption of mains appliances, you can fit a monitoring product and 'trip device' called a Fuse Control.

Problems at peak periods

Caravanners have been quick to grasp the benefits of having a mains supply, so it is hardly surprising that manufacturers have responded by offering water heaters, space heaters, fans, chargers, air conditioners and other appliances that operate on 230V. This hasn't been without its problems.

It is true that some sites can offer a hook-up output as high as 16A from an individual supply pillar. But this presumes that all visitors are not hoping to run an array of appliances *at the same time*. In winter when the evenings are dark and temperatures low, more and more caravanners switch on an electrically operated space heater, a colour TV, an array of lights, and keep the hot water storage heater and fridge running on mains as well.

When this happens, the supply is simply unable to cope and posters displayed at Caravan Club sites have urged members to exercise careful vigilance over the draw on current.

In reality, if a site is full in winter and if caravans are coupled into the hook-ups on *every* pitch, the *actual* supply available is far lower than 16A at each hook-up point. It has even been stated that a simultaneous demand of *more than 5A* from every hook-up is likely to lead to a site supply failure.

Whilst it is true that cabling and components could be upgraded to provide a full 16A from every supply socket simultaneously, the cost of the installation would run into millions of pounds. This, of course, would influence the cost of staying at the site.

Coupling procedure

For safety's sake, a strict procedure should be followed:

1. Check that the site supply pillar looks safe and doesn't have an array of badly coupled cabling and adaptors. On some sites abroad, adherence to safety standards in the height of the season leaves a lot to be desired.
2. Ensure the switch on the caravan's mains control unit is OFF.
3. Unwind the cable into large, loose coils and trail it towards the coupling pillar making sure it lays flat on the ground. Never leave it tightly wound on a drum because it might get hot and in extreme cases the insulation can melt.
4 Couple the blue female plug (with recessed tubes) into the input socket of your caravan. *Connect this end of the cable first.*
5. Then couple the other end of the cable to the site supply. On some of the Caravan Club sites the plug has to be inserted and then rotated clockwise to engage the contacts.
6. Stow any surplus cable out of the way in loose coils under the caravan to ensure it doesn't get in the way.
7. Switch on the supply at the mains Consumer Unit in your caravan, and then test the trip button to confirm that the residual current device is responding by switching off instantly. Reset the safety switch.
8. Having coupled up, it's wise to check polarity – there may be a warning light on your Mains Supply Unit. Failing this, you can purchase a polarity tester and the product from W4 Accessories is stocked at most caravan accessory shops. Fit this into one of the 13A sockets, switch on and check the display lights in conjunction with the information on the tester's label.
9. If it is confirmed that the polarity of the supply is reversed, refer to the later section which describes the implications of this reversal.

Disconnection

1. Switch off the supply at the caravan mains control unit.

Always make a point of coupling the blue female plug with the recessed tubes into your caravan *before* coupling the male plug to the socket on the hook-up pillar.

Operation of the safety cut-out, called an RCD, can be confirmed by pressing a test button on the Consumer Unit.

A polarity tester from W4 Accessories is available from most caravan accessory shops.

2. Disconnect the cable from the supply pillar. On some sockets – especially on Caravan Club sites – you have to press a red release button in order to withdraw the coupling plug

3. Recoil the cable and disconnect from the caravan.

Polarity

In the UK, it has been traditional for switches to create a break in the live cable serving an appliance or lamp fitting. In other words when a light is switched off, current is prevented from reaching either the bulb or its socket. On the other hand, the neutral wire remains permanently connected to the lamp fitting.

On the Continent the arrangement is different because the switches used abroad create a break in both live *and* neutral connections, a system known as double-pole switching. This is undoubtedly a very safe arrangement. It means that if the live and neutral feeds are reversed – a situation referred to as 'reverse polarity' – the supply current is still unable to reach an appliance or a light fitting.

Unfortunately reverse polarity can be very dangerous for the UK tourist whose caravan is normally only fitted with single-pole switches. When you switch off an appliance it is true that it ceases to function. But if we take a lamp as an

On some sites, it is necessary to depress a release button before withdrawing the hook-up connector.

example – *the light fitting remains live* because polarity reversal means that the switch creates a break in the neutral cable which leads *out* of the unit.

In a situation of reversed polarity, the usual advice is to cease using a supply – just in case you accidentally touch a live connection.

To overcome the problem, some caravanners take a second Continental adaptor intentionally wired up with reversed connections and duly marked with a bold label to indicate the reversal. This effectively remedies the problem at the supply point itself.

Another precautionary measure is to fit an RYD live/neutral polarity changeover unit which is manufactured by Jenste. This is often fitted in

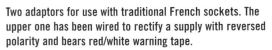

Two adaptors for use with traditional French sockets. The upper one has been wired to rectify a supply with reversed polarity and bears red/white warning tape.

Some caravanners buy a second Continental adaptor and change over the live and neutral cables to suit hook-ups which have reversed polarity.

The RYD live/neutral changeover device is available by mail order from its manufacturer, Jenste.

Like any mains component, this should be installed by a competent electrician; the connections are clearly labelled.

pleasure boats, and as the photograph shows, the connections are clearly marked enabling a competent DIY electrician to follow them.

As a result of IEE regulations, caravans manufactured since 1994 now have a double-pole switched RCD and double-pole MCBs so the level of protection is improved. Regrettably however, 13A sockets with single-pole switches are still fitted in spite of the fact that double-pole sockets are now available in the UK.

If double-pole switched sockets, together with a double-pole switched RCD and double-pole switched MCBs are fitted, the danger posed by a hook-up with reversed polarity is now eliminated as far as the caravanner is concerned. On

It's possible to purchase double-pole switched sockets in the UK, as the marking shows on this product; but they are not always easy to find.

the other hand, some appliances, e.g. lap-top computers, might be polarity-sensitive, in which case damage could occur.

Mains system components

Bearing in mind that a towed caravan is subjected to some destructive movements on bumpy roads, the specifications for a mains system are different from those which apply to wiring in our homes.

Only the correct components for caravan installations should be used. So if you purchase a pre-owned caravan which contains a DIY mains installation, it is imperative that this is checked by a qualified electrician before being put into commission.

As regards owner installation, some very good kits are available and enable a competent and careful practitioner to install a mains supply where one hasn't already been fitted. Kits from suppliers like Powerpart or W4 Accessories, for example, are stocked in many caravan accessory shops. Purchasing a full kit of parts in this way ensures you have components of the correct type and quality.

Many people would entrust this work to a

Safety

When purchasing a pre-owned caravan, ask if there is a signed Inspection and Completion Certificate to verify that the mains installation meets the technical requirements set out in BS 7671. If not, an inspection should be carried out by one of the following specialists, either:

■ an approved contractor of the National Inspection Council for Electrical Installation Contracting (NICEIC), or

■ a member of either the Electrical Contractors Association (ECA) or the Electrical Contractors Association of Scotland.

If an inspection certificate doesn't exist, it is in the purchaser's interests to arrange for the caravan to be inspected before the mains provision is put into service. To find out your nearest NICEIC specialist telephone 0171 582 7746, or to find an ECA member, telephone 0171 229 1266.

DIY mains wiring is possible; the Powerpart Mains wiring kit is supplied with full fitting instructions.

qualified electrician, of course, but *some* DIY enthusiasts undoubtedly have the knowledge and ability to fit one of these kits themselves. Simple electrical connections will have to be made but a lot of the work only involves carpentry.

As regards the provision itself, this should comprise:

1. A caravan hook-up cable with couplings.

The couplings are 16A industrial products which have to be blue in colour and compliant with BS EN 60309-2. Plugs and sockets of this pattern are often seen on building sites and at other industrial locations. Hook-up points on caravan sites in the UK have been equipped to receive these couplings for many years and this pattern is now required at new sites in European Member States.

In addition, the coupling lead has to be heavy duty three-core flexible PVC shielded cable in which the cross-sectional area of each core is 2.5 mm^2. This coupling lead should be 25m long (+ or –2m) and should meet BS EN 60309-2.

A longer cable should not be used, nor for that matter is it deemed acceptable to link up more than one extension lead.

Note: *If you want to connect the supply lead to a 13A socket at home – perhaps to pre-cool a refrigerator prior to departure – you'll need an adaptor. Furthermore, since the coupling cable from your house is not protected by the RCD in your caravan's consumer unit, it is strongly recommended that you fit a portable RCD to the supplying socket. These are sold at DIY stores. Other adaptors will also be required to connect into many of the hook-up pillars used abroad.*

2. Caravan Inlet

At the caravan end of the supply lead, the blue plug is designed with deeply recessed tubes to eliminate any chance of making accidental contact with the live connectors. The caravan itself will correspondingly be fitted with a 16A inlet to meet BS EN 60309-2.

The location of the inlet socket should not be higher than 1.8m above the ground. Curiously

in some mid-eighties caravans (e.g. imported Homecar models) the socket was often positioned above head height which was most inconvenient.

A surface-mounted input socket is no longer considered suitable if installed below the floor. Even if fitted with a protective cap these sockets

Sudden downpours are not unusual and since the sockets on hook-up cable are not designed to be immersed in water, the reason for not linking separate extension leads is obvious here.

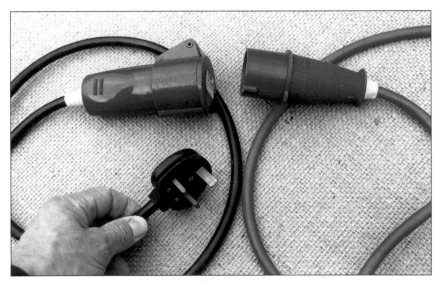

If you want to couple up a caravan supply lead to a 13A domestic socket at home, you'll need a special adaptor.

When supplying a caravan's 230V system at home from a domestic 13A socket using the hook-up cable and an adaptor, it is strongly recommended to add a portable RCD as well.

Wall-mounted inlets sometimes include a release lever which has to be depressed in order to withdraw the connecting plug.

Even when there's a protection cap, face fitting inlet sockets are no longer considered acceptable for installation below the floor.

To afford good protection, some face fitting sockets are located in a locker – but never use a locker containing gas cylinders or gas supply pipes.

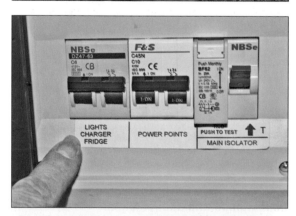

This label helpfully indicates the function of each switch on the consumer unit. Unfortunately some manufacturers fail to include stickers like this.

In the Sargent PSU 2007 electrical control unit, the left side deals with 12V circuits; the right contains the mains RCD and three MCBs.

are easily damaged by road dirt and debris. However, if you don't want to cut into the wall of your caravan to have a boxed socket with hinge lid fitted, a face fitted socket can be installed in an exterior locker as long as it is not a locker used for gas cylinders or gas supply pipe.

As a point of interest, some sockets now feature a retention catch and a release lever to prevent the plug from being accidentally withdrawn.

3. A permanently installed connection to the caravan consumer unit

The first length of cable inside a caravan which runs from the inlet socket to the mains consumer unit is *not* protected by the Residual Current Device (RCD). Only the wiring runs, sockets and appliances that are in the circuit *after* the RCD are protected by the safety trip switches.

For this reason the run of cable here should be continuous and as short as possible. In any event it shouldn't exceed 2m and it must either be installed within conduit or attached to the structure securely using insulated clips. These should be no further apart than 0.25m on a horizontal run and 0.40m on a vertical run.

This part of the internal system should be carried out using 3-core PVC flexible cable in which each core has a cross-sectional area of 2.5 mm^2. This is the same as the cable specified for the outside coupling lead.

4. Consumer unit

To meet regulations, a mains control or 'consumer unit' has to fulfil several functions. It should be fitted with:
• an isolating switch,
• over-current protection (achieved by miniature circuit breakers or MCBs),
• a double-pole residual current device (RCD) to comply with BS4293, BS EN 61008-1 or BS EN 6AN 1009. This should: create a break in all live conductors; react to a residual operating current of 30mA; and have an operating time not exceeding 40 milliseconds at a residual current of 150mA.

A number of products meet these requirements although there are several variations in design. For instance many caravans are fitted with a stand-alone consumer unit. Products from Hager are well-known examples. On the other hand, there are also instances where the mains consumer unit is integrated into a larger control system which incorporates controls and fuses for 12V systems as well. This is the case with the Power Box from BCA Leisure and the PSU 2007 electrical control unit from Sargent Electrical Services.

Further variations will be found in respect of the MCB provision. Many units are fitted with one MCB rated at 5 or 6A which protects lighting circuits, battery charger circuits and fridge circuits from overload situations. A second MCB rated at either 10A or 16A is designated to afford protection to the socket outlets fitted in the caravan. In some installations a third MCB is included as well.

A mains system in a caravan must include an earth bonding wire which is connected to the chassis and marked with a warning tag.

5. Bonding requirements

To meet the regulations, a bonding cable no less than 4mm^2 has to be connected from the RCD earth to the chassis and to any other conductive parts with the exception of the aluminium wall panels on a caravan. So if a metal sink is fitted, this must be bonded – just as it should be in a modern house.

The cable will have a green and yellow sheathing and the point of connection should bear a warning tag advising users not to disconnect it.

Note: *Some caravanners express concern that although an earth wire is attached to the chassis, corner steadies are often lowered on to wooden or plastic blocks, thus preventing earthing to the ground. However, earthing via this route is not necessary – earthing is carried out via the earth pin on the hook-up socket in accordance with the procedure detailed in* BS 7671: 2001(IEE Wiring Regulations, Sixteenth Edition).

6. Internal connecting cable

Connections from the consumer unit to appliances, e.g. the refrigerator and the 13A sockets, must be made with 1.5 mm^2 *flexible cable*. To fulfil IEE regulations, this has to be fixed permanently and whereas running it within conduit is acceptable, clips are more commonly used. These should be spaced no further apart than 0.25m on horizontal runs and 0.4m on vertical runs.

The reason for specifying *flexible* cable whose conducting wires are multi-stranded is the fact that it is more able to absorb jarring movements at points where connections are made. The twin and earth flat PVC sheathed cable used for connecting up 13A sockets in our homes should *not* be used for connecting up the 13A sockets in a caravan. Its single strand copper conductor is not sufficiently resilient.

Normally the cable runs will be unbroken. However, if there is a need to connect lengths of cable in the installation, this should be achieved using a junction box fitted in an accessible location.

7. Switches, sockets and spurs

The 13A sockets in a caravan are fitted into either a flush fit or surface-mounted box. It is important

that the plugs on appliances carry a fuse of the correct rating. Many 13 plugs are sold with a 13A fuse, but if you are using this for a table lamp, it is important to change this for a 3A fuse – as you should at home. Manufacturers of appliances like TV sets and hair dryers will similarly specify the fuse needed in the plug.

As a rule, the switched sockets fitted in caravans are seldom double-pole switched types. In view of the recurring problem of reversed polarity experienced on many sites abroad this is a pity.

Where an electric space heater, an electric water heater and a refrigerator are fitted, these should be coupled directly into their own fused spur socket outlet. These sometimes carry a red neon indicator and this switched control should be as close to the appliance as possible.

Normally a battery charger is fitted into a mains system as well and if one of these is added in an upgrade project, the manufacturer's instructions regarding connections should be followed. Some are stand-alone items whereas other chargers are installed within the casing of a mains and 12V fused distribution unit.

Installation requirements

If you have purchased an older caravan and want a temporary mains installation, the easiest way to do this is to purchase the Powerpart Mobile Power Unit. This is a self-contained product that offers

INVERTER WAVE FORMS AND BATTERY CAPACITY

■ Some electrical equipment only operates properly on 230V if the wave form from a power-serving appliance replicates that of a mains supply; electronic-contolled appliances like curling tongs are a case in point. A 'pure sine wave' inverter is most likely to achieve this but these are comparatively expensive. In practice, most caravanners' needs are met by a 'modified (or quasi) sine wave' inverter. Dealer literature should clarify this issue and particularly clear explanations are provided in Road Pro's annual catalogue.

■ The leisure battery serving an inverter should have an Ah capacity at least 20% of the inverter's wattage. Thus a 70Ah (minimum) battery is needed to run a 350W inverter.

The Consumer Unit supplied with a Powerpart Mains Kit is pre-wired in order to make the installation much easier.

The Powerpart Portable Mains Unit is ideal for use in an older caravan when the owner doesn't want to fit a permanent installation. It's also useful in an awning.

three 13A sockets and the unit is pre-connected with hook-up cable. It carries the full complement of protective devices like the RCD and MCBs that would be found in permanent installations. But not only can you take this portable product with you when selling a caravan: it is a protection system you can also use whenever operating DIY power tools at home.

However, if you want to fit a permanent mains system, it is recommended that a kit is purchased. Some have pre-connected consumer units in which the input supply cable, output cable for the sockets and earth cable are already coupled up and hanging from the box. In reality, you still need to take off the front casing to gain access to the screw fixing holes, but a pre-connected unit certainly simplifies the installation.

When fixing the consumer unit, choose a location where it is easy to see and where its control switches are accessible. In addition you will almost certainly need to strengthen the wall panel or furniture panel on which it is going to be located. This is easily done by glueing and screwing a base piece of 9mm (⅜in) plywood to the surface as a reinforcement. Cut this to the size of the consumer unit and use an impact adhesive like Evo-Stik.

A similar strategy is likely when fitting 13A sockets. The standard 3mm decorative ply used in caravans is not sufficient to provide a stable base. Nor does it offer sufficient depth for the threads of the fixing screws.

When the installation is complete, you should have it checked by a qualified electrician before putting it into commission.

In order to screw a Consumer Unit in place, the cover has to be removed to reveal the fixing holes on the back plate.

A Consumer Unit should be located where it is easy to see and control – but the recommendation was not followed in this 1999 model.

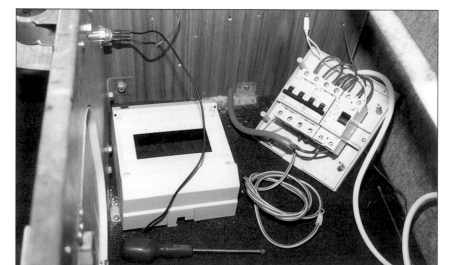

A short adaptor lead is needed before you can couple your caravan's hook-up lead to the domestic 13A three-pin socket fitted on most leisure generators.

The Sterling Pro PowerQ from Road Pro is an inexpensive 350Watt modified sine wave inverter whose output suits most caravanners' 230V needs.

Portable Generators

In a remote location a generator can be extremely useful; but on a crowded site its noise is undoubtedly intrusive.

In the previous chapter the subject of damage to switched-mode battery chargers as a result of generator power surges was fully explained. Equally it was pointed out that the latest Honda EU 10i and EU 20i generators incorporate the Company's pioneering inverter technology circuitry which creates a smooth output and is claimed to meet the needs of all types of sensitive mains appliances.

Unlike the industrial, noisier generators, these portable leisure products are normally fitted with a domestic-type 13A socket. This means you'll need to purchase an adaptor before you can couple your hook-up lead.

Also required is some type of generator cover for use when it's raining. Several products are available, and a 'mini tent' from Sew and So's is particularly neat because its edges can be folded down and then zipped so that the cover becomes a generator carrying bag.

In conclusion, when a leisure generator is used with thoughtful care and a polite regard for neighbours it can be particularly useful. This is especially true if you prefer to use remote farm locations that often aren't equipped with mains hook-up points. However, if you are intending to purchase a generator in order to operate a microwave oven, check the advice in the accompanying technical tip panel.

Inverters

Another way to gain mains power is to draw current from the 12V system and to convert it into a 230V supply using an inverter. Products like the Sterling inverters from RoadPro and PRO Watt models are two well-respected product ranges; however, there are many other makes on sale.

Permanently installing an inverter is usually straightforward. It should be located near the battery, fixed securely and connected to the live and neutral battery terminals. The device can then run mains appliances providing their wattage doesn't exceed the rating of the inverter. Larger inverters designed to run high wattage appliances are also available in the Driftgate 2000 and Sterling ranges.

Without doubt, where lighting and low wattage appliances are concerned, an inverter is excellent, but its supplying battery effectively limits the possibilities. For example a 250W inverter – even if 100% efficient – would draw more than 20A from a battery when working to its limit. In consequence a 60Ah battery would be completely discharged in less than three hours.

Note: *In practice, no inverter is 100% efficient, so the discharge rate is also affected by unavoidable power loss. Also note the Tip Box referring to 'wave forms'.*

On the other hand, you often want to use an appliance for a short spell and since a sound battery has a self-recovery element, using an item like a hair dryer or shaver is unlikely to create difficulties. Even comparatively high wattage appliances can be used briefly with some inverters without necessarily discharging a battery totally.

To enjoy the benefits of mains lighting, and to run low wattage appliances, the value of an inverter is unquestioned – especially if you have a 120Ah battery in your caravan.

It is common nowadays for manufacturers to equip caravans with a microwave oven, but their quoted output ('cooking power') is far less than the input needed for their operation.

Water systems

In order to carry out servicing, repairs and precautionary winterising jobs, it is important to know how a caravan's supply and waste systems work.

Like many services in a modern caravan, the water system has become increasingly sophisticated. Electrically driven pumps are standard nowadays and nearly all new caravans have a hot and cold water supply.

At the same time, some features are disappointing. Even when a high quality pump is fitted, the connecting supply pipes cannot always be described as 'state of the art' plumbing.

In waste water systems, for example, it is not unusual for water to empty from a sink or basin at a sluggish rate – a feature that can so easily be improved. Curing a problem like this is discussed later and recommendations for improvements are proposed throughout the chapter.

Moreover, to ensure that owners of a wide range of models can identify the system they have fitted, the chapter also looks at the different components installed over the last 40 years or so.

Fresh water supply

As caravans became more sophisticated, one of the changes was the move away from manually operated pumps. Electric pumps are now a standard feature. This change was prompted by a desire to provide hot – as well as cold – water at the sink, coupled with a decision to introduce hot showers in caravans. Running a shower is not something that can be achieved using a footpump!

Notwithstanding the benefit of these creature comforts, the earlier manual systems undoubtedly had their merits.

Pre-electric systems

Some 1970s caravans are still in use and very few will be fitted with an electric pump or a water heater. These 'cold water' caravans rely either on a hand-operated pump mounted on the sink – like the Whale Flipper, or a foot pump fitted at floor level – like the Whale Tiptoe model.

In the case of foot-operated products, water is delivered from a faucet – the name given to a permanently-open outlet. This is different from a tap which has a mechanical system for physically arresting the flow of water.

As a rule, hand or foot pumps are very reliable and continue to be used in cabin cruisers as well as caravans. Parts are therefore available for the more popular models. As regards the rest of the system, it merely comprises the supply pipe – though there may also be a non-return valve fitted near the input point.

A non-return valve is a small component fitted within a run of pipe. It is connected up so that water will only pass in one direction, namely towards the sink outlet. Its purpose is to prevent water from draining back through the system every time you stop using the pump.

If we look at the pipe needed in a system driven by a foot pump, there are only two lengths. These are:

- a feed pipe to the pump that couples to the inlet point on the caravan,
- a run from the output side of the pump to the faucet on the sink.

The sheer simplicity of the system is its attraction. Anyone owning an older model who uses sites equipped with a washroom and who doesn't mind boiling a kettle to get washing-up water might be advised to make no changes to the arrangement. There is hardly anything to go wrong in a cold water system.

Electrically pumped systems

Hot and cold systems require *many* more components. These include:

- an inlet socket,
- a non-return valve,
- an electric pump,
- a battery to power the pump (*see* Chapter 7),
- a switch to activate the pump,
- a pipe system,
- a drain down point,
- a water heater (*see* Chapter 10),
- taps and shower controls.

This is a simplification, however, and several *different* types of electric pump are in use. Accordingly this has an influence on the type of inlet socket fitted. Equally there are three types of switches for setting a pump in motion. These are:

This inlet with integrated filter, introduced into the Truma Ultraflow water range in 2006, was installed on some 2007 caravans.

....

- a button switch (e.g. Whale BS7204) or a foot switch (e.g. Whale FS7210). In practice these are seldom used;
- switches built into each tap – one for hot, one for cold and referred to as 'microswitches';
- a pressure-sensitive switch located in one of three places – fitted in a supply pipe, integrated within an inlet socket, or built into the pump.

Although these are the main features fitted in caravans, you will often come across other arrangements as follows:

Winter inlet
Some owners fit an additional water input point inside a caravan so that the water container can be brought indoors when caravanning in sub zero temperatures. *Carver* used to supply an installation kit for this winterising arrangement. The water container would be placed in the shower tray and the alternative input mounted on one of the internal walls in the washroom. When two inputs are created you need to fit a blocking plug into the one not being used.

Direct coupling pitches
Using this system you can connect up permanently to a water supply point that exclusively supplies your pitch. The provision is appearing on a growing number of large caravan parks and a special coupling hose is all that's needed to take advantage of the service. For instance, the Whale 'Aqua Source' includes an adaptor so you can couple into either a Whale Watermaster Socket or a Carver Compact inlet. The product has a pressure-reducing valve so the mains supply won't damage the couplings in the caravan's plumbing system. Equally, when the Carver 'Waterline' inlet became unavailable the Truma Waterline continued in its place.

Note: *The supply hose is fitted **in place of** a submersible pump, and taps provide water using mains pressure just like at home. However, if your caravan is fitted with an inboard diaphragm pump the coupling cannot normally be used unless the pipework is modified to bypass this component.*

Winter inlet conversion proposed by Carver in the 1990s

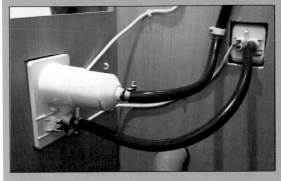

1. The additional socket on the right is mounted on an interior wall of the shower compartment.

2. When there's frost outside, the water container is placed in the shower tray.

3. A blocking plug has to be fitted on the exterior socket before water is drawn from the inlet inside the caravan.

Since an increasing number of sites are fitting water taps to serve individual pitches, some caravanners use direct coupling systems like this.

The early Whale 'Aqua Source' direct coupling only fitted Watermaster inlets; later versions had an adaptor to fit Carver Compact inlet fittings too.

An inboard water tank is fitted on the 1999 Bessacar Cameo.

Inboard water tank

For several years the manufacturers of some 'up-market' UK caravans dispensed with the idea of using external water containers and followed the Continental practice of installing a fixed tank indoors. The 1999 Bessacarr Cameo was one example. However, it is usually very inconvenient to tow a caravan to a water supply point for topping-up the tank, so owners either purchase a long hose to reach distant taps or take a portable water container for replenishment. Frankly, this rather defeats the object of the exercise so Avondale introduced a combined system.

Using a Shurflo external wall coupling and an internal diaphragm pump, Avondale first started fitting combined water systems on its Landranger models.

The combined system in this Bailey Senator has an instruction label to show which 'open' and 'close' combinations of the manual control valves are needed to achieve the three pumping options available.
(Photographs courtesy of Bailey Caravans)

Combined systems

To provide owners of Landranger caravans with the best of both systems, Avondale introduced a fresh water supply facility which included an inboard diaphragm pump, a fixed tank, and an external wall inlet for coupling-up to a portable water container. This system used a pump and wall coupling made by Shurflo.

Shortly afterwards Whale developed a similar facility and this has been installed in Bailey Senator models as shown below. The arrangement incorporates manual valves for controlling and diverting water and Bailey has affixed a clear diagram alongside the pump to illustrate how to select the operating mode you want to engage. The pumping alternatives are as follows:

1. You can operate the internal pump to draw water from an external water container to serve your caravan in the usual manner.
2. You can alter the valves so that the internal pump draws water from an external container and directs it into the inboard tank.
3. Moving the valves into a third configuration allows the pump to draw water from the inboard tank; a supply container outside isn't needed.

Note: *Whale also offers electrically-operated valves and a remote control panel which can be fitted in place of the manual levers.*

Although this supply system might seem complicated, it offers several benefits. For example, the facility is especially appropriate for owners who use their caravan in frosty conditions. An external portable container is only used briefly to top up the tank, and since this is fitted indoors its contents are far less likely to freeze.

Of course, water is heavy (one litre weighs a kilogram; one gallon weighs 10lb) so a caravan should never be towed when there's water remaining in its internal tank. Apart from adding considerable weight to the outfit, a part-filled tank creates serious instability as the water swirls around inside.

Taste filters

In recognition of the unpalatable characteristics of some types of tap water, many caravans are fitted with a taste filter. This should not be confused

Filter systems

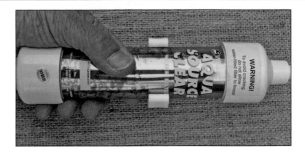

The Whale Aqua Source Clear has to be fitted into the water supply hose or plastic pipe; its narrow diameter is ideal in tight places.

Since Carver ceased trading, Truma UK has continued to supply some of the replacement components including the in-line 50 Carver Crystal filter.

Some of Carver's wall-mounted inlets house taste filters which need a removal key, or you can cut a slot in the end of a hardwood batten.

The filter on a Carver Crystal Mark III inlet can be removed by hand but strong fingers are needed to disengage the 'O' ring connections.

The Truma Ultraflow system includes two types of wall-mounted inlet; this model includes a housing to accommodate Truma's taste filter.

Since a filter intercepts a variety of water-borne items, it's essential it gets replaced periodically. The Truma inlet includes a reminder dial.

If you have an internal diaphragm pump rather than a submersible, Whale offers this AquaSmart filter for water containers with a wide neck.

If a caravan has a high output diaphragm pump, fitting a Nature Pure Ultra fine filter purifies water as well as improving its taste.

with the grit filter fitted on many pumps. Nor should it be confused with water treatment units in which bacteria are killed by an infra red lamp or by a sophisticated intercepting filter. Taste filters are normally fitted with charcoal and they must be changed at periodic intervals.

There are many different types of taste filter, some of which are clipped into a run of supply pipe like the Whale Aqua Source Clear, whereas others are mounted in a housing that forms part of the wall-mounted coupling inlet. Filters in the former Carver range have continued to be supplied and labelled by Truma, and this service was still being operated in 2008. Replacement spare filters include: Crystal 1 and 2, Crystal 3, and Crystal in-line 50.

The photo panel above shows some of the more popular filter systems.

Handy tip

If you cannot obtain a purpose-made key to unscrew a Carver cartridge filter from the inlet housing, cut a wide slot in the end of a hardwood batten to engage with its release flange.

On many older caravans it is not unusual to find a GP74 electric pump coupled up with a GP51 foot pump.

Centrifugal pumps

One of the earlier types of electric pumps is the Whale GP74. The Mk5 version weighs only 245 grams (8oz) and can achieve a maximum output of 11 litres (2.42 gallons) per minute. This is normally fitted in a cupboard below the sink and it is a type of pump that has to be primed before it delivers water.

Priming means that air has to be expelled from the casing and water introduced in its place before pumping can take place. Once primed, a small paddle wheel or 'impeller' then pushes water along the supply pipe and a good flow rate is usually achieved.

Devices using an impeller are often referred to as 'centrifugal pumps' – or by the more descriptive title, 'pusher pumps'. These are not used solely in caravans. For example a centrifugal pump with an impeller is normally used for emptying a domestic washing machine. However, since the pump is installed below a washing machine's drum, the effect of gravity means water being emptied from the machine dispels air in the pump automatically. In a caravan where a GP74 pump is fitted, you could achieve the same effect by putting your fresh water container on the roof.

This is completely impracticable, of course, so

caravans fitted with a GP74 pump also have a foot pump alongside such as the Whale GP51.

Every time air gets into the system – such as during towing, or if you draw every bit of water from your water container – you need to operate the foot pump to re-prime the pump. This should only require a few foot strokes, after which the system will keep on working until air is pulled into the pump again.

The system was fitted in many early 1980s caravans and one of its advantages is that if the auxiliary battery completely discharges, you can still pump water to the taps using the foot pump on its own. This is because water can be driven *through* the casing of a centrifugal pump, even when its impeller is stationary. This is not the case with diaphragm pumps (the self-priming devices mentioned later).

In spite of the benefits offered by an inboard electric pump such as the GP74, it is no longer fitted in new caravans. The submersible pump has taken its place.

Submersible pumps

The previous section has explained the purpose of pump-priming, and the characteristics of a centrifugal or 'pusher pump'. In effect the submersible pump is much the same as the inboard GP74 previously described.

For instance the casing of both pumps houses 12V electric motor which drives a small impeller or 'paddle wheel', protected by a filter.

The clever feature about submersible units, however, is the fact that they become automatically 'primed' merely by dropping them into a water container, but occasionally air bubbles can get caught in the casing and water doesn't flow as it should – a point explained in the box below.

Without doubt, a good quality submersible pum

Since the mid-1980s, most UK caravans have submersible pumps; versions of Whale Watermaster Premium and Highflow pumps fit Truma Crystal II, Truma Compact, and Whale inlet sockets.

Although there's a filter on submersible pumps, grass, dust and dirt can get through the mesh; prise it off occasionally to check nothing's crept underneath.

Technical tip

When a submersible pump is lowered into a water container, air bubbles sometimes remain caught in the casing. Even though the motor turns at its usual speed, you find that water isn't delivered at the taps.

To dislodge the bubbles, disconnect the feed pipe from the caravan's input coupling where this is possible. Keeping the pump below the surface of the water, swing the feed pipe so that the unit bumps several times against the side of the water container. This helps to dislodge trapped air which is then released through the upper end of the disconnected hose or from the lower end of the pump.

Trapped air is not unusual and in newer submersible units like the Whale 881, an air release hole has now been included in the top of the casing.

will give unfailing service for many years. However, cheap units have been supplied in the past in a bid to keep caravan prices down. The problem with low quality pumps is that if the casing becomes damaged, water finds a way in and ruins the electrical components. Successful repairs are seldom possible and the product has to be thrown away.

For this reason, anyone embarking on a long and important holiday abroad is always advised to take a spare. If your pump fails while you're away, finding a replacement with the correct type of coupling is often very difficult.

As regards the coupling-up procedure, the favoured system today is to have a socket mounted in the wall of the caravan and a mating plug on the feed pipe from the pump. When withdrawing the connection it may demand a firm pull. This is because there are both electrical terminals to release as well as a leak-free water connection. To ensure there are no leaks, a rubber 'O' ring is fitted and this is why the coupling is tight.

Having a detachable pump is current practice. However, around 1990 many caravans were fitted with Carver's Mk1 Crystal system. It features a permanently connected roll-away double core hose. Water flows along one channel, the electric cables run through the other. When leaving a pitch, there's nothing to disconnect and the whole unit is simply rolled up and stowed in a compartment fitted in the side of the van. It's a clever idea although repeatedly rolling up the hose eventually leads to damage.

This type of double hose is sometimes stocked by dealers and Whale use a similar product on some of their pumps too. On the other hand, if they decide to dispense with the roll-up, fixed hose idea, some owners fit a replacement inlet which takes a detachable pump complete with hose and coupling.

To help in these circumstances, Carver used to sell blanking plates to reduce the size of an aperture if necessary, but these are now hard to track down. Today, therefore, owners renovating an old caravan and needing to fit a smaller inlet point would probably need to create a blanking cover themselves, using sheet plastic cut to size.

Booster pump upgrade

A product that few caravanners are aware of is a booster pump, such as the Whale Superline 99. At first sight, this looks like a submersible pump except that it has an inlet nozzle at one end of the casing and an outlet at the other. Since it features an electric motor which drives an impeller, the pump has to be primed before it can push water through its casing.

Operating on its own, the Superline 99 has a maximum output of 12.3 litres (2.7 gallons) per minute and fits into very restricted spaces. Provided it is used in conjunction with a foot pump for priming, it can take the place of the slightly bulkier GP74.

When renovating an older caravan many owners fit new water inlets, although these often require alterations to the original aperture.

However, a particular strength is its ability to work *in conjunction with* a submersible pump. By fitting it within the water supply pipe and by connecting it up to the same switched supply cable that activates the submersible unit, the two units will operate together. This can boost an otherwise sluggish flow – though a better strategy might be to dispense with centrifugal pumps altogether and to fit a high quality diaphragm pump.

Diaphragm pumps

More expensive caravans are often fitted with a self-priming diaphragm pump rather than a submersible unit. Instead of its electric motor operating an impeller (i.e. a paddle wheel), it drives what is known as a 'wobble plate'. As this plate revolves, it bears against tiny pistons which are pushed back and forth in turn. Adjacent diaphragms follow the movement and operate a valve assembly.

The reciprocating action of the pistons is very small – usually around 3mm – so it is essential that grit doesn't get into the mechanism. This is why a diaphragm pump is always fitted with a grit filter and its gauze should be periodically inspected and cleaned as shown in the photographs below and overleaf.

Diaphragm pumps are well-engineered products and are considerably more expensive

Removing the grit filter from a Whale Clearstream pump

1. A wide-bladed screwdriver is used to undo the filter cover on the Clearstream pump. It is usually a tight fit.

2. The gauze is easily removed for cleaning – and the water pipe does not have to be disturbed.

Removing the grit filter from a Whale Evenflow pump

1. On an Evenflow pump, the hose has to be disconnected from the filter.

2. When a plastic collar has been removed, the two sections of the filter housing can be parted.

3. The mesh filter is seated in the middle of the casing.

The Shurflo Trail King filter

The clear plastic filter on a Shurflo pump is screwed on to its inlet socket.

than submersibles. Normally they give fault-free service although there are after-sales repair and overhaul facilities to cure problems that can arise. For instance, Leisure Accessories undertakes repairs of Shurflo pumps, a product manufactured in the United States, and also the POSIflo range. There's a similar service offered by Whale Pumps for the Evenflow, Clearstream, Smartflo and AquaSmart models. Parts for Fiamma pumps can be ordered by caravan dealers from the wholesaler, Nova Leisure.

If you do find the motor doesn't operate, carry out the following check procedure before sending the pump away for repair:

1 Check the pump switch on the main control panel is *on*.
2 Switch on some of the other 12V appliances to confirm the battery hasn't become totally discharged. Even better – put a meter on the battery terminals to confirm its condition.
3 If the control panel has a separate fuse for the water pump, check that it hasn't 'blown'.
4 Open a couple of taps to ensure the switching is activated and leave them open.
5 Locate the pump and see if there's an in-line fuse on its live lead. Inspect the fuse and change if necessary.

6 Put a test lamp across the terminals of the pump – or better still, use a meter.
7 If the power is definitely reaching the pump, then it can be deduced that it is the motor that requires attention. Using the appendix address list at the back of this book, contact the supplier to find out about repair services.

Note: *If the motor operates, your supply vessel is full, but no water is delivered at the taps, it might be caused because a sealing 'O' ring in the pump chamber is perished, stretched or damaged. If air gets into certain parts of the assembly, a pumping action cannot take place. Sealing washers can fail occasionally and this is not an unusual source of pumping problems.*

The diagram opposite shows the components in a typical Shurflo unit and spares are available. However, repair work is not normally a DIY option. It is true that dismantling this type of pump is fairly straightforward but putting it all back together again can be a particularly testing task!

As regards performance, diaphragm pumps are impressive. For instance, the open flow rate of a Whale Aquasmart pump is 5.5 litres per minute and the maximum lift is 3m (10ft). The open flow rate of a Whale Smartflo pump is 8 litres per minute; and the maximum lift is also 3m (10ft).

Another benefit is that if the motor is left running accidentally and in a dry state, it is unlikely to overheat. This is not the case with a submersible pump which is soon damaged if left running.

However, there are disadvantages, too. Unlike in-line and submersible non-priming pumps, it is not possible to drive water through the chambers of a diaphragm pump. This means you cannot fit a back-up foot pump to provide an alternative service if the battery fails.

Equally, when preparing for winter, a diaphragm pump will not permit water in the pipework on the 'tap side' of the system to be drained off via a low level drain cock. In other words, to release residual water from 'upstream' pipes, you either need to fit a second drain cock or disconnect the supply pipes on the outlet side of the pump. You can generally

Technical tip

If a diaphragm pump seems unduly noisy, this is often caused because the mounting screws on its base are driven in so tightly that the rubber feet become compressed. The result of this is that the base on which the pump is mounted acts like a sounding board and amplifies the noise – a principle used to full effect on many electric guitars.

To solve this, loosen the fixing screws a little, or if necessary, order some replacement rubber feet. Don't try to suppress the noise by wrapping the pump with an insulating material; this could lead to overheating.

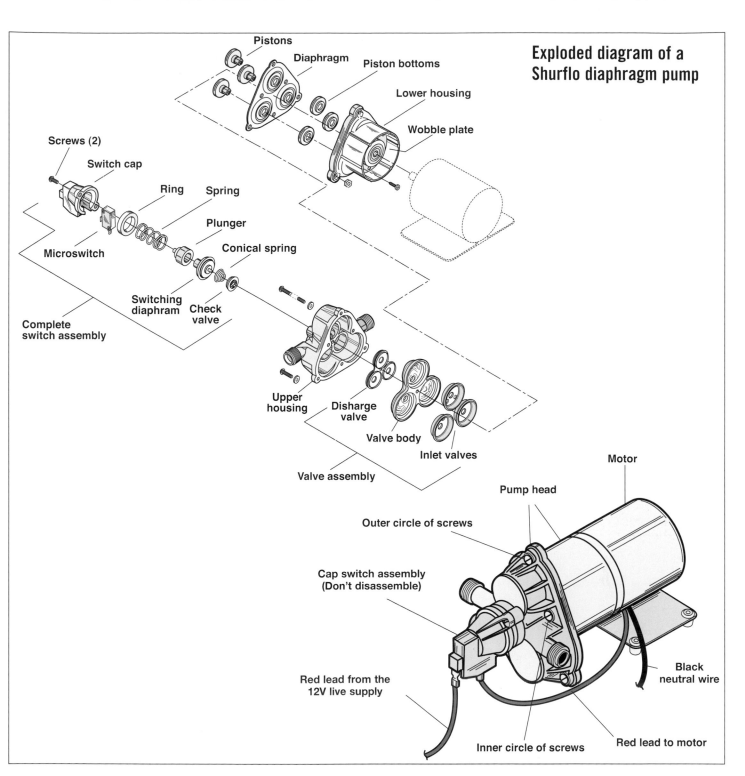

Exploded diagram of a Shurflo diaphragm pump

Pistons
Diaphragm
Piston bottoms
Lower housing
Wobble plate

Screws (2)
Switch cap
Ring
Spring
Plunger
Conical spring
Microswitch
Switching diaphram
Check valve
Complete switch assembly

Upper housing
Disharge valve
Valve body
Inlet valves
Valve assembly

Motor
Pump head
Outer circle of screws
Cap switch assembly (Don't disassemble)
Red lead from the 12V live supply
Inner circle of screws
Red lead to motor
Black neutral wire

confirm which is the outlet connection by reference to a flow direction arrow moulded on the casing.

Noisy operation is another regular complaint and the tip box opposite explains how this can often be reduced.

Finally, the delivery of water is sometimes subject to surges because the motor might produce irregular pulses due to battery condition. To resolve this, a surge damper is often built into the pipe supply. This helps to smooth out the flow of water and if you fit one yourself, make sure it is mounted vertically with its connection at the bottom.

All major parts are available to repair a Shurflo pump and the manual gives exploded diagrams and part number listings *(courtesy of Leisure Accessories Ltd)*.

To create a smooth delivery of water, a diaphragm pump often needs to be supported by a surge damper; the Whale damper *must be* mounted vertically as shown.

Pump switching

The two most common ways to switch a pump motor into operation have been mentioned earlier. As a general rule, caravans fitted with submersible pumps usually have a microswitch fitted within the tap assembly – though there are exceptions.

To confirm that a water pump is activated by microswitches in the taps, look under the sink or basin. Normally there will be microswitches on both the hot and cold supplies so look for one pair of cables connected to the microswitch for the cold tap outlet and a second pair of cables serving the microswitch on the hot tap.

The alternative system for activating pump operation involves the installation of a pressure sensitive switch, which is normally situated in one of three places:

1. Within the mechanism of a diaphragm pump as shown in the photograph below.
2. In-line – meaning the switch unit is mounted within one of the main supply pipes.
3. As an integral part of a wall connection socket – as in the case of the Whale Watermaster coupling.

As a point of interest, there is no obligation to use the pressure-sensitive switch in Whale's Watermaster unit. Other terminals on the product allow a coupled submersible pump to be triggered by a microswitch on the tap instead. In other words, if your caravan has one of these wall-mounted inlets it is possible to make a change from one type of switching to the other without too much alteration to the wiring.

The operating principle of a pressure-sensitive switch is described in the box opposite. In addition there are two further points to keep in mind.

1. The sensitivity of the switch is usually adjustable to compensate for a battery losing its power and also to reduce sensitivity in a supply system that has tiny air leaks in some of the pipe connections.
2. The slightest drop in pressure in the water pipes will often cause a pump motor to trip into action for two or three strokes. This can be rather distracting, especially at night, so the caravan manufacturer normally includes a pump isolating switch – usually mounted on the 12V fused distribution and control unit. It thus becomes a habit to turn off the pump last thing before going to bed.

Microswitching versus pressure – sensitive switching

So which is the better system – pressure-sensitive switching or a microswitch arrangement? In truth, neither is fault-free. The false 'tripping' of pressure-sensitive switches has already been mentioned; also microswitches sometimes get damp in the casing and the motor is switched into action without even turning the tap.

Different locations of pressure-sensitive switches

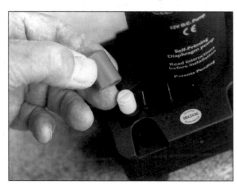

1. Within the pump: Adjusting point on a Whale Clearstream pump.

2. Within the pump: Screw hidden by silicone on a Whale Evenflow.

3. Within the pump: Centre screw (of five) on a Shurflo Trail King.

4. In-line: Whale pressure switch with adjusting wheel on top.

5. In wall socket: There's switching in this Whale Watermaster inlet.

6. In wall socket: Setting adjustment screw on a Watermaster inlet.

Pressure loss

A pressure-sensitive switch is able to detect a drop of pressure in the water supply pipes.

As soon as the tap is turned, the opening creates a loss of pressure in the pipes which is detected at once, whereupon the pump is automatically set in motion. This generally works well. However, a small pressure loss can also occur at a faulty connection in one of the pipes. This might not be serious enough to cause a water leak, but it sends a false message to the pump which briefly comes to life.

Locating the leak and re-forming the joint is the best answer, but you can often cure the problem by making an adjustment to the setting control on the switch to make it less sensitive.

Caravanners often report that their battery becomes mysteriously discharged whenever they've been out for the day. Not unusually this is because the pump has been running intermittently and unnoticed for prolonged spells due to false switching.

Changing a faulty microswitch fitted to the side of a tap is shown in the sequence photographs on this page. It is much easier on recent designs of tap even though gaining access beneath a sink or basin demands a measure of human flexibility. With this in mind, it is pleasing that changing a microswitch on Elite taps from Whale is wholly done from above the worktop.

Taps

In some of the latest caravans, taps look much the same as the fittings used at home. However, if the flow rate on a pump is modest, full-size domestic taps are rather disappointing when delivering water.

In reality, smaller and less pretentious fittings are used in the majority of caravans and these

Handy tip

Many caravans have a double tap system for the hot and cold water supply. If a microswitch fails on one of the supplies – let's say it's the hot supply that cannot be switched into operation – you can sometimes temporarily solve this by 'cheating the system'. This is how you do it:

1. Open the hot tap a generous amount. Nothing will come out because we've established the microswitch has failed.
2. Now, very gently turn the neighbouring cold tap (or any other tap in the caravan for that matter) listening for a tiny click to indicate its switch is activated.
3. Don't open this tap any further – it just needs enough to trigger the microswitch.

Hey presto! The pump will be set in motion but the water will come from the hot tap which was opened a generous amount.

Changing the microswitch on a Whale Elegance mixer tap

1. Reaching under the sink, locate and slip off the rectangular spring collar.

2. Leave the terminals in place, but ease the switch from its mounting pillars.

3. When you are in a more comfortable position, detach the electrical terminals – they can be fitted either way round.

4. The forefinger shows the tiny switch button on the casing; modern microswitches are usually sealed units.

Changing the microswitch on a Whale Elite mixer tap

1. To take off the operating lever, remove the hot/cold indicator to reveal an attachment screw.

2. With the tap lever removed, lift off the switch activating plate, *noting its position very carefully*.

3. Use a small screwdriver to prise the microswitch from its location.

4. Ease the switch clear, so that the connecting terminals can be reached.

On older taps, the design included a soft connecting hose that was squeezed by a clamp to arrest the flow of water.

The disadvantage with flexible hose is that kinks easily develop.

Handy tip

If your caravan has a microswitching system and the pump doesn't operate when one of the taps is turned on, there's an easy way to establish if the fault lies in the switch. This presumes the tap is one where the terminals for the switching cables are easily accessible and you've established that the pump is activated when any of the other taps are used.

1. Ensure that the pump circuit is switched on at the main control panel.
2. Disconnect the two wires that go to the faulty tap.
3. Touch their terminal tags together whereupon the pump should immediately respond.

In effect you are simply doing the job of a switch by creating continuity in the supply cables. If the pump still doesn't respond, you've established that the microswitch cannot be blamed for the fault.

display a more appropriate feeling of scale. It is interesting to note that the Elite taps from Whale adopt a lever operating system – currently fashionable in domestic situations – but these are appropriately scaled down to suit the caravan setting.

As regards principles of operation, whenever there is more than one tap in the system, each unit must have a physical means of arresting the flow of water. Whilst a faucet is fine for a single outlet, as described earlier, you cannot fit two faucets in a caravan since both would deliver water at once whenever the pump starts to operate.

To achieve a mechanical closure, taps used in the 1980s have a short length of soft hose connected to the delivery nozzle. This is merely pinched by a sliding bar in the same way you would pinch the neck of a balloon to prevent it losing air. It seems rather rudimentary, but it works surprisingly well. Since then, more sophisticated mechanisms have been employed.

On taps which operate a microswitch to activate the water pump, the best examples are those where changing the switch is straightforward. On a few imported taps, the microswitches are sealed inside the unit. This is wholly unsatisfactory because if one of the microswitches fails, the entire tap unit has to be replaced.

Pipes and fittings

One of the most disappointing features in a fresh water supply system is the use of flexible hose and clipped joints. Whilst this may prove adequate in the short term, kinks often develop in pipe runs after several seasons. With the passing of time, hose becomes less flexible, kinks become permanent, and flow rates are affected.

Many caravanners then blame the pump for the poor flow of water. But if all the pipe runs are carefully checked, there will usually be a kink – typically at a point where the pipe has to negotiate a sharp corner. On older caravans, this frequently occurs where the pipe comes from underneath the 'van and takes a sharp upward turn through the floor.

Leaks can be another problem. Couplings formed using worm-drive clips (Jubilee clips), can have variable success. Where cheaper substitutes are used, the integrity of joints is often poor.

Several reputable caravan manufacturers still persist with this primitive form of plumbing which is surprising. A much better system is available. Semi-rigid plastic pipe and push-fit couplings have been available in the caravan industry for several seasons. But the product has a much longer history. Food quality semi-rigid pipe was used behind bars in pubs and clubs as long ago as the mid-1960s.

Now it is being used by some caravan manufacturers as well, though sadly not all. The system is not difficult to install and a range of components is available. Push-fit drain-down taps, in-line taste filters, right-angle channelling for preventing kinks, adaptors for linking up with traditional connections and a full range of couplings are available. Push-fit components are included in the water component ranges from both John Guest and Whale. A similar system was also used in ABI caravans several seasons ago although the 10mm bore size of the pipe was narrower than Whale's 12mm product.

Replacing flexible hose with semi-rigid pipe is an improvement job that many DIY owners

Using black 90° channelling from the John Guest product range, semi-rigid pipe is supported and doesn't kink on sharp bends.

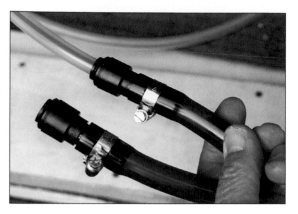

Adaptor couplings can be purchased in order to combine sections of flexible hose with semi-rigid pipe.

successfully carry out. If it proves easier to retain part of an orginal hose system because of access problems, you can fit a combined arrangement using adaptor couplings.

Waste water removal

Criticisms of the plumbing for waste water were voiced at the beginning of the chapter. There is no doubt that the rigid PVCu waste and cistern overflow pipes available from a builders' merchant provide a much better system than one constructed with a narrow flexible hose. Indeed a domestic pipe was used under the sinks of Vanroyce caravans before production ceased. There was also a domestic-type water trap for keeping smells in the pipe from seeping into the caravan. It is most pleasing that an idea described and illustrated in the First Edition of this manual in 1993 was adopted several years later by Vanroyce designers. However, rigid waste pipes are not often fitted in touring caravans and are more likely to be seen in coachbuilt motorhomes.

The long-running tradition in touring caravans has been to fit 19mm (¾in) convoluted flexible hose, and its pronounced ridges on the inside catch grains of rice, peas, and other water-borne debris. During a winter lay-up this decays, with

Frost damage

Many caravans are not built with a drain-down tap in the supply system, so frost can cause damage to pipe joints or key components e.g. an in-board pump. Since residual water is held in pipes on account of the system's non-return valve it is therefore necessary to disconnect a pipe to drain off the water before the onset of winter.

Fitting a Whale drain-down tap is a much better answer and this should be positioned 'upstream' of the non-return valve. As a rule, these one-way valves are usually situated near the main input point. Moreover, in a caravan fitted with a diaphragm pump, a drain-down tap is needed on the 'up-stream' side of the pump as well, for reasons explained in the earlier section describing these units.

When parking-up a caravan before the start of frosty weather, always leave the taps and the shower control open. If there's residual water remaining in a downturn loop of pipe, it will expand when it freezes. This expansion then causes a build-up of pressure in the pipe, which puts components and couplings at risk. Leaving taps open provides pressure release points, without which bad damage can occur, as shown in the photograph. Moreover, as pointed out on page 199, lever taps *must* have their lifted lever aligned in the central position so that both hot and cold supply pipes are given a pressure relief outlet.

This lever-type shower control wasn't left open in a central position, and when residual water started freezing the increase in pressure was sufficient to split its casing apart.

the result that smells enter the caravan via the sink, basin and shower tray outlets.

Furthermore, if you look under caravans, you will often find the waste hose has pronounced sags between the fixing clips. This helps residual water to collect and stagnate.

Equally if you inspect the hose in kitchen and bathroom cupboards, you will sometimes see that sections of the run are installed with scarcely any fall. It is little wonder that water can be so slow to discharge from a sink or basin.

The waste hose in this 1999 caravan is level in places and its ridged construction will certainly trap food particles.

Internal ridges on cheap convoluted hose have a tendency to trap food particles, which later decay and cause smells.

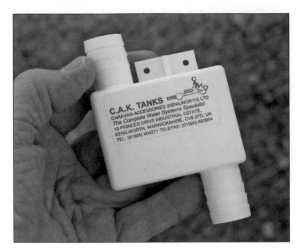

This compact trap was introduced by CAK accessories. A large range of adaptors is also available.

The trap from DLS Plastics, also available from CAK, has an interceptor bowl which is removable for cleaning.

To improve flow rates, some manufacturers now fit a larger waste hose with a 25mm (1in) diameter. In a few models you will also find rigid pipe, but it's seldom larger in diameter than the 25mm PVCu product used for the overflows of domestic toilet cisterns.

It's also disappointing that caravans are rarely equipped with Supaflex waste hose, which has a smooth lining inside; curiously it is frequently installed by motorhome manufacturers. The smooth surface inside this type of hose means that food particles are unlikely to get caught, so it's worth considering in a DIY improvement project. Supaflex is sold by CAK, which specialises in water components for caravans and operates a mail order service. In fact the highly informative CAK annual catalogue should be on every DIY caravanner's book shelf.

Another answer would be to fit a completely new waste water system using domestic PVCu rigid pipe; this is described in the final section of the chapter.

Water traps
In modern housing, unpleasant pipe smells are not able to enter our living spaces because sinks, washbasins and toilet pans have deep water traps or 'U' bends which act as odour barriers. The author started adopting this principle when revising waste systems in his caravan and motorhome sinks in the 1980s. As mentioned above, the idea was subsequently used in Vanroyce caravans in the late 1990s.

Even if you periodically use proprietary pipe and tank cleaning products like Wastemaster Supercleaner from F.L. Hitchman, caravan waste pipes often become smelly. That's why you should always put a plug in your sink, basin and shower tray if your caravan is left unused for long spells during the winter.

Fortunately some component manufacturers have also recognised the benefit of fitting water traps under sinks and basins in caravans, and two components have been introduced as shown above. Fitting these retrospectively is sometimes possible although it's usually necessary to fit pipe adaptors when coupling them up.

Direct waste water coupling
It was pointed out earlier that several caravan sites offer facilities which enable caravanners to couple-up directly to a standpipe tap. Similar provision is sometimes made for waste water discharge too. At the time of writing, the practice is still comparatively unusual but the accompanying photos show a direct coupled arrangement in operation.

A long piece of standard convoluted hose and a Y adaptor are coupled to the caravan.

Here the site owner has made two hose-sized inlets as part of the waste disposal point.

General improvements

A number of alterations can be made to either the fresh or waste water systems. Changing your pump or altering the pipe arrangement is unlikely to present problems.

Diaphragm pump upgrade

The quality of submersible pumps supplied with recent caravans has improved considerably but inboard diaphragm pumps offer a number of advantages. For example, to fit a General Ecology Ultra Fine Water purifier, you need the output of a good quality diaphragm pump to drive water through its complex filter. Bear in mind that this American purifier is capable of converting dirty canal water into pure, crystal clear and palatable drinking water.

Diaphragm pumps can also be repaired whereas submersible pumps are throw-away items. They're well engineered, and are the preferred choice in many 'up-market' caravans and motorhomes. If you fit one to replace a submersible model, alterations are going to be needed to the external coupling-up point. However, some owners retain the original coupling and merely cut the submersible unit away from its flexible feed hose.

In this DIY project a Whale diaphragm pump was installed with a Nature-Pure Ultrafine water purifier (middle) and a surge damper (right).

Compare the specifications before purchasing. This Whale Smartflo has an 8-litres-per-minute output and is designed for caravans with two outlets.

Points to note:

Cable size – As explained in Chapter 7, it's important to avoid voltage drops and you must use the type of flexible cable recommended by the manufacturer. Typically a diaphragm pump will be wired using 2.5mm² cable.

Fuse rating – Although there will be a fuse in a caravan's 12V control panel, check that this matches the pump specialist's recommendation. Some models have an in-line fuse holder near the pump and the rating of the fuse will be given in the instructions.

Filter – This is critically important for protecting the mechanism inside and there are several different types, as shown earlier. The pump should be installed where you can reach it easily for checking and cleaning the filter.

Flow direction – There is both an inlet and outlet coupling and you'll often see an arrow marked on the casing to show flow direction. A drain-down tap fitted to a T coupling is recommended on the upstream side.

Couplings – The manufacturers often include several types of coupling to fit the threaded connections, recognising that some caravans will have a flexible fresh-water hose whereas others are fitted with push-fit semi-rigid pipe.

Noise – The earlier technical tip box pointed out that some pumps appear noisy in operation but this is often caused by screwing down the unit so tightly that the rubber feet are over-compressed. The base then amplifies the noise.

Disabling switch – A pump disabling switch is needed, and it can prove helpful to operate this

before bedtime; sometimes a pressure-sensitive switch causes brief but occasional 'false starts', and this can be distracting.

Pressure sensitive control – Most diaphragm pumps have a built-in pressure-sensitive mechanism. The instructions should explain this more clearly and provide details about the way pump activation can be fine-tuned.

Surge damper – Sometimes the flow of water from a tap can be irregular and the motor runs in a pulsing manner. This is usually solved by fitting a surge damper, which smoothes out irregularities in the flow.

Warning: *Anyone tackling this job needs an understanding of basic caravan wiring, and cables which supplied the original pump will have to be connected differently. For instance, diaphragm pumps are usually operated by a pressure-sensitive switch, whereas the pump being replaced may have been activated by microswitches in the taps. A wiring diagram for the new pump should be included in the installation instructions.*

Semi-rigid pipe with push-fit couplings

This is much better than a hose-and-clip system, which is susceptible to kinked hose and leaking connections. Good quality stainless steel worm-drive clips (e.g. 'Jubilee' clips) are reliable but some manufacturers save pennies by fitting poorer quality versions. With push-fit couplings, this problem doesn't arise and a connection is

To create good joints, the end of a pipe must be cut squarely; an inexpensive tool for the job is sold by Whale.

Pipe is pushed into a coupling. There may be initial movement but keep pushing until it is fully home.

To detach pipe, a collar in the coupling is pushed inwards while you pull the pipe firmly out of the fitting.

These brass adaptors from Whale accept a flexible hose on one end; the other end pushes into pipe couplings.

normally very reliable. Conversely a connection is easily disengaged by depressing a small collar in the coupling (called a 'collet') at the same time as the pipe is pulled from the fitting.

If you decide to upgrade the fresh-water plumbing system in your caravan, it isn't always easy to reach all the hose fittings and connections. In this case, you can always retain the hard-to-reach hose runs and fit an adaptor to accept semi-rigid pipe where there's good accessibility.

The 'Quick Connect' semi-rigid pipe sold by Whale is referred in the catalogues as 'tubing' and it comes in 12mm, 15mm and 22mm external diameters. The 12mm version is usually fitted in caravans. There is also John Guest 'Speedfit', which is used in the building industry; this range includes 'cold forming' channelling (pictured on page 138), which ensures kinks will not develop when a pipe is taken around a 90° corner.

Warning: *More recently-manufactured 12mm semi-rigid pipe can jam when fitted into the older push-fit couplings made in the 1990s. It's wise to purchase modern products rather than mixing-and-matching old and new components.*

Upgrading taps

Caravan taps are much more attractive now than they used to be. If you are upgrading an older

caravan, choosing a new product is quite difficult and it helps to see examples already fitted and operating in a caravan before you spend a lot of money.

You also have to be certain that the worktop or basin where a new unit is going to be fitted offers sufficient space to accommodate its base. Furthermore, if you are replacing a traditional mixer tap with a single pillar lever tap like a Whale Elite model, the location might have a large hole which you'll need to cover with a filler plate. This was necessary in the project pictured below, in which a piece of thin plywood was used to cover two holes left in the worktop when the original taps were removed.

In addition you have to consider whether you're content to use a tap which incorporates microswitches in its housing. Equally you would want to check how easy these switches are to replace once the tap's been installed.

Finally you need to take into consideration the way the tap would be coupled to the hose or semi-rigid pipe that's already fitted in the 'van. The photos show some of these issues.

Warning: *Read the instructions with regard to winter precautions. Residual water sometimes gets left in taps and if this freezes it can cause irreparable damage. With a mixer tap operated by a lift-up lever, you must centralise and leave the lever lifted when a caravan's in store for the winter.*

Broken microswitches on the tap in this 1988 ABI couldn't be replaced, and to fit a lever tap required a ply plate.

Protective caps mark the hot and cold inlets and wires are connected to the microswitch hidden underneath the lever.

The Elite tap is made for push-fit pipe but this adaptor from Whale has a ribbed nozzle to make a hose and clip connection.

This brushed steel tap from Whale's marine range is supplied with twin braided tails underneath and couplings.

Waste water pipe upgrade

This project involves the installation of rigid 32mm (1¼in) PVCu pipe, which is available from most builders' and plumbers' merchants. It is sold with a wide range of fittings, and if installed with care and forethought you can create a waste system with a fall (i.e. a slope) throughout every part of the entire run. The reward for your time and thought is a system which allows water to discharge from a sink or a basin at a noteworthy rate.

Two features present potential problems. Firstly your existing caravan sink and basin will probably have a narrow diameter outlet and waste plug. It *is* possible to change this for a large diameter domestic outlet but with ABS plastic sinks this can be difficult to achieve. An easier solution is to retain the small outlet and to leave a short tail of the original hose as shown in the photographs.

A second problem is negotiating chassis members when creating a fall in the pipe below the floor. Fortunately AL-KO and BPW chassis have openings in the main members and these can be used to advantage.

With regard to the final discharge point where water has to drain into a waste container, it is wise to create a threaded end piece with protective cap so that vermin cannot find an entry point when the caravan is out of use. On the site, this can also be made to couple with a short removable spout which is angled into the waste container's inlet. As an alternative to a spout, you can buy a short length of car radiator hose which has a large enough diameter to fit over the end of the plastic pipe.

Before construction work begins it is *very* important to get your caravan parked level. From then onwards, each length of waste pipe is fixed with a fall and checked with a spirit level. This means that whenever your caravan is parked on a level pitch in future, your waste pipes will always have a slope throughout the entire pipe run.

When working under the floor, blocks of different thicknesses can be screwed and bonded to the ply using Sikaflex-512 Caravan to create a gentle slope in the pipe runs and to accept pipe brackets. Do *not* drill chassis members.

Warning: *You will find that most types of adhesive sold for bonding lengths of rainwater downpipe or PVCu waste pipe is easy to use, especially if it is sold with a brush in the lid. However, observe the instructions with care, recognising that the strong smell of this 'solvent weld' adhesive should not be inhaled in restricted areas. Some people find it addictive. Also remember to leave the system to dry for at least 24 hours before testing it out with water.*

Conclusion

Modern caravans have some impressive features and sophisticated appliances. Aspects of their plumbing systems, however, are often less impressive and this is an area of attention where a knowledgeable and careful DIY owner can carry out several worthwhile improvements.

When sections are cut, roughen the surface *and* the mating surface inside the couplings using emery cloth.

Apply solvent weld to both faces, insert the pipe fully, twist it back and forth once, and wipe off excess adhesive.

Some dummy 'dry runs' and pre-checks allow you to create larger sections which can be glued up on a workbench.

To couple the new system to old hose under a sink, leave a tail to drape inside a vertical run of the PVCu pipe.

10

Contents

Gas supply systems and appliances

Liquefied petroleum gas (LPG) is heavier than air, non-poisonous and easily transportable in purpose-made cylinders. It is a convenient fuel for cooking and heating but caravanners should be mindful of safety whenever the gas is used.

Even though a few caravan hobs are fitted with a 230V hotplate, liquefied petroleum gas (LPG) is the principal fuel used for cooking and heating. However, this is a highly flammable product, so the caravanner must observe all safety advice relating to its use. It also helps to understand some of the characteristics of LPG and to recognise the respective merits of the two types used by caravanners, namely butane and propane.

Characteristics of the gas

Many caravanners are surprised to learn that in its natural state, liquefied petroleum gas (LPG) is odourless. This could be a dangerous feature because leaks might pass unnoticed, so the suppliers add what is known as a 'stenching agent' and its unpleasant smell soon warns of a fault in the supply system.

Another important feature about LPG is that it is heavier than air. In other words if gas leaks from a faulty cylinder valve or a poor connection in a supply pipe it will start to accumulate at floor level. This is potentially very dangerous.

To ensure leaking gas escapes, low level ventilators are installed in caravans. There are also escape outlets referred to as 'drop out' holes situated directly under gas appliances. It is most important that these vents are kept unobstructed.

The same provision has to be made in gas cylinder lockers, and escape outlets *must* be situated at the lowest point of a storage compartment. Unfortunately some gas lockers have been constructed with vents in the access door, but not at the lowest point as they should have been. If gas were to seep from a faulty cylinder valve, this could have dangerous consequences.

A further point to recognise is that there are two

types of LPG: butane and propane, both of which are suitable for use in caravans. However, when changing from the liquefied form into vapour they attain different pressures. To ensure that a caravan's appliances are supplied with gas at the required pressure, a device called a 'regulator' is required.

Until recent developments in regulator design, gas supplied from a butane cylinder has required a butane-specific regulator; conversely, gas supplied from a propane cylinder has needed a propane-specific version. In 2003, however, a new type of regulator was introduced which could deal with either butane or propane; this is discussed later.

The two types of LPG are different in a number of other respects as well:

BUTANE

■ **Butane** has a higher calorific value than propane which means it is a more efficient heat producer. Accordingly butane is the preferred choice when conditions are suitable.

■ **Butane** does not change from its liquefied state to a gas vapour if temperatures fall below 0°C (32°F) at atmospheric pressure. For this reason it is not the preferred gas of winter caravanners.

■ **Butane** is heavier than propane. Although the smallest Calor Gas cylinders for the two products are the same size, the propane version holds 3.9kg (8.6lb) whereas an identically sized cylinder of butane holds 4.5kg (10lb) of liquefied gas.

PROPANE

■ **Propane** changes from a liquefied state into a gas in temperatures as low as −40°C – so it is ideal as a winter fuel. Regrettably, many Continental gas suppliers only seem to supply butane cylinders for leisure use, though some

The higher calorific value of butane makes it a more efficient heat producer than propane.

Since propane gas vaporises in much lower temperatures than butane, it is the preferred product for winter caravanning.

processing companies add a small quantity of propane to butane cylinders in order to give improved cold weather performance.

■ **Propane** in its liquefied state is lighter than butane. That is why in two cylinders of identical size, there is less propane by weight than butane.

■ **Propane** has a vapour pressure around five times that of butane and before the introduction of universal regulators in 2003 you had to fit a propane-specific regulator. This topic is discussed in more detail in a later section on pressure regulation.

The range of supplier-filled cylinders

In earlier editions of this Manual, only the products from Calor Gas Ltd and Campingaz were reviewed. Now there are several other specialists marketing gas cylinders for caravanning and other leisure uses and the sale of owner-refillable cylinders has also generated interest.

Notwithstanding these developments, Calor products are still a dominant force in both the UK domestic and leisure markets. For instance, large cylinders are supplied to home owners, although Calor's 19kg propane products are too heavy and bulky to transport in touring caravans. Remember, too, that a cylinder should never be transported horizontally, in order to prevent liquefied gas from seeping through the valve mechanisms.

Equally a gas cylinder should always be mounted securely in a caravan gas locker;

standing a cylinder outside a caravan is potentially dangerous and is strongly discouraged by the caravanning clubs. As regards the Calor Gas range of leisure industry products, these are listed in the table on page 147. It's an impressive array and it is a pity that Calor products cannot be purchased abroad.

In contrast, Campingaz is available in over 100 countries worldwide and cylinders are available in most European countries. But there are exceptions. Campingaz is not available in Finland or Sweden and is seldom stocked in Norway.

Also bear in mind that Campingaz cylinders only contain butane, which can present a problem for winter caravanners. It is believed that a small amount of Propane is added to improve performance in cold environments but this strategy is not revealed on the cylinders' markings. Furthermore, only the 907 cylinder is suitable to meet the typical consumption requirements in modern caravans. This is the *largest* cylinder in the Campingaz range and it only holds 2.72kg of butane: even the *smallest* butane cylinder in the Calor Gas range holds 4.5kg of butane.

Both Calor Gas and Campingaz continue to be popular in the UK, but choice increased further when BP introduced two 'Gas Light' cylinders in 2006. These are being marketed in conjunction with Truma UK and the corrosion-proof, glass fibre reinforced material used for the cylinders is claimed to be half the weight of an equivalent steel cylinder. Part of its structure is semi-transparent, too, so you can see the level of the LPG inside.

Even when thought to be empty, a cylinder might seep remnants of LPG through a control valve; so *never* transport one horizontally like this.

The 907 cylinder holding 2.72kg of butane is the only Campingaz cylinder of practicable use; the small 901 cylinder is intended for camping.

In some caravan lockers the smaller 5kg BP Gas Light cylinder is accommodated more easily than its taller partner.

Many caravanners purchase an adaptor to couple-up with the Gas Light cylinders' 27mm clip-on valves.

OWNER-REFILLABLE PORTABLE LPG CYLINDERS
Notwithstanding the cost-saving benefits of owner-refillable gas cylinders, both The Camping and Caravanning Club and The Caravan Club adopted a policy NOT to encourage members to invest in such equipment. There are concerns over the acceptability and safety of re-filling portable cylinders on an autogas forecourt; moreover, forecourt staff are seldom classed as 'competent' to carry out the task or give advice. This is likely to invalidate a Company's insurance.

Then in June 2007, a trade association known as the LPGas Association (since re-named UKLPG) also made the formal statement: *It is our advice that user owned (sic.), portable LPG cylinders should not be refilled at Autogas refuelling sites'.* This refers to cylinders which have to be removed from a caravan for refilling directly from the nozzle of an LPG pump. The Association then added:

Vessels which are attached to a vehicle for heating or cooking (on camper vans or similar) present similar risks on filling to those for propulsion purposes and may be permitted to be re-filled at Autogas refuelling sites provided they:
■ *remain in-situ for refilling; and*
■ *are fitted with a device to physically prevent filling beyond 80%; and*
■ *are connected to a fixed filling connection which is not part of the vessel.*

Fixed systems which meet these criteria are available from Gaslow International Ltd., MTH Gas Systems Ltd., and RPi Engineering.

Two sizes of Gas Light cylinders have been introduced holding 5kg and 10kg of propane respectively. However, some caravan lockers might not be able to accommodate the larger product, which is 587mm high; both have a diameter of 305mm. As regards coupling-up, Gas Light cylinders have a 27mm clip-on valve and many owners need to purchase an adaptor as shown above.

In response to the BP weight-saving initiative, Calor also launched a new lightweight cylinder in Autumn 2007. Known as the Calor Lite, this is filled with propane; it is made using recyclable lightweight steel and fitted with plastic handles.

The Calor Lite cylinder is also fitted with a level indicator which uses the float mechanism originally introduced in 2005 for use with the Company's Patio Gas propane cylinders.

Though slightly taller, Calor Lite 6kg cylinders are otherwise the same dimensions as existing 6kg Calor Gas 'heavy' cylinders; they also employ the screw-thread 'pole' couplings fitted on the Company's 3.9kg, 6kg and 13kg 'heavy' propane cylinders. When filled with 6kg of propane, a Calor Lite cylinder weighs a total of 10.52kg.

By comparison, the alloy collar on Calor's equivalent 'heavy' cylinder records a tare (i.e. cylinder-only) weight of 17lb 6oz – i.e. 7.88kg – and when added to the gas content (6kg) totals 13.88kg. In other words the new Calor Lite cylinder is 3.36kg (about 7.4lb) lighter than its big brother, which is a significant saving in weight.

Owner-refillable cylinders

Cylinders which caravan owners refill themselves are another recent development and several safety issues have been raised. See Safety panel alongside. The main attraction of a self-fill product is the fact that gas drawn from an LPG pump at a filling station is considerably less expensive than gas supplied with an exchange cylinder. In other words, an owner who goes caravanning regularly, especially in winter, might recuperate the cost of a refillable cylinder and its installation fairly quickly.

There are also advantages if you travel abroad because the Autogas stations which supply gas-powered cars dispense propane – which is the chosen fuel of many caravanners too. Sometimes a coupling adaptor might be needed but these are available from gas specialists.

However, there are important safety issues to consider and it has been reported that some fuel stations do not permit members of the public to refill portable cylinders on their forecourts. This hasn't been helped by the fact that some self-fill cylinders are not equipped with an automatic shut-off valve; this is important because a gas cylinder must never be filled to more than 85% to 87% of its total volume. Over-filling can have disastrous consequences, especially if you drive with an over-full cylinder in your caravan; a change in air pressure can cause the contents to expand.

The Calor Lite cylinder on the right is paired up here with its equivalent 6kg standard propane cylinder on the left.

The Calor Patio propane gas cylinder launched in 2005 has a float system which indicates when the gas level is low.

Although a float system works best during the later stages of consumption, the facility is fitted on Calor Lite cylinders.

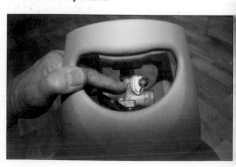

Cylinder sizes

Note: *The weight in kg with its approximate equivalent in lb relates only to the gas itself. On Calor products this is clearly marked on the cylinder. It does not relate to the total weight of both the cylinder and its gas content.*

Campingaz cylinders

0.45kg (1lb) butane
1.81kg (4lb) butane
2.72 kg (6lb) butane
- Campingaz cylinders are painted blue.

Note: *Only the Type 907 Campingaz 2.72kg butane cylinder is a practicable proposition for the caravanner. The two smaller cylinders might be kept for emergency back-up to operate a cooker burner but they are really intended for camping use.*

BP Gas Light cylinders

5kg (11.02lb) propane
10kg (22.04lb) propane
- BP Gas Light cylinders are coloured green and white.

Calor Gas cylinders

3.9kg (8.6lb) propane
4.5kg (10lb) butane
6kg (13.2lb) propane
7kg (15.4lb) butane
13kg (28.7lb) propane
15kg (33lb) butane,
19kg (41.9lb) propane
6kg (13.2lb) propane Calor Lite cylinder introduced 2007
- Calor Gas butane cylinders are painted blue
- Calor Gas propane cylinders are painted red.
- Calor Patio gas (propane) cylinders are green.

Note: *The larger cylinders, notably 13kg propane, 15kg butane and 19kg propane are often used on permanent pitches but are normally too large for safe transport. Locker compartments are not designed to accommodate cylinders of these sizes.*

Gaslow owner-refillable cylinders

6kg (13.2lb) propane
11kg (24.3lb) propane
- Gaslow cylinders are coloured yellow.

For this reason, a refillable cylinder must be fitted with an automatic cut-off valve that is activated when the contents reach 80% of the total volume. Unfortunately some refillable products lack this all-important feature and you have to monitor the rising level through a sighting point in the side of the cylinder. This can be difficult to judge with accuracy, especially at pumps which dispense the fuel at a brisk pace.

In response to this legitimate safety concern, Gaslow, a long-established gas specialist, embarked on the design of a safe, caravan-specific installation. The project started with the manufacture of yellow portable cylinders which would be installed to act like the fixed tanks used on many motor caravans. With capacities (in gas weight) of 6kg and 11kg respectively, these carry a 15-year warranty and qualify for replacement after that period for a small fee. The complete Gaslow installation kit now offered to caravanners includes:

- a 6kg or 11kg cylinder fitted with a European Pi approved filler valve that shuts off when the cylinder is 80% full,

....

Sold with a date stamped on the collar, Gaslow's cylinders have a 15-year warranty and an exchange facility.

- an over-pressure release valve fitted on both sizes of cylinder,
- a 0.6m length of semi-flexible, rubber-free, stainless steel pipe, and
- a filler coupling for mounting externally on the wall of a caravan; this is the type used on many LPG-converted cars.

....

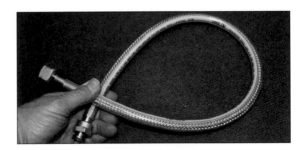

A Gaslow stainless steel coupling has a braided cover protecting a semi-flexible stainless steel ribbed pipe.

The refill inlet mounted on the wall of a caravan is the same pattern as many of the couplings fitted on LPG-powered cars.

Several combinations of cylinders are possible and this Gaslow installation includes an automatic changeover regulator.

■ Before taking to the road, it is important to turn off the gas supply at source. Although there are gas cocks in modern caravans to cut off the supply to different appliances within the system, the best precaution is to turn off the supply *at the cylinder*. This should be part of every caravanner's routine prior to departure.

■ Always transport a cylinder in its *upright* position. If a cylinder is laid on its side, the liquefied gas *might* escape from a faulty valve. When it is acknowledged that in the transfer from liquid to vapour there's approximately a *two hundred times increase in volume*, the potential hazard is clearly apparent. A tiny quantity seeping through the valve becomes a very large amount of gas.

When carrying out the fitting work, a cylinder (or cylinders) must be installed in the caravan locker and fixed just like purpose-made gas tanks. The cylinder then has to be coupled-up to the stainless steel pipe, which must be appropriately secured and permanently connected to a wall-mounted filler. Three optional filling adaptors are also available from Gaslow to match different European coupling systems.

To refill a cylinder in a Gaslow installation, the caravan has to be towed to a fuel station equipped with LPG facilities. Since this might be inconvenient, some owners pair a Gaslow product with a dealer-exchange cylinder. Various combinations of cylinder are possible and Gaslow also supplies manual and automatic changeover regulators.

Purchase procedures

The suppliers of gas cylinders operate different systems for marketing their products. For example, if it is decided to use Calor Gas or BP Gas Light cylinders, a caravanner has to enter into a hire agreement and pay a one-off fee. Cylinders remain the property of the gas supplier and if you subsequently decide to cease using the product, you can return the cylinder, submit the hire contract papers and have some or all of your payment returned. At present, Calor Gas Ltd returns the full amount: returned BP Gas Light cylinders are credited with a reduced refund.

Within the Calor hire arrangement, you are not normally 'locked-in' to using one particular type of gas or size of cylinder. Admittedly, market trends sometimes place restrictions on the exchange of particular cylinders. However, it is usually permissible to trade-in an empty *butane* cylinder, to pay the gas refill fee, and to receive a full *propane* cylinder instead. Similarly you can usually exchange a small cylinder for a larger one, and vice versa.

It's a different arrangement with some of the other products. For example, you are required to purchase a Campingaz cylinder yourself. It becomes your personal property and, when empty, it will be exchanged on payment of a gas fee for a refilled replacement.

Incidentally, some caravanners complain about the cost of a gas refill but don't appreciate what

Cylinder state

Assessing the amount of gas remaining in many types of cylinder can be difficult and several retro-fit devices are sold to give an indication of the 'fill' level.

Some owners monitor consumption by weighing a full cylinder on bathroom scales before it is put into commission. The information is noted down or recorded on a sticky label which is then attached to the cylinder. Since the quantity of gas in a full cylinder is expressed in weight, it is easy to calculate what proportion of the gross figure is gas and what proportion relates to the weight of the empty cylinder (called the tare weight).

Furthermore, when embarking on a trip with a part-used cylinder, a further check on the bathroom scales will indicate how much weight has been lost since the cylinder was new – and correspondingly, what weight of gas is remaining.

takes place in respect of cylinder refurbishment. For instance, a supplier of LPG like Calor Gas subjects returned cylinders to rigorous inspections. Refilling plant operatives carry out leak-testing checks, undertake periodic repainting work and fit new valves when needed. Safety issues are taken very seriously and unserviceable cylinders are speared through the sides with a spike and then scrapped to prevent unauthorised recommissioning.

Storage arrangements

The traditional location for the transport of gas cylinders on a caravan has been the draw bar, sometimes referred to as the 'Λ frame'. In the late 1960s, the cylinders were clamped on this part of the chassis and exposed to the elements. Locker boxes mounted on the draw bar came later and were fitted in the 1970s and early 1980s. However, by 1986 almost all caravans were built with an integral forward locker which is aesthetically more pleasing. The only problem is that some owners overload this with a number of weighty holiday items, thereby exceeding the permitted nose weight of the caravan.

More recently, Avondale has designed caravans whose cylinder locker is built into a side wall. This is usually located close to the axle, which is a good position for the transport of heavy items. Only in a 2009 prototype model was this moved to a less satisfactory location at a rear nearside corner. Heavy weights at the extreme rear can contribute to instability problems.

Another point of importance made in the earlier chapter on 12V systems is that a gas locker should never be used to accommodate electrical appliances – particularly a leisure battery. Leakage can occur at a gas cylinder valve and if a spark is generated when you are coupling wires to the terminals of a battery, an explosion could easily occur. It is therefore concerning that some caravans built in the 1980s were equipped with a cage for a leisure battery that was mounted alongside the gas

Side-located gas lockers situated near the wheels contribute to good weight distribution.

cylinders. Hopefully the batteries on these models have since been refitted elsewhere by vigilant owners or workshop technicians.

In addition to the importance of segregating gas cylinders from electrical appliances it is not permitted to run any power cables inside a gas cylinder locker *unless* they run within a sealed conduit. This is why a gas locker must *not* be fitted with a light. Some manufacturers overcome this by fitting a weather-protected lamp outside the locker on the A-frame fairing, suitably angled to cast light inside as required.

In addition, Bailey Caravan designers have noted that LED lights are totally sealed and do not have tungsten filaments like conventional bulbs. After protracted discussions with The National Caravan Council it was agreed that an LED light could be mounted within Bailey's lockers provided its wires are external and a protective casing is used to enclose the fitting. See Appendix B regarding power-supplying low voltage devices which measure the 'fill state' of gas cylinders.

On return home, many owners remove gas cylinders from the caravan as a precautionary measure. This is fine, but storage of the cylinders at home presents new problems. Under no circumstances should cylinders be left in a cellar, for example, since leaking gas would have no means of escaping. In fact the *Gas Safety (Installation & Use) Regulations* state clearly that propane cylinders must not be stored inside any dwellings. Nor should they be stored anywhere that lacks low level ventilation outlets. An outside shed or outhouse might prove suitable; but it's safer to adopt the practice of the suppliers whose cylinders are kept in a roofed storage cage situated well away from any source of flame.

Pressure regulation

Gas appliances made for use in caravans are calibrated to operate at specific pressures. To ensure gas is delivered at the required pressure a regulator is therefore needed in the supply system. For example, the point was made earlier that propane has a vapour pressure about five times that of butane. Furthermore, gas supplied from a cylinder won't always be delivered at a stable and consistent rate. This depends, in part, on whether a cylinder is full or nearly empty.

To achieve a consistent flow of gas at the required pressure a device called a 'regulator' is fitted in the supply system. A diaphragm in the regulator ensures that the operating pressure needed by gas appliances is achieved. However, the pressures adopted in European countries have differed in the past. For instance, appliances in pre-September 2003 UK caravans run on gas pressures between 28mbar and 37mbar whereas in Germany appliances have been set to run at 50mbar. In consequence, different regulators have been fitted in the past.

When more and more caravans started to be manufactured, exported and imported throughout Europe, the need for universal gas supply specifications became abundantly clear. Action was prompted after the publication of BS EN1949 and manufacturers responded by making radical changes to caravan gas systems. As regards UK caravans, the installation of a new type of cylinder coupling and regulation arrangement took effect from 1st September 2003. The standard is also complemented by BS EN 12864:2001, which is specifically concerned with regulators, including the types installed in touring caravan gas systems. However, the altered recommendations are not applied retrospectively so older caravans continue to use the original appliances and regulator systems.

To clarify how this affects owners, some general information about regulator operation is given next, followed by the products fitted in: 1. Caravans manufactured in the UK up to 31st August 2003; 2. Caravans manufactured from 1st September 2003 onwards.

Gas regulators

The gas regulators fitted in caravans have a diaphragm inside which stabilises the flow of gas and ensures that it is delivered at the pressure required. The device must be weather-protected and for its diaphragm to operate correctly a tiny breather hole in the casing must never get blocked. This is one of the reasons why gas cylinders and regulators should be secured in a gas locker rather than used outdoors. For instance, if rain gets into the breather hole in winter it might start to freeze, whereupon operation of the diaphragm would be badly affected.

Apart from ensuring that dirt doesn't get into the breather hole, there is nothing in a caravan regulator to service or adjust. Accordingly its casing is sealed, and these devices normally give unfailing service for several years. As regards cylinder-mounted products, opinion is divided about their life expectancy. Some specialists advise that it is good practice to fit a new regulator every five years; others quote ten years. Obviously if there are doubts about a regulator's operation you should fit a replacement at once.

Cylinder-mounted regulators

Although caravan gas installations changed in September 2003, the majority of caravans currently in use are older models built to use cylinder-mounted regulators. Their gas appliances run on either butane or propane *provided* you fit a cylinder-mounted regulator specific for your chosen gas. In other words if you use butane in summer and propane in winter you merely have to purchase a butane regulator (usually blue in colour) *and* a propane regulator (which is usually red). This system works well, but if you tour outside Britain your UK regulators won't fit the cylinders sold abroad – apart from the widely available Campingaz 907 cylinder.

Technical tip

If you ever get a frightening tall flame on a stove burner, this is 'over-gassing', which is usually caused by a faulty regulator. The condition typically occurs when a regulator's tiny breather hole gets blocked with dirt, thereby upsetting the operation of its diaphragm. This blockage can also occur in winter if rainwater gets into the breather hole and then freezes.

A regulator will fail to work properly if the breather hole on its casing gets blocked.

Both types of gas are being used in this caravan and the owner has purchased two regulators to suit the different connections.

The sealing washer on regulators intended for Calor's 4.5kg butane cylinder must be changed regularly.

Technical tip

A butane-specific regulator is rated at 28mbar, which is described as 28cm/11.2in water gauge. A propane regulator is rated at 37mbar, alternatively described as 38cm/14.8in water gauge. This means that when a gas engineer conducts tests by connecting up a manometer (which is essentially a 'U' tube holding water) the pressure induces a difference between the two water levels of 28cm (butane) or 38cm (propane).

Also be aware that the cylinder couplings on butane and propane regulators are intentionally different to ensure that pressure regulation is appropriate for the type of gas you are using. The different pressure ratings and the test procedures for the two types of regulator are given in the adjacent technical tip panel.

Coupling a regulator directly to a gas cylinder is a safe and effective system which has not been troubled by the problems that have affected many post-2003 caravans (discussed later). Its shortcoming is based on the fact that there are so many different gas connections on cylinders sold in Britain and across mainland Europe. Let's look at this more closely.

To connect to a propane cylinder intended for caravanners the regulator is manufactured with a carefully machined and threaded insert (male) which achieves a tight fit within the receiving socket (female) of the cylinder. No washer is involved – merely a close metal-to-metal register. The coupling method is the same on all Calor Gas propane cylinders for caravanners and you'll need to keep a spanner handy. An inexpensive open-ended spanner to suit the coupling is sold at caravan accessory shops.

Regrettably butane couplings are less straightforward because there are several different types. For instance on a 4.5kg Calor cylinder, there's a threaded female nut; this has to be positioned over the threaded male outlet and tightened anti-clockwise. The reverse thread often surprises newcomers to caravanning and a spanner is needed once again. Moreover, there's a small washer held within the regulator coupling nut which must be changed periodically. Spares are available for a modest sum from any Calor specialist.

On both the Calor propane cylinders and the Calor 4.5kg butane cylinders a robust turn wheel on the top opens or closes the gas supply valve. However, when caravanners find it necessary to use Campingaz there are two alternative strategies. Firstly, you can purchase a purpose-made Campingaz regulator as shown in the panel of photos on page 151. Secondly, you can purchase an adaptor that screws into the top of the Campingaz butane cylinder. This adaptor, shown in the photo sequence, incorporates a control valve, and its threaded outlet matches the cap nut fitted to a regulator designed for Calor's 4.5kg butane cylinder.

It is the larger butane cylinders from Calor Gas that adopt a different coupling method. The regulator needed now has to have a special clip-on coupling. Moreover, the on/off control now forms part of the regulator itself whereas on the smaller 4.5kg product the turn wheel was part of the cylinder.

If you fit BP Gas Light cylinders for use in a pre-September 2003 caravan you will need to purchase a 37mbar propane cylinder-mounting regulator as shown in the photo panel opposite.

To summarise, if you intend to use all types and sizes of Calor Gas cylinders intended for

Disconnecting a 541 regulator from a 7kg Calor Gas butane cylinder

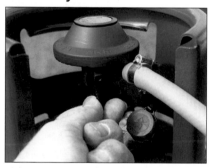

1. When the control knob points to the 6 o'clock position, the gas supply is ON.

2. Turn the control knob to the 9 o'clock OFF position to close down the gas supply.

3. With the control knob in the OFF position, the disconnecting lever can be lifted and the regulator removed.

4. The orange safety cap must be replaced on the cylinder even if it's empty.

caravanners, you need to purchase three different cylinder-mounting regulators. These are:

1. A Calor screw-on propane regulator – tightened with an open-ended spanner.
2. A Calor screw-on butane regulator to suit 4.5kg cylinders and tightened with an open-ended spanner.
3. A Calor 541 clip-on butane regulator to suit 7kg and 15kg butane cylinders.

If using a Campingaz 2.72kg 907 cylinder you must purchase either a Campingaz butane regulator with on/off tap and hose nozzle or an adaptor which offers a threaded coupling point for a Calor butane regulator as described in point 2 above and pictured below.

For information on coupling BP Gas Light propane cylinders to pre-2004 model caravans, consult Truma UK.

For information on coupling Gaslow owner-refillable cylinders see the various combinations described in the annual catalogue.

The accompanying photo sequence shows some of these products, including an unusual cylinder-mounted regulator set at 30mbar to operate appliances in post-1st September 2003 caravans and later models. This is an alternative to the wall-mounted 30mbar regulators normally installed in recent caravans; it has been fitted in some German models.

Wall-mounted butane/propane regulators

It is wholly illogical to expect caravanners to purchase an array of regulators to suit different types of gas cylinder. Moreover, since a regulator is an essential part of a caravan's gas system it would be reasonable to expect one to be included with every new caravan being sold. These points, together with the need to adopt universal practices among EU member states, prompted the publication of two new standards: BS EN 1949:2002 and BS EN 12864:2001.

Under these recommendations, the purchase and installation of a regulator no longer becomes the responsibility of a person buying a new caravan. In consequence a regulator complying

Open-ended spanners sold by dealers tighten the regulators on Calor propane cylinders and Calor 4.5kg butane cylinders.

One of the alternatives for a Campingaz 907 butane cylinder is to fit a purpose-made Campingaz regulator with on/off control.

Another alternative on a Campingaz 907 cylinder is an adaptor which offers a threaded coupling for a Calor butane regulator.

This propane 37mbar regulator fits the push-on connection of a BP Gas Light cylinder for coupling to pre-1st September 2003 caravan systems.

Gaslow sells a wide range of regulators and this adaptor type fits Norwegian, Spanish, Portuguese and Southern Irish cylinders.

Some German manufacturers have not fitted wall-mounted 30mbar universal regulators and supply this 30mbar type for post-1st September 2003 'vans.

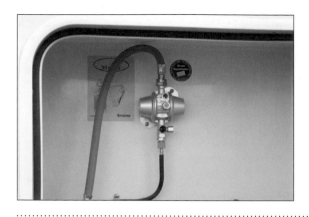

This GOK 30mbar regulator has a test connection point on the lower part of the casing; the downturn in the hose at the top could be eliminated by adding a 90 deg elbow joint as described under 'Blockages in gas supply'.

The CLESSE regulator has been fitted in Avondale caravans; its high mounting point in the gas cylinder locker is a good feature.

with EN 12864 annex D is now included as part of the fixed gas system. The device is mounted permanently by the caravan manufacturer on a wall or ceiling of the gas cylinder locker, and it usually has a test point as part of the regulator itself or in a location just downstream of the assembly. It was also decided that wall-mounted regulators would operate at a pressure of 30mbar.

Three gas component manufacturers introduced products which fulfilled the new standards, namely GOK (supplied by Truma), CLESSE (from Comap) and RECA (from the Cavagna Group).

The new standards raised a number of issues and these can be summarised as follows:

■ Technical literature distributed by Calor Gas Ltd and supported by the NCC clearly states that new butane/propane regulators should *not* be installed retrospectively in pre-1st September 2003 caravans, i.e. those models fitted with the former supply system and its different appliances. The Company reported: 'The gas pressures of the new regulator and your existing installation are NOT compatible.' (Leaflet published February 2003 *New Requirements for LPG in Caravans*.)

■ In the previous section in this chapter it was pointed out that previously-fitted cylinder-mounted regulators were rated at 28mbar (butane) and 37mbar (propane). In contrast, the new 'universal' regulator operates in conjunction with both butane and propane; it delivers gas to a caravan's supply system at a standard pressure of 30mbar.

■ Gas appliances installed in caravans fitted with this revised system also have to be manufactured to run at a standard pressure of 30mbar and this must be clearly shown on a label affixed to the product.

■ The hose which connects the regulator to the supplying cylinder *must*: a) carry a High Pressure rating; b) be marked accordingly on the side; and c) be supplied with factory-fitted couplings on both ends. Under no circumstances should low pressure hose and conventional hose clips be used on the revised system; unregulated gas being drawn from a cylinder is emitted at a high pressure.

■ The overall length of the new high pressure coupling hose must not exceed 450mm (about 18in), and many different versions are sold so that a UK caravanner can purchase one to suit the connections on cylinders sold in the European country being visited. (Longer hoses up to a maximum length of 750mm are permitted where cylinders are mounted on a pull-out tray arrangement.)

■ In Britain it was decided that the new universal butane/propane regulators would be wall-mounted in a caravan's gas lockers, a practice followed in several countries in mainland Europe. It was surprising, therefore, that some German caravans built in 2004 for sale in the UK were exhibited with an unmounted universal 30mbar dual gas regulator for direct cylinder-mounting. This arrangement defeats the object of creating an easy connection facility for caravanners wishing to use other cylinders sold throughout Europe.

Low pressure hose used with cylinder-mounted regulators can be fastened with hose clips, but this is *not* acceptable on hose used for gas flowing at high pressure.

Whatever its colour, high pressure hose must have clear labelling on the sides and show the date when it was manufactured.

Coupling hose used in post-1st September 2003 caravans must have factory-fitted connections. Normal hose clips are not permitted.

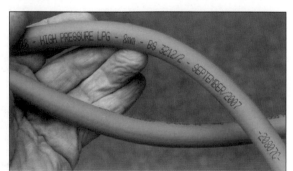

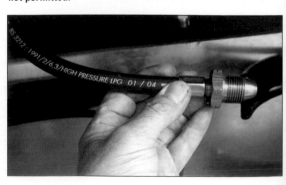

■ In view of the many types of different couplings on portable gas cylinders, there are not always coupling hoses to suit every type of connection. However, adaptors are available to couple up with high pressure hose connections; examples include adaptors for the clip-on couplings used on Calor 7kg and 15kg butane cylinders.

■ The specification of flexible hose has to be stamped on its side. It is *not* rubber; it is a special compound resistant to damage by LPG, and its colour does *not* signify its high or low pressure rating. For instance, there are examples of black Low Pressure hose and black High Pressure hose – hence the importance of checking the markings on the side.

■ Under the new system, a factory-fitted regulator forms part of a supplied caravan's fixtures and fittings. It therefore receives a manufacturer's soundness check together with the rest of the installation before it leaves the factory.

Standardising the gas supply systems in European caravans makes good sense. It's very helpful, for example, if you want to spend a long winter sports holiday in the French Alps because you merely need to buy a coupling hose to suit the French cylinders. However, there is a matter to bear in mind which affects caravanners who want to tour from country to country: you have to avoid collecting an array of different empty or part-full cylinders because there would be no space to store them safely in your caravan.

Blockages in gas supply

Following the installation of wall-mounted 30mbar regulators, a growing number of reports were received after mid-2005 of gas starvation occurring in caravans and motorhomes. Investigations found that an oily substance was getting into – and sometimes passing through – the regulator mechanisms. It was believed that the fluid could upset the operation of regulators, thereby contributing to the irregular supply of gas to appliances.

Attempts to identify the origin of the liquid led to wide speculation, and investigation teams were hindered by the fact that the condition was unable to be recreated in laboratory conditions. However, when samples of the liquid were analysed the 'oily' residue was found to contain phthalates, which form part of the plasticising agent used in the manufacture of gas hose.

It was also noted that when cylinder-mounted regulators were fitted prior to September 2003, the gas being fed into the copper supply pipes was already at a *low* pressure and no one reported the incidence of 'oily' contaminants in the system. However, with a wall-mounted regulator, the connecting hose accepts gas straight from a cylinder's outlet at *high* pressure. When gas appliances are not in operation, the regulator closes and the pressure of gas subsequently held within the hose is the same as that in the cylinder. No one had anticipated that in certain conditions, condensation would form in the high pressure connecting hose. Nor was it widely recognised that the condensation could absorb some of the plasticising chemical used to improve the long-term flexibility of coupling hose. This process produced the so-called 'oily fluid'.

If a regulator is mounted lower than the outlet from a gas cylinder, the slope on a connecting gas hose makes it easier for condensation accumulating inside to discharge into the regulator through gravity and to upset its operation. Any looping downturn in a hose can also act as a collecting point for residual moisture.

To see a more detailed commentary on this unexpected problem and to learn about the curative measures which dealers are carrying out, it is recommended that caravanners experiencing gas blockages read the definitive statement from The National Caravan Council (NCC). This was published in January 2007 and a copy of the NCC paper can either be accessed on the www.thecaravan.net website, or obtained from the Council direct using the address in Appendix.

One of the dealer-modifications is to remount regulators at a higher location wherever possible. Alternatively some regulators are being fitted with an elbow extension joint on the top of the casing to achieve an increase in height and to eliminate any slope that heads towards a regulator's inlet.

During this routine service, it was found that the 'oily substance' thought to cause blockages had passed through the regulator and into the main supply pipe.

This caravan had several gas blockages so its dealer fitted an extension pipe and elbow above the regulator; now the hose can achieve an unhindered slope back to the cylinder.

Flexible hose for LPG is made from a special composition material to comply with British Standard 3212. It is *not* rubber and the hose may be either Type 1 or Type 2 as defined in the British Standard.

Type 1 (low pressure) has an 8mm diameter bore to fit the LPG nozzle connections on cylinder-mounted regulators and a caravan's main pipe inlet. It has a pressure rating of 50mbar. Type 2 (high pressure) has many bore sizes including examples with an 8mm diameter. The material is made to a higher specification and Type 2 hose will withstand a greater pressure of 17.25bar.

Confirmation of a hose's specification is printed on its sides as shown in the earlier photographs. At one time the colour of hose was an indicator of type but this is no longer the case. For example, black hose is sold in both low and high pressure versions.

The idea is to allow any accumulating condensate to drain back by gravity towards the cylinder. Moreover, some owners are having Gaslow stainless steel flexible pipe fitted instead of the flexible hose containing plasticisers.

In many instances owners have been able to have remedial work carried out through the warranty covering their caravan and it should be emphasised that the incidence of problems is not high. According to the NCC, gas blockages have only been reported on around 4% of models. Furthermore, as soon as the condition became apparent manufacturers raised the height of regulators during production.

Notwithstanding the inevitable criticism of installations and products, The National Caravan Council categorically states in its explanatory paper that 'nobody has done anything wrong, but collectively a set of circumstances has arisen that created the problem.' The Council also points out that the problem is not a safety issue, although modifications should *not* be made by individuals who want to experiment with a revised system of regulation. *Equally, as stated earlier in this chapter, no work on gas systems should be attempted by an unqualified person.* On this note, if your caravan's gas appliances are not working as expected and you suspect there may be a blockage problem, get things checked by a qualified gas engineer with experience of LPG in leisure vehicles.

Supply pipes

General points about coupling hose

Normally only one flexible hose is permitted in a gas system but two are acceptable if an automatic cylinder changeover device is installed. Details about high and low pressure hose and their respective couplings have been given in the previous two sections but there are a few general notes to add before considering the fixed pipe system:

• When a cylinder-mounted regulator is fitted, the hose which is pushed on to its ribbed union (i.e. connecting nozzle) must be secured with a hose clip to create a sound, gas-proof joint. Correct practice is shown in the first two photos of a 541 regulator in the sequence on page 150.

The requirements of The Gas Safety (Installation and Use) Regulations 1998 are stringent but exclude touring caravans from their scope except where they are hired out in the course of a business. To undertake gas system work on non-business caravans an operator must be deemed to be 'competent'. This can be achieved by passing relevant examinations such as ACS or ACoPs and where the person has attended a recognised training course. Some caravan owners insist on repair work being undertaken by a CORGI engineer as an assurance of competence. *Note: CORGI stands for 'Council for Registered Gas Installers'. At the time of writing CORGI has lost gas registration scheme rights and a company called Capita assumes this responsibility from 1st April, 2009.*

• Flexible hose deteriorates very little when kept in stock at a suppliers. In use, however, it is affected by LPG and will need changing periodically.
• The hose bears a date on the side to indicate when it left the factory; this may be a year of so *before* you make the actual purchase depending on stock turnover. Keep a record of the date when you have a new hose fitted.
• Noting the installation date is strongly advised because coupling hose needs to be replaced at regular intervals. The *Calor Gas Dealer Directory 1995* recommends this is done at five-year intervals or whenever there's evidence of deterioration. For instance, you sometimes find that it loses resilience prematurely and stretches at ribbed unions (connecting nozzles).

On a caravan fitted with cylinder-mounted regulators, the inboard end of the connecting hose is fitted to a bulkhead connector and secured with a clip.

On account of the risk of a serious accident, neither the rigid gas supply system nor the connections to gas appliances should be modified, repaired or coupled up by non-qualified DIY enthusiasts. In the Calor Caravan Check Scheme booklet (May 1995 Edition) it states, 'Gas installation is an expert's job and by law must only be undertaken by an experienced gas fitter.'

This view is endorsed here and technical descriptions about the supply system are provided for information only. In reality the task of connecting up copper gas pipe using a proprietary compression coupling is not difficult – particularly for anyone familiar with the similar pressure fittings used in domestic plumbing. But the inexperienced person will not know how much to tighten a coupling to achieve a leak-proof joint. Over-tightening can deform the pipe and a leak is inevitable – as it is if the coupling is under-tightened. So the instruction is clear: leave this to a competent LPG fitter.

Safety

A competent and practically-experienced owner should find no difficulty in replacing the flexible hose on a pre 1st September 2003 gas supply system. However, fit *new* clips every time you replace the hose, and avoid using clips whose drive serrations cut into its surface. Then confirm that the joints at both ends are gas-proof; the later section in this chapter entitled 'Leak detection' describes the test procedure.

As regards the rest of a supply system, this should always be entrusted to a competent gas engineer. The Gas Safety (Installation and Use) Regulations 1998 provide further guidance.

Compression fittings feature three items: a cap nut, an olive and the component itself.

The fixed pipework

Although copper is used most frequently on modern caravans, steel or stainless steel gas pipes are sometimes fitted instead. Pipes should be secured with clips at recommended intervals not greater than:

500mm for copper pipes
1,000mm for steel or stainless steel pipes

When metal clips are used to secure runs of pipe, these should be the type manufactured with rubberised inserts to prevent metal-to-metal contact.

Supply pipes of the following sizes are installed ('OD' stands for outside diameter):

5mm (³⁄₁₆in) outside diameter (OD) = feed to a gas lamp; seldom used today.
6mm (¼in) OD = feed to many types of appliance e.g. the fridge.
8mm (⁵⁄₁₆in) OD = main trunk feed in a caravan; feed for space heating appliances.

Pressure couplings are made to suit the pipe diameters, with reducers permitting branches to adopt different sized pipes from the main trunkway. The diagram above shows key components such as the 'olive' and the 'cap nut'.

When a compression coupling is formed, the *Dealer Information Booklet* published by Calor Gas states that jointing compounds should not be used. 'Best practice' requires that seals are made with *dry* joints although some fitters ignore this and smear the olive with jointing compound from Plasticoll or a dark red paste called 'Calortite'. Any surplus Calortite on fittings has a nasty tendency of getting on to clothing.

Bending copper gas pipe is often done by hand; but for more precise work, especially when forming a tight bend, a pipe bending tool is used. This supports the walls of the pipe and prevents kinking. It follows the same principle of operation as a pipe bender used for domestic plumbing.

As regards the final coupling to appliances, this often employs a thread-to-thread union rather than a compression fitting. In this instance, a purpose-made

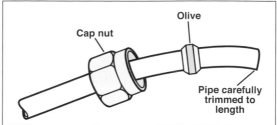

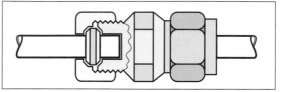

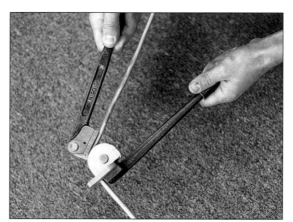

LPG jointing paste *is* required to seal the threads.

In modern installations, it is also necessary for individual appliances to be controlled by a separate gas cock (sometimes called an isolation valve). If an oven were to give trouble on holiday, for example, you could completely shut down its gas supply whilst leaving other appliances still usable.

Changeover systems

Unexpectedly running out of gas is usually annoying. Even if there's a new back-up cylinder, the task of disconnecting a coupling from an empty cylinder and connecting up a replacement is a nuisance. This is particularly aggravating when it is raining, a meal is being cooked, or it's during the night when a heating system is needed

When connections are formed, the cap nut is fitted on the supply pipe first, followed by the olive. The pipe is then inserted into the coupling as far as the stop point and the cap nut tightened.

As a cap nut is tightened, the olive bears harder against the shoulder of the fitting and is squeezed inwards, gripping the gas pipe tightly.

For precise work, bending copper supply pipe is done with a pipe-bending tool.

Isolation valves (or 'gas cocks') are fitted in a gas supply system so that individual appliances can be controlled separately.

Technical tip

The use of diluted washing up liquid for checking the integrity of gas joints is common practice. However, specialist engineers point out that it contains salts which are fine for cleaning dishes but these additives can corrode the components used in gas systems. If a proprietary leak detection fluid is unobtainable, washing up fluid MUST be washed off with clean water when a test is completed.

This manual changeover from Gaslow is intended for use with Calor 4.5kg butane cylinders.

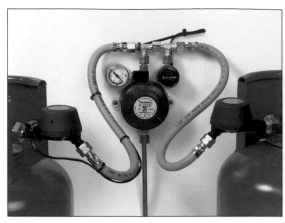

The Triomatic gas regulator from Truma was introduced in the UK in 1998.

Many engineers use a special pump to fill the supply pipes with air, whereupon the ability of the system to retain the air is checked on a gauge.

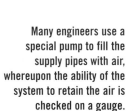

for warmth. Mindful of this, many caravanners use two cylinders and purchase a changeover device.

Even a manual changeover permits a hasty reinstatement of gas because both cylinders are already pre-coupled to provide a supply. Manual devices are available to suit caravans with either cylinder-mounted regulators or wall-mounted versions.

Alternatively there are automatic changeover products which are able to sense when a supply is reaching exhaustion and then bring the back-up cylinder into commission. Like manual changeover systems, these automatic devices are available for pre-September 2003 caravans as well as models fitted with the more recent 30mbar supply system.

Changeover devices from Truma have been available for over ten years and Gaslow has also been prominent in supplying products for a long time. In particular, Gaslow's sales literature presents a very clear description of around six different configurations to meet caravanners' requirements. Moreover, a photograph earlier in this chapter shows a changeover unit fitted to a pair of Gaslow's refillable propane cylinders.

As a useful addition to Gaslow's changeover

products, the Company's gauges can be fitted to give a visual warning of a cylinder's supply. However, a Gaslow gauge will only provide this information *when an appliance is in use and consuming gas*. As a secondary function, these compact components also help to detect a leak in a supply system as described in the following section.

Leak detection

Although the installation or modification of existing supply systems should not be undertaken by unqualified DIY owners, it is always wise to keep a watchful eye on gas pipes – and a nose as well. The smell of leaking gas is easily detectable.

Many caravan owners also have a leak detector fitted and some types are available that an owner could fit themselves. In addition, if an owner wants reassurance that couplings are sound, there's no reason why he or she shouldn't check them using a leak detection liquid.

The procedure is to have the system switched on at the cylinder and to keep all appliances off. Cigarettes and naked flames must be extinguished. Couplings are then coated with either a proprietary leak detection product or a solution made of diluted washing-up fluid, but see the Technical tip box on page 155. Once it has been applied, check for bubbles – which indicate a leak. It is usual to apply the mixture with a small brush and to hold your fingers around the joint to prevent the fluid running away. If you find a leak, switch the system off at once and get the coupling replaced by a gas engineer.

A more convenient way to monitor a system is to fit a Gaslow gauge at the gas supply cylinder. These products were mentioned earlier because they have an additional function of indicating the amount of gas in a cylinder. Testing is carried out as follows:

1. Turn off *all* gas appliances.
2. Turn *on* the gas supply cylinder; the gauge should show a green segment.
3. Turn *off* the gas supply at the cylinder.

The leak detector from Alde is installed in the main supply pipe – bubbles in the sighting glass indicate a passage of gas.

The Strikeback 12V alarm from Van Bitz activates a penetrating siren when it detects LPG, and numerous other gases too.

4. Provided there is no major leak, gas will be held in the supply pipes and the gauge will remain green for a prolonged period.
5. Using a standard Gaslow product, if the gauge remains green for at least a minute, the system is considered to be satisfactory.
6. Over a longer period however, the gauge will eventually return to the red sector.

Note: *Registered gas installers use much larger gauges and run tests over a 10 minute period. These trace even very small leaks in a system.*

Another way to keep a long-term check is to have an Alde leak detector fitted into the supply line by a gas engineer. This incorporates a small glass sighting chamber filled with a glycol liquid. To conduct the test you switch the gas supply on and turn all appliances off. When a red test button on the top of the detector is depressed, a regular flow of bubbles in the sighting chamber gives away the fact that gas is escaping somewhere in the system.

Different again are leak detectors that give an audible warning when a sensor detects gas. This type of device *could* be fitted by a careful DIY owner. For instance, the Van Bitz Strikeback electronic gas alarm warns occupants of a leak using a loud siren. The device has to be connected to a 12V DC supply and mounted on a secure base in an appropriate location. Since LPG is *heavier* than air, it is best to fit gas-sensing devices like this in a low position.

Cooking appliances

Cooking facilities in a caravan consist of a hob as a standard item; some models include an oven, too. In British models, a grill is also included as part of the hob.

Caravans built abroad are often different and a grill is not normally included. In fact the importers of foreign products often have to fit different appliances in order to make a kitchen more acceptable to the British public.

A large number of imported caravans also lack electronic ignition devices to light their hob's burners, a facility which has been commonplace on UK models since the early 1990s. Many Cramer hobs, for example, require the owner to keep a box of matches or a hand-held lighter in the kitchen.

Many of Cramer's hobs need either matches or a hand-held product like this Zippo gas lighter to ignite the burners.

Like most UK caravans, this prototype 2009 Avondale is fitted with an oven and grill as standard.

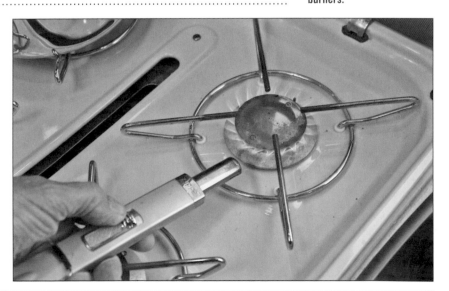

Since 1994, flame-failure devices have been fitted on each burner on a hob.

It is important for a gas engineer to test the operation of all cooking appliances on a regular basis.

Since 1994, it has also been mandatory to have a flame failure device (sometimes called a 'flame supervision device') fitted to all gas burners. If the gas on a burner blows out, the device immediately cuts off its supply. You will see the small probe that projects into the flame of the burner; when this is hot, an electric current is generated. The current then flows to an electromagnetic gas valve that stays open all the time the probe is hot. However, as soon as the flame is extinguished, current is no longer produced, the electromagnet in the gas valve fails and a small spring closes off the supply. The only point to note with this system is that you need to override the gas valve when lighting the burner in order to give the probe time to heat up. That's why a gas control has to be held down for a few seconds when igniting a burner.

Routine servicing and safety check

• Apart from cleaning, there are no servicing tasks on cookers that an owner can carry out.
• Like all gas systems, the cooking appliances *must* be checked by a competent gas engineer in accordance with manufacturer instructions. This is one of the tasks that should come within an annual service check.

• If a gas flame flickers yellow and soot is left on saucepans, this is usually a sign of an incorrect gas/air mixture. The condition is symptomatic of incomplete combustion and when it occurs there may be a release of carbon monoxide. This can be serious so the appliance should be checked by a competent gas engineer. Indeed the fault *must* be remedied before the burner is used again.

Space heating appliances

On the grounds of safety, an open burner 'gas fire' is no longer used in caravans. Unenclosed burners are considered dangerous because:
• something could fall on to the exposed flame,
• oxygen is taken from the living space while the heater is in operation,
• waste products are discharged into the living area as well.

In extreme cases there might be a risk of carbon monoxide poisoning, so appliances now have to be 'room sealed' and are referred to as 'space heaters' rather than 'gas fires'. Room

Never use a hob to heat the interior; when a burner is uncovered, a locker above a hob can get dangerously hot.

Safety

■ Make sure your kitchen is equipped with
 1. A fire blanket
 2. A dry powder fire extinguisher.
■ Select a situation for the Fire Blanket and Extinguisher that is easy to reach *without* being too close to the location where a stove fire might develop.
■ Use the fire blanket on fat fires, rolling it over at the sides to cover your fingers – thus providing protection from the flames.
■ Never use cooking appliances to heat the interior. A case has been reported where an open burner, not covered with a saucepan and left operating for a prolonged period, caused a kitchen fire. In addition, there have been fatalities from carbon monoxide poisoning where cooking burners have been left alight all night at a low setting to provide heating.
■ Ventilation is essential in a kitchen and permanent vents will be installed. These are needed to provide oxygen for combustion and to provide an escape for the products of combustion. Additionally, ventilators help with the removal of steam which causes condensation.

Two air connections are fitted to room-sealed heaters – one admits air for combustion whereas the other is the flue for exhaust fumes.

The fins on this Carver heat exchanger help to release warmth created by the gas burner to the interior of the caravan.

Carver Products

In this section, there are several references to Carver space and water heaters. These appliances have been fitted in many caravans but the company ceased manufacturing caravanning products in 1999. However, spare parts, accessories, and similar appliances are available from Truma UK whose address appears in the Appendix. In addition the Henry-GE Water heater was introduced in 2005 and manufactured along the lines of the Carver Cascade GE. Most of its parts are also claimed to be compatible with those of the Carver product. The complete product or individual components are obtainable from Caravanparts.net whose address is given in the Appendix.

sealing means the burners are housed in a chamber which is completely sealed off from the living area. Air for combustion is drawn directly into this sealed chamber from the outside and in a similar way, exhaust gases are returned outside via a flue.

Heat generated in the combustion chamber then has to reach the living area. The objective is achieved by directing the hot air through a 'heat exchanger' which is purpose-designed to release heat efficiently. Many heat exchangers are thus manufactured with moulded fins – rather like the fins on an air-cooled motorcycle engine.

In consequence it is the heat exchanger that warms the interior rather than the gas flames themselves. To assist in the distribution of heat, many appliances also have a fan which directs warmed air along a network of ducts. Outlets in

this system then ensure that heat is distributed throughout the interior at low level instead of immediately rising to the ceiling. Closed rooms like a shower cubicle can also be supplied with warm air via the ducting.

On the rear of some Carver and Truma fans it is also possible to adjust the proportion of heat being directed along the two outlets served by the fan. So if one end of the caravan seems cooler than the other, the diversion lever offers the opportunity to adjust the distribution of heat as an adjunct to the butterfly control flap on the duct outlets.

Many practically skilled owners add a ducting system to their caravans; using proprietary components from Truma, the task can be fairly straightforward. Hiding the ducting discreetly is the main challenge although it *is* possible to obtain

On some of the heaters from Truma and Carver, the balance of air released into the ducts from the fan can be adjusted.

Many heaters can be fitted with a blown air ducted system using one of the manufacturer's kits.

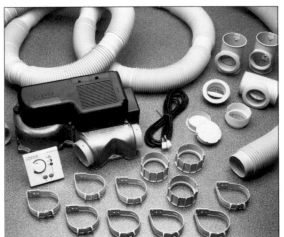

The Carver Fanmaster houses a 230V heating element and includes a reset button to recommission the heater if it has automatically shut down through overheating.

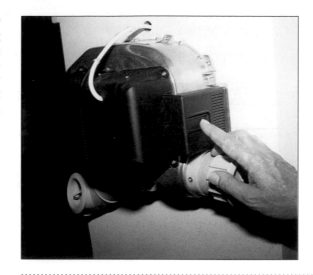

The Carver 4000 Fanmaster provides heat from either a gas burner or a mains element fitted behind the heat exchanger.

specially reinforced sections to take routeways *beneath* the floor without too much loss of heat.

In 1994, Carver went one step further by introducing the Fanmaster which combined a 230V heating element within the heat distribution fan unit. With everything contained in the same appliance, a caravanner has the choice of either distributing warm air from the gas burners or creating warm air from a mains element. Both systems, however, should not be operated simultaneously.

In January 1995 this was made available as an 'add-on' appliance which could be fitted to a number of space heaters. Products like the Carver 1800, 2000 and 3000 heaters could be upgraded using the appropriate fitting kit. But with two heating levels provided by 1kW and 2kW elements, the 8.3A and 4.2A rating of a Fanmaster has implications for a site's 230V hook-up capabilities.

When using this Fanmaster unit it is essential that at least one outlet remains open whenever the heater is running. However, in the event of overheating an automatic cut-out safety switch comes into operation. The device is reset as follows:

1. Wait until the appliance has cooled down.
2. Open all the outlets.
3. Disconnect the mains supply at the consumer unit.
4. Reset the trip button by pressing the push switch on the side of the casing.

Unfortunately the reset switch can be difficult to locate and operate, especially when the casing is mounted out of sight in the bottom section of a wardrobe.

Other makes of space heater have overheat cut-out devices too, but check the reset advice in your user instruction leaflet. Some types have to be left for a short period, whereupon the operating system resets automatically and the unit is then safe to use again.

As regards ignition, heaters installed in caravans in the 1980s and early 1990s like the Carver Trumatic SLP 3002 were fitted with a push button Piezo igniter. These are reliable but will

not operate if the spark gap is incorrect or if the high tension cable from the switch has become damaged. Similarly, the push button assembly on the SLP 3002 sometimes fails. Spares are available, however, from Truma.

Some owners later had the Piezo ignition system on Carver space heaters changed for an electronic auto ignition unit. Conversion kits introduced in May 1996 were subsequently available for Carver's 1800, 2000 and 3000 models.

As regards more recent developments, both the Truma Ultraheat and the Carver Fanmaster 4000 are space heaters where the electrical heating elements are located behind the rear of the heat exchanger but within the main casing itself. In other words heating elements were no longer built into the fan housing.

In the case of the Trumatic Ultraheat 230V auxiliary heater, this can be fitted on several Truma appliances between the heat exchanger and the metal installation box at the rear. Most Truma S series heaters can be thus equipped (see Company brochures), and the three power settings are:

• 500W (2.2A)
• 1,000W (4.5A)
• 2,000W (8.5A)

On a Carver 4000 Fanmaster space heater, the 230V heating elements are mounted within the main casing, to the rear of the heat exchanger.

If fitted to a Trumatic S 3002 P heater, the outputs from these settings are entirely separate from the heater's rated thermal output of 3,400W when operating on gas. Note that the current draw when running on mains power is substantial on the higher settings, and being able to gain the full potential of this product depends on the output current available from a caravan site's hook-up.

Since space heaters like the Truma S 2200, S 3002 and S 5002 are fitted in a large number of UK caravans, it is useful to have an understanding of their key components. This is strictly for general interest; as stated already, repairs and servicing work on gas appliances must only be carried out by competent gas specialists who have attended training courses run by appliance manufacturers.

In large caravans you will also find 'wet systems' in which radiators are used. The 3000 Compact central heating system from Alde, for example, is installed in high specification models from Vanmaster. Reports from owners indicate that it is extremely efficient.

Routine servicing and safety check

Like cooking appliances, space heaters also need an annual safety check and service. This is not something an owner should tackle.

Several tasks will be carried out including checks on the shape of the gas flames. The shape of a flame will inform competent and experienced gas engineer about operational efficiency.

One of the problems in caravans is that there are periods when gas appliances might not be used for an extended spell. This is when dust and cobwebs can accumulate. It often comes as a surprise to learn that the humble spider often upsets gas appliances. For instance filaments of a spider's web across a pilot light can distort the shape of the flame and prevent the main burner from igniting. Equally, a spider ball or a dead insect caught in the trumpet-shaped venturi through which combustion air is admitted to the burner is a common cause of flame distortion.

It is the same with the flue. Even a spider's web spun across a flue roof outlet can upset exhaust efficiency enough to prevent a space heater switching from pilot to main burner. So general cleaning is one of the elements of servicing and the labour charge for this is modest.

To summarise:
• There are no servicing tasks on gas heating appliances that an owner can carry out.
• The operation of space heating appliances must be checked by a competent gas engineer in accordance with manufacturer's instructions – an element that should come within a caravan's annual service check.
• In addition to checking the appliance, the flue will also be given a safety and efficiency check.
• Ensure that you are given a written account of the servicing work as explained in Chapter 13.

Trumatic S Series heater detail

Many UK caravans are fitted with Trumatic S series space heaters as standard; they can also be retrofitted to replace products like Carver's.

In this cut-away model used for training purposes, the removal of the upper part of its heat exchanger shows the ignition burner alight but not the main burner.

On modern space heaters the burners are completely enclosed in a sealed heat exchanger. To confirm that a burner's alight the flame can be checked through a viewing port.

The control wheel on top of a heater is coupled to this assembly by a steel spindle. A copper thermal sensor tube controls the main burner and mustn't get covered by carpet.

This heater has been removed and inverted for servicing. Operation is often upset when spiders/moths get into the copper (or stainless steel) air intake.

The air intake is now removed for cleaning-out. The main burner is on the left; the ignition burner has a spark igniter, and the tip of a thermocouple element is visible at the rear.

To run the automatic ignition system a small battery is fitted which triggers a microswitch. One of the tasks during a full service is to replace the battery and clean its contacts.

The electric auxiliary Ultraheat unit fits to the rear of a heat exchanger and helps raise the temperature quickly; many caravanners leave it on a low setting at night.

Water heating appliances

Availability of hot water is a great asset and few caravans are built now without the inclusion of a water heater. There are three main types:
1. Instantaneous water heaters e.g. the Morco, the Rinnai.
2. Storage water heaters e.g. the Carver Cascade Rapide GE, the Maxol Malaga, the Truma Storage.
3. Water heaters integrated with a space heater e.g. the Trumatic C range, and Alde 3000 Compact.

Instantaneous water heaters have lost their popularity recently on account of the fact that the gas burner is exposed, a constructed flue above the unit is now a requirement, and the appliance takes up valuable wall space. On the other hand instantaneous appliances can produce hot water without any delay and continue to produce it all the time there's a cold water supply and gas to heat it.

Storage heaters have the advantage of being inconspicuous, they can easily be mounted in a bed box and their operation uses a remotely sited control panel. Their balanced flue is discreet, too, and more recent versions incorporate a mains heating element as an adjunct to the gas burner; both can be operated simultaneously to speed up heating time. Notwithstanding the twin source of heat, the storage vessel still takes time to heat up from scratch and the quantity of available hot water is limited, too. There's also the matter of weight. Few people drain down the water before taking to the road and water is significantly heavy. A Carver Cascade, for example, holds 9 litres (2 gallons) thereby taking up 9kg (20lb) of payload capacity. Alternatively the Truma Ultrastore 10-litre model now being fitted in the majority of UK caravans holds 10kg (22lb) of water.

After its debut in the mid-1980s, the Carver Cascade underwent a number of improvements. In recognition of this, Carver manufactured upgrade kits for owners who wanted to improve earlier models. For instance, the Cascade 2 could be upgraded to achieve the faster drain-down time of the Cascade 2 Plus using a special kit.

In addition the Cascade 2 Plus GE included a 680W mains electricity heating element. However, the later Cascade Rapide included an 830W heating element and if you bought a tank repair kit this included a replacement 830W element instead. Incidentally, on the more recent models an overheat reset button was situated behind a cover flap, as shown in the accompanying photo.

Upgrades were undertaken by dealers and some experienced DIY owners. Now there is the Henry GE water heater, which has all the main features of a Carver Cascade product. Retaining the original design of Carver's water heater made good sense because it was not only popular, it was also a conveniently compact appliance.

While the Carver Cascades were the most common storage heaters fitted in earlier UK caravans, the Maxol Malaga and its partner the Malaga E with a 230V heating element were also fitted in caravans, including models in the Fleetwood 1995 range. In addition, water heaters bearing the name of the Belling Malaga were fitted in the Bailey Hunterlite range from 1997 onwards. Finally, Propex has introduced the Malaga MkIIIG and GE 13.5-litre models, both of which are available from suppliers like CAK.

However, it is the Truma Ultrastore which is most often installed in caravans now being manufactured in the UK and mainland Europe. There are 10- and 14-litre versions, although it is the smaller one which is normally chosen for touring caravans. Both models can be equipped with an additional 850W (3.7A) electric heating element.

Routine servicing and safety check

It is important that a water heater is inspected and serviced regularly at an approved dealership. As with other gas-operated appliances, servicing and repair work fall outside the scope of DIY endeavour. Draining-down work, however, is an exception.

Frost will seriously damage a water heater. For instance, in a storage heater the casing that holds the water can be torn away from its seating and couplings as soon as freezing water starts to expand. In an instantaneous water heater like the

If a Carver Cascade 2 overheats it has an emergency cut-out; a reset button is on the end of the casing.

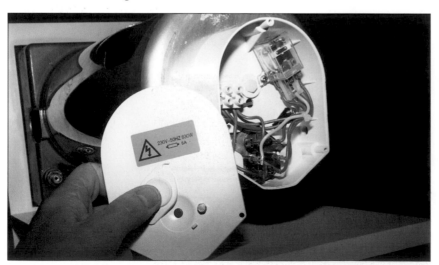

On earlier models, the drain down plug on a Cascade 2 had to be left open for a considerable time.

Although its name and manufacturer has changed, the key features of this water heater now available from Propex is its box-like casing which lends itself to bed locker installations.

Rinnai, extreme damage can be sustained within the labyrinth of narrow bore water pipes.

There are two ways to ensure this doesn't happen. One is to fill the entire system with potable anti-freeze. This strategy is favoured in the United States and a potable anti-freeze is now available under the Camco accessory range sold by ABP Accessories, Leicestershire. All you have to do is to pump the recommended quantity into the system via your water container, and leave it there until the weather improves. The only point to bear in mind is that some manufacturers of water heaters may not approve of using potable anti-freeze in case it damages components like water seals.

The alternative to using potable anti-freeze is to drain down a water heater in strict accordance with its manufacturer's instructions. The procedures vary, however, and whereas a Carver Cascade has a threaded bung to remove, the Truma Ultrastore has a simple lift-up lever. Early Cascades often take an hour or more to drain down completely, but later models discharge water much more rapidly because the manufacturer added an air relief valve on the top left of the external flue plate.

Instantaneous water heaters can also take time to drain down completely and if a receptacle can be left for a day or so underneath the outlet, so much the better.

On a Trumatic 'Combi' space and water heating appliance (more commonly installed in motor caravans), there is also an automatic 'dump valve'. When temperatures approach freezing point, a sensor activates a release valve and the contents of the water heater are drained-off automatically. It's a clever system, except some owners complain that they sometimes lose all the water during overnight stops on winter expeditions.

Differences aside, a key feature is to open all the hot and cold taps and leave them like that all through a winter lay-up. With regard to lever-type mixer taps, always make sure the lever is centralised and lifted to ensure that both the hot and cold outlets can release a pressure build-up if water trapped in the pipes starts to freeze and expand. Moreover, if the drain-down procedure involves removing a bung, replace this in a loose but secure manner so that spiders and insects are unable to force an entry.

Time spent here is well-rewarded; having frost-damaged appliances repaired can be a costly business.

Truma Ultrastore water heaters are being fitted by many caravan manufacturers as basic equipment. Both the gas burner and a 230V element (if fitted) can be used simultaneously.

As with all gas appliances, the control systems are complex and repair work should not be attempted by DIY owners. The Ultrastore has an over-temperature safety cut-out.

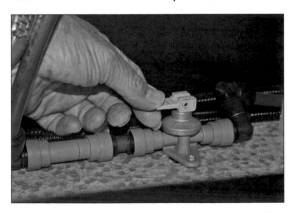

All makes of water heater can be irreparably damaged if water held in the system starts to freeze. The drain-down tap for a Truma Ultrastore heater is conspicuous.

11 Contents

Operation and efficient use

Installation

Servicing

Refrigerators

As well as being one of the most useful appliances in a modern caravan, a refrigerator is an important contributor to comfortable living. However, successful operation is only achieved if the appliance is correctly installed, used properly and regularly serviced.

The provision of refrigerators in touring caravans goes back to the early 1970s. In those days this was an optional item in more expensive models – although by modern standards the devices were rather rudimentary. For instance, models like the Morphy Richards Astral had to be lit with a match and the burner could only be reached from an access hatch outside the caravan.

On older fridges, cooling would sometimes cease because an airlock had developed in the refrigeration unit. To solve this, it would be necessary to remove the appliance, turn it upside down for several hours, and then reinstate it. Invariably this temporarily cured the problem but it often involved quite a lot of dismantling and reassembly work.

In contrast, today's caravan refrigerators are supplied with sophisticated ignition and cooling control systems. They also keep the contents cool, even during very hot weather. However, to achieve full efficiency, a caravan fridge has to be:

- installed in the manner laid down by the manufacturer;
- used in accordance with the manufacturer's recommendations;
- fully serviced at appropriate intervals.

These points might seem self-evident, but in practice, it is not unusual to find that a caravan manufacturer has not carried out the installation properly. Equally there are many owners who disregard advice contained in the user-instructions. Finally, it is not unusual to find a fridge that hasn't been serviced since the day it left the factory.

The aim of this chapter is to look into these issues more closely; in some cases, readers may note the technical points and want to undertake corrective measures themselves like fitting better wall ventilators, but do not presume that the content is solely directed at the practical person. On the contrary, the final section is included to inform owners what tasks a service engineer should carry out when undertaking a full refrigerator service. The illustrated text demonstrates what is involved and underlines why a refrigerator, like any gas-operating appliance, needs periodic attention.

At no point is it necessary to understand the chemistry of refrigeration. However, a broad grasp of the cooling process is helpful and this is explained below, albeit in non-technical language.

Operation and efficient use

A caravan refrigerator is rather different from the appliances fitted in our kitchens at home. It is true that chemicals have to be circulated around a network of pipes – whether it's a fridge at home or in a caravan. Moreover, as the refrigerants circulate the chemicals change state and draw heat out of the food compartment in the process – but this is where the similarities end.

■ **Compressor refrigerators** – In a normal domestic appliance, refrigerant chemicals are circulated by a compressor whose operation is activated by a thermostat. A compressor is sometimes heard coming into operation whenever additional cooling is needed. However, in a busy kitchen at home the hum of a compressor often passes unnoticed, whereas in the close confines of a caravan it is much more conspicuous. Although

Product identities

For many years, the refrigerators fitted in leisure vehicles were manufactured by Electrolux. However, in 2001, the leisure appliance division of Electrolux became an independent company and the name Dometic was adopted. This had been a brand name in the US for a number of years. In 2003, many appliances were still bearing both Dometic and Electrolux badges which was rather confusing. However, in 2004 the licence to use the Electrolux name expired. In this chapter both names are used because thousands of caravans are fitted with products previously manufactured by Electrolux. Only more recent models have appliances bearing the Dometic badge, and aftersales advice covers both products. Norcold is another manufacturer of absorption refrigerators. These products were launched in the UK in 2002 and are being marketed by Thetford. Several caravan manufacturers are now installing Norcold appliances.

Waeco is also a prominent manufacturer of leisure refrigerators but these are compressor models which only run on a 12V supply; they are often fitted in small motor caravans sometimes referred to as 'camper vans'. Then, in 2007, Dometic and Waeco amalgamated; the headquarters is now based in Dorset.

small 12V compressor fridges *are* sometimes fitted in campervans and lorries, absorption refrigerators are the preferred option in touring caravans.

■ **Absorption refrigerators** – In this type of refrigerator, the chemicals are circulated by the application of heat rather than by a compressor pump. Since the system has no moving parts and is completely silent, absorption refrigerators are ideal for use in caravans, motorhomes, hotel rooms and hospitals.

In the context of caravanning, the heat used to circulate the chemicals can come from one of three sources, namely:

1. A gas burner drawing from the caravan's gas supply.
2. A 230V heating element drawing from a mains hook-up.
3. A 12V supply drawn from the towcar when its engine is running.

Under normal conditions, each of the alternatives will achieve efficient cooling although it's important to point out that the 12V option is not controllable. When operating in this mode, the fridge operates at a consistent level and altering the fascia cooling control makes no effect whatsoever. This is not the case, of course, when the appliance is run on mains electricity or gas.

It is also important to point out that on some holiday sites, the sheer number of caravanners drawing mains electricity means that the nominal 230V supply can actually drop as low 195V. The tip box on this page adds advice on this point.

Choosing the operating mode

On most caravan refrigerators you have to select the heat source yourself to suit the circumstances. Only the Automatic Energy Selection (AES) refrigerators carry this out without need for owner intervention. Working under a computer monitoring system, the AES fridge has a built-in priority programme. For instance, on-site the AES system will choose 230V mains; if this is not available or the supply drops below 200V, gas will automatically be selected instead. Furthermore, when you take to the road, it recognises that gas appliances should not be operated during towing. Even if you haven't turned off the gas cylinder control valve, it switches over automatically to 12V operation as soon as the engine is started.

Following this arrangement through further, when entering a petrol station and switching off the engine, the refrigerator will not return to gas operation until a period of 15 minutes has elapsed. This is a safety precaution in case you've forgotten to turn off the gas cylinder.

Although AES refrigerators leave the caravanner with very little to do apart from switching on and setting the cooling level, they are still comparatively unusual. Cost is one of the reasons although they have been fitted to more expensive caravans and are often installed in coachbuilt motorhomes.

Advice to owners

To get the best from a refrigerator, there are a number of measures you can take:

Prior to departure

Before taking to the road, pre-cool the food compartment by running the refrigerator for three hours or more. During this pre-cooling period it is helpful to load some non-perishable items, like bottles of mineral water.

If your caravan is parked at home, it is often possible to couple the hook-up lead to a 13A socket so that the fridge can be operated from a mains supply. However, you will need an adaptor and should also fit a portable Residual Current Device (RCD) into the socket as well, in order to provide protection to anyone passing the trailing lead to the 'van. The function of an RCD was described in Chapter 8, *The mains supply system*, and a portable unit bought from a DIY store was illustrated on page 123.

On the road

Always remember to switch to 12V operation when taking to the road. As mentioned in Chapter 10, *Gas supply systems and appliances*, the supply cylinder should be turned off as a safety measure. On a model which has a tiny 'porthole' in the bottom of the food compartment, check here to confirm the gas flame is extinguished.

Do not regard 12V operation as 'second best'. On the contrary, cooling in this mode is just as good as it is under gas or mains. However, there is no thermostatic control and the natural movement of the caravan prevents over-freezing. In the unlikely event that you suffer from over-cooling when towing in cold conditions, fit winter covers on the external ventilators.

On site

Once on site, keep the following tips in mind:

Ignition problems

If attempts to ignite the burner are unsuccessful, this may be because there's air in the gas line. Repeated attempts usually purge the air but if there's continuing difficulty, the appliance is probably due for a service. Cleaning and realigning the ignition electrode is one of the servicing tasks.

Handy tip

If your refrigerator is operating on mains electricity on a busy site, you may find the cooling level is disappointing. This often happens because the 230V supply drops as low as 190–195V on account of the large number of caravanners hooked into the system. If this occurs, select the gas operating mode. This should result in the fridge achieving better cooling.

Avoid over-packing a refrigerator; air must be able to circulate around the contents.

Placing washed lettuce in a plastic bag helps to prevent condensation forming on the cooling fins in the food compartment.

Covering the silver cooling fins with a drinks pack will seriously affect cooling performance.

Cooling fins

The silvered cooling fins at the back of the food compartment draw heat from the interior, so it is most important that these are not covered. Items like canned drink packs should never be pushed hard against the fins. Equally, water droplets or frost on the cooling fins reduce operating efficiency, so remember to cover damp vegetables or put them in a plastic bag – especially freshly washed lettuce. Similarly, wipe excess moisture from food cartons.

Voltage drops

Take note of the problem of mains voltage drops on crowded holiday parks described earlier.

Packing food

Make sure that plenty of space is left around the items on the shelves. For the contents to cool, air must be allowed to circulate inside the cooling compartment. Also make sure that strong-smelling food like cheese or onions is packed in a sealed plastic bag.

Door use

Open your fridge door as briefly as possible. Regrettably several recent caravan kitchens incorporate a decorative door that hides the fridge completely – including the controls. This means you have to lose cold air just to alter a control or to confirm the red 12V light is working when setting off. It is a poor design feature.

Winter covers

When outside temperatures fall below 10°C (50°F) Dometic advises that winter covers are fitted over the ventilators. Unfortunately some of the 'budget' vents fitted on cheaper models may not have matching covers. Some owners try to overcome this by partially covering the fins with cooking foil. It may help to prevent over-cooling but the arrangement is neither glamorous nor entirely effective.

On arrival home

Remove all food and leave the refrigerator door partially open in order to let air circulate around the storage compartment. Normally the manufacturer fits a catch which keeps the door slightly ajar during periods of storage. A variety of devices are fitted for this purpose, some of which are better than others.

In some Dometic refrigerators this provision is completely missing, although a replacement catch is available to remedy the situation. Problems also arise when caravan manufacturers fit a false door cover and add a conventional catch that isn't designed to engage in a part-open position. These are poor features because the failure to allow air to circulate around an empty food compartment often leads to the formation of mould inside.

At the end of a caravanning season, Electrolux/ Dometic technical staff recommend that a food compartment is cleaned with a weak solution prepared using a teaspoonful of bicarbonate of

This false wooden front allows the user to check or adjust the controls without having to open the fridge door unnecessarily.

Winter covers are recommended when outside temperatures fall below 10°C (50°F).

Before taking to the road, always turn off the gas supply at the cylinder; then turn the fridge to its 12V operating mode to protect food in the storage compartment.

Note that on Electrolux fridges made prior to 1992 with a gas thermostat, the burner flame isn't extinguished merely by turning the temperature control to its lowest setting. Some owners misunderstand this and drive away with the fridge operating on both 12V and a low gas flame. Apart from being potentially dangerous this can damage the appliance. As a guide, any model with a red button on the control panel that has to be depressed during lighting is one of the earlier appliances.

More recent models do incorporate a gas shut-off valve in the control knob, but it is still recommended that the supply be turned off at the cylinder as a precautionary measure, whenever taking to the road.

soda dissolved in one litre of warm water. Do not use household detergents because some products are thought to cause fridge linings to develop cracks. The manufacturers of Thetford fridges used to recommend domestic detergents in their 'user instructions' booklets but now recommend use of the Company's own 'Bathroom Cleaner' instead. This is specially formulated to clean plastics; note that Thetford also labelled batches of this product as 'Plastics Cleaner'.

Needless to say, if you are not planning to use the caravan for an extended period, consider having the fridge serviced in readiness for the next trip.

Installation

Different makes of refrigerator have model-specific requirements so the points below present no more than an overview of typical installation recommendations. That said, to achieve efficient cooling a refrigerator must be fitted in accordance with its manufacturer's instructions. It is therefore disappointing to report

Aggressive domestic cleaners caused some fridge liners to crack so Electrolux recommended owners to mix this treatment.

Refrigerator storage catches

The strut for this Thetford fridge door looks fragile but it effectively prevents the magnetic closer from shutting the door completely.

It seems perverse that a caravan manufacturer removed this effective door catch in order to add a cosmetic door panel.

This additional wooden panel fitted by a caravan manufacturer has a standard cabinet catch so the door cannot be held ajar.

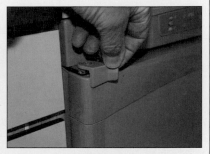

These catches fitted on some Electrolux fridges held a door secure during towing but lacked a facility for holding it ajar.

This replacement catch from Electrolux meant that a door could be modified by forming a hole for its nib so that it could be held ajar.

If a fridge isn't cleaned properly and its door isn't held slightly open when not in use, mould soon forms inside and may leave permanent marks.

Thetford initially recommended normal domestic cleaners but now advises caravanners to use the Company's 'Bathroom Cleaner'.

If the surface above a fridge gets hot, it is likely the appliance has not been fitted correctly.

that some caravan manufacturers have failed to fulfil some requirements that are expressed with unquestionable clarity in refrigerator installation manuals. For instance, there are models from well-respected manufacturers that fall short in respect of the clearly stated ventilation requirements.

Although an appliance with a poorly-formed ventilation facility is certain to achieve a measure of cooling, its full potential is unlikely to be realised. In the heat of summer, for example, its shortcomings will often become apparent much to the discontent of the owner. When this occurs it is often the refrigerator itself which is wrongly blamed for a mediocre performance.

Self check

To enable the cooling unit at the rear of a caravan refrigerator to operate properly, the rear

of a refrigerator should be completely sealed off from the living quarters. There are different ways of achieving this but in most cases aluminium shielding is fitted around the back of the casing. Sealing off the rear of an appliance is necessary because the interior of a caravan can get exceedingly hot when parked in the sun – much hotter inside than out. If this heat reaches the refrigeration unit on the rear of the casing, its operating potential will be significantly reduced.

Furthermore, if the installation has been carried out correctly, cold wind blowing into the wall ventilators will not be able to penetrate the living space. Some caravans can be very draughty inside and in most cases this is the result of deficiency in the shielding arrangement.

You can check the installation of your refrigerator as follows:

• If your refrigerator is located below a draining board or work top, put your hand on the surface when it is operating. If it is warm, there's a strong likelihood that the appliance hasn't been shielded off effectively.

• Check for draughts in the kitchen on windy days. Wind blowing through external fridge vents should never reach the interior. This is a sure sign that the shielding system at the rear of the appliance doesn't meet the fridge manufacturer's specifications.

• Look through the outer vents. If your caravan has one of the more recent Dometic and Electrolux ventilators, you will be able to detach the grille from its frame to see even better. Peering through, you should not be able to see light in the caravan interior, nor inside the kitchen furniture. To seal off the rear of the appliance, aluminium sheet is usually used – with sealant applied around apertures enclosing pipes or cables.

• It may help to remove kitchen drawers when looking from inside your caravan. Once again, the grilles should not be visible.

• If you find that a length of sponge or glass fibre quilt has been wedged on top of the casing instead of a metal deflector, this is an unsatisfactory substitute. It is unlikely that this will keep draughts out on windy days because sponge or similar material can compress or become detached.

• To achieve cooling at the rear of the appliance, ventilators of the specified size are essential. On some caravans you will find them reduced in size; others may be lined with an insect gauze which reduces the effective area quite considerably. In reality, if a fridge has been correctly installed and sealed at the rear, insect gauze is unnecessary. It is essential that air from outside can enter, unhindered, at a low level and then be passed back outside above the top of the casing.

• Vents should not be completely obstructed by a caravan door. Regarding Dometic and Electrolux appliances, technical staff have recommended that the distance between the open door and the vents should be at least 50mm (2in). Equally, ensure that parts of an awning do not cover a ventilator. On some caravans, a fully open door

Installation inspection

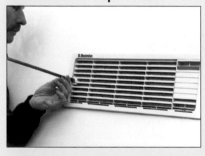

1. On recent ventilators, it is easy to remove the grille.

2. Withdraw the upper section of the flue assembly.

3. Detach the complete grille from its support framework.

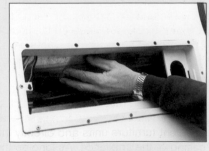

4. Inside the uppermost vent, a tilting deflector shield should be visible.

When a caravan door is fully opened, check it doesn't touch the flue cover or obscure the ventilators.

On a badly installed fridge, a tilting deflector shield can sometimes be made from aluminium sheet and fitted retrospectively. Sealing-off the cooling unit at the rear of an appliance from a caravan's interior is important.

also restricts the outflow of exhaust gases from the flue outlet. This is most unsatisfactory.
• Some owners presume that 'winter covers' are intended as draught excluders. This is certainly not the case: their purpose is to prevent *overcooling*.

If your refrigerator installation fails in any of the above respects, the following section gives a brief summary of the key features. Using this information, some readers will undoubtedly respond by undertaking corrective measures themselves. Others will prefer to seek the advice of their caravan dealer. However, this is only a summary and to obtain more detailed installation information, you should contact the customer service department of your appliance's manufacturer. Addresses and telephone numbers are listed in the Appendix at the end of this book.

Key installation elements

When taking all points of installation into account, there are seven specific areas of attention:

1. Achieving a level location.
2. Structural fixing.
3. Ventilation.
4. Flue.
5. Mains connection.
6. Low voltage connection.
7. Gas connection.

Achieving a level location

The circulation of refrigerant chemicals is hindered if a fridge isn't level. So anyone who is refurbishing an older caravan and wants to fit a refrigerator would start by parking the caravan in a level plane. Thereafter, a spirit level is used when installing the appliance so that when the job is completed you know that if the 'van is level, the fridge will be level as well.

On older Electrolux refrigerators, the reference point for verifying a level plane is the shelf in the small freezer compartment. Of course, a very short spirit level is needed to take a reading here. The exception is the RM123 which has a sloping shelf and on this model the spirit level should be placed on the base of the food storage cabinet.

Note: *i) All Electrolux refrigerators manufactured before 1986 had to be completely level to operate. A tilt in excess of 2–3° could impair operation. Since this date, all higher specification models are described as 'tilt tolerant'. Some models will operate at an angle of 3° (e.g. RM122 and RM4206); others operate at 6° (e.g. RM4217, RM4237, RM4271, 6 Series, 7 Series and 8 Series models).*
ii) On the road, a fridge will seldom be level, particularly when driving along a carriageway with pronounced camber. However, as long as a level position is achieved periodically – which is the case on normal roads – chemical circulation will take place and cooling will occur.

Structural fixing

When being towed, a caravan receives a considerable shake-up, especially on bumpy roads, so a refrigerator needs to be carefully secured. Dometic and Electrolux both recommend that wooden blocks are fitted on the floor at the rear of the unit as shown in the diagram on page 170. Equally, if the support afforded by adjacent kitchen units is in doubt, blocks can also be fitted on the floor to support the sides of the casing.

In the past, mechanical fixing at the sides has often been achieved by driving screws through adjacent furniture units and directly into the metal casing of the appliance. As long as the fixings penetrated no further than 12mm (½in), the interior plastic lining wouldn't be damaged. However, models like the RM2260 and RM2262 were then

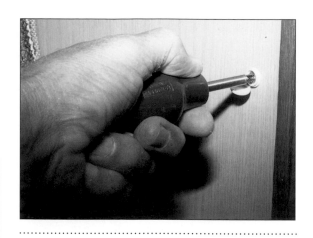

Sealing off the rear of refrigerators

The need to create a sealed compartment at the rear of a fridge which is completely isolated from the living area is not merely to prevent draughts causing a nuisance. It is also to achieve operational efficiency. For instance, when a caravan is parked in the sun, temperatures in the living area get far higher than temperatures outside the caravan. If this pronounced heat is allowed to reach the labyrinth of pipes on the rear of a fridge – called the cooling unit – its operation will be significantly compromised. The importance of having a sealed ventilation pathway is described in the main text. And since this vital feature is clearly explained and illustrated in many refrigerator installation manuals, it is inexcusable that some caravans have been built in the past with no shielding at all.

Correct installation is important and the need to fit a metal shield deflector at the rear is emphasised by the manufacturer.

manufactured with a projecting flange around the front which incorporates fixing points.

Even better are the Electrolux fridges made since 1994 which incorporate pre-formed holes in the sides of the food compartment. This means that long screws can be driven from the inside outwards, thereby achieving anchorage from adjacent structures – usually kitchen cupboards. The screw heads are then concealed by a white plastic cap that matches the inner lining of the food compartment.

Overall, a successful structural installation will achieve three objectives:

• The fridge will be in a level position when the caravan is parked on level ground.
• It will not shake loose even when towing on very rough roads.
• The appliance will be easy to remove and reinstate to facilitate servicing.

Ventilation

Some very small refrigerators fitted in the 1980s did not use wall-mounted ventilators. Their food compartment was less than 1cu. ft and nowadays these models are seldom seen. The 'internal venting' employed for these appliances would certainly not meet the requirements of the larger refrigerators that caravanners now expect.

On today's appliances, it is important that the cooling unit on the back of the casing is completely sealed off from the caravan interior. This point has already been mentioned and owners can check the installation using the test procedures given earlier.

Bridging the gap left between the rear of an appliance and a caravan wall is normally achieved with aluminium sheet. To eliminate the need to fabricate this, Electrolux introduced a pre-formed surround referred to as the IK1 kit which fitted most popular models. However, this assembled structure didn't always suit caravans with end-kitchen installations on account of the larger-than-usual gap between the wall and the rear of an appliance. Moreover, while some caravan manufacturers purchased IK1 units, others preferred to produce their own version. Regrettably, on a few caravans no form of shielding was fitted at all.

Once a sealed ventilation path has been created using the shielding, air from outside will be drawn in via a low vent. This air will rise and pass across the pipes, burner assembly and other cooling unit components whereupon it will absorb some of the heat created in the refrigeration process. It rises by convection until it meets a tilting deflector shield that should be mounted on top of the refrigerator casing. The warmed air is thus redirected outside

Installation details

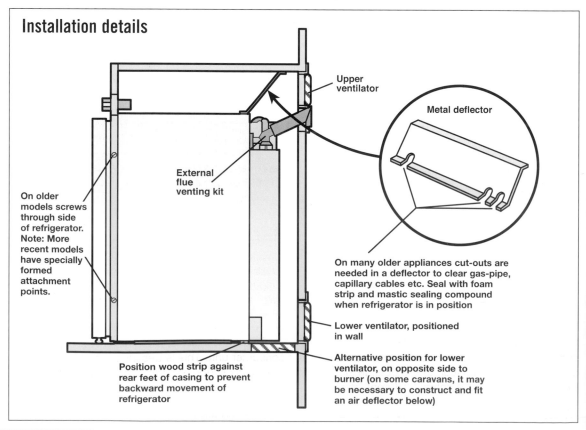

Upper ventilator

Metal deflector

On older models screws through side of refrigerator. Note: More recent models have specially formed attachment points.

External flue venting kit

On many older appliances cut-outs are needed in a deflector to clear gas-pipe, capillary cables etc. Seal with foam strip and mastic sealing compound when refrigerator is in position

Lower ventilator, positioned in wall

Alternative position for lower ventilator, on opposite side to burner (on some caravans, it may be necessary to construct and fit an air deflector below)

Position wood strip against rear feet of casing to prevent backward movement of refrigerator again via the upper vent as shown in the illustration on the previous page. Regrettably this important deflector shield has not been fitted by some caravan manufacturers.

Achieving an unhindered passage of air across the rear of a refrigerator is important and in a correct installation the warmed air will rise naturally. In a correctly installed fridge, there is seldom any need to fit a fan to accelerate air movement. Notwithstanding this advice, some caravanners like to add a 12V operated fan within the sealed section at the back. Cooling fans to suit any make of three-way absorption fridge can be purchased using the CAK mail order service. In addition, Dometic introduced a thermostatically-controlled ventilating fan in 2007.

The efficiency of the provision is also influenced by the ventilator units as well. Their size is important and minimum dimensions will be given by the manufacturer. For instance, on Dometic and Electrolux refrigerators of 2 cu. ft. storage capacity or less, the ventilators should provide at least 240cm^2 of free air space. Models offering more than 2cu. ft. storage require ventilators achieving at least 300cm^2 free air space. Note that this is reduced if an insect gauze is added on the inside of the grille.

The A1609 and A1620 ventilators made by Electrolux certainly achieve these requirements although they are comparatively expensive. It's for this reason that several manufacturers fit other types – although these alternatives might lack the leak-proof design of the appliance manufacturer's units, in which case driving rain could penetrate. Equally some of the less expensive ventilators are not made to accept winter covers, although this problem also occurs with earlier types of Electrolux ventilator, too.

Owners of older caravans often decide to upgrade their fridge ventilators to more recent versions since these accept winter covers and integrate the flue outlet neatly within the design. This improvement work necessitates increasing the dimension of the aperture and you should check there are no obstructions before cutting into the sides of a caravan.

The position of ventilators relative to the appliance is another issue. In a Dometic or Electrolux installation, the top vent should be located so that its upper edge is at least 55mm (2in) above the casing of the refrigerator. On the other hand, the lower vent can either be positioned in the side wall or in the floor. If the latter option is preferred it should be situated as far from the burner as possible so that draughts don't extinguish the flame. It may also need a deflector plate fixed under the floor so that dirt isn't driven into the vents when the caravan is being towed.

Flue provision

When the gas burner is in operation, an efficient flue system is essential for conducting waste products from combustion to the outside air. Note that this facility is entirely different from the ventilation provision described earlier. In consequence, the flue outlet and cover plate on

Sections of aluminium sheet are prepared around the fridge so that its cooling unit is completely sealed off when the unit is installed.

older models used to be mounted separately from the ventilation grilles and a cast alloy fitting with a draught shield was fitted on the side of caravans.

It was partly a quest to improve the external appearance of the fittings that led Electrolux to introduce the A1620 grilles in 1994. These combined both the flue outlet and the upper ventilation outlet into a single plastic-moulded unit. However, the flue outlet was still a separate assembly from the ventilation arrangement for the cooling unit, even though it was now accommodated in the same frame. An outlet in an A1620 grille can be seen in the sequence of photographs on page 168 showing an installation inspection.

Further amendments were made later when Dometic introduced large capacity fridge freezers, although these are more commonly installed in motorcaravans. In these models, combustion gases from the flue share the upper area of the ventilation zone near the metal deflector shown in the installation drawing on page 170. From this point onwards, warmed air from the cooling unit and flue gases no longer have separate outlets and both discharge together through the upper ventilator. In this arrangement it is obviously essential that the ventilation zone is effectively and completely sealed so that flue gases cannot enter the living area.

Mains connection

Making a 230V mains connection is usually straightforward. Typically a refrigerator is supplied with a length of three-core flexible cable and a pre-fitted 13A fused plug. This is intended to couple into an adjacent socket wired as a separate spur and protected by a miniature circuit-breaker on the caravan's mains consumer unit. This is described in Chapter 8, *The mains supply system*. The rating for the plug's fuse on most compact leisure refrigerators is 5A, but check your fridge manufacturer's recommendation.

Key electrical components needed in a 12V cooling system

■ A fuse on the fridge supply cable should be situated as close to the positive terminal of the towing vehicle's battery as possible. Towbar fitters usually recommend a 15A fuse.

■ A device has to be fitted which will activate the flow of current to operate a fridge on its 12V setting as soon as the towcar's engine is running. As discussed in Chapter 3, *Towcar preparation*, this might be a mechanical make/break relay or an electronic switching device. This provision means that a supply is automatically terminated as soon as the engine ceases to run.

■ The total length of live and neutral cable from the vehicle battery to the fridge *and* back should be as short as possible to minimise the voltage drop. Equally the gauge of cable specified by the fridge manufacturer should be fitted. Aware of owner criticisms relating to disappointing 12V performance Electrolux increased the recommended gauge on several occasions. At one time 2.00mm² cable was specified; this was later changed to 2.5mm² cable. In 2000 some Dometic refrigerators were recommended to have a 6.00mm² supply cable; in 2006 RM7601/7605 models were recommended to have 10.00mm² cable. Check the specification for your model and be aware of allegations that some caravan manufacturers have disregarded fridge manufacturers' recommendations and have fitted thinner cable.

■ Although the supply could go directly to a fridge, it is usually routed via a caravan's 12V fused distribution control panel. Typically these have a separate switch for the refrigerator supply and another fuse, normally of 10A rating.

■ Depending on whether the car/caravan connection employs a 12S coupling or a 13-pin coupling, the standardised pin allocations given in Chapter 3 should be used.

■ A 12V feed needed to run an electronic device to ignite the gas burner on a fridge is usually coupled to a caravan's leisure battery rather than the towcar's battery. Normally it has its own in-line 0.5A or 1.0A fuse.

Low voltage connection

Although an absorption refrigerator will work well from a 12V supply, its performance is impaired if the actual voltage reaching an appliance has fallen below this level. It was pointed out in Chapter 7,

The 12 volt supply system, that voltage drops occur when a connecting cable is too long and/or too thin. The recommendation of the fridge manufacturer should always be strictly observed and it is interesting how the specification has changed in the last few years.

At one time Electrolux recommended the use of 2.00mm² cable but this was later altered to 2.5mm² cable. In 2000 the installation manual for AES refrigerators specified 6.00mm² cable, which is very much thicker. In 2006 the recommended coupling cable for RM7601/7605 models was a prodigious 10.00mm². This undoubtedly helps to minimise voltage loss and it is unfortunate that the coupling blocks into which the cable has to be connected are sometimes too small to accommodate a core of this size. This means that some of the copper strands have to be nipped off, which is counter-productive.

That aside, the typical wiring features in a supply for an Electrolux or Dometic product are shown in the drawing below. This should be read in conjunction with the panel on the left and the points covered in Chapter 3, *Towcar preparation*. Information on wiring the supply to 12S and 13-pin connections is also given in that chapter.

The 12V supply that operates the refrigerator's cooling system is usually taken from the vehicle's alternator and this has to be an *ignition-controlled supply* (in other words the current only flows when the engine is running).

However, an additional, *permanent supply* is also needed for the electronic igniter which lights the burner when you switch over to gas operation. At one time a gas burner would be lit by a Piezo crystal spark created when you depressed a red

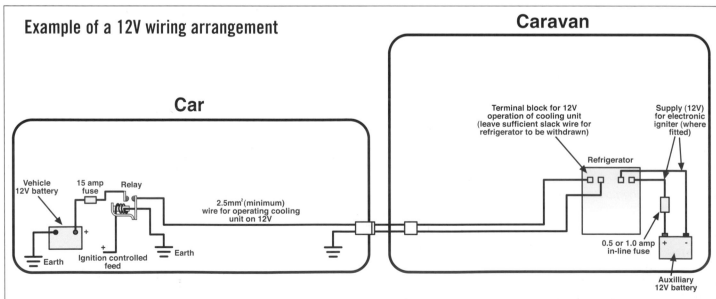

Example of a 12V wiring arrangement

Car

Vehicle 12V battery — 15 amp fuse — Relay

2.5mm²(minimum) wire for operating cooling unit on 12V

Earth

Ignition controlled feed

Earth

Caravan

Terminal block for 12V operation of cooling unit (leave sufficient slack wire for refrigerator to be withdrawn)

Supply (12V) for electronic igniter (where fitted)

Refrigerator

0.5 or 1.0 amp in-line fuse

Auxilliary 12V battery

■ This shows a typical wiring arrangement found on 1990s caravans. Check the box above for additional information.

■ As described in Chapter 3, mechanical make/break relays in a towing vehicle are fitted less often; electronic switching devices are now used in most towing vehicles.

■ The recommendation to use 2.5mm² cable for supplying 12V to a refrigerator has been superseded; cable with a more substantial gauge is often recommended instead.

button, but most refrigerators now have electronic ignition instead. It has many advantages although it *does* need a 12V feed. Its current consumption is very small, however, so the supply is normally taken from the caravan's auxiliary battery as shown in the diagram opposite.

Gas operation

Requirements in the gas supply include:

• The need for an independent gas cock in the supply to the fridge. This is usually situated adjacent to the appliance in a kitchen cupboard.
• Copper feed pipes of 6mm (¼in) outside diameter (OD). The final connection to the appliance must not be made with flexible gas hose.
• A flue arrangement is needed as described earlier.
• An ignition system. In the early 1970s, the gas burner had to be lit with a match. However, push-button ignition in which a Piezo crystal is used to generate a spark soon replaced this system. In the mid 1980s, electronic ignition was introduced and this is now more commonly fitted.
• Gas escape provision must be included when a unit is installed. Accordingly a purpose-formed 'drop-out' hole of 40mm (1⅝in) is normally needed, thus providing a direct outlet to the exterior. In some instances the lower ventilator grille can achieve this objective, but if fitted with one of the older types of winter covers, it then fails to meet the requirement.
• At one time, the union for coupling to a caravan's gas supply system was on the top of the appliance just behind the fascia controls. This means the appliance needs a generous length of copper gas pipe on top so that it can be pulled forward from its housing in order to reach the coupling that has to be disconnected. An improved arrangement was introduced in 2000 on AES models where the coupling was situated just behind the upper ventilator where it could be reached easily. On Electrolux fridge-freezer models like the RM4501, the coupling was situated at the bottom of the appliance, thus offering access via the lower ventilator.
• Whilst it is true that an experienced DIY owner would be able to secure a fridge within a kitchen unit, the final connection of a gas supply should be entrusted to a competent gas engineer as defined in Chapter 10. The joint is normally formed using an approved threaded coupling. In a thread-to-thread union, a jointing compound like Calortite is used.

Recent innovations

Since Thetford introduced refrigerators manufactured by Norcold a few years ago, competition between suppliers has become increasingly acute. In response to the arrival of these new appliances, caravan manufacturers like Bailey have fitted both Dometic and Thetford products in different models in order to evaluate their respective merits.

Several new innovations have appeared too, and on Dometic Series 7 models the gas burner doesn't have a traditional flame failure device; it is

Controls on many Electrolux fridges confused owners so Dometic introduced simple fascias which also prevent more than one operating source from being activated simultaneously.

As regards the design of the storage compartments and their overall finish, Thetford-badged products are little different from the majority of Dometic appliances.

Some of the recent Norcold refrigerators being marketed within the Thetford range of products are equipped with LCD screens on the fascia panel.

Older refrigerators had their gas connection point illogically positioned just behind the fascia panel. On this AES model it's easily reached by removing the upper ventilator.

Removable freezer compartments

Not everyone wants a freezer compartment and some owners prefer to have a fridge that just offers conventional storage facilities. Noting these different preferences, some Dometic 8-series models are manufactured with this patented clip-in and removable freezer section. This example is fitted in 2009 Bailey Pageant models.

On initial inspection, this 8-series Dometic fridge has a freezer compartment at the top of the food compartment.

But not everyone wants to store frozen food and on this appliance the compartment is only clipped in place.

It merely takes a few seconds to unclip and slide the compartment away from its mounting point.

Conversion complete and storage space is greatly increased; but the compartment is soon reinstated if needed.

fitted with a special electronic gas valve instead. Furthermore, once commonplace features like a gas flame inspection port at the bottom left-hand side of the food compartment have been omitted. And on the Series 7 models, the gas supply turns off automatically when cooling reaches the specified level.

Developments continue and the photographs on the previous page show further examples of recent features.

Servicing

As with any gas-operated appliance, periodic servicing is very important. This not only ensures that the refrigerator operates efficiently; it is a safety element too.

In spite of this, some caravanners *never* have their fridge serviced – and the appliance seems to perform well, season after season. But there's nothing more annoying if it finally fails on holiday, especially when there's a spell of hot weather.

Recognising the different levels of use, Dometic and Electrolux have recommended that servicing should be carried out every 12 to 18 months to ensure optimum performance. In practice, servicing work is fairly straightforward; the job that often takes a disproportionate amount of time is removing the appliance from the caravan and transferring it to a work bench. Unfortunately caravan manufacturers often fit the appliance early on and then build furniture around it, making its retrieval – and reinstatement – annoyingly difficult.

Since much of the servicing operation demands competence and experience working with gas appliances, it is not a task that a DIY enthusiast should tackle. On the other hand, a labour charge might be saved if an owner were able to remove the refrigerator from its housing. Reinstatement could also be considered, although remaking the gas connection and carrying out a leak test should be conducted by a gas service engineer. Only a few of the more recent refrigerators are claimed to permit servicing operations with the appliance left in situ. Furthermore, some service engineers assert that cleaning loose rust and carbon deposits from a burner tube flue is extremely difficult if an appliance isn't transferred to a bench.

As regards the charge normally made to service a Dometic refrigerator, this is made-up of three elements:
• The workshop's normal labour rate will be payable for removal and reinstatement of the appliance.
• The service work itself takes about an hour to complete and is charged according to the labour rate.
• Parts like a new gas jet are charged extra, but in normal circumstances the overall cost of parts is modest.

The photographs opposite highlight the key tasks that your dealer should carry out. The work breaks down into the following:

• With the fridge on a bench, the service engineer will remove the flue outlet pipes that are connected to the top of the burner tube. This tube is effectively a chimney clad in an insulating material. Wrapped within its insulation are the heating elements for 12V and 230V operation.
• A baffle is lifted out of the burner tube. This is a twisted piece of sheet metal suspended on a wire and its position within the tube is critically determined by the length of this wire. One servicing task is to clean off any carbon deposits from the baffle.
• At the base of the burner tube, a metal windshield enclosing the burner is removed.
• The burner assembly is disconnected next and pulled away from the base of the burner tube. Using a special wire brush supplied by Dometic, the engineer will clean all carbon deposit from the tube.
• The burner assembly will be cleaned, too, including the tip of the flame failure probe called the 'thermocouple'.
• The burner is now unbolted in order to gain access

Problem solving

If a refrigerator doesn't work on gas, check:

■ **The fridge's selection switch is set to gas operation**
■ **The gas cylinder isn't empty and its control is switched on**
■ **The gas control valve near the appliance is switched on**
■ **If it has been serviced in the last 18 months.**

If a refrigerator doesn't work on 12V:

■ **Ensure the fridge's selection switch is set to 12V operation**
■ **Remember that this option only works when the engine is running**
■ **Check all fuses related to the 12V supply**
■ **Get an electrician to check that a 12V supply is reaching the fridge's connector block.**

If a refrigerator fails to work on 230V check:

■ **The fridge's selection switch is set to 230V operation**
■ **The mains is connected and the consumer unit's RCD and MCBs are switched on**
■ **The refrigerator 230V plug is in the socket and the switch is on**
■ **The fuse is intact if a 13 Amp plug is fitted.**

Thermocouple operation

Gas only flows to the burner when the tip of the thermocouple has warmed up and the operating valve has opened. During the warming-up period, you have to open the valve manually by holding in the gas control knob for a few seconds.

When the tip is heated, a tiny current flows from the thermocouple; it then activates an electromagnet that holds open a spring-operated gas valve. The valve is behind the fascia panel and forms part of the gas control itself. However, the attachment nut that holds the connecting wire in place sometimes shakes loose, thus preventing the current from reaching the electromagnet. In consequence the thermocouple will not hold open the gas valve and the flame goes out as soon as you release the manual override control knob. During a service, the tightness of this nut will be checked.

to the tiny gas jet. This will be replaced; under no circumstances should the original jet be cleaned since the size of its aperture is critical. Even brushing it with a finger tip can upset the delivery of gas. There are also many jet types to suit different models.

• After reassembly, the tip of the ignition probe is positioned to achieve the 3mm clearance needed for a spark gap.

• The thermocouple's connecting nut behind the fascia will be checked for tightness. The importance of this is described in the box on page 174.

• After a general inspection of the appliance, a bench test will be carried out to confirm the fridge is fully operational. It will then be reinstalled in the caravan and all couplings to gas and electrical supplies will be reconnected and checked.

Some of the operations carried out during a service

1. In most cases an appliance is disconnected, removed from its location and transferred to a bench.

2. A metal shield at the rear is removed in order to reveal the burner at the bottom right of a casing.

3. The burner assembly is unscrewed and gently eased away from its location to avoid falling carbon deposit.

4. The sloping T-shaped flue section on top of the burner tube is unscrewed and detached.

5. The twisted flue baffle attached to a wire is lifted out of the burner tube and cleaned.

6. A purpose-made hard bristle brush from Dometic is used to clean carbon deposit from the burner tube.

7. The burner and tip of the thermocouple is cleaned; the spark clearance gap is reset.

8. Gas jets vary according to model and must be replaced; cleaning is *not* acceptable.

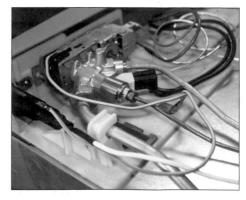

9. Wires behind the fascia are inspected and the nut securing the copper flame-failure coupling is checked.

Improvements and repairs

A caravan can be improved in a number of ways. This selection of projects shows some of the jobs that an owner might like to consider

Modern caravans feature an extraordinary array of products, and owners of older models are naturally envious. However, it is often possible to upgrade a caravan and this chapter features eight improvement and repair jobs.

Many readers will use this for reference and arrange for the work to be carried out at a caravan dealership. Others, however, will tackle the projects themselves. Whichever strategy you follow, bear in mind the following points:

• Don't over-spend on upgrades presuming that the full cost of new items will be reflected in a dealer's trade-in price. Adding a thousand pounds of accessories seldom adds the same value to a caravan's resale price.
• Experienced DIY enthusiasts know it is often unwise to do everything themselves. Enlist the help of experts where necessary.
• Note warnings in earlier chapters concerning safety issues. For example, the completion of

gas and flue connections must be carried out by a competent specialist.
• Remember that caravans have a specified maximum payload and it can be easy to exceed the limit. If additional appliances are installed, the extra weight will take up some of the payload previously available for your personal effects.
• If heavy accessories are added, stability and noseweight may be affected. Fitting a heavy item in a location well away from the caravan's axle can upset weight distribution and towing characteristics

With these points in mind, remember that fitting a new appliance may be relatively straightforward. With good instructions from the manufacturer, an installation is often achievable by owners who have practical experience and the appropriate tools.

On the other hand, repairing appliances, dismantling assemblies and diagnosing problems is usually much more involved. This type of work nearly always needs a qualified expert.

Structural alterations

Some installations may involve making structural alterations. Revising fixed furniture is not normally a major undertaking but timbers used in the body construction present a more serious challenge.

If you have to form an aperture in an external wall, avoid cutting through a structural member – unless you are able to create alternative

reinforcement. Furthermore, it is important to line an aperture cut in a wall panel using timber inserts. In a bonded wall (as described in Chapter Five), this necessitates cutting away a small amount of block insulant so that battens can be inserted, as shown in the photograph below left.

When a hole is cut in a caravan, a framework of softwood battens is needed to reinforce the aperture and to provide a solid material for fixing screws.

After a metal/timber bonding sealant such as Sikaflex-512 Caravan has been applied, sections of the timber framework are held in place using G cramps.

Improvement and repair projects

The photographs in this chapter show work in progress. More detailed information is provided in manufacturers' instructions which should be read thoroughly. The times quoted relate to DIY installations; experienced service engineers are likely to complete the work more quickly.

Fitting a Fuse Control

Comments: *A caravan site Reception can tell you how many amps (i.e. how much current) can be drawn from a 230V supply pillar before it 'trips out'. In practical terms you then have to calculate your likely current consumption (amps) using the wattage rating of each 230V appliance. However, components such as a built-in battery charger often get overlooked, and their current-draw varies, according to the charge level of the battery being revived.*

Fitting a 'Fuse Control' offers three benefits:
1. A digital display informs you how many amps are being drawn whenever mains appliances are in use.
2. The current-draw of individual appliances can be confirmed using the display.
3. You can set a trip switch by selecting a cut-out point just below the site's supply limit. If you then start drawing too much current, the Fuse Control switches off automatically whereas the site supply remains intact. After disconnecting the last appliance that caused an overload,

you then reset the Fuse Control to regain your supply of mains power.

Since this is a mains supply component, many owners would wisely entrust the installation of a Fuse Control to a qualified electrician. Furthermore, although the instructions supplied are adequate they could be better. Bear in mind, too, that when fitted, the Fuse Control comes between a caravan's inlet socket and the mains consumer unit with its RCD protection and MCBs. In consequence the consumer unit which is 'downstream' in the supply doesn't offer protection if the Fuse Control isn't wired correctly.

Not that there is much to do beyond cutting the caravan's 2.5mm² flexible supply cable, coupling the live, neutral and earth cables to both the IN and OUT terminals on a connection block and then mounting the unit securely. The author reported to the supplier that a larger connector block was needed and that clamps should be provided to secure the 2.5mm² cables. A revised model has since been introduced with minor alterations.

■ **Time taken: approximately 3 hours.**

Measuring just 110 x 110 x 60mm (4¼ x 4¼ x 2³⁄₈in) the Fuse Control is a compact unit that takes up little space.

The IN and OUT connector blocks on the circuit board are clearly labelled but could be larger, with wider spacing between the cables.

Making good connections needs dexterity and it was easier to complete the electrical connections before mounting the unit.

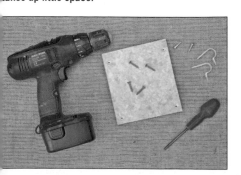

The 3mm ply used for caravan furniture is too thin for mounting a Fuse Control so an additional base was cut using faced 15mm ply.

In the absence of the type of cable clamp fitted in a 13A plug, the cables were secured by clips fitted just outside the casing.

Now in use, the Fuse Control reveals that a connected 230V appliance is drawing 1.5A; self-set tripping is a great idea too.

Choosing and fitting a solar panel

Comments: *It is wrong to regard the purchase of a solar panel as a money-saving strategy. When a 70W panel and regulator can cost around £450 and an 85Ahr battery is sold for around £50, it would take many years to recuperate the cost of a solar system. Buying a new battery every two years might work out less expensive.*

In essence solar systems are convenience products, because they provide a useful trickle charge for a leisure battery. This is particularly beneficial when stopping on sites with no mains hook-ups, and also during storage periods. That said, caravanners opt for several types of solar panels. As the accompanying photographs show, some are content to have a portable product rather than one which is permanently installed on their 'van. Many panels are also heavy and clumsy; an aluminium frame and a protective panel of heavy-duty glass needs sturdy support when fitted to the roof of a caravan. Fortunately, some useful installation brackets are now available which make the task easier.

Slightly more expensive are lightweight, semi-flexible frameless panels, which are protected by an ethylene vinyl acetate plasticised surface.

(These are often bonded to the decks of boats, and don't get damaged when members of the crew walk across them.) The price of such panels has become increasingly cheaper. Note that an all-important solar regulator must alway be fitted in the output supply from any panel. As usual, the hardest task is hiding the runs of wiring which link the panel to the leisure battery via the regulator.

GB-SOL, based in South Wales, manufactures flexible panels in 35W and 70W versions; these weigh 2 and 3kg respectively. The larger version is shown here, and this was installed using adhesive sealant and no further fixings. Only one hole has to be drilled in the roof and that is for the cable. Although inexpensive solar regulators work well in protecting a battery from over-charging, a Steca product was installed here on account of its useful monitoring facilities. For instance, the model chosen can keep an ongoing total of all the amp hours produced, and displays the information in both numerical and diagrammatic form. It also features a built-in resetting electronic fuse.

Once you have worked out how to gain safe access to your caravan's roof, and how to hide the cable, this is an easy product to fit. Removing it to transfer to another caravan might be much harder.

■ **Time taken: approximately 8 hours.**

Framed panels with glass protection can be quite heavy, so many caravan owners use portable panels rather than roof-mounted ones.

To double the output, some manufacturers sell hinged solar panels that open and close like a book.

Mounting a heavy panel on the roof of a caravan can often be difficult but these brackets from Run By The Sun can help.

Another useful type of bracket available from Run By The Sun is this one designed to support the corners of a solar panel.

The semi-flexible encapsulated panels from GB-SOL are available in 35W and 70W versions and will bond direct to a roof.

On a bright day a panel often produces around 20V, which would ruin a 12V battery; this is one of the reasons for fitting a regulator.

A connection block complete with a generous length of cable to suit customer needs is mounted on the front of GB-SOL panels.

Removing some interior lights helped confirm if any obstructions were in the roof void and revealed where the cable could be fitted.

Plastic strips covering joints in the plywood ceiling panels were unclipped; this also revealed other potential cable routeways.

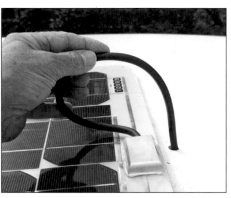

The panel was temporarily laid in position and a hole was drilled through the roof material to take the pre-coupled cable.

The aluminium backing of a GB-SOL panel can flex provided its curvature gains no more than 40mm over a one-metre length.

Having thoroughly cleaned the roof surface, the panel was put in its intended position and masking tape used to define its perimeter.

A generous application of white Sikaflex-512 Caravan was placed around the perimeter; remnants of black 512 were used too.

Weight discs held the panel down in its curving profile; 24 hours later a further beading of sealant was added at the edges.

The cable from the panel was taken through into a wardrobe. The Steca PR1010 regulator's connection block is at the bottom edge.

A small strengthening panel of 9mm ply was stuck inside the wardrobe to give a secure mounting point for the fixing screws.

Additional 2.5mm² automotive cable was then taken from the solar controller to the leisure battery, with in-line fuses fitted at both ends of the run. On a clear day and in direct line with a strong sun, the Steca PR1010 records a little over 3A.

Flat-screen TV support arms

Comments: *Many of the latest flat-screen portable televisions designed for mobile leisure users are supplied with VESA fixings on the back of the casing. These fittings are more likely to be found on freestanding 15in models and larger; the two versions of VESA threaded couplings are mounted at the four corners of a square at either 75 or 100mm centres. A range of matching mounting brackets is available, some of which are for direct wall mounting or for use with articulating single or double-length arms. These can also be used in conjunction with quick-release plates which allow a TV set to be easily removed from a caravan and then remounted on a bracket fitted in your house.*

Provided you purchase a flat-screen set with VESA mountings, support brackets are available from electrical specialists such as Grade U.K. Versions with or without a quick-release plate are easy to attach to a TV; a less straightforward attachment is at the other end. Caravan shelves, cupboards and furniture are often built using 3mm decorative ply, which needs to be strengthened by bonding-on some additional 15mm ply in order to cope with the weight of the set. When it is being towed a caravan is subjected to considerable forces, and its rise and fall on poor road surfaces can soon cause a support arm to come adrift from a weak mounting point.

The B Tech BT 7513 articulating arm unit shown here can support a maximum weight of 15kg (33lb) as long as the wall fixing is sound. The manufacturer is certainly anxious to encourage careful workmanship by stating in the instruction sheet that failure 'to mount this bracket correctly may lead to serious injury and/or death'.

■ **Time taken: bracket assembly 20 minutes; wall-mounting time will vary.**

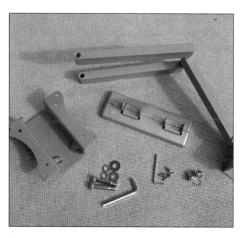
Several types of bracket are available. This one features a double arm and tilting facility which allows a screen to be aligned.

On this television the four VESA couplings are used to attach a carrying handle/support base which has to be removed.

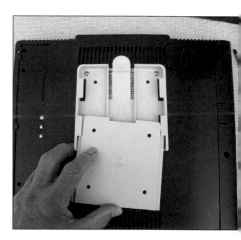
With the rear handle removed, a quick-release assembly can be fitted to the TV using its VESA threaded coupling sockets.

Good kits include well-illustrated assembly instructions; this one also included two hexagonal spanners to tighten the assembly bolts.

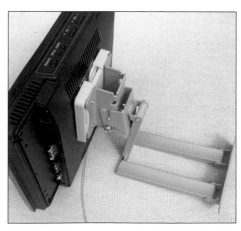
The brackets can also be assembled so that a television is able to be adjusted by rotation on a pivot fitted to the outer end of the arm.

There is no need to fit the quick-release clamp shown here but it permits tool-free removal of a TV set when a caravan is not in use.

Removable external directional TV aerials

Comments: *For many years caravans have included an omni-directional roof aerial as a standard fitment. The fact that this type of aerial can receive both analogue and digital TV signals without any need to alter its position is a useful feature. Less pleasing is the fact that even with the assistance of a 12V amplifier and signal control unit, omni-directional aerials are not as effective as the directional types which have to be orientated correctly when you arrive at your destination. In areas of poor reception omni-directional products often give disappointing results and are frequently unsuitable for the reception of Freeview digital TV. This has led many owners to purchase a directional aerial in spite of the fact that their caravan may already be fitted with an omni-directional product.*

The products from Grade U.K. shown alongside enable you to erect an aerial pole to the side of your caravan with awning rail clamping. This in turn will provide elevation for a directional aerial, of which there are many types on sale. However, the coaxial cable from an aerial has to be taken to the TV set and the practice of draping it through a part-open window is not only inconvenient but can also pose a security risk: fitting an external coupling socket eliminates the need to use a window.

■ **Time taken: 1–2 hours including the coupling socket.**

To obtain a signal in areas where an omni-directional aerial performs poorly, many caravanners purchase a directional aerial.

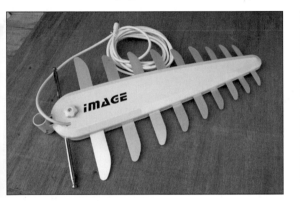

The Image directional aerial from Grade UK is easy to pack and can be mounted either horizontally or vertically to suit the transmitter.

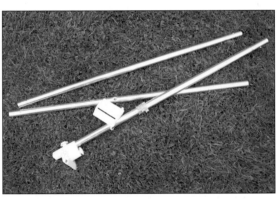

Lightweight interlocking poles elevate an aerial, and some are made to attach to a caravan's A-frame using the jockey wheel clamp.

Brackets are available to support a portable mast using a caravan awning rail; there are also wall fittings with adhesive pads.

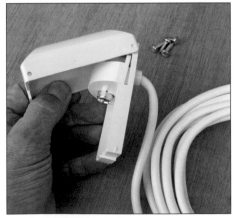

Weatherproof couplings for wall-mounting have pre-wired cable to use inside a caravan; the external socket takes the aerial's cable.

To replace an omni-directional roof aerial with a permanent elevating-pole model, Grade UK sells a blanking plate for the roof.

Installing a Grade UK Status 530 directional aerial

Comments: *Although a directional aerial usually achieves better reception than an omni-directional model, it has to be orientated in accordance with the location of the nearest transmitter. It also has to be inclined correctly because the signals from a transmitter are either horizontally or vertically polarised. Equally, the TV has to be retuned whenever you move to a new location.*

Orientating an external aerial to achieve a good signal is made more difficult when a TV set is located indoors and isn't visible through a window. Communication between two people doesn't always achieve a good result quickly and the task is certainly less pleasant when it's raining. This led to the development of aerials which can be adjusted from indoors when the antenna itself is mounted outside.

Of course, the mast has to be lowered before a caravan is towed on the road, and the longer the pole, the greater the intrusion indoors. For this reason Grade UK developed the Status 530/5 so that its short 485mm mast, when lowered, could be accommodated in a typical ceiling locker: alternatively the 530/10 has a 920mm mast which is usually fitted so that it can be lowered into either a wardrobe or a purpose-made locker.

These two models both include an FM radio antenna and a power pack which can either amplify or reduce a signal as required.

Before fitting a roof-mounted product, the structure of a caravan roof must be carefully checked. Moreover, when a caravan is still within

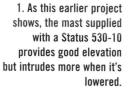

1. As this earlier project shows, the mast supplied with a Status 530-10 provides good elevation but intrudes more when it's lowered.

its warranty period it is likely that the installation of a product which necessitates cutting holes in its structure will invalidate the terms of cover. Owners of 'vans under warranty should check the position most carefully. Such matters must be taken seriously.

When the author was invited to fit one of the first prototype 530/10 models on behalf of Grade UK, the issue of roof strengthening and weatherproofing was given special attention. Consequent to this operation, the product was slightly modified by the manufacturer prior to going on general sale. Now, after eight years in use, the 530/10 has performed without fault and there is no evidence of either roof fatigue or water ingress.

As regards the installation illustrated here, this shows the short mast 530-5 version, which is less intrusive when lowered indoors. Although there are times when the higher an aerial, the better it performs, a long pole requires greater roof reinforcement, especially in gusting winds. This can be achieved by bonding a wooden block in the roof void, bearing in mind that the removal/reinstatement of a small section of ceiling ply is less conspicuous when it falls within a wardrobe or locker. Note that this aerial was being fitted on an imported caravan which had a 'cosmetic' roof rack. However, its cross members did not limit clearance when the aerial was lowered.

■ **Time taken: approximately a full day depending on whether roof strengthening is needed.**

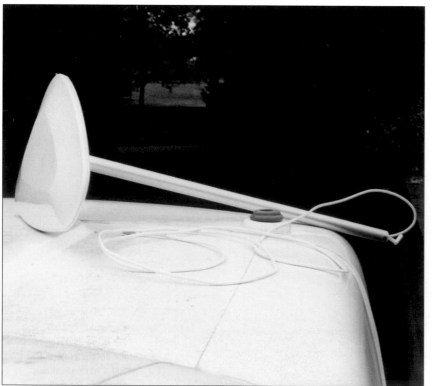

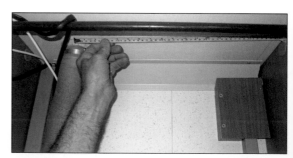

2. Using a flue pipe as a reference point, measurements were taken inside a wardrobe to check where pole brackets might be fitted.

3. On the roof, measurements were now taken from the flue outlet cover to establish that there were no obstructions outside.

4. Cutting and drilling templates are included, although in this instance the position of a pilot hole was marked using a collar.

5. Using a cordless drill, a pilot hole was drilled from inside. This was then enlarged using a 45mm hole saw from outside.

6. The external mounting plate is supplied with a foam seal and is fixed in place using the three 16mm screws supplied in the kit.

7. The mounting foot with its central sleeve and weatherproofing gaiter is fitted next and secured with three 32mm screws.

8. The antenna, which is pre-fitted to its mast, is now fitted from outside. When the 'van is parked level the mast must be vertical.

9. The pre-connected coaxial cable and mast now project inside the wardrobe and both the locking plate and collar are fitted.

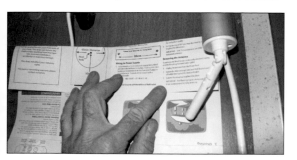

10. A convenient location was chosen for the power pack inside the wardrobe, and the template providing its fixing holes is offered up next.

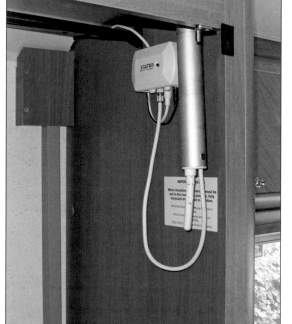

12. The cables are shortened, coaxial plugs are fitted as described in the detailed instructions and a warning label is affixed to the wall.

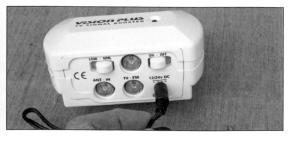

11. The markings on Grade UK's power packs are very clear and a plug with a length of wire is supplied for connecting to a 12V supply.

Comments: *Since Thetford first introduced fixed cassette toilets in the 1980s, numerous variations on this basic theme have appeared. At one time only bench-style products were installed, but it wasn't long before swivel bowl products appeared as well. Since these allow space to be utilised more efficiently their use by caravan manufacturers is steadily increasing.*

There are also differences between products fitted in touring caravans as opposed to motor caravans, particularly in respect of the source of flushing water. In motor caravans, flushing water is often drawn from the main fresh water supply tank, whereas in touring caravans it is drawn from a source built into the body of the toilet. An advantage of the latter system is that you can use additives like Thetford's pink Aqua Rinse in the flushing supply. A disadvantage is the fact that the limited capacity of the supply calls for frequent replenishment. This independent supply also mustn't be overlooked when water needs to be drained-down at the onset of frosty weather.

Since there are several dissimilar designs of fixed cassette toilet in a range of around ten models, it is impossible to present a detailed commentary here about every repair operation. Furthermore, those repairs that have to be undertaken out of sight, in the dark, and within the waste tank itself are not really feasible projects for an untrained amateur to tackle. As shown later, the service technicians who are able to carry out these (sometimes) unpleasant tasks have access to a training tank section like the one shown here. In consequence, the illustrations focus on some of the less difficult repair and maintenance jobs.

■ **Time taken: Variable, but the task of replacing a 'Lip Seal' valve can be completed, first time, in around 30 minutes.**

Useful tips

If an electric flush isn't working, some models draw 12V from the leisure battery; others use small batteries that might need changing.

Service technicians learn how to replace components in a waste tank by practising procedures with one of these dummy training tops.

A float which signals when the tank is nearly full has a magnet to activate the gauge. Floats break if you swirl water around too forcibly.

If you check closure blade operation when the tank is removed, reset the knob parallel to the side before reinstating the tank.

General points

In 2006 Thetford changed the name of 'Plastic Cleaner' to 'Bathroom Cleaner'. The foam is easy to use and leaves a shine.

Check an appliance's instruction leaflet on how to drain down the flushing water. The bung here is only for removing the final drops.

The swivelling drainage outlet on a cassette can be pulled from the main body of the container when turned to a release position.

Like several of the moving components fitted to a cassette, the swivel outlet has an 'O' ring; these need replacing if leaks appear.

Replacing a lip seal

Note: *To confirm the date when your toilet was manufactured, the code number printed on a sticker affixed to the underside of the waste tank is its completion date printed backwards (year/month/day).*

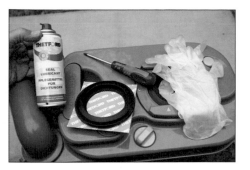

1. Basic equipment, but get the right lip seal. Toilets manufactured up to 15 June 2000 had a different pattern from the later ones.

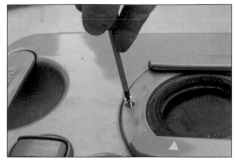

2. There were changes to the lip seal assembly and earlier models lacked a slider plate. But removal of screws is easy.

3. Prise off the two side flanges with a small screwdriver. This reveals six more crosshead screws to remove.

4. Put the screws in a safe place before lifting off the plastic frame that holds the lip seal in its recess.

5. Look most carefully at the lip seal when you remove it because there's a right and wrong way to fit it.

6. Liberally spray the new lip seal with Thetford's 'Seal Lubricant'. Perhaps protective gloves should have been worn from the start.

7. An old towel is handy for cleaning the seating ridge on which the lip seal is mounted. Clean the closure blade too.

8. Apply more seal lubricant to the blade, and the seating ridge. Fit the new lip seal the correct way up and reinstate the whole assembly.

Replacing an 'O' ring on the blade control knob

1. This is one of the items which has to be removed using touch alone by placing your hand into the tank with the blade fully open.

2. This photograph of the dummy training top shows how you use a screwdriver to depress the spring lugs which keep a knob in place.

3. When the knob has been pulled out of its housing, you can see the spring lugs on either side that you depressed with the screwdriver.

4. Like most of the components attached to a waste tank, the blade control knob has an 'O' ring that needs replacing if liquid seeps out.

Comments: *Many caravanners prefer stabilisers which are mounted near a tow ball and attached alongside a caravan A-frame. Their surfaces provide a large area of friction, and if the main arm is like a single leaf-spring, vertical movements (called 'pitching') are reduced as well. One of the earliest examples was made by Scott, and the Bulldog is still a popular product. The principle was adopted earlier on cars and this type of shock absorbing device can be seen mounted vertically at the front of many pre-war vehicles.*

However, one of the disadvantages of these products is that they have to be stored and fitted separately: in contrast, ball-acting devices form an integral part of the special coupling head fitted on many recent caravans. This is certainly a more convenient arrangement, but in operational terms the surface area of the friction pads is small.

The Winterhoff ball-acting product is fitted to BPW chassis and benefits from the fact that its two friction pads apply pressure at the front and rear of a tow ball. This means that they can remove unwanted deflections in both lateral and vertical planes. Earlier models from AL-KO only had pads acting on either side of a tow ball, which meant that they did not resist unwanted vertical movements.

Later AL-KO ball-acting stabilisers have the addition of friction pads in the fore and aft position too, although these lack the clamping effect that is adopted for the side pads. For this reason they might not arrest pitching movements as much as the clamping pads fitted on a Winterhoff product.

As regards the success of ball-mounted friction stabilisers in general, these devices are faced with a tough task when a long caravan starts to swing from side to side. The bearing surfaces are not large, and if there is paint on a tow ball, or the slightest hint of grease, their effects are considerably reduced. The pads are also likely to wear out fairly quickly, although AL-KO suggests that if they are cared for properly and kept grease-free they may not need replacing for around 20,000 miles.

The accompanying sequence of photographs shows the friction pads being changed on a recent AKS 3004 stabiliser. These are made of a special plastic compound, whereas on the early AKS models the pads enclosed a separate insert of brake-like friction material. You could also adjust the pressure applied by each pad by turning its threaded stem with a flat-bladed screwdriver. On the recent models, adjustments are made instead by fitting shims; this is the name given to very thin spacer washers made for the job.

Note that this is only a brief insight into AL-KO's products. A very helpful leaflet available from the Company or downloaded from the Internet gives a wealth of useful information about operational efficiency and user care.

■ **Time taken: Approximately 80 minutes.**

The AL-KO 3004 is a standard fitting on many modern caravans in place of a conventional coupling head product.

The pads on early 3000-series stabilisers had a separate friction material. The recent black ones have a type of plastic compound.

Changing the friction pads on an AL-KO 3004 stabiliser

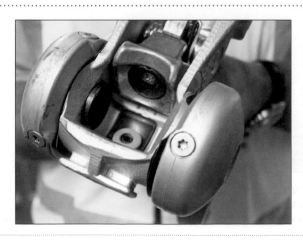

1. The side friction pads move inwards to clamp tightly to the tow ball sides. The rear one here doesn't move once installed.

2. Arrows on side castings need to be related to the moulded recesses in the red plastic. The position here indicates little wear.

3. If the two arrows align with this part of the recess when the clamp has been activated, the side pads need replacement.

4. This red/green indicator reveals if the front/rear fixed pads are worn and need replacing or whether the 50mm tow ball has worn.

5. The first step in a pad replacement operation is to grasp the red plastic 'soft dock' moulding at the front and to ease it firmly upwards.

6. To remove the screw which secures the stabiliser handle you need a torx spanner, which AL-KO can supply if required.

7. Prise out the red side caps with a small screwdriver, then give a sharp tap using a punch to unseat the stems of the stabiliser pads.

8. The pads might have one or two spacer shims or none at all. Note what is used and remember which sides the shims were fitted.

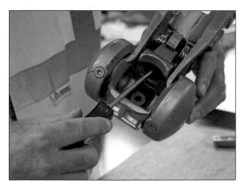

9. A screwdriver is required to remove the rear fixed pad and to provide the access needed, its coupling handle should be lifted.

10. Before removing the front pad, the safety indicator should be pushed outwards and held with a 14mm open-ended spanner.

11. All four pads are now removed. The side units with their shims are on the right; the fore and aft pads are shown on the left.

12. New front and back pads are screwed in place; stems of the side pads are then pushed into each side. Now test on a tow ball.

13. Applying the side handles still disconnected from the handle shows that the left-hand pad needs an extra shim to level the arrows.

14. With the arms still working independently, these two arrows show their pressure is equalised. Only now should you refit the red handle.

Fitting a motor moving device from PowrWheel

The wheel-driving mechanisms are sometimes unattractive but the latest model from Truma is enclosed in a smart casing.

It is possible now to have movers fitted to twin-axle caravans but these require a very robust machine which is much more costly.

Comments: *Since Carver first introduced the 'Caravan Mover' in the late 1990s, many other manufacturers have introduced similar products. Different refinements have also appeared, although the broad principles have been much the same. Most manufacturers have also purchased similar motors from an independent specialist.*

The benefit of having one of these devices fitted is especially evident if you have to park a caravan in a restricted space. It's no secret either that many owners are unable to reverse a caravan with confidence and accuracy. Then there are elderly and disabled owners who are not in a position to manoeuvre a caravan manually either on a site or back at home.

The disadvantages of these products are their cost, which is often close to a four-figure sum, and weight. As stated earlier in this chapter, have your caravan weight checked before purchasing one of these heavy devices. Also remember that even a good leisure battery can be soon discharged if used to perform manoeuvres for an extended period.

There are also stand-alone, portable motorised devices that attach to a caravan's coupling head as an alternative strategy. They involve little attachment work and do not add weight to a caravan if carried in the back of a towcar. However, permanently installed movers have become extremely popular in the UK and the PowrWheel example shown being fitted here is only one of several products.

■ **Time taken: A full day.**

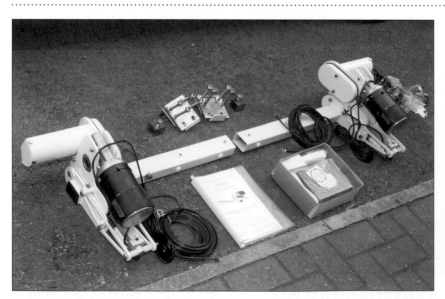

1. The motors and brackets of a Powr Touch Powrmover (2008 model) are laid out for checking. Installation involves *no* drilling.

2. The two 12V motors have reduction gearboxes which can be driven independently on a single-axle caravan.

3. Manufacturers of modern chassis do not permit drilling so the PowrWheel units are supplied with sturdy clamping devices.

4. A plate together with powder-coated clamp brackets fastens to a lightweight chassis; only non-standard chassis need welding.

5. The bracket clamps firmly to the chassis side members and 'U' bolts support the bar on which the motor is mounted.

6. As soon as both motors are supported by the chassis members, a cross bar is inserted through apertures in both assemblies.

7. Once the bar is centralised midway between the motor supports, it is fastened in position with captive bolts to brace both units.

8. It is important that the friction rollers are both aligned equally with the tyres, so the motor units are adjusted if necessary.

9. Wooden spacer blocks are also supplied to ensure that both rollers are set at the right distance from the tyre tread.

10. When the position of the motors is correct, stop blocks are fitted either side to prevent an active motor from sliding along the chassis.

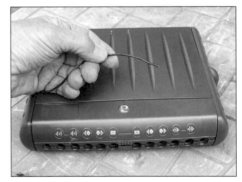

11. The mechanical work is complete. Now the main radio-controlled unit with its aerial has to be installed inside the caravan.

12. The number of wires attached to the product may look daunting but the control unit is well marked and the instructions are clear.

13. Because of its close proximity to the motors, which keeps cables as short as possible, this control box is fitted in the wardrobe.

14. The latest remote control unit has a red line drawing showing the caravan and its draw bar. This makes its operation much more clear.

Servicing and seasonal preparation

Like any other road-going vehicle, a caravan has to be serviced regularly. There are seasonal tasks to carry out too, particularly if a caravan is unused for long periods.

The need to keep a car serviced regularly is never questioned. It is, therefore, rather surprising that some caravanners do not realise that their caravan should be serviced as well.

Servicing

Many jobs might be included under the heading of 'servicing' but some stand out as particularly important. For instance, it is essential that safety items like the brakes are periodically adjusted; the operation of road lights needs checking, too. It is also essential to carry out regular damp checks to confirm there are no leak points in a caravan's bodywork – a subject discussed in Chapter 5.

Then there are the appliances and if a refrigerator, a heater, an oven or a hob are never serviced, there could be more than a risk of malfunction. An unchecked fault here might lead to the release of carbon monoxide.

So it is most important that a caravan is regularly serviced. This raises two questions – what needs to be done, and who should carry out the work?

Servicing development and expectations

Before the establishment of clear codes of practice, some self-styled 'caravan specialists' used to charge a substantial fee for servicing work but failed to provide customers with written documentation stating what service operations had actually been carried out. Doubts about dealer-competence were confirmed in the late 1980s when the author was asked by a sceptical, non-technical owner to inspect his caravan immediately after it had been given a 'dealer service'. It was soon apparent that the brakes had not been checked at all by the 'caravan specialist'. Not only was there a substantial amount of brake dust inside the assemblies; the linings on the leading edges of its brake shoes were worn perilously close to the metal.

Suffice it to say, the receipt of a dated, signed service schedule with warning comments on 'wear items' like tyres is essential, and both the dealer and customer should have copies. In reality, the poor level of care described above was probably not typical. Many servicing specialists conduct their work in a professional manner. A detailed service schedule will be available for inspection *before* a caravan is submitted and a completed copy is given to the customer at the time of collection. Comments on matters like brake shoe condition, tyre wear and so on are entered on the form.

Also included on the job list is a damp test as described in Chapter 5, and the results of this should also be given to the customer, albeit on a separate form. Normally a dealer takes readings using 50 or more check points indicated on line drawings, and information should be recorded on these diagrams where appropriate.

The condition and operation of both gas and electrical supply systems will similarly be checked and recorded on the service schedule document. However, a good workshop will also offer to provide *additional* inspection services, a dated certificate from an independent approved CORGI-registered gas contractor and a similar certificate from an NICEIC, ECA or ECA (Scotland) approved electrical contractor/member. This will be charged as an additional service, of course, but these optional independent reports can be very useful when buying or selling a caravan.

Without doubt, there have been wide discrepancies in the quality of services offered to caravan owners. Anxious to establish benchmarks for service quality and to create identifiable and consistent levels of customer care, The National Caravan Council has been increasingly involved in raising standards, as mentioned later.

Service schedules

When the First Edition of *The Caravan Manual* was published in 1993, it did not include a list of servicing jobs – usually referred to as the 'service schedule'. At the time, surprisingly few dealers worked with a job list and most operations were concerned with brake and road-light checks and adjustments. From a nationwide perspective there was undoubtedly a lack of consistency in this all-important aspect of caravan care.

To provide caravanners with more servicing information in the 1996 Second Edition, the author visited many dealers and joined training courses organised by the manufacturers of caravans, chassis, cooling appliances, towbars, space heaters and water heaters. Additional investigative work included familiarisation visits to water system manufacturers (e.g. Carver, Optimus and 'Whale'), and bodywork repair specialists (e.g. Crossley Coachcraft). Using the knowledge gained, the recommendations of many specialists were then brought together and a detailed service schedule was drawn-up and presented in the new edition.

The compilation of operations prompted many discussions, and the schedule was subsequently extended and refined for the 2000 Third Edition. During the research it was helpful to shadow an accreditation examiner inspecting a potential 'Approved Workshop' (White Arches Caravans). Shortly afterwards The National Caravan Council convened a meeting with the author and the published schedule was used as a model during discussions concerned with the ongoing development of 'Approved Caravan Workshops'. This national accreditation scheme is described later.

To raise standards further there is now a City & Guilds Examination in Caravan Engineering (Touring Caravans and Motorhomes), and in the practical part of the test examinees have to carry out a full service using a detailed service schedule. It has been especially informative seeing the scope and depth of scrutiny that was exercised when candidates took a practical examination conducted at Lowdham Leisureword in Nottinghamshire. Prior to taking this City & Guilds Examination, students under tuition are given a copy of the *Caravan Industry Training Organisation Engineers' Handbook* which outlines procedures associated with each service operation.

The caravan owner is the beneficiary of these many improvements, and further innovations and ideas are under discussion. Rightly so, because

At this AL-KO Kober training course, participants learn the procedures involved when checking a ball-operating stabiliser coupling.

new products are being introduced all the time. To give one example, a large proportion of recent caravans are supplied with either an AL-KO Kober or BPW Winterhoff ball-acting stabiliser built into the coupling head. Like brakes and bearings these need periodic checks, so an inspection and operational evaluation has been added to the standard service schedule job list given here.

Another debate is also in progress relating to gas-operated appliances. In existing service schedules, gas appliances like a cooker, space heater, water heater or refrigerator are given what is described as an 'operation check'. Taking a space heater as an example, a service specialist who is conducting a standard service operation is only required to:

• check that it is correctly installed in accordance with its manufacturer's specification,
• check that its flue and the termination point of the flue are undamaged,
• check the burner flame visually, as long as it is accessible without needing extensive dismantling work, and
• check that a flame failure device is operating satisfactorily.

An examiner shadows a candidate who is carrying out a service operation during the City & Guilds Examination in Caravan Engineering.

Although the burner on a Carver Crystal or Henry GE water heater is located behind a shield, this only take a few minutes to remove; in consequence the flame shape and colour are easy to check visually.

Stabiliser checks

In spite of their contribution to safe towing, stabilisers are seldom checked during a service operation. Equally, many owners do not realise that some products need to be inspected, checked and adjusted. Traditionally stabilisers haven't been a service item because blade-types are removable assemblies that couple-up with both a towcar and its caravan. However, ball-acting stabilisers are normally an integral part of a caravan's coupling head and these are now fitted as standard on most new models. Like all friction-dependent devices, these need attention if grease or a coating gets on to their friction surfaces. Even if a caravanner ensures that their car's towball is always completely clean, grease sometimes contaminates the friction pads after a caravan has been moved around a storage facility by a tractor or other vehicle. AL-KO Kober states that friction pads on its AKS coupling head stabilisers can sometimes be cleaned with reasonable success using a degreasing agent but in most cases it is preferable to fit new pads. And since coupling head stabilisers are now permanent fixtures, checking and reporting their condition is deserving of inclusion on a service schedule list.

Removing the burner of a Carver Crystal or Henry GE water heater is easy for an experienced gas technician, so removing any dust with an air line is quite often carried out within a basic habitation service.

Equally, the service specialist is required to notify an owner in writing if in his or her opinion the appliance itself needs to be serviced. In other words nothing is likely to have been taken apart, and no attempt will have been made to remove insects or spiders from gas assemblies.

A similar abbreviated check will be made of a refrigerator in operation, but the service technician is unlikely to clean the burner tube, replace the gas jet or perform the other service tasks that its manufacturer recommends should be carried out annually. Some of these operations were shown in Chapter 11.

It comes as no surprise that caravan owners often blame a dealer for poor workmanship if a gas appliance fails to work just a few weeks after a four-hour standard service has been carried out. In reality, many caravanners are simply not aware that some appliances need to be serviced separately as one-off operations in order to comply with their manufacturers' recommendations. Judging from readers' letters sent to caravanning magazines, this situation

An invoice issued after a caravan has been serviced should include an itemised section showing the charge for grease, other lubricants and spare parts like replacement hub nuts.

is seldom made clear to owners at service workshops. Moreover, this might explain why many refrigerators never receive a full service as laid down by their manufacturers.

The position regarding individual appliances should be clearly stated on written schedules so that owners can take the appropriate steps to keep their gas appliances up to scratch as, and when, appropriate. Of course, an alternative might be to embrace the work on individual appliances within a basic service. However, this is not really feasible because caravans are built to dissimilar specifications, have different types of appliances fitted, and may contain products whose recommended service intervals are greater than the 12-monthly period applicable to basic habitation work. On account of these variables, it would be scarcely possible to quote a fixed charge rate for 'all-in servicing' operations.

Recognising that some workshops already conduct damp tests and refrigerator servicing as separate operations, there might be good sense in offering three levels of caravan service such as:

- **Bronze** – External light check, brake check/adjustment, stability check, and road safety elements.
- **Silver** – The preceding operations together with basic habitation service with damp check, as at present, and in compliance with warranty conditions.
- **Gold** – The preceding operations together with a full service of gas appliances, with a 'Prices from…' quotation to reflect the dissimilarities in caravan equipment.

Charges

On an average size caravan with a typical complement of equipment, The National Caravan Council advises that a thorough 'basic service' usually takes around four hours. When related to the hourly labour rate charged by the workshop, you can soon calculate what this is likely to cost. However, members of the Approved Workshop scheme are obliged to display service charges in their reception area.

Not that the labour element is the only cost feature. There are also charges for lubricants and replacement parts. On older caravans, for example, brake drum retention nuts are secured with replaceable split pins; on newer models the 'one-shot' nuts described in Chapter 4 also have to be renewed every time the brake drums are removed. Flexible gas hose is normally replaced too, on caravans that employ gas cylinder-mounted regulators. All these elements are 'chargeable' and should be itemised on an invoice.

It should also be pointed out that some workshops often carry out minor repairs during the course of a service without additional labour charges, provided there's time available within the normal four-hour booking. For instance, if the

If an 'easily curable' gas leak is detected and the work is proceeding well within the four-hour time period allotted for a habitation service, it is often remedied there and then.

....

gas system is found to have a small leak at one of the couplings, the tightening of the connection is often carried out there and then.

Similarly if a fluorescent light tube is faulty, a replacement will usually be fitted and noted down on the invoice's parts list. However, you should enquire about the workshop's policy when you book-in your caravan; typically it's in your interests to get small jobs carried out at once rather than having to make a further appointment in the future.

More expensive jobs, of course, might also appropriately be carried out while a caravan is in the workshop. However, if something like a new water pump needs to be fitted a service centre would be expected to contact an owner before embarking on such a repair, since pumps can be costly items. This is another procedure to check with your dealer; unexpected bills are never welcome.

Approved Workshop Scheme

Recognising that workshops throughout the country lacked consistency when carrying out habitation services, an initiative was launched some years ago by The National Caravan Council in conjunction with The Camping & Caravanning Club and The Caravan Club.

After lengthy discussions, a nationwide chain of Approved Caravan Workshops was established in 1999. The idea proved successful, and in 2003 centres specialising in motor caravan servicing were also brought into the scheme. At that point the name was changed to 'Approved Workshops' and the scheme's publications included an 'Independently Assessed' red banner.

Before being accepted into the scheme, service centres wishing to gain approval have to undergo a lengthy and elaborate inspection conducted by an independent agency. The appointed agency also administers the scheme on a day-to-day basis. The national caravanning clubs mentioned above and The National Caravan Council can provide enquirers with addresses of Approved Workshop members. However, approvals are not 'set in stone' and re-examination inspections are conducted

annually to ensure that the required standards are maintained.

During the early planning stages, the Inspection Agency met with National Caravan Council specialists and the author to discuss the content of service schedules. These schedules are also the subject of periodic reviews in order to reflect changing needs and the introduction of new caravan components.

The accompanying panel gives further information about the scheme, which certainly provides caravan owners with assurances of a high standard of workmanship, procedural consistency, receipt of a detailed invoice and a clear customer complaints procedure. Centres are also obliged to display a full tariff of charges in their service reception area, and that's something owners usually want to see before making a booking.

Carrying out servicing work

As the schedule overleaf indicates, there are many different operations involved in a standard service. There is also a wide variety of staff experience and competency at different service centres. At an Approved Workshop, the qualifications of staff and the training courses they have attended are usually displayed in the service reception. The industry also benefits from employees who have repaired caravans for most of their working lives. However, small companies sometimes enlist the help of external qualified gas and electrical specialists when specific certification work is required.

As regards DIY caravan owners, we all have different background experiences, different skills, different competencies and different collections of tools. Without doubt, some routine jobs on a service schedule are not safety-critical and can easily be carried out by most DIY enthusiasts using inexpensive hand tools. Tasks like checking road lights, inspecting tyres, changing water filters, lubricating a jockey wheel and greasing corner steadies are just a few examples.

....

Cleaning away grit with a wire brush and applying a light film of grease to corner steady spindles is a job which many owners tackle themselves. Unlike work on a caravan brake assembly, no special tools are needed.

Approved Workshops no longer bear the word 'Caravan' on their wall plaques; some are more specifically concerned with motor caravans.

Approved Workshops

The number of Approved Workshops is ever-increasing, although it should be noted that some participating companies specialise in either touring or motor caravans.

In one information leaflet, the Approved Workshop scheme is described as 'rigorous, uncompromising and designed to offer you, the customer, an assurance of first class service and value for money.' This a praiseworthy intention and the scheme offers many benefits to caravan owners, as its publicity leaflets explain.

Note: *There is no implicit suggestion that workshops which are not members of the Approved Workshop scheme are not able to provide owners with a professional and high standard of service. Some most definitely do offer good service and workmanship; but there are others which don't.*

Having checked, cleaned and lightly greased parts of the brakes on this modern 'van, a technician needs to reinstate the drum and use a calibrated torque wrench on the retaining hub nut. Few owners possess such expensive specialist tools.

Sometimes a hub puller is needed to remove a difficult brake drum.

Well-equipped service centres have a ramp which affords excellent access to the underside of a caravan.
(Photograph courtesy of Crossley Coachcraft)

When cleaning the brake surfaces using emery cloth, a trained technician is aware of the importance of using a mask; safety goggles might be needed, too.

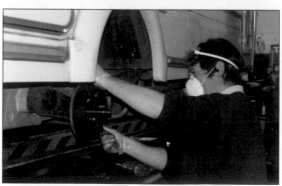

Looking at more involved jobs, some DIY car owners might have the tools required to remove difficult brake drums, adjust brakes, torque-check hub nuts, check tyres and tackle maintenance work on the undergear using information contained in Chapter 4. For others, who don't want to spend over £200 on the type of torque wrench needed for checking flanged hub nuts, tasks like that would be a step too far.

However, irrespective of an owner's self-chosen level of personal involvement, wearing the correct safety gear and achieving safe access is essential; in fact, recent legislation has resulted in many service technicians being more aware than DIYers of current health and safety issues. In addition, workshops that are equipped with a caravan ramp are also at a clear advantage when access is needed to chassis components and running gear.

As regards work involving a gas supply system and gas appliances, this must be entrusted to a competent and appropriately qualified person. This point was emphasised in Chapter 10 and the matter of qualification was explained. In a similar way, installation checks on a 230V mains supply system should be entrusted to a qualified electrician familiar with caravan wiring practices.

Since the experiences and qualifications of caravan owners are all different, there is no simple prescription as to what elements in a standard service operation we could or should not tackle ourselves. It should be self-explanatory that under no circumstances should an owner embark on work if they are ill-equipped and doubtful about what it entails. As a further caveat, don't forget that during a caravan's warranty period, its manufacturer would require all servicing work to be undertaken at the specified intervals and by one of its approved dealers. In addition the warranty documents have to be signed, dated and stamped as specified.

Purchasing pre-owned caravans

In the light of the points made above, purchasing a pre-owned caravan, either privately or from a dealer, is often accompanied by an uncertainty about its operational condition. It is no secret that

This fully trained service specialist is using a manometer to check the integrity of a gas supply system – not a task for an unqualified DIY owner.

Typical Standard Service Schedule

Make:　　　　　**Model:**　　　　　**Year:**　　　　　**Chassis number:**　　　　　**Vehicle Identification no.**

Section 1: Chassis and Running Gear

	Comments
1. Check coupling head; lubricate as necessary	☐ ....
2. Lubricate over-run piston using grease gun	☐ ....
3. Check hand brake operation and adjust	☐ ....
4. Check breakaway chain/cable.	☐ ....
5. Check and lubricate jockey wheel	☐ ....
6. Check and lubricate corner steadies.	☐ ....
7. Remove wheels/drum assembly. Remove dust	☐ Shoe condition ....
8. Check tapered bearings if fitted; clean, re-grease	☐ ....
9. Adjust brakes, commencing at drum	☐ ....
10. Replace split pin or 'one shot' stub axle nut	☐ ....
11. Torque 'one shot' nut to manufacturer's data	☐ ....
12. Check tyres, remove stones, check pressures	☐ Tyre condition ....
13. Replace wheels and torque check nuts/bolts	☐ ....
14. Check operation, grease spare wheel rack if fitted	☐ ....
15. Check pads on ball-acting stabiliser if fitted	☐ ....

General report: ....

Section 2: Gas

	Comments
1. Carry out pressure test on system	☐ ....
2. Replace washer on butane regulator if fitted	☐ ....
3. Replace flexible hose and hose clips if fitted	☐ ....
4. Fridge: Light, test for cooling, check gas drop-out holes	☐ ....
5. Cooking appliances: Light and verify operation	☐ ....
6. Check space heater operation; check gas drop-out holes	☐ ....
7. Check water heater operation, check gas drop-out holes	☐ ....
8. Certificate of gas system integrity if requested	☐ ....

Report on gas appliances: ....

Section 3: Electrical

	Comments
1. Check RCD and MCBs on central unit	☐ ....
2. Test 13 amp mains sockets	☐ ....
3. Test 12V sockets	☐ ....
4. Check integrity of wiring and fuses	☐ ....
5. Check operation of all interior lights	☐ ....
6. Check road lights, reflectors, awning lamp	☐ ....
7. Certificate of Mains Check appended if requested	☐ ....

Report on the electrical system: ....

Section 4: Water systems

	Comments
1. Check operation of water pump, clean grit filter	☐ ....
2. Check waste & fresh water system for leaks	☐ ....
3. Flush through with purifying cleaner	☐ ....
4. Change charcoal water filter, if fitted	☐ ....
5. Check toilet flush and blade operation	☐ ....

General comments on water systems: ....

Section 5: Body-work and General Condition

	Comments
1. Carry out damp and seepage tests.	☐ ....
2. Look for poor sealant /potential leak points.	☐ ....
3. Confirm window operation; lubricate if needed.	☐ ....
4. Check/oil door lock; oil hinges.	☐ ....

Comments on bodywork/general condition: ....

Section 6: Fire warning systems

	Comments
1. Check fire alarm operation/ battery	☐ ....
2. Check expiry date on extinguisher	☐ ....
3. Check fire blanket location/fixing	☐ ....

Work completed by: 　　　　　Date: 　　　　　Official stamp:

Statement of Standard Labour Charges 　　　　　£ ___ : ___

Total cost of parts and lubricants, itemised on invoice 　　　　　£ ___ : ___

SUB-TOTAL 　　　　　£ ___ : ___

Value-Added Tax 　　　　　£ ___ : ___

TOTAL: 　　　　　£ ___ : ___

Additional Service Options: Note that gas appliances are only given an 'operation check' during a basic habitation service. To perform a full service on a refrigerator, space heater, water heater and cooker as specified by their respective manufacturers, the workshop requires owners to make an additional booking. These tasks sometimes involve the dismantling and disconnecting of appliances. To verify that this enhanced service work has been carried out, an appliance-specific, dated certificate is issued on completion. Price quotations are available on request.

Service Intervals: The use of a caravan cannot be easily gauged in miles. In the case of average use, a caravan should be serviced every 12 months. However, anyone who uses a caravan regularly and extensively should submit it for servicing more often.

some caravans and individual appliances have *never* been serviced, and in consequence some elements are in a woefully unsatisfactory state.

When purchasing from a dealer's forecourt, it is important to enquire whether the quoted price includes the completion of a full service prior to collection. The word 'full' means that the caravan has received a refrigerator service, cooker inspection and gas heating appliance service as recommended by their respective manufacturers. Naturally, this might not be needed if these operations have been carried out recently and there are signed, dated certificates confirming the scope of the work. In reality, however, this paperwork is seldom available.

If it is decided to purchase a caravan with no service documentation and there's evidence of owner modifications and fitments of uncertain provenance, it is strongly recommended that the 'van is thoroughly checked and fully serviced before being put into commission. Caravans 'sold as seen' may offer many hours of pleasurable renovation, but don't be misled into thinking that their gas systems are safe just because there's a flame on a hob. Furthermore, unseen items like brake shoes might be unacceptably worn.

Pre-storage tasks

If you are not going to use your caravan for several months, certain tasks have to be carried out. This is especially true when laying it up for winter.

Outdoor tasks

❏ Select a suitable location
Make sure the caravan is parked in a place where damage cannot be caused by falling branches, slates or tiles. Even a conker can cause a dent on an aluminium roof panel. Remember too, that trees leave a green algae deposit during a long storage period.

Try to avoid parking under trees during a winter lay-up. Not only are falling branches a danger: green deposits are most unsightly.

❏ Remove the awning
Make absolutely certain that your awning is dry before packing it away for winter. Brush off bird lime and clean the plastic skirts if necessary. If the awning has been left dirty or if it has been used under trees which exude sticky substances, a thorough wash is needed. Often it's best to re-erect it for cleaning and there are products you can use such as *Awning Cleaner* from Camco. Tent cleaners sold in outdoor activity shops can also be helpful. Finally, check that damp hasn't found its way into any of the pole sections.

❏ Chock the wheels so you can leave the handbrake off
Over an extended lay-up, handbrake mechanisms sometimes seize up, leaving the brakes locked on. If you can park on level ground, chock the wheels, lower the corner steadies, and disengage the handbrake. Bear in mind that even on a mild slope, some of the plastic chocks sold in caravan accessory shops have a nasty tendency to slip on smooth, hard surfaces.

❏ Decide whether to remove the wheels, substituting axle stands
Tyre walls can sustain damage if a caravan is left unmoved for a long period – especially if they're exposed to sunlight. Storing the wheels avoids this and also makes theft more difficult. Winterwheels from PGR can be put in place of removed wheels, although axle stands are better because they also relieve the suspension system. The stands used must be robust and have a wide base.

❏ If you decide against removing wheels, consider security clamps
Thefts of laid-up caravans are all too common. Fit at least one security device. A close fitting wheel clamp is an excellent deterrent, but use a heavy duty version. Remember that electronic systems are of no use when the battery is flat.

Parking on level ground, chocking the wheels and lowering the corner steadies usually means you can avoid applying the brakes. This ensures they won't seize-up in the 'on' position.

Although a plastic cover helps to keep a coupling head protected from severe weather, make sure that air can circulate around the mechanism.

It usually makes sense to remove cylinders because gas lockers are easily forced open by thieves. However, store them as advised in the text.

❏ **Protect the coupling head**

Fit a loose-fitting plastic cover that will protect the coupling head while also allowing air to circulate around it.

❏ **Remove the gas cylinders and transfer to a safe, ventilated store**

Transfer gas cylinders to a lockable, well-ventilated shed. If you leave cylinders in a caravan locker box, they may get stolen and could be a fire risk. Never store cylinders in a cellar or a location where leaks of this heavier-than-air gas would be unable to escape. Ensure the cylinders are kept upright.

❏ **Cover a gas pipe outlet with a fabric bag and an elastic band**

If spiders decide to nest in an exposed length of flexible gas hose, you might suffer from gas blockages when the caravan is put back into commission. Avoid using a plastic bag since this will retain any condensation.

❏ **Remove battery to a place where it can be periodically charged**

A battery will soon be ruined if left in a discharged

Tie a fabric bag over a gas supply hose to keep out spiders and insects during a period of storage.

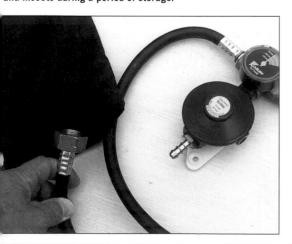

condition. Transfer it to a garage or workshed where you can monitor its condition and recharge when necessary. Trickle chargers often sold for keeping the batteries of Classic cars in sound condition are also used by caravan owners.

❏ **Spray 12N, 12S and 13-pin connections with a moisture-repellent like Tri-Flow**

Brass pins and sockets get coated with a deposit that affects their electrical contact. Spray them with a moisture repellent like Tri-Flow; this won't damage the plastic part of the plug.

The circuitry in trickle chargers allows them to be coupled to a battery for long periods. Charging is activated automatically when the level drops too low.

The pins on connection plugs and sockets should be sprayed with a moisture repellent like Tri-Flow.

Once all the taps have been opened at the sink, basin and shower, a Truma Ultrastore heater is drained-down by lifting a yellow lever tap alongside the appliance.

❑ Block off water supply inlets
Keep out spiders and insects. A water inlet, or outlet, provides a pleasant home for them in winter – and blockages later.

❑ Replace the water filter
Arguably this could be left until Spring, but doing the job in late Autumn means you can get 'off the mark' quicker when the new season arrives. What's more, the price of the filter might be higher next season.

❑ Drain off a water heater
Repairing a frost-damaged water heater is costly and drain-down procedures will be given in the

Owner's Manual. On a Carver Cascade this involves removing an external drain plug, which is shown at the end of Chapter 10. On a Truma water heater there's a yellow lift-up release tap situated indoors adjacent to the appliance.

❑ Empty the flushing water from a cassette toilet
If you own a Thetford 'bench-style' cassette toilet, check the vertical tube clipped inside the access door that shows water level. Pull it from the clip and hold downwards to drain off the remaining water. Then empty the top-up bowl in accordance with the manufacturer's instruction leaflet. Check instructions applicable to the different types of swivel bowl models.

❑ Polish out serious marks on exterior bodywork
Remove body stains under fitments or guttering before the onset of winter. Several products are now available which will do this and cleaning work was discussed in Chapter 5. If time permits, apply a coating of polish for additional seasonal protection.

❑ If planning to fit a breathable cover, ensure the caravan is clean, free of dust and surface dirt
This is particularly important for acrylic windows, but never cover these with cling film – it is believed that this practice causes crazing cracks to later appear all over the surface. Position protection pieces over sharp corners so that holes are not worn in the fabric during windy spells. Make sure it is secure.

Fitting a caravan cover

1. Cover manufacturers usually supply protective pieces to fit near the sharp corners of awning rails.

2. To protect the sharp edges of a circular roof ventilator, bubble-wrap plastic was taped in place.

3. To lift a cover over the roof of a large caravan it often helps to elevate it using a broom.

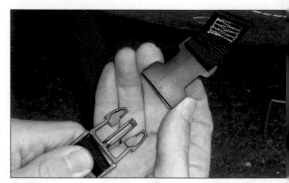

4. Strong winds can cause fabric to flap and damage paintwork, so secure the retaining straps tightly.

Indoor tasks

❏ **Consider removing residual water in pipes by disconnection**

Many water supply systems have a non-return valve near the point of entry. This ensures water doesn't drain back to the water container whenever taps are turned off but residual water in the pipes can freeze. Plastic hose sometimes copes with the expansion, but it is always advisable to disconnect a low level pipe to drain off the water. Better still – fit one of the drain-down taps shown in Chapter 9, *Water systems*.

❏ **Remove any interior stains before they set for good**

Stains should always be removed as soon as possible. If left too long, they will become permanent. Guidance is given in Chapter 6, *Interior maintenance and improvements*, on stain removal and the cleaning of furnishings.

❏ **Leave the fridge door open using the second catch position**

If you shut the fridge door completely, the interior will start to smell unpleasant. Start by wiping out the interior using one of the cleaners described in Chapter 11, *Refrigerators*. Then leave the door ajar using the second catch position.

❏ **Clean appliances**

Degrease the oven and hob with a proprietary cleaner. Remove dust from the burners using a stiff brush, but don't be tempted to use a wire brush – this can easily damage a jet.

Clean off the black streaks which often form below body fixings.

❏ **Leave taps and shower controls open**

As described in Chapter 9, leaving taps open releases any build-up of pressure if residual water in pipe-runs starts to freeze. To achieve this with a lever mixer tap, ensure that its control is lifted and left in a central position.

❏ **Put plugs in the sink, basin and shower tray to keep out smells**

On most caravans, the waste pipe consists of a convoluted hose which may hold residual water where it sags under the floor. Insert plugs to prevent waste pipe smells entering the caravan.

Remove the rust and dust from your hob using a stiff brush.

To release air pressure in the pipes serving a hot/cold lever tap, ensure that its lever is lifted and left positioned centrally.

Caravan waste water pipes seldom have water traps under sink outlets; to prevent smells rising into the interior, fit plugs during storage periods.

household cleaner – this can irreversibly damage the seal. Dry thoroughly and then apply either olive oil or Thetford's Toilet Seal lubricant. Never use any other type of vegetable oil or Vaseline. Leave the blade open throughout the storage period; this prevents it from becoming stuck in the closed position.

❑ Remove mattresses and cushions, or cover rusting bed box hinges

Ideally, transfer mattresses indoors. If left in the 'van, damp may cause hinges on bed boxes to leave rust marks on the underlining. Alternatively cover the hinges temporarily with sticky tape or lay old towels under the mattresses.

❑ Make list of repair jobs for Spring recommissioning – or do them now!

If you need any parts, order them at the end of a season. Delivery is quicker in winter.

Pre-season tasks

After a long lay-up period – especially during the winter – a caravan will need some preparatory work before it is ready for your first trip away in the new season. It is often surprising how quickly the exterior and interior surfaces bear the marks of an extended storage period.

Pre-season tasks include:

❑ Shower heads

Make sure no residual water is left in the shower head. If you have a submersible pump, check similarly that no water is trapped in its casing.

❑ Toilet

Double-check that the holding tank has been emptied and flushed out. Clean the rubber seal using Thetford Bathroom Cleaner or a luke warm diluted solution of washing-up liquid. Never use a

Pre-storage work on a toilet cassette

1. Clean around the seal using Thetford Bathroom Cleaner or a diluted solution of washing-up liquid.

2. Dry the seal completely with a cloth.

3. A special maintenance spray is available to protect toilet seals.

4. An alternative seal lubricant is olive oil. Once applied, leave the blade *open* throughout the storage period.

Dial-type tyre pressure gauges are noted for their accuracy; ideally the pressure required should fall midway in the range because this is where a gauge is usually most accurate.

....

❏ Check the tyres
Check the tyre pressures, including the spare; and carry out a visual check of the side walls; look carefully at both sides to confirm there's no sign of cracking or premature failure. Make a further tyre check after your first trip.

❏ Check the handbrake
Make sure the brake operates freely by pulling/releasing the lever several times.

❏ Reinstate furnishings
Replace the cushions and any other soft furnishings that have been transferred to a warm storage base.

❏ Services
Carry out a run of all the services. Couple-up a gas cylinder and make sure the gas appliances are working. Note that it may take several moments for

air to be purged from the supply pipes. Reinstate the leisure battery – take a reading with a voltmeter if you own one to ensure it achieves 12.7V or more.

❏ Water filter
If the system has a cartridge fitted and you didn't replace it at the end of the previous season, fit a new one.

❏ Sterilise water system
It is wise to start the season by running a sterilising solution through the water pipes. A product like Milton is often used which is available from any good chemists. Milton is the product widely used for sterilising babies' feeding bottles.

❏ 12N, 12S or 13-pin couplings
Check the connections are sound by coupling-up to your towcar and testing both the road lights and the internal 12V systems. It is not unusual for grit and damp to get inside the car sockets during the winter. If the systems seem wildly at fault, this is often a sign that the earth return connection needs attention.

❏ Clean the caravan
Use a brush to remove webs, insects, and dust from around the doors and locker lids. Similarly clean the awning channel; a purpose-made brush is available from W4 Accessories which can be inserted into the channeling to scour the inner trackway completely.

❏ Servicing
If you didn't complete the season with a service, be certain to arrange this in good time. If you are intending to book-in your 'van at a dealership, do this at the earliest possible opportunity. It can be especially hectic at the start of a season. Now enjoy the caravanning season ahead in comfort and safety!

After a long storage period it is wise to run a mixture of Milton, diluted as stated in its instructions, through all the pipe runs of your caravan.

Reinstate the leisure battery having checked its charge with a voltmeter.

Establishing the age of a caravan

Whereas cars have a Vehicle Registration Document, there is no obligatory form of registration to accompany a caravan. It can therefore be quite difficult to establish a caravan's age. Chassis plates, for example, are not always helpful and there's no doubt that some second-hand models on sale are older than the seller suggests. The notes which follow record some of the changes that have occurred and these provide helpful clues for anyone trying to establish when a caravan was manufactured.

1970s caravans:

■ Caravans of this period are heavy and were built very differently from post 1980 models.

■ Bargain buys for around £500- £800 certainly exist and sometimes provide a pleasant introduction to caravanning. But be careful if you're not prepared to carry out repairs or improvements yourself.

■ Spares can be difficult to obtain for earlier models - particularly spare parts for appliances, fittings for furniture, chassis items and coupling components.

■ Locker boxes to house gas cylinders - previously clamped to the draw-bar and open to the weather - became common after 1971.

■ Refrigerators like the Morphy Richards models of the early 1970s had to be lit using a match and often failed to provide cooling because of an air lock.

■ Chassis made by firms like B&B, Peak, and CI need periodic painting.

■ The running gear of the period employed spring suspension and shock absorbers; damaged items may be difficult to replace.

■ To reverse a 1970s caravan, you usually need to operate an over-ride catch on the coupling head before starting the manoeuvre. This is an annoying chore.

■ In the early 1970s, fluorescent lights became popular but gas lamps were often fitted, too, in order to provide back-up lighting.

■ In the early 1970s, water pumps were usually foot or hand-operated devices.

■ Body-work construction comprised a framework made of wood. This skeleton structure was clad with aluminium sheet on the outside and coated hardboard or plywood on the inside.

■ Insulation was poor on most 1970s 'vans. Usually fibre glass wool was placed in the void between the wall panels - but this slumps down in time leaving cold spots.

■ Floors were made from plywood with supporting joints underneath and seldom had any form of insulation.

■ Windows were single glazed and glass was used. However, in November 1977 it became obligatory for new caravans to be fitted with safety glass.

■ In response to legislation, the industry introduced acrylic single-glazed windows comprising a frame-less moulded pane. Aluminium frames were discontinued overnight.

■ Not long afterwards, double glazed versions of these 'plastic' windows became the standard fitting.

■ After 1st October 1979, it became mandatory for new caravans to have a rear fog lamp. Absence of a fog lamp suggests a 'van is an earlier model.

■ From October 1979, a double plug system was used - the 12N plug for caravan road lights; the 12S plug was reserved for internal supplies.

1980s caravans:

■ A new approach to building was introduced using pre-manufactured bonded sandwich floors and wall panels; most manufacturers soon adopted the system.

■ New computer-designed lightweight chassis were introduced around 1980.

■ On lightweight chassis, coil springs hitherto fitted with shock absorbers were replaced by a rubber-in-compression suspension system.

■ A few chassis as late as 1984 were still painted, but galvanising was more usual now as a standard finish.

■ In April 1989, all caravans manufactured had to have auto-reverse brakes; a manually operated lever fitted to the coupling head became obsolete. Automatic brake disengagement mechanisms were now built into the drums.

■ More and more low voltage appliances appear in caravans including electric pumps, reading lights, fans and stereo systems. Now a separate "leisure battery" becomes an essential item.

■ Fused distribution panels were introduced so that 12V appliances could be operated on separate supply branches and fused independently.

■ In the mid 1980s, caravans lost their symmetry and became wedge shaped using sloping fronts to achieve better fuel economy.

■ After 1986, virtually all gas storage lockers were built into the body itself. A separate locker box mounted on the draw bar was not often fitted.

■ From the mid 1980s many caravans were equipped with water heaters; the Carver Cascade storage heater was particularly popular.

■ Around 1987, the cassette toilet arrived, revolutionising bathroom design and vastly improving emptying arrangements.

■ From 1st May 1989 smoke alarms had to be fitted to all new caravans *and* all pre-owned 'vans sold by a dealer.

1990s caravans:

■ Road lights set high on the sides - called marker lights - became obligatory on caravans over 2.1m wide and manufactured after 1st October 1990.

■ Combustion Modified High Resilience foam (CMHR) became mandatory in caravan upholstery supplied after 1st March 1990.

■ From April 1991, all fabrics have to be a fire-resistant type.

■ The first AL-KO Kober side-lift jack was introduced in the early 1990s

■ Hardly any caravans were sold in the 1990s without a 230V supply system as standard.

■ In 1992, ALKO- Kober announced that their latest lightweight chassis must *not* be drilled - even for mounting a stabiliser bracket on the draw bar.

■ CRiS (Caravan Registration and Identification Scheme) was introduced in 1992 and UK-manufactured caravans were issued with a Vehicle Identification Number (VIN). This is supplied with the owner-information pack, recorded at CRiS headquarters and etched on windows.

■ Around 1992, BPW chassis and running gear was fitted with maintenance-free sealed bearings.

■ The AL-KO Euro-axle with sealed bearings appeared in 1994 models. The bearings are well engineered, but after a brake assembly has been cleaned an expensive torque wrench is needed to tighten the nuts securing the drums.

■ Since 1994, flame failure devices have been fitted on stoves.

■ In Spring 1995, the Abbey Domino was launched with GRP impact-resistant sheet on its side walls instead of aluminium panels. Other models followed with this repairable cladding.

■ From 1st January, 1996, gas appliances have to bear a CE mark to indicate they meet European standards.

■ In caravans manufactured from 1997 onwards, a small 'tamperproof' tag containing the Vehicle Identification Number is hidden in the body; it can only be identified using a CRiS "reader" device.

■ In the latter part of the 1990s, reeded and stucco surfaces were used less and less on external walls. Smooth aluminium finishes became popular again.

■ In 1998, BPW introduced a castellated tined (ie spiked) lock nut instead of 'one-shot' nuts for retaining brake drums; they can be used more than once.

■ AL-KO Kober introduced a 'universal' Vario chassis with bolt-together main members in Spring 1999. Models of different lengths in a manufacturer's range can be built using the same chassis sections.

■ In Spring 1999, AL-KO Kober introduced the Euro Over-Run Automatic Self-adjusting Brake. This detects movement when a 'van is parked on a backward facing slope and re-applies a slipping brake automatically.

■ A CRiS Scheme was launched in 1999 in which caravans manufactured *before* 1992 can be retrospectively CRiS

registered and tagged. If buying a pre-owned, CRiS registered, 'van, its age can be verified; warning is given if it's a reported stolen model or one still subject to loan repayments.

■ Around 1999 Carver ceased manufacturing appliances for the caravan market; Truma agreed to sell Carver spares for several more years.

2000 and later caravans:

■ From 2000, Truma space and water heating appliances took Carver's place and became a standard installation in many caravans.

■ Number plates fitted on caravans after 1st September 2001 have to comply with BS AU 145d and registration plates must bear this code.

■ Tyres for 13in wheels are hard to obtain so Swift and Explorer caravans were fitted with 14in wheels in 2001. Bailey followed suit in 2002.

■ From 1st September 2003, manufacturers supplied caravans with a wall-mounted 30mbar gas regulator instead of requiring owners to purchase cylinder-mounted 28m bar butane or 37m bar propane regulators.

■ Electrically driven, fixed moving devices gained popularity. Carver's Caravan Mover, introduced in the 1990s, set a standard; many other makes have followed.

■ After a slow start in the 1990s, Thetford's swivel bowl cassette toilets which take up minimal floor space became more popular than bench-type models.

■ Around 2003 Thetford introduced Norcold absorption refrigerators into its range of products; several manufacturers started to fit these appliances.

■ AL-KO Kober AKS coupling head stabilisers were being fitted to more and more caravans as a basic equipment item. Models built on a BPW chassis have a dark blue WS3000 stabiliser manufactured by Winterhoff.

■ In 2005, some wall-mounted 30mbar gas regulators were reported as being contaminated with an oily substance. Dealers then remounted regulators higher in the gas locker and fitted a 90deg elbow at the top.

■ Around 2006, several caravans built on AL-KO Kober chassis were equipped with a locking plate to prevent wheel rotation on parked 'vans.

■ In 2007 AL-KO introduced the ATC, a safety device which identifies excessive lateral instability in a caravan and applies its brakes to help bring it back into line.

Note: *Fuller information on the developments listed here is given in the earlier chapters.*

Standards, regulations and legal issues

In Appendix A - *Establishing the Age of a Caravan* - reference is made to some of the regulations which have altered the design and specifications of caravans over the last 40 years. For example, a rear fog lamp became a legal requirement on caravans constructed on and after 1st October 1979. This, in turn, necessitated changes to the wiring in a caravan's towing plug.

Not that 'regulations' are the only initiators of change. For instance UK caravan manufacturers started fitting 13-pin plugs on models made on and after 1st September 2008. This alteration was prompted by European-wide recommendations laid down in European Norms/British Standards. Without doubt it was a logical decision to take but there isn't a legal requirement to fit 13-pin couplings. In fact owners are at liberty to fit 12N and 12S plugs if they want to.

What's also important to recognise is that even new legal requirements are seldom applied retrospectively. Hence owners of models built **before** 1st October 1979 do not have to upgrade their caravan by fitting a foglamp even though that became a legal requirement for all later models.

In addition to providing examples of changes in Appendix A, this book has also made continuing references to regulations, standards and codes of practice throughout the text. For instance, changes in the law regarding towing brackets received a detailed explanation in Chapter 3. Now, in this Appendix, a summary of standards and regulations mentioned earlier is brought together under a single heading. It also reveals that there is an ever-increasing unification of standards that have hitherto been applied in other European countries.

The adoption of European Standards for Caravans

The establishment of common standards throughout member States of the European Community has many merits. Although small differences might be needed in Export models such as door position, a benefit of having European Norms means that a compliant caravan made in one country doesn't have to undergo further approval tests in the country which imports it.

The implementation of a European Norm structure thus creates a situation of free trade between partner countries. This undoubtedly helps the British caravan manufacturers that are exporting models to several of our European partners.

Other benefits include the fact that vehicle manufacturers cannot insist that you only fit their own design of towing bracket. The whole principle behind free trade means what it says - as long as alternative products on sale fulfil the relevant standards.

Technical Tip

Up to 31st September, 1998, the manufacturers of UK caravans worked within the recommendations of British Standards, particularly BS4626. However, during 1998 many new European Norms were adopted in this country and given the status of British Standards. So from 1st October, 1998 manufacturers in this country worked to European Norms, particularly EN 1645.

Legal issues and 'standards'

As regards a motor vehicle used for towing, this is subject to a prodigious array of legally binding requirements, most of which fall beyond the scope of this book. Caravans, too, have to achieve compliance in respect of brakes, road lights and dimensions.

However, most of the interior features in a caravan, often referred to as 'habitation elements', are covered by 'standards' rather than 'regulations'. Whilst a 'standard' is an advisory recommendation, a 'regulation' is legally binding.

Although it is not usually mandatory for a caravan manufacturer to adopt European Standards, the position changes if key elements become embraced in the law. Two example of this are as follows:

1. The fitting of European Type Approval tow bars that met the criteria laid down in Directive 94/20/EC (now EU Regulation 55) was not a legal requirement in the UK **until** an amendment was made in the Road Vehicles (Construction & Use) Regulations 1986. Compliance with the Directive then became legally binding and took effect from 1st September, 1998. Implications of this were explained in Chapter 3.

2. Recommended procedures relating to the installation of LPG in Caravans are given in BS EN 1949. However, the legal position in the UK is set down in The Gas Safety (Installation and Use Regulations) 1998. Indeed the guidance contained in this manual which relates to work on gas appliances adopts the Regulation's statement that: 'No person shall carry out any work in relation to a gas fitting **unless he is competent to do so.'**

Notwithstanding this important difference between a 'standard' and a 'regulation', most manufacturers voluntarily decide to comply with published standards. In some instances, 'British Standards' continue to be applicable: others are now subsumed within Europe-wide recommendations described as European Norms. The resulting status of a publication is verified when its identification number is prefaced with the 'BS EN' designation.

However, most UK caravan manufacturers also adopt BS EN recommended practices on account of their association with Britain's caravan trade organisation, the National Caravan Council (NCC). A large proportion of UK caravan and component manufacturers are members of the NCC and among its many initiatives is the establishment of a 'badge of approval scheme'. This brings with it another tier of terminology, namely 'Codes of Practice'.

Codes of Practice and the NCC Approval Scheme

British touring caravans that achieve approval under the NCC scheme have to fulfil criteria that go above and beyond British and European Standards. The NCC's Code of Practice 302 (Touring caravans) not only embraces all relevant legislation but adds further self-imposed demands. These are rigorously applied when a caravan submitted for NCC approval is placed before professional inspectors for scrutiny. The Touring Caravan Certification Scheme gives a benchmark of quality and all models which meet the requirements of this Scheme carry a badge to denote their compliance.

Of course, some caravans - especially models imported from abroad - do not carry the NCC badge. Without doubt, many imported caravans are well-built, but one feature that hasn't met a key requirement in the NCC Code of Practice is the position of the entry door. A caravan door is usually installed on the opposite side from a British model. In other words in this country, when an imported caravan is parked on the nearside, its door opens directly on to the road which is potentially dangerous.

Keeping up-to-date

Understandably, regulations and standards are constantly coming under review and by the time you read this section, it is possible that several new proposals may have been discussed, approved and implemented. For this reason you should always seek guidance about current requirements and practices.

Needless to say, members of the two major Caravan Clubs are kept up-to-date through the pages of members' monthly magazines and by their respective Technical Departments. In addition, staff from the National Caravan Council often attend major indoor exhibitions. Although the Council is principally a trade organisation, free leaflets are distributed to the public including the NCC's Advice Sheets: 'Coupling up a caravan to a car' and 'Correct Attachment of Breakaway Cables'.

Revisions

As stated already, revisions are always under discussion. For example it was pointed out in Chapter 10 *Gas supply systems and appliances* that electrical equipment is not permitted in a gas cylinder locker. Disallowing supply cables in a gas cylinder locker is to ensure that there is no potential source of ignition. In practice, however, one well-known gas appliance specialist is manufacturing a gas cylinder fill-indication device which operates using a 12V supply; equally, some of the changeover devices attached to cylinders are similarly reliant on low voltage electricity. These issues have drawn attention to related inconsistencies published in EN1949:2002, EN 1648-1 (Electrical systems in leisure vehicles) and IEC 60357. Clarification is clearly needed so EN1949 is currently under

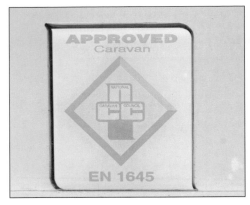

From 1st October, 1998, manufacturers in the UK worked to European Norms, particularly EN 1645. This is shown on the badges applied to UK touring caravans which have achieved approval under the NCC Certification Scheme.

discussion and amendments are planned for publication in 2009. Not surprisingly part of the draft revisions are taking account of the present use of extra low voltage (ELV) equipment for gas supply control and for equipment that monitors gas content in cylinders.

This helps to show that standards, regulations and codes of practice are always under review and subject to changes.

The main standards currently applying to touring caravans are:

BS EN 1645-1	Caravan habitation requirements
BS EN 1645-2	Caravan payloads
BS EN 27418	Vocabulary and terminology
BS EN 1648-1	12V DC extra low voltage electrical installations
BS EN 721	Ventilation requirements in caravans
BS EN 722-1	Liquefied fuel heating in caravans
BS EN 1949	LPG installation in leisure accommodation vehicles
BS EN 12864	Low pressure non-adjustable gas regulators
BS EN 60335-1	Specification for safety of electrical appliances
BS EN 60335-2-29	Specification for safety in battery chargers
BS EN 60309-2	Mains site sockets, caravan inlet sockets and connections on hook-up leads
BS 7671, IEE Wiring Regulations 16th Edn, and IEC Standard 364	Mains electricity installations and components
BS 4293, BS EN 61008 or BSEN 6 AN 1009	Requirements for RCD devices installed in caravans
BS 1363	Issues regarding 13Amp 3 pin sockets
BS EN 6765 Pt4	Specification for undergear
BS EN 3	Fire extinguishers; detail about manufacturing features

Caravan number plate

A caravan must bear the same registration number as its towcar and be illuminated at night. Plates fitted to caravans after 1st September, 2001 must comply with BS AU 145d and be marked with the BS AU number. To purchase a number plate involves the presentation of several documents to the plate fabricator to verify that you are the owner of the towing vehicle.

Contact addresses

Please note: This address list was correct at the time of going to press. It includes specialist suppliers and manufacturers whose products and services have been mentioned in this book. Several of the firms have web sites and these are easy to locate using search engines.

Abbey and Ace Caravans - See The Swift Group

A.B. Butt Ltd,
(Now marketing solar systems as Run by the Sun; contact unknown)

ABI Caravans Ltd,
(Ceased manufacturing touring caravans, in 2001)

ABP Accessories,
27 Nether End,
Great Dalby,
Leicestershire,
LE14 2EY
Tel: 08700 115111
(Importer of Camco products)

**A-Glaze surface sealant.
(See Creative Resins Distribution)**

Adria Caravans,
Hall Street,
Long Melford,
Sudbury,
Suffolk,
CO10 9JP
Tel: 0870 774 0007
(Adria and Fleetwood caravans)

Alde International (UK) Ltd,
14 Regent Park,
Booth Drive,
Park Farm South,
Wellingborough,
Northamptonshire,
NN8 6GR
Tel: 01933 677765
(Central heating systems, Gas leak detector)

AL-KO Kober Ltd,
South Warwickshire Business Park,
Kineton Road,
Southam,
Warwickshire,
CV47 0AL
Tel: 01926 818500
(Chassis, running gear, security, stabilisers, wheel carriers)

Apollo Repair Chemicals,
Available from Leisure Plus,
Unit 3, Airfield Industrial Estate,
Hixon, Staffordshire, ST18 0PF
Tel: 01889 271692
(Wholesaler distributing Apollo delamination kits)

Arc Systems,
13 Far Street, Bradmore,
Nottingham, NG11 6PF
Tel: 0115 921 3175
(Repair of all types of Carver heater)

Autac Products Ltd
London Road, Macclesfield,
Cheshire, SK11 7RN
Tel: 01625 619 277
(Purpose-made 13-core cables for caravans)

Auto Glym,
Works Road, Letchworth,
Hertfordshire, SG6 1LU
Tel: 01462-677766
(Caravan and car interior/exterior cleaning products)

Autovan Services Ltd,
32 Canford Bottom, Wimborne,
Dorset, BH21 2HD
Tel: 01202 848414
(Major body repair and rebuilding work)

Avondale Coachcraft Ltd,
(Ceased manufacturing caravans in 2008)

Bailey Caravans Ltd,
South Liberty Lane,
Bristol, BS3 2SS
Tel: 0117 966 5967
(Manufacturers of Bailey caravans)

BCA Leisure Ltd,
Unit H8, Premier Way,
Lowfields Business Park, Elland,
North Yorkshire, HX5 9HF
Tel: 01422 376977
(Trade supplier of Powerpart mains kits, the Power Centre & Powerpart Mobile; see Pennine Leisure)

Belling Appliances - See Glen Dimplex.

Bessacarr Caravans – See The Swift Group

BP Gas Light – See Truma UK

BPW Ltd,
Legion Way,
Meridian Business Park,
Leicester,
LE19 1UZ
Tel: 0116 281 6100
(BPW chassis and Winterhoff stabilizers)

Bradleys,
Old Station Yard,
Marlesford,
Suffolk, IP13 0AG
Tel: 01728 745200
(SMART repairs and Mail Order ABS repair kits; paint products for plastic)

Brink UK Ltd,
Unit 7,
Centrovell Industrial Estate,
Caldwell Road,
Nuneaton,
Warwickshire, CV11 4NG
Tel: 01203 352353
(Towbars)

Brittania Specialist Fitting Services,
Unit 6, Wadehurst Industrial Park,
St. Philips Road,
St. Philips,
Bristol,
Avon, BS2 0JE
Tel: 0117 955 1011
(Specialist installer of towbars and towing systems)

British Rubber Manufacturers' Association Ltd,
6 Bath Place,
Rivington Street,
London, EC2A 3JE
Tel: 020 7457 5040
(Trade Association for the tyre industry)

Buccaneer Caravans - See The Explorer Group

Bulldog Security Products Ltd,
Units 2, 3, & 4,
Stretton Road,
Much Wenlock,
Shropshire,
TF13 6DH
Tel: 01952-728171
(Bulldog stabilisers, SSK stabiliser importer, security devices)

C.A.K. Tanks – See Caravan Accessories

Calor Gas Ltd,
Athena Drive,
Tachbrook Park,
Warwick,
CV34 6RL
Tel: 0800 626626
(Supplier of butane, propane and LPG appliances)

The Camping & Caravanning Club,
Greenfields House,
Westwood Way,
Coventry,
CV4 8JH
Tel: 024 7647 5448

**Camco Products -
See ABP Accessories**

Campingaz
Coleman UK Inc.,
Parish Wharf Estate,
Harbour Road,
Portishead,
Bristol, BS20 9DA
Tel: 01275 845024
(Supplier of Campingaz butane and LPG appliances)

Caravan Accessories (CAK Tanks) Ltd,
10 Princes Drive,
Kenilworth,
Warwickshire, CV8 2FD
Tel: 0844 414 2324
(Water accessories, interior equipment)

The Caravan Club
East Grinstead House,
East Grinstead,
West Sussex, RH19 1UA
Tel: 01342 326944

Carafax Ltd,
Rotterdam Road,
Sutton Fields Industrial Estate,
Hull, HU7 0XD
Tel: 01482 825941
(Cartridge sealants)

The Caravan Centre,
Unit 3A,
Gilchrist Thomas Industrial Estate,
Blaenavon, NP4 9RL
Tel: 01495 792700
(Specialist breakers supplying
caravan products)

Caravanparts.net,
Unit 5,
Grovehill Industrial Estate,
Beck View Road,
Beverley,
East Yorkshire,
HU17 0JW
Tel: 01482 874878
(Supplier of caravan parts and the
Henry-GE water heater)

The Caravan Seat Cover Centre,
Cater Business Park,
Bishopsworth,
Bristol,
BS13 7TW
Tel: 0117-941 0222
(Re-upholsterer, loose covers, and
foam supplier)

**Carcoon Storage Systems Int.
Ltd,**
Orchard Mill,
2 Orchard Street,
Salford,
Manchester,
M6 6FL
Tel: 0161 737 9690
(Trickle battery charger: Mail
Order)

Carlight Caravans
(Ceased manufacturing caravans
in 2004)

**Carver spares – See Miriad
Products and Truma (UK)**

CEC Plug-In-Systems,
(Contact your caravan dealer)

Ceuta Healthcare,
41 Richmond Hill,
Bournemouth,
Dorset,
BH2 6H7
Tel: 0800 0975606
(Milton sterilising products and
water treatment additives)

Coachman Caravan Co Ltd,
Amsterdam Road,
Sutton Field Industrial Estate,
Hull, HU7 0XF
Tel: 01482 839737
(Manufacturers of Coachman
caravans)

**Compass Caravans Ltd – See
The Explorer Group**

**The Council for Registered Gas
Installers (CORGI),**
1 Elmwood,
Chineham Park,
Crockford Lane,
Basingstoke,
Hampshire, RG24 8WG
Tel: 0870 401 2200

Creative Resins Distribution,
7, The Glenmore Centre,
Eurolink Industrial Estate,
Castle Road, Sittingbourne,
Kent, ME10 3GL
Tel: 01795 599880
(Supplier of A-Glaze surface
treatment)

CRiS
Dolphin House,
New Street,
Salisbury,
Wiltshire, SP1 2PH
Tel: 01722 413434
(Caravan Registration &
Identification Scheme)

Crossley Coachcraft,
Unit 33A, Comet Road,
Moss Side Industrial Estate,
Leyland,
Lancashire, PR5 3QN
Tel: 01772 623423
(Major body repair and rebuilding
work)

**Crown Caravans - See The
Explorer Group**

B. Dixon-Bate Ltd,
Unit 45,
First Avenue,
Deeside Industrial Park,
Deeside,
Clwyd, CH5 2LG
Tel: 01244 288925
(Towing accessories including
cushioned towball units)

D&J Industries,
19 Woodlands Drive,
Colsterworth,
Lincolnshire, NG33 5NH
Tel: 01476 860815
(Trail-A-Mate hydraulic jack)

**David's Isopon resin, filler paste
and U-Pol**
(From car accessory stores)

DLS Plastics,
Occupation Lane,
Gonerby Moor,
Grantham,
Lincolnshire, NG32 2BP
Tel: 01476 564549
(Plastic waste water plumbing
components)

Dometic Group,
Dometic House,
The Brewery,
Blandford St Mary,
Dorset, DT11 9LS
Tel: 0844 626 0133
(Formerly Electrolux Leisure;
amalgamated with WAECO
in 2007: Air conditioners,
refrigerators, Seitz windows,
Cramer cookers)

Driftgate 2000 Ltd,
Little End Road,
Eaton Socon,
Cambridgeshire, PE19 3JH
Tel: 01480 470400
(Manufacture/repair XCell Mains
inverters)

EECO,
Exhaust Ejector Co Ltd,
Wade House Road,
Shelf,
Nr. Halifax,
West Yorkshire, HX3 7PE
Tel: 01274 679524
(Replacement acrylic windows
made to order)

Elecsol Europe Ltd,
47 First Avenue,
Deeside Industrial Park,
Deeside,
Flintshire, CH5 2LG
Tel: 0800 163298
(Elecsol batteries)

**Electrical Contractors
Association (ECA),**
ECA ECSA House,
34 Palace Court,
London, W2 4HY
Tel: 020 7313 4800
(Mains supply system checking)

**Electrolux Appliances – See
Dometic Group**

**Elddis Caravans - See The
Explorer Group**

Elsan Ltd,
Elsan House,
Bellbrook Park,
Uckfield,
East Sussex,
TN22 1QF
Tel: 01825 748200
(Manufacturer of toilets and
chemicals)

Evode Ltd,
Industrial Division,
Common Road,
Stafford,
ST16 3EH
Tel: 01785 272727
(Manufacturer of Evo-Stik
Adhesives)

Exide Technologies Ltd,
6/7 Parkway Estate,
Longbridge Road,
Trafford Park,
Manchester, M17 1SN
Tel: 0161 786 3333
(Exide Gel and Lead/Acid Leisure
Batteries)

The Explorer Group,
Delves Lane,
Consett,
Co Durham, DH8 7PE
Tel: 01207 503477
(Manufacturer of Buccaneer,
Elddis, and Compass models)

Farécla Products Ltd,
Broadmeads,
Ware,
Hertfordshire,
SG12 9HS
Tel: 01920 465041
(Caravan Pride acrylic window
scratch remover and GRP surface
renovator)

Fenwick's,
Fir Tree Farm,
Chorley,
Cheshire,
CW5 8JR
Tel: 01270 524111
(Caravan cleaning and care
products)

**Fiamma water pumps and water
tanks**
Contact your motorcaravan
dealers for Fiamma products.

Flavel Leisure,
Clarence Street,
Leamington Spa,
Warwickshire,
CV31 2AD
Tel: 01926 427027
(Flavel cookers and hobs)

F.L. Hitchman,
46 The Trading Estate,
Ditton Priors,
Bridgnorth,
Shropshire,
WV16 6SS
Tel: 01746 712242
(Suppliers of portable water
containers and cleaning chemicals)

**Fleetwood Caravans –
See Adria**

FFC (Foam for Comfort) Ltd,
Unit 2,
Wyther Lane Trading Estate,
Kirkstall,
Leeds, LS5 3BT
Tel: 0845 345 8101
(New foam supplier, composite bonded foam specialist)

Froli Kunststoffwerk Fromme GmbH,
Liemker Strasse 27,
D-33758 Schloss Holte-Stukenbrock,
Germany.
Tel: 49 (0) 52 07 - 95 00 0
(Froli bed support systems)

Gaslow International,
Castle Business Park,
Pavilion Way, Loughborough,
Leicestershire, LE11 5GW
Tel: 0845 4000 600
(Refillable gas systems, Gaslow gauges, regulators, couplings and components)

GB-Sol,
Unit 2,
Glan-y-Llyn Industrial Estate,
Cardiff Road, Taffs Well,
Cardiff, CF15 7JD
Tel: 029 2082 0910
(Semi-flexible lightweight solar panels)

General Ecology Europe Ltd,
St. Andrews House,
26 Brighton Road,
Crawley, RH10 6AA
Tel: 01293 400644
(Nature Pure Ultrafine water purifier)

Glen Dimplex Home Appliances,
Stoney Lane,
Prestcot,
Merseyside, L35 2XW
Tel: 0871 22 22 503
(Belling, New World, Stoves, Vanette appliances)

Grade UK Ltd,
3 Central Court, Finch Close,
Lenton Lane Industrial Estate,
Nottingham, NG7 2NN
Tel: 0115 986 7151
(Status TV aerials, Flat Screen TV and accessories)

Grayston Engineering Ltd,
115 Roebuck Road,
Chessington,
Surrey, KT9 1JZ
Tel: 020 8974 1122
(Trade supplier of tow car spring assister kits)

Hammerite Paints
Available from DIY stores

Häfele UK Ltd,
Swift Valley Industrial Estate,
Rugby,
Warwickshire, CV21 1RD
Tel: 01788 542020
(Furniture components and hardware)

Hawke House Marine Ltd,
Unit E1,
Heritage Business Park,
Heritage Way,
Gosport,
Hampshire, PO12 4BG
Tel: 02392 588588
(Cut-from-roll Vent Air-Mat; mattress anti-condensation underlay)

HBC International A/S,
Fabriksparken 4,
DK9230 Svenstrup,
Denmark
Tel: +45 70227070
(Professional dent repair system for aluminium panels)

Hella Ltd,
Wildmere Industrial Estate,
Banbury,
Oxfordshire, OX16 3JU
Tel: 01295 272233
(Hella towing electrical equipment)

Hodgson Sealants,
Belprin Road, Beverley,
North Humberside, HU17 0LN
Tel: 01482 868321
(Manufacturers of caravan sealants)

International Tool Co Ltd,
Interlink Way South,
Bardon Hill, Coalville,
Leicestershire, LE67 1PH
Tel: 08449 395910
Mail Order, Dial-type tyre pressure gauges

Jablite insulation
From Builders' Merchants

Jenste,
The Stables,
Pashley Farm,
Ninfield Road,
Bexhill-on-Sea,
East Sussex, TN39 5JS
Tel: 01424 893880
(RYD Live/neutral polarity changeover unit)

Jonic,
Unit 5, Woodgate Park,
White Lund Industrial Estate,
Morecombe,
Lancashire, LA3 3PS
Tel: 01524 67074
(Memory foam, fitted sheets, mattress protectors, duvets)

John Guest International,
Horton Road,
West Drayton,
Middlesex, UB7 8JL
Tel: 01895 449233
(Speedfit push-fit semi-rigid plumbing)

Johnnie Longden Ltd,
Unit 24,
Dawkins Road Industrial Estate,
Poole,
Dorset, BH15 4JD
Tel: 01202 679121
(Caravan Accessories including components for older caravans)

Kenlowe Ltd,
Burchetts Green,
Maidenhead,
Berkshire, SL6 6QU
Tel: 01628 823303
(Radiator cooling fans and automatic transmission oil coolers)

Kewal Trailer Products,
206 Longfield Road,
Albert Hill,
Darlington,
County Durham, DL3 0RR
Tel: 01325 359789
(Towing electrical products)

Kingdom Industrial Supplies Ltd,
610 Bancrofts Road,
Eastern Industrial Estate,
Chelmsford,
Essex, CM3 5UQ
Tel: 01245 322177
(Gramos Kits for repairing ABS plastic)

Knott (UK) Ltd – See Miriad Products Ltd

Labcraft Ltd,
22B King Street,
Saffron Walden,
Essex,
CB10 1ES
Tel: 01799 513434
(Lighting and 12V products)

Leisure Accessories Ltd,
Britannia Works,
Hurricane Way,
Airport Industrial Estate,
Norwich,
NR6 6EY
Tel: 01603 414551
(Diaphragm pump repairs and POSIflow, FLOking sales)

Lunar Caravans Ltd,
6 Sherdley Road,
Lostock Hall,
Preston,
Lancashire, PR5 5JF
Tel: 01772 337628
(Manufacturer of Lunar caravans)

Marlec Engineering Ltd,
Rutland House,
Trevithick Road,
Corby,
Northamptonshire, NN17 5XY
Tel: 01536 201588
(Wind and solar systems)

Magnum Mobiles and Caravan Surplus,
Unit 9A,
Cosalt Industrial Estate,
Convamore Road,
Grimsby, DN32 9JL
Tel: 01472 353520
(Caravan surplus stock)

Maypole Ltd,
54 Kettles Wood Drive,
Woodgate Business Park,
Birmingham,
West Midlands, B32 3DB
Tel: 0121 423 3011
(Towing accessories, electrical items)

Maxol heaters – See Propex

Maxview,
Common Lane,
Setchey,
King's Lynn,
Norfolk,
PE33 0AT
Tel: 01553 813300
(Maxview TV dishes/aerials)

Merlin Equipment,
Unit 1, Hithercroft Court,
Lupton Road,
Wallingford,
Oxfordshire, OX10 9BT
Tel: 01491 824333
(PROwatt Inverters)

Mer Products Ltd,
Whitehead House,
120 Beddington Lane,
Croydon,
Surrey, CR0 4TD
Tel: 020 8401 0002
(Distributor of Mer Car Care products)

Miriad Products Ltd,
Park Lane,
Dove Valley Park,
Foston,
South Derbyshire,
DE65 5BG
Tel: 01283 586060
(Accessories; UK distributor of Knott running gear & BPW chassis)

Morco Products Ltd,
Morco House,
Riverview Road,
Beverley, HU17 0LD
Tel: 01482 325456
(Instantaneous Water Heaters)

Munster Simms Engineering Ltd,
277 -279 Old Belfast Road,
Bangor,
Co Down, BT19 1LT
Northern Ireland.
Tel: 028 9127 0531
(Whale water products and semi-rigid pipe)

The National Caravan Council,
Catherine House,
Victoria Road,
Aldershot,
Hampshire,
GU11 1SS
Tel: 01252 318251

National Inspection Council for Electrical Installation Contracting, (NICEIC)
Warwick House,
Houghton Hall Park,
Houghton Regis,
Dunstable,
LU5 5ZX
Tel: 01582 539000
(Independent voluntary body for electrical installation matters)

National Trailer and Towing Association,
1 Alveston Place,
Leamington Spa,
Warwickshire, CV32 4SN
Tel: 01926 335445
(Trade Association for all aspects of towing and equipment)

The Natural Mat Company,
99 Talbot Road,
London, W11 2AT
Tel: 020 7985 0474
(Anti-condensation mattress underlay)

O'Leary Spares and Accessories,
314 Hull Road,
Plaxton Bridge Road,
Woodmansey,
East Yorkshire,
HU17 ORS
Tel: 01482 868632
(Caravan parts and accessories)

Paintseal Direct,
34 Cross Street,
Long Eaton,
Nottinghamshire, NG10 1HD
Tel: 07783 300 377
(Paint protection system containing DuPont™ Teflon®)

PCT,
Holbrook Industrial Estate,
Holbrook,
Sheffield, S20 3GH
Tel: 0845 123 1111
(Towbar manufacturers and towing electrics)

Pennine Leisure Supplies,
Unit G9,
Lock View,
Elland,
West Yorkshire, HX5 9HD
Tel: 01422 313 455
(Wholesaler of Accessories and BCA Leisure products)

PGR Products Ltd,
Unit16 Allenby Business Village,
Crofton Road,
Lincoln,
Lincolnshire, LN3 4NL
Tel: 01522 534538
(Sectional TV mast, security, winter wheels)

Powrwheel Ltd,
6 Priory Industrial Estate,
Airspeed Road,
Christchurch,
Hampshire, BH23 4HD
Tel: 01425 283293
(Caravan motorised movers)

Propex Heatsource Ltd,
Unit 5,
Second Avenue Business Park,
Millbrook,
Southampton, SO15 0LP
Tel: 023 8052 8555
(Space heaters and Malaga Water heaters)

Protimeter plc,
Meter House,
Fieldhouse Lane,
Marlow,
Buckinghamshire, SL7 1LW
Tel: 01628 472722
(Caravan moisture meters)

Purple Line Ltd,
2 Lady Lane Industrial Estate,
Hadleigh,
Suffolk, IP7 6BQ
Tel: 0870 444 8688
(Caravan accessories including Kojack)

Pyramid Products Ltd,
Byron Avenue,
Lowmoor Road Industrial Estate,
Kirkby in Ashfield,
Nottinghamshire, NG17 7LA
Tel: 01623 754567
(Caravanning accessories)

Remis UK,
(Caravan blinds – Order through dealer)

Reich UK,
91 Hednesford Road, Cannock,
Staffordshire, WS12 5HL
Tel: 01543 459243
(Importer of motorised movers, accessories including the Fuse Control)

Right Connections UK Ltd,
7 Churchill Buildings,
Queen Street,
Wellington, Telford,
Shropshire, TF1 1HT
Tel: 0871 226 2030
(Towbar vehicle-specific wiring kits)

Ring Automotive Ltd,
Gelderd Road,
Leeds, LS12 6NA
Tel: 0113 213 7389
(Vehicle lighting, towing and general accessories)

RoadPro Ltd,
Stephenson Close,
Drayton Fields Industrial Estate,
Daventry,
Northamptonshire, NN1 5RF
Tel: 01327 312233
(Suppliers of chargers, inverters, satellite TV systems, electrical accessories)

Ronseal Ltd,
Thorncliffe Park,
Chapeltown,
Sheffield,
South Yorkshire, S35 2YP
Tel: 0114 246 7171
(For suppliers of Tri-Flow penetrating lubricant with Teflon®)

RPi Engineering Ltd,
Wayside Garage,
Holt Road,
Horsford,
Norwich,
Norfolk, NR10 3EE
Tel: 01603 891 209
(Refillable gas installations)

Ryder Towing Equipment Ltd,
Alvanley House,
Alvanley Industrial Estate,
Stockport Road East,
Bredbury,
Stockport, SK6 2DJ
Tel: 0161 430 1120
(Electrical towing equipment)

Sargent Electrical Services Ltd,
Unit 39,
Tokenspire Business Park,
Woodmansey,
Beverley,
Hull, HU17 0TB
Tel: 01482 881655
(Electrical control systems and low voltage panels)

Selmar Guardian Chargers
Tadmod Ltd,
Galliford Road,
Malden,
Essex, CM9 4XD
Tel: 0161 859444
(Selmar stage chargers, from marine specialists)

Sew 'n' Sews,
42 Claudette Avenue,
Spalding,
Lincolnshire, PE11 1HU
Tel: 01775 767 633
(Bespoke awnings, cover systems, bags and generator covers)

SF Detection Ltd,
4 Stinsford Road,
Nuffield Industrial Estate,
Poole,
Dorset, BH17 0RZ
Tel: 01202 645577
(SF350 Carbon monoxide detectors)

Ship Shape Bedding,
Turners Farm,
Crowgate Street,
Tunstead,
Norfolk,
NR12 8RD
Tel: 08704 464233
(Cut-from-roll DRY Mat™ Anti condensation mattress underlay)

Shurflo Ltd,
5 Sterling Park,
Gatwick Road,
Crawley,
West Sussex,
RH10 9QT
Tel: 01293 424000
(Shurflo diaphragm water pumps)

Sika Ltd,
Watchmead,
Welwyn Garden City,
Hertfordshire, AL7 1BQ
Tel: 01707 394444
(Sikaflex Cartridge Sealants)

The Society of Motor Manufacturers and Traders,
Trade Sections Department,
Forbes House,
Halkin Street,
London, SW1X 7DS
Tel: 020 7235 7000
(Publishers of SMMT booklet *Towing and the Law*)

Solar Solutions,
Stepnell Reach, Unit 1,
541 Blandford Road,
Poole,
Dorset, BH16 5BW
Tel: 01202 632488
(Solar panel accessories)

Sold Secure Trust,
5c Great Central Way,
Woodford Halse,
Daventry,
Northamptonshire,
NN11 3PZ
Tel: 01327 264687
(Test house conducting security device testing)

The Stabiliser Clinic,
Holme Grove,
Bypass Road,
Garstang,
Preston,
Lancashire, PR3 1NA
Tel: 01995 603745
(Stabiliser testing and overhaul service)

**Stoves plc –
See Glen Dimplex**

Swift Group Ltd,
Dunswell Road,
Cottingham,
Hull, HU16 4JX
Tel: 01482 847332
(Manufacturer of Abbey, Bessacarr, Sprite, Sterling & Swift caravans)

Tetroson brake and clutch cleaner -
Available from automotive factors.

The 12Volt Shop,
9 Lostwood Road,
St Austell,
Cornwall, PL25 4JN
Tel: 01726 69102
(Twelve volt electrical components)

The Caravan Medic,
Head Office, 12 Church Square,
Leighton Buzzard,
Bedfordshire.
Tel: 08080 373737 (National Call Line)
(Franchise repair scheme; replicating textured panels for localised repairs.)

Thetford (UK) Spinflo,
4-10 Welland Close,
Parkwood Industrial Estate,
Rutland Road,
Sheffield,
S3 9QY
Tel: 01142 738157
(Norcold refrigerators, toilets and treatments, Spinflo cooking appliances)

Thompson Plastics (Hull) Ltd,
Bridge Works,
Ferry Road,
Hessle,
East Yorkshire,
HU13 0TP
Tel: 01482 646464
(Manufacturer of acrylic-capped ABS body mouldings)

Towing Electrics Ltd,
Unit 3F, Moss Industrial Estate,
Woodbine Street East,
Rochdale,
Lancashire,
OL16 5LB
Tel: 01706 638065
(Caravan and Towing relays)

Towsure Products Ltd,
151-183 Holme Lane,
Hillsborough,
Sheffield,
S6 4JR
Tel: 0870 60 900 70
(Accessory supplier and towbar manufacturer)

Towing Solutions Ltd,
The Old Dyehouse,
London Road Terrace,
Macclesfield,
Cheshire,
SK11 7RN
Tel: 01625 433251
(Complete towing installation service, Publisher of 'How to Pass the Towing Test: B+E explained')

Trade Grade Products,
Unit 2, Thorne Way,
Wimborne,
Dorset,
BH21 6FB
Tel: 01202 820177
(Injection adhesive kits for repairing delaminating floors)

**Tri-Flow Suppliers –
See Ronseal**

Truma UK,
Park Lane,
Dove Valley Park,
Foston,
South Derbyshire,
DE65 5BG
Tel: 01283 586050
(Space and water heating systems, gas components, water systems, caravan mover, Carver spares)

Trylon Ltd,
Unit J, Higham Business Park,
Bury Close,
Higham Ferrers,
Northamptonshire,
NN10 8HQ
Tel: 01933 411724
(Resins, glass and guidance on glass reinforced plastics)

Tyre-Line Original Equipment Ltd,
Cedar House,
Sopwith Way,
Daventry,
Northamptonshire, NN11 5PB
Tel: 01327 701000
(Trade supplier of tyres to caravan manufacturers)

Tyron UK,
Castle Business Park,
Pavilion Way,
Loughborough,
Leicestershire,
LE11 5GW
Tel: 0845 4000 600
(Tyron Safety Bands)

Van Bitz,
Cornish Farm,
Shoreditch,
Taunton,
Somerset, TA3 7BS
Tel: 01823 321992
(Gas alarm, Battery Master)

VanMaster Touring Homes Ltd,
Unit S32,
Standish Court,
Bradley Hall,
Bradley Lane,
Standish,
Wigan,
WN6 0XQ
Tel: 01257 424999
(Manufacturer of VanMaster caravans)

Vanroyce Caravans,
(No longer in manufacture)

Varta Automotive Batteries Ltd
Broadwater Park,
North Orbital Road,
Denham,
Uxbridge,
Middlesex,
UB9 5HR
Tel: 01895 838989
(Gel-type, non-spill leisure batteries)

V & G Caravans,
107 Benwick Road,
Whittlesey,
Peterborough,
Cambridgeshire,
PE7 2HD
Tel: 01733 350580
(Replacement replica panels in GRP)

W4 Ltd,
Unit B, Ford Lane Industrial Estate,
Arundel,
West Sussex,
BN18 0DF
Tel: 01243 553355
(Suppliers of 230V kits, socket testers, and ribbon sealants)

WAECO International,
(Battery chargers, inverters and electrical accessories)
See Dometic

Watling Engineers Ltd,
88 Park Street Village,
St. Albans,
Hertfordshire, AL2 2LR
Tel: 01727 873661
(Designer/manufacturer/fitter of towing brackets)

Whale Products - See Munster Simms Engineering Ltd,

Winterhoff coupling head stabilisers - See Miriad Products Ltd and BPW Ltd

Witter Towbars,
Drome Road,
Deeside Industrial Park,
Deeside, CH5 2NY
Tel: 01244 284500
(Towbar systems and cycle carriers)

Woodfit Ltd,
Kem Mill,
Whittle-le-Woods, Chorley,
Lancashire, PR6 7EA
Tel: 01257 266421
(Hinges, fittings, hardware, wire storage baskets and catches)

ZIG Electronics Ltd,
Saxon Business Park,
Hanbury Road,
Stoke Prior, Bromsgrove,
Worcestershire, B60 4AD
Tel: 01527 556715
(Low voltage control components, chargers, and gauges)

Zippo UK Ltd,
Unit 27,
Grand Union Centre,
336B Ladbroke Grove,
London, W105AS
Tel: 020 8964 0666
(General purpose large-size gas lighters)

Index

Acknowledgements

This manual touches on many technical subjects and to ensure accuracy in words and illustrations, a large number of specialists gave advice; parts of the manuscript were also checked for accuracy.

The author and the publisher would like to thank the following people:

Derek Bedson, Bedson Advisory Ltd

Nick Howard, Technical Director, Bailey Caravans Ltd

Paul Jones, Marketing Manager, AL-KO Kober Ltd

Gordon King, Commercial Director, BCA Leisure Ltd

John Lally (Director General) and staff at the National Caravan Council

Nigel Lea, Towing Solutions Ltd

Simon McGrath, Editor of Publications, The Camping and Caravanning Club

Louise McIntyre, Editorial Co-ordinator, Haynes Publishing

Barry Norris, Technical Manager, The Camping and Caravanning Club

Martin Spencer, Technical Manager, The Caravan Club

Barry Williams, Head of Publications, The Caravan Club

Additional photographs loaned by:

The Explorer Group (Cover illustration and interiors)

Andrew Jenkinson (Buccanneer Photographs)

Bailey of Bristol, (Water system and interiors)

Carlight (Exploded illustration)

The Caravan Club (Towcar of the Year)

Crossleys (Body repair)

Sika (Sealant applications)